BE

DISCOVER
TUSCANY

Edited and designed by
D & N Publishing,
Ramsbury, Wiltshire.

Cartography by
Hardlines, Charlbury, Oxfordshire.

Although we have made every effort to ensure the accuracy of all the information in this book, changes do occur. We cannot therefore take responsibility for facts, addresses and circumstances in general which are constantly subject to alteration.

If you have any new information, suggestions or corrections to contribute to this guide, we would like to hear from you. Please write to Berlitz Publishing at one of the above addresses.

Photographic Acknowledgements

All photographs by Jon Davison and © Berlitz Publishing Company Ltd. except for the following: Ancient Art & Architecture Collection 52, 67 (lower), 68, 84, 88, 89, 90/91, 215 (lower), 217, 308; Jason Best 218, 225, 226, 306/307; Colorific! 215 (upper), 216, 227; Jean Hall 53, 310; Neil Ray 221.

Front cover: Church of San Biagio, Montepulciano (Jon Davison/Berlitz)

Back cover: The Campanile, Florence (Jon Davison/Berlitz)

Photograph previous page: typical Tuscan landscape at Via di Chiana.

 The Berlitz tick is used to indicate places or events of particular interest.

Phototypeset, originated and printed by C.S. Graphics, Singapore.

BERLITZ®

DISCOVER
TUSCANY

Jack Altman

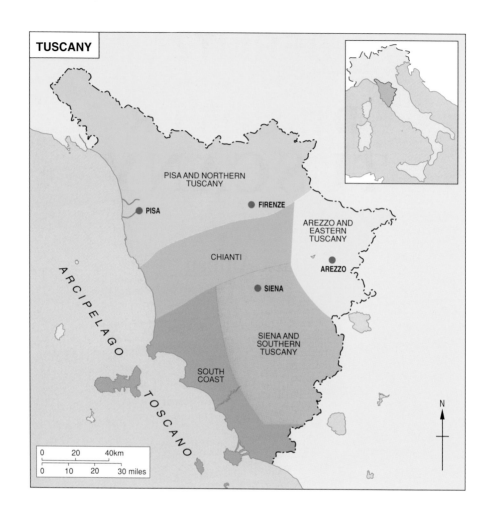

TUSCANY

PISA AND NORTHERN
TUSCANY

● PISA

● FIRENZE

AREZZO AND
EASTERN
TUSCANY

CHIANTI

● AREZZO

● SIENA

A R C I P E L A G O

SIENA AND
SOUTHERN
TUSCANY

SOUTH
COAST

T O S C A N O

0   20   40km
0   10   20   30 miles

N

Contents

MAPS: Tuscany 4, 8; Pisa and North-west Tuscany 164; North-east Tuscany 184; Chianti 196; Chianti Classico Region 202; Siena and southern Tuscany 220; South coast 258; Arezzo and eastern Tuscany 290; Tuscany coastal strip 314.

Town Plans: Arezzo 291; Florence 120; Island of Elba 281; Lucca 185; Pisa 166; San Gimignano 206; Siena 222/223.

TUSCANY: FACTS AND FIGURES

All the Nuts and Bolts for a Successful Journey

In principle – and in Tuscany, we're talking about the pleasure principle – there are no terrible problems about organizing a holiday here: no weird diseases, no serious signs of civil war. Italians are, in general, the most easy-going of people, but a minimum of advance planning will make things even easier.

Italy is a fast-changing country and Tuscany's tourist infrastructure and telephone system are undergoing constant renewal. As a result, the many addresses, telephone numbers and other detailed information may change from one moment to the next. Our 'facts and figures' are as accurate as we can make them, but we beg your understanding for any alterations there have been by the time the book reaches you.

In Renaissance days, Montepulciano was an outpost of Medici power in southern Tuscany. Today, it looks peacefully out over vineyards famous for their red vino nobile, smooth and heart-warming as the surrounding landscape.

When to Go

The best times for visiting any part of Tuscany are spring to early summer (late March to mid-June) and the autumn of the wine harvest (September and October).

In high summer, Florence, sitting in its basin of the Arno valley, becomes for most people an unbearable oven. If school holidays or office-imperatives impose a July or August vacation, make sure you spend most of the time in the cooler, airier Tuscan hills with day-trips *into* steaming Florence rather than the other way round. If you have children and are not renting a villa with a swimming pool, plan on at least a couple of days at a beach resort.

The winter months (November to March) are mostly wet and piercingly cold, but can have unpredictably pleasant

AVERAGE MONTHLY TEMPERATURES

The following official figures are for Florence; elsewhere in Tuscany from June to
September, subtract about 3°C (5-6°F).

	Jan	Feb	Mar	Apr	May	Jun	Jul	Aug	Sep	Oct	Nov	Dec
°C max.	9	12	16	20	24	29	32	31	28	21	14	10
min.	2	2	5	8	12	15	17	17	15	11	6	3
°F max.	48	53	59	68	75	84	89	88	82	70	57	50
min.	35	36	40	46	53	59	62	61	59	52	43	37

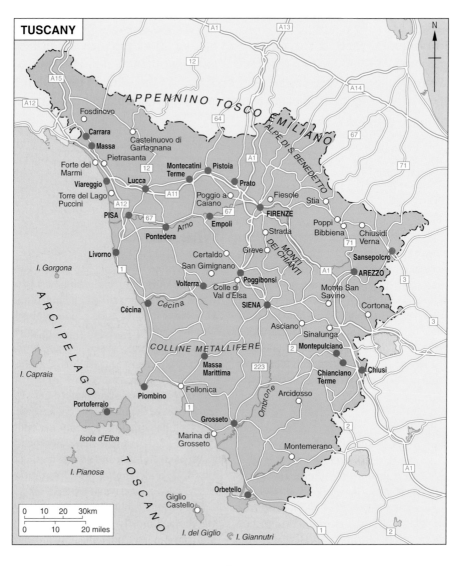

weather. A few days' break can be rewarded, between centrally heated museum-visits, with an hour or two nursing a cappucino in the sun. Remember that many resort hotels close off-season, though some, like the Mediterranean beaches, are best when they are deserted, particularly old-fashioned 'palazzi'.

For How Long?

Ideally, say the connoisseurs, Tuscany deserves a lifetime. Failing that, any first-time visit for less than a week would be too frustrating.

One week is a minimum. This would allow, for example, a couple of days in Florence, two days through the Chianti country, a day or two in and around Siena – with trips to San Gimignano and Volterra. Alternatively combine Florence with Pisa and its coast and hinterland – Lucca and Carrara. **Two weeks** enable you to follow your sightseeing with a longer period of relaxation at a beach resort. **Three weeks** or more would let you do real justice to Florence and Siena, and add in Arezzo and the rich, relatively unexplored country. Tuscany is at its best when you spend a lot of time there doing nothing at all.

Travel Documents for Motorists

To take a car into Italy, you should have:
- Valid national driving licence, International Driving Permit or pink European Community licence. It is advisable to carry a translation (free from automobile associations).
- Car registration papers.
- Green Card (an extension to your regular insurance policy making it valid specifically for Italy); if you plan to stay in Italy for more than 45 days, you must take out Italian insurance.
- Red warning triangle. This should be placed in an emergency at least 30m (100ft) behind the car.
- National identity sticker for both cars and caravans (trailers).

*L*ike many things in Italy, handling traffic is an art rather than an exact science. Two wheels are the ideal solution for weaving in and out of the congestion – and for hassle-free parking.

Passports and Visas

Visitors from the European Community countries need only a national identity card to enter Italy. Citizens of most other countries must have a valid passport. Tourists from South Africa must have a visa. Though European and North American residents are not subject to any health requirements, visitors from further afield may require a smallpox vaccination. You should check with your travel agent before departure.

You must be at least 18 years old to drive a car in Italy. Drivers of motorcycles (any two-wheeler over 49cc) need the same documents as car drivers. Drivers entering Italy in a car not their own must have the owner's written permission.

How to Get There

In this highly competitive age, transport conditions, timetables and fares change rapidly. Before deciding how you are going to get to Tuscany, check with your local travel agent and the Italian Tourist Office in your home country for the latest situation. They will help you with timetables, budget and personal requirements.

By Air

Tuscany's main international gateway (with services from London, Paris, Frankfurt, Rome and Milan) is **Pisa** (Galileo Galilei Airport) in the southern suburb of San Giusto. Only one hour by train from Florence, it is also particularly convenient for those starting or finishing their stay at a beach resort.

Florence itself has a smaller airport on the north-west edge of town at Peretola served by London's Stansted airport and several charter flights.

Rome (Leonardo da Vinci at Fiumicino) is a good gateway airport for those planning to rent a car and start their tour of Tuscany on the beach resorts of the southern coast. It is a 90-minute drive to the Argentario peninsula.

Approximate flying times from main cities are: London to Pisa, Florence or Rome, 2 hours; New York to Rome, 8 hours; Los Angeles to Rome, 15 hours; and Sydney to Rome, 26 hours.

Charter Flights and Package Tours

All-inclusive arrangements are available (air fare, accommodation, sightseeing and airport transfers, combining Florence with, say, Pisa, Siena and/or the Chianti country) or arrangements can be made on an individual basis tailor-made to your personal requirements with an independent itinerary. Check local travel agents or the Compagnia Italian Turismo (CIT), Italy's national travel agency and tour operator. If you're flying by charter with an independent itinerary in mind, check fly-drive possibilities combining airfare and car rental. The Italian National Tourist Office (*see* page 27) has lists of recognized tour operators.

By Road

The Channel Tunnel and car ferries link Britain with France, Belgium and Holland. Car-trains run in the summer months. Once on the continent, you can put your car on a train to Livorno (starting points include Calais and Paris). The modern network of European roads is such that you can now drive from the Channel coast (or via the Tunnel, from Paris) all the way to Florence or Pisa without leaving a motorway.

Motorways in Belgium and Germany are toll-free. In France and Italy you pay according to the distance travelled. At the Swiss border you have to buy a sticker (*vignette*), which is valid for the current year if you want to travel on the motorways. This should be displayed on the windscreen (windshield). In Austria, tolls are only levied on a few motorways, including the Brenner Autobahn into Italy.

By Coach

Eurolines operate regular coach services from London and major continental cities to Florence and Pisa. The coaches are modern and stop for breaks and meals, but it can be a strenuous journey and the service is not especially cheap. In Britain, tickets may be booked through any National Express agent. Return tickets are valid for up to six months. Information on routes, timetables and fares may be obtained from:

Euroline
13 Lower Regent Street
London SW1 4LR
Tel. (071) 730 0202.

By Rail

The European national railways offer a wide variety of bargain tickets. Many of the rail-passes mentioned below must be obtained before leaving home. Other conditions may change from time to time and some offers may be withdrawn or replaced. As an indication of what may be available, we give you here the current range of possibilities.

The **Eurailpass**, an individual ticket available to people residing outside Europe and North Africa (Tunisia, Algeria, Morocco), is valid for first-class unlimited railway travel in 20 European countries, including travel on some buses and many ferries and steamers.

The **Eurail Youthpass** for those under 26 years of age allows one or two months unlimited second-class rail travel. Surcharges are imposed on fast trains, like EuroCity (EC), InterCity (IC), French TGV and Italian Rapido (R), and for certain ferry-crossings during high season.

The **Eurail Flexipass** for North Americans, Mexicans, Australians and New Zealanders offers five days of unlimited first-class travel within a 15-day period; the 21-day pass permits nine days' actual travel. The **Eurail Youth Flexipass**

allows 15 days of second-class travel within two months.

For Europeans under 26, the old *Interrail* ticket has been abandoned and a new type of ticket called **Domino** has been introduced. Check with your travel agent for full details.

Overnight services with sleeping compartments leave from London's Victoria Station via Dover, Calais, Basel and Milan to **Florence**. Services through the Channel Tunnel to Paris run via Dijon and Genoa to **Pisa** or via Lausanne and Milan to **Florence**.

What to Pack

The rule should be as little as possible. One of the unpredictable hazards of Italian life is the national pastime of *sciopero* (labour strikes). When they do happen, the most commonly affected places are airports and railway stations, so that you may find yourself carrying your bags long distances. However, even without being unduly pessimistic, a light load in a hot country is always a good idea. Be sure to add one extra, fold-away bag to bring out at the end of the trip for your gifts.

Clothes

From May to September, you will need only the lightest garments that should preferably be cotton, plus a good sunhat and sunglasses. In winter and early spring (November to April), remember this is hill country, so bring pullovers and a raincoat. Warm clothing may be necessary for evenings in the hills any time of year. Italians appreciate elegance everywhere, even on the beach, but that does not mean formal wear. The keynote is *casual* elegance. Some first-class hotel dining-rooms or

Many who have conducted a lifelong love affair with Florence make straight for Piazzale Michelangelo. The panorama is reassuring (previous pages).

top-rated restaurants may require men to wear a jacket.

When visiting churches, dress modestly – no undervests or other clothes that bare the flesh. Shorts should be considered a taboo for men and women alike, and women should cover their shoulders. A light scarf is acceptable.

For the town, take either flat shoes, moccasins or sandals. High heels are a mistake anywhere. Comfortable walking shoes are essential both for the hill towns and the rough stone terrain of the Etruscan archaeological sites. In case you decide to hike in the Apennines, take more sturdy shoes and warmer clothing.

Electrical Appliances

Italy has 220 volt, 50 cycle electric current. Sockets are of the standard European type with two cylindrical prongs.

A pocket torch (flashlight) with plenty of extra batteries is a precious companion for either exploring the darker churches and Etruscan tombs by day, a walk in the hills at night or the power-failure (very rare, but not unknown in remoter villages).

Health Matters

If your health insurance does not cover foreign countries, take out a short-term policy for the risk of illness or accident while you are on holiday. Visitors from European Community countries are entitled to the same health cover as the Italians, but must have a special form from their governmental health authorities.

If you need medical care, your hotel receptionist will help you find an English-speaking doctor (or dentist). Local Health Units of the Italian National Health Service are listed in the telephone directory under *Unità Sanitaria Locale*. First aid services (*Servizio di Pronto Soccorso*) function day and night at most hospitals, major railway stations and airports.

Note two telephone numbers that we hope you will never need:
Emergency: 113
Ambulance in Florence: 215–555.

Pharmacies

The *farmacia* is open during normal shopping hours (*see* OPENING HOURS, page 29), but an all-night service is available in at least one pharmacy in every town. Florence has three:
Comunale N°13
Santa Maria Novella Railway Station
Tel. 289–435;
Molteni
Via Calzaiuoli 7r
Tel. 289–490;
Taverna
Piazza San Giovanni 20r (near Duomo)
Tel. 284–013.

The opening schedule for other duty pharmacies is posted on every pharmacy door and in local newspapers Your hotel should know the closest.

Bring along an adequate supply of prescribed medication as you cannot be sure that the Italian equivalent brands will conform to all the specifications.

14

Public Toilets

Most museums and art galleries have public toilets. Restaurants, bars, cafés, large stores, the airports, railway stations and car parks all have facilities. On the whole, they are clean and in good order.

Toilets may be labelled with either the symbol of a man or a woman or the initials WC. Beware of Italian signs that might mislead you: *Uomini* is for men, *Donne* for women; *Signori*, with a final *i*, is for men, *Signore*, with a final *e*, is for women.

Fuel and Oil

Prices are set by the government. (The old discount-coupons for tourists were, at publication time, no longer being issued, but the system may be resumed. Check with the Italian National Tourist Office.) Petrol (gasoline) is available in super (98-100 octane), unleaded (95 octane), normal (86-88 octane) and diesel. Remember: 40 litres are a fraction more than 10 US gallons.

Filling stations generally provide full service from 7am to 12.30pm and from 3.30pm to 7.30pm in summer, closing a half hour earlier in winter. Many stations close on Sunday. Most have a self-service

Getting Around

By Car

In general, driving in Italy is an acquired skill that the fearful compare to brain surgery and the more self-confident to that of any challenging sport requiring fast reflexes and a healthy instinct for survival. It takes on an added zest on the winding roads of Tuscany's hill-country. For that reason, Tuscany's drivers pride themselves on being more disciplined than most Italians, but that remains a relative and highly subjective judgment.

Florence is Tuscany's only city subject to the special stress of metropolitan driving. In any case, most Tuscan towns have placed their city centre (*centro storico*) off limits to private cars. If you must drive in town, be firm but not reckless. In a traffic jam, advance steadily, moving confidently forward. You may cause trouble and win no gratitude by courteously waving on another driver to cut in ahead of you. Most Italians have Formula One reflexes for whipping in and out of available spaces – without your help.

Every country has a toy-car that actually works: France's Deux-Chevaux, Britain's Mini. In Italy: the Cinquecento.

15

pump that can be used outside these hours. They take banknotes of various denominations. Stations along the motorway (*autostrada*) are open 24 hours a day.

*T*here's a wonderful sense of freedom wheeling around the country roads of the Tuscan hills. In this case, it's the meandering highway 68 from the coast to Volterra.

Speed Limits

On the *autostrada* toll highways the speed limits are 130kph (80mph) on weekdays, 110kph (68mph) on weekends and holidays; on other main roads the limit is 90kph (55mph). The limit in built-up areas is generally speaking 50kph (30mph). Speeding fines are high and the police, increasingly vigilant, will ask you to pay on the spot. If you don't do this, the charge is much higher later, and these days, the computer will track you down!

Rules of the Road

Drive on the right, pass on the left. When overtaking or remaining in the left-hand lane, keep your directional indicator flashing. Traffic on major roads has right of way over that entering from side roads. At the intersection of roads of similar importance, the car on the right has priority. That's only the theory. In practice, be very careful. Take nothing for granted.

Seat belts are compulsory. Drive with dipped (low-beam) headlights in tunnels.

The use of car horns is prohibited in towns and cities, but not outside built-up areas. However, Italian drivers make use of their horns all over the place, but much less aggressively than they used to. It is even worth learning to sound your own horn whenever it could help warn of your pending arrival.

Roads: Autostrada and Others

Apart from the *autostrada* (motorway/expressway/turnpike), the road network comprises: *strada statale* (state road), *strada provinciale* (provincial road) and *strada comunale* (local road). Access signs to the *autostrada* are green. Toll charges are regulated according to vehicle size and distance travelled, are controlled by a ticket and paid either at the exit or with a flat rate when entering the motorway.

Road Conditions

The ACI (*Automobile Club d'Italia*) operates a Rome-based 24-hour telephone assistance centre staffed with multilingual personnel who give nationwide information on road and weather conditions: Tel. 06–4212.

Accidents and Breakdowns

To report an accident, the all-purpose emergency number is 113, with telephones at regular intervals on the *autostrada*. The ACI assistance number is 116. The service is not free so take out international breakdown insurance before leaving home.

Parking

The *centro storico* of almost all Tuscan towns is closed to private cars from 7.30am to 6pm, Monday to Friday. If you are staying in the city centre of Florence, Siena or another major town, find a supervised parking lot (*parcheggio custodito*) or multi-level garage (*autorimessa*) near your hotel and leave your car there for the duration of your stay. (*See* CRIME, page 28, about leaving valuables in the car.) In Florence, tow-away zoning is strictly enforced. It costs a fortune to retrieve your car from municipal garages, and they close on Sundays and holidays. For parking in a 'Zona Disco' in outlying areas and country towns, you need a parking disc (*disco di sosta*), obtainable from service stations. Place it visibly inside your windscreen (windshield), and when set to your time of arrival, it will indicate your departure limit.

Road Signs

Most road signs employed in Italy are international pictographs, but the LANGUAGE GUIDE at the back of the book contains some of the written signs you may come across.

Car Hire/Rental

For the best deal, reserve your car from home. This can be done either through your travel agent as a package with your flight and hotel booking or directly through a major international car rental company. Check whether the deal includes unlimited mileage, what kind of insurance is included, and if the car has to be returned to its starting point. Some companies charge extra if, for instance, you pick up the car downtown and drop it off at the airport. This may nonetheless be the most desirable arrangement for Florence, where you may not need the car until you start your out-of-town excursions.

To rent locally, consult the telephone directory's yellow pages under *Autonoleggio* and then be prepared to bargain: weekend rates, unlimited mileage, third-party or full insurance coverage can all

make a difference. Major companies usually have English-speaking staff. You will need a driving licence and passport or national identity card. The minimum age is 21 or 25 depending on the company and the car's engine size, or even 30 if an upmarket car is involved. To hire you must have held a licence for at least one year. Without a credit card, the required cash deposit may be prohibitive, as are the prices of chauffeur-driven cars, available through the major rental companies.

By Train

The Italian State Railway (*Ferrovie dello Stato*) offers a service that has fares among the lowest in Europe. Choose your train carefully, as journey times vary considerably. The following list describes the various types of train:

TEE Trans-Europ-Express, first class only with surcharge; seat reservations essential.

EuroCity (EC) International express; first and second class.

InterCity (IC) Intercity express with few stops; luxury service with first and second class.

Rapido (R) Long-distance express stopping at major cities only; first and second class.

Espresso (EXP) Long-distance train, stopping at main stations.

Diretto (D) Slower than *Espresso*, it makes a number of local stops.

Locale (L) Local train stopping at almost every station.

Tickets (*see also* HOW TO GET THERE, BY RAIL, page 11) can be purchased and reservations made at a local travel agency or at the railway station. Better-class trains have dining-cars or self-service cars that offer food and beverages at reasonable prices. If you don't have a reservation, arrive at the station at least 20 minutes before departure; Italy's trains are often crowded.

By Bus

The closing-off to private cars of most towns' *centro storico* has made the municipal bus service a real boon in places like Florence and Pisa. Buy your ticket before getting on board, from tourist information offices, newspaper shops, tobacconists and bars, and get it punched in the automatic machines inside the bus. For a prolonged stay in Florence, the tourist office can give you information about one-week tickets or other fare bargains.

Consider the hour's ferry trip from Piombino to the island of Elba a mini-cruise. Not so boisterous as a cross-Channel ferry, but then the booze is the same price at both ends.

Country buses are an attractive alternative to trains, particularly good for day-trips and picnics. Services operate from Florence's Santa Maria Novella Railway Station. Other towns' tourist offices will give you details of timetables and fares.

By Taxi

Your best chance of finding a taxi is at railway station cab ranks or near the major hotels. Taxis are relatively cheap by north European and American standards, *if* the meter is running. Extra charges for luggage and night, public holiday or airport trips should be posted in four languages inside all taxis. A tip of at least 10% is customary. Beware of non-metered unlicensed taxis whose rates are just like their eloquent Italian name: *abusivi*. Inquire about out-of-town charges before starting the journey.

By Ferry

If you are including the island of Elba in your itinerary, the ferry ports are at Piombino (1 hour to Elba) and Livorno (3

hours), with several competing companies at the harbour. In high season, be sure to book a return passage. For people without cars, there is a daily Florence-Piombino train in summer, taking you directly to the ferry port.

Internal Flights

If you are on a grand Italian tour involving other major destinations before or after Tuscany, Alitalia, Italy's national airline, and its domestic affiliate ATI (*Aero Trasporti Italiani*) have a good interior network. Detailed information is available at travel agencies and Alitalia offices. Inquire about special family group fares, and rates for children, young people/ students and senior citizens. There are also discounts on night flights and weekend tickets.

The address of the Alitalia office in Florence is: Lungarno Acciaiuoli 10r. Tel. (055)–27881

Maps

Tourist offices give away street plans of the city centres featuring a selection of local information and useful telephone numbers. More detailed city maps are on sale at news-stands. The best overall map of Tuscany is published by the Touring Club of Italy (TCI), and is available in bookshops. In the national parks and mountain regions, information offices provide detailed hiking maps drawn to a scale of 1/25,000. Among the better maps of Italy that you will find at home are those published by Hallwag, Kümmerly & Frey, and Michelin.

Travellers with Disabilities

Italy is not in the vanguard of amenities for tourists who are disabled, hard of hearing or blind. Public transport is not yet equipped to lift wheelchairs onto buses, but assistance is available at airports and

If you don't feel like taking pictures yourself, the colour slides on sale at the souvenir stands can be of remarkably good quality these days. In this case, at Piazzale Michelangelo in Florence, you can always compare the commercial shot of the cathedral with the real thing just over the left.

railway stations, and some trains have special facilities for transporting wheelchairs. Hotels increasingly do provide appropriate amenities and lists of these establishments are available from the Italian National Tourist Office and CIT Italian travel agency in your home country.

Museums are also beginning to install elevators for access to exhibition halls on upper floors. By law, all new public buildings must facilitate access for the disabled. In the majority of towns in which the *centro storico* is closed to private traffic, cars for disabled people are allowed in, with specially reserved parking places.

Money Matters

Currency

The *lira* (plural *lire*, abbreviated *L.* or *Lit.*) is the Italian monetary unit.
• Banknotes: L. 1,000, 2,000, 5,000 10,000, 50,000, 100,000;
• coins: L. 10, 20, 50, 100, 200, 500.

The lowest denominations are increasingly rare, so shopkeepers often round up amounts or in some cases give out sweets (candy) in place of very small change.

Changing Money

As a general rule, carry your passport for all exchange transactions. The advantage of the banks' better exchange rate should be weighed against the frequently tiresome wait at their counters. The bank rate will be better than in restaurants or shops, but you may prefer paying your hotel's commission as a fee for the convenience.

Automatic cash-dispensers, handling 17 different foreign currencies with major bank-cards, are most convenient of all, but come with a generally hefty commission on the daily exchange rate. They are available at the airports, railway stations and sometimes at larger tourist information offices.

Credit Cards and Traveller's Cheques

Shops, banks, hotels and an increasing number of restaurants accept major credit cards. The frequently posted *CartaSi* sign means that a wide range of cards are accepted. Traveller's cheques and Eurocheques are best cashed at the bank or your hotel. Some petrol stations will accept Eurocheques.

Tipping

A service charge is added to most restaurant bills, but it is customary to leave an additional tip. It is also in order to tip bellboys, doormen, hat check attendants,

HOW MUCH TO TIP

Hotel porter, per bag	L.-1,500
Hotel maid, per day	L.-1,500
Lavatory attendant	L.-400-500
Waiter	5-10%
Taxi driver	10-15%
Hairdresser	up to 15%
Tour guide	10-15%

garage attendants, and the like. The chart above will give you some guidelines.

Where to Stay

Hotels
The tourist authorities class establishments, known as *Hotel* or *Albergo*, by stars from five (luxury) down to one. Our own listing of HOTELS AND RESTAURANTS (*see* pages 334-345) has grouped these categories into a triple price range of high, moderate and low. Rates vary according to region – as well as location, season, class and services offered – and are fixed in agreement with the regional tourist boards in Florence and the Tuscan provincial administrations.

Breakfast is usually optional. During high season at beach resorts, many hotels require guests to stay a minimum of three nights on half-board terms. Even if prices are listed as *tutto compreso*, all-inclusive of local taxes and service charges, check that the VAT sales tax (*IVA*), 18% for five-star hotels, 9% for other categories, is included.

It is advisable all year round to book well in advance; in the high season it's essential. At coastal resorts, where many establishments stay open for only half the year, the low season is mid-April to June and September. Reservations may be made through travel agencies or by writing directly to the hotel; in the latter case, request written confirmation of your booking. If looking for a hotel on the spot, tourist offices (*see* page 27) can supply local hotel lists.

Hotel reservation service: requests for bookings can be made in writing to CRAT (*Consorzio Regionale Aziende Turistiche della Toscana*), c/o FIAVET
Via Martelli 5
Florence
Tel. (information only, not reservations) 055–294–900.

Pensioni
The term *pensioni* covers everything from simple family-style boarding houses to comfortable small hotels (breakfast included). They tend to offer fewer facilities and may not have a restaurant; when there is one, you could well be treated to some excellent Italian family cooking.

Motels
Motel chains, operated in many cases by oil companies like AGIP, are mushrooming and improving in service. Many have a swimming pool, tennis courts and other sports facilities.

Self-catering
Villa rentals in Tuscany are a long-established tradition, to the point where

Grand old resort hotels, like this one at Montecatini Terme, have become part of the dream landscape of Italian cinema. They provide the backdrop of many a masterpiece by Fellini. All sense of time is lost in the never-never land of a health spa.

large numbers of British residents have caused the region between Florence and Siena to be nicknamed *Chiantishire*. Tuscany rental agencies advertise in the British and American press.

For families staying a week or more at a beach resort, a furnished apartment (*appartamento ammobiliata*) or villa is an economic and convenient alternative to a hotel. Tour operators offer self-catering packages that include travel to and from Italy. Lists of operators are available from the Italian National Tourist Office (*see* page 27).

On the spot, check local newspaper advertisements or regional tourist offices for lists of companies and agents handling villa and apartment rentals.

Farm Holidays

Green tourism in Italy is growing in popularity. You can stay on a farm in Tuscany, in a spartan cottage, a modern farmhouse or a 17th-century castle, and enjoy threshing, grape harvesting or mushroom gathering, fishing, horse-riding or golf. There are three organizations:

Agriturist
Associazione Regionale Toscana
Piazza San Firenze 3
50122–Florence
Tel. 055–287–838, fax 055–230–2285;
Turismo Verde Regionale
Viale Lavagnini 4
50129 Florence
Tel. 055–489–760;
Terranostra Regionale
Via dei Magazzini 2
50122 Florence
Tel. 055–280–539, fax 055–236–0288.

Monasteries and Convents
Some Roman Catholic orders take in guests at very reasonable rates. They provide clean, comfortable rooms as well as meals. For information, write to the regional tourist information office (*see* page 27).

Youth Hostels
Tuscany has a dozen youth hostels (*ostelli per la gioventù*) scattered across the region, each open to holders of membership cards issued by the International Youth Hostels Federation. As for hotels, you must book well in advance in the high season. Membership cards and information are available either from your national Youth Hostels Association or, more expensively, from Tuscany's regional office at the Florence hostel. The following all serve at least breakfast:
Florence
Europa-Villa Camerata
Viale Augusto Righi 2/4
Florence
Tel. 055–601–451, fax 055–610–300;
Chianti
San Michele (closed mid-October to
   February)
Via Casole 42
Lucolena
Greve in Chianti
Tel. 055–851–034;
Ostello del Chianti (closed November
   to February)
Via Cassia
Tavarnelle Val di Pesa
Tel. 055–807–7009;

*T*oday, if a beach is uncrowded, it's probably because it's polluted. This one at Forte dei Marmi is fine – crowded and safe for bathing.

Siena
Guidoriccio (3km [2 miles] north of
  Siena city centre)
Via Fiorentina 89
Località Stellino
Tel. 0577–52212;
San Gimignano
Ostello della Gioventù
Via delle Fonti
Tel. 0577–941–991;
Eastern Tuscany
San Marco (closed mid-October to
  February)
Via Maffei 57
Cortona
Tel. 0575–601–392;
North Coast
Ostello Apuano (closed October to mid-
  March)
Viale delle Pinete 89
Partaccia
Marina di Massa e Carrara
Tel. 0585–780–034;
Northern Tuscany
Il Serchio (groups only)
Via del Brennero
Salicchi
Lucca
Tel. 0583–341–811.

Camping

There are a couple of hundred official
campsites in Tuscany, graded like the hotels by stars. Most of them are equipped
with electricity, water and toilet facilities.
Addresses and full details of amenities for
the whole Tuscany region are given in the
directory *Campeggi in Italia*, published
annually by the Italian Touring Club
(TCI), Corso Italia 10, 20122 Milan, and
available in most Italian bookshops. A free
list of sites with location map is available
from the Italian National Tourist Office
(*see* page 27) or from:

Federcampeggio
Via Vittorio Emanuele II
PO Box 23
50041 Calenzano (Florence).
  Campsites in July and August are invariably very crowded. Check with the local tourist offices about reservations.
  Many campsites require the *International Camping Carnet*, a pass that entitles
holders to modest discounts and insurance
cover throughout Europe. It can be obtained through your camping or automobile
association, the TCI or Federcampeggio.

Day Hotels (Albergo Diurno)

Situated mainly around the big railway stations, these modest establishments provide
low-price daytime facilities, including
bathroom, hairdresser and left-luggage, but
not overnight accommodation.

Tourist Information Offices

Take advantage of their services both in
your home country and the local offices in
Tuscany. The Italian National Tourist Office (*ENIT, Ente Nazionale Italiano per il
Turismo*) publishes detailed brochures with
up-to-date information on Florence and
Tuscany. They cover transport, accommodation, including campsites, and suggestions
for special cultural or other itineraries.
  Locally, you will find municipal or regional tourist information offices in practically all the towns mentioned in our
sightseeing chapters. Besides details of local monuments, museums and other at-
tractions, the offices can be particularly
helpful with information (but not reservations) for last-minute accommodation
needs. The addresses for offices outside
Italy, and for those in the nine provincial

TOURIST INFORMATION OFFICES INSIDE AND OUTSIDE ITALY

The following addresses are for Italian National Tourist Offices in English-speaking countries and for local information offices in Tuscany's nine provincial capitals and other major towns.

Offices Overseas

Australia and New Zealand: c/o Italian Government Tourist Office, Lions Building, 1-1-2 Moto Akasaka, Minato Ku, Tokyo 107; tel. 03–3478–2051.

Canada: 1 Place Ville-Marie, Suite 1914, Montreal, Quebec H3B 3M9; tel. 514–866–7669, fax 514–392–1429.

Eire: 47 Merrion Square, Dublin 2; tel. 01–766–025, fax 01–764–514.

South Africa: London House, 21 Loveday Street, PO Box 6507, Johannesburg 2000; tel. 11–838–3247.

United Kingdom: 1 Princes Street, London W1R 8AY; tel. 071–408 1254, fax 071–493 6695.

USA (Chicago): 500 N Michigan Avenue, Suite 1046, Chicago, Illinois 60611; tel. 312–644–0996, fax 312–644–3019.

USA (Los Angeles): 12400 Wilshire Boulevard, Suite–550, Los Angeles, California 90025; tel. 213–820–0098, fax 213–820–6357.

USA (New York): 630 Fifth Avenue, Suite 1565, New York, New York 10011; tel. 212–245–4961, fax 212–586–9249.

Offices in Tuscany

AREZZO: Piazza della Repubblica 28; tel. 0575–377–678.

CARRARA: Viale XX Settembre 46; tel. 0585–843–370.

Cortona: Via Nazionale 70; tel. 0575–630–352.

Fiesole: Piazza Mino da Fiesole; tel. 055–598–720.

FLORENCE: Via Manzoni 16; tel. 055–234–6284.

Forte dei Marmi: Viale Achille Franceschi 8; tel. 0584–80091.

GROSSETO: Viale Monterosa 206; tel. 0564–454–510.

LIVORNO: Piazza Cavour 6; tel. 0586–898–111.

LUCCA: Via Vittorio Veneto 40; tel. 0583–493–639.

Massa Marittima: Palazzo del Podestà; tel. 0564–902–256.

Montalcino: Costa del Municipio 8; tel. 0577–849–321.

Montecatine Terme: Viale Verdi 66a; tel. 0572–772–224.

Orbetello: Piazza della Repubblica; tel. 0564–860–560.

PISA: Piazza del Duomo; tel. 050–560–464.

PISTOIA: Palazzo dei Vescovi, Via Roma 1; tel. 0573–21622.

Portoferraio (Elba): Calata Italia 26; tel. 0565–914–671.

Prato: Via Cairoli 48; tel. 0574–24112.

Radda in Chianti: Piazza Ferrucci 1; tel. 0577–738–003.

San Gimignano: Piazza del Duomo 1; tel. 0577–940–008.

SIENA: Piazza del Campo 56; tel. 0577–280–551.

Viareggio: Viale Carducci 10; tel. 0584–962–233.

Volterra: Via Turazza 2; tel. 0588–86150.

capitals and other major towns are shown in the information box on page 27.

Photography and Video

Hand-held photographic equipment, but not tripods or flash, may be used in museums and churches, but sometimes for a small fee. Make sure you have the right kind of film for Tuscany's very bright light.

Crime, Police and Lost Property

Crime

The watchword is prudence not paranoia. Criminologists have observed that nervous people attract criminals just as fear attracts aggressive dogs. Nonetheless it is only realistic to acknowledge that petty theft in Italy is an endless annoyance and tourists are always easy targets. By taking a few simple precautions, you can reduce the risk or ease the pain and inconvenience caused by loss or theft of your belongings.

- Make sure you have insurance to cover theft or loss of personal effects while abroad.
- Take traveller's cheques and change only a minimum of cash. Keep your record of traveller's cheque numbers (and passport) separate from the cheques.
- Leave documents and unneeded valuables in the hotel safe. Carry money and credit cards in an inside pocket or a pouch inside your clothes. (If you must strap a 'banana-bag' around your waist, remember it has become an obvious target for thieves, so don't put *all* your valuables in it.)

- Don't carry your handbag slung loosely over your street-side shoulder; it becomes an invitation to thieves on motorbikes or in cars.
- Photocopy your tickets, driving licence, passport and other vital documents to facilitate reporting a theft and obtaining replacements. Leave one set of photocopies at home and carry another set *separately* from the originals.
- Never leave valuables in your car when parked, not even in the boot (trunk). Leave a car containing luggage only in the care of a parking attendant.

Any loss or theft should be reported at once to the nearest police station, if only for insurance purposes. Your insurance company will need to see a copy of the police report.

Police

The municipal police (*Vigili Urbani*), dressed in either navy blue with white helmets or all-white, handle city traffic and other city police tasks. They are courteous but rarely speak a foreign language, except for a few interpreters wearing a badge. The *Carabinieri*, who wear brown or black uniforms, deal with major crimes and demonstrations. The *Polizia di stato* (national police) man Italy's frontiers, airports and railway stations.
Emergency number 113.

Lost Property

Save time and energy by appealing only to senior staff at hotels or museums. For items lost on the train, you should talk to the conductor or, when you get off, to the stationmaster.

Florence's lost-property office is the Ufficio Oggetti Smarriti, Via Circondaria 19; for property lost on trains, go to Piazza dell'Unità 1.

Emergencies

If your hotel receptionist or a police officer is not at hand, you can telephone these numbers, from anywhere in Italy, 24 hours a day:

All-purpose	113
Carabinieri	112
Fire	115
Road assistance	116
Emergency pharmacy	192

Embassies and Consulates

Your diplomatic representatives are there only for the direst emergencies, not to help out with cash or lost plane tickets. Except for the Florence-based consulates of the United Kingdom and USA, the following addresses are all in Rome.

Australia
Via Alessandria 215
Tel. 06–832–721.
Canada
Via G. Battista de Rossi 27
Tel. 06–855–341.
Eire
Largo del Nazareno 3
Tel. 06–678–2541.
New Zealand
Via Zara 28
Tel. 06–851–225.
South Africa
Via Tanaro 14-16
Tel. 06–841–9794.
United Kingdom (consulate)
Lungarno Corsini 2, Florence
Tel. 055–284–133.
USA (consulate)
Lungarno Vespucci 38
Florence
Tel. 055–239–8276.

Opening Hours

Tuscany is part of Italy so the times we give are constantly subject to change and whim. In most parts of the region, the after-lunch siesta is still sacrosanct.

Banks are generally open from 8.30am to 1.30pm and again for an hour or so in the afternoon, Monday to Friday.

Currency-exchange offices at the airports and railway stations are open later and weekends, too.

Churches generally close for sightseeing at lunchtime, approximately noon to 3pm.

Museums and **art gallery** opening hours are erratic and constantly changing their opening times. Most open at 9 or 9.30am with a break for lunch. The commonest closing day is Monday. In any case, check the latest situation at the tourist information office.

Post Offices normally open from 8.15 or 8.30am to 2pm, Monday to Friday, and until noon on Saturday. Florence's main post office, Palazzo delle Poste, Via Pellicceria, is open from 8am to 7pm, Saturday 8.15am to noon.

Shops are closed Monday morning, open Tuesday – Saturday 9am to 1pm and 4 to 7.30pm. Food shops open an hour earlier. Hours are more flexible at some of the beach resorts. These hours apply also to pharmacies, except those on a special-duty rota (*see* PHARMACIES page 14).

Public Holidays

When a national holiday falls on a Thursday or a Tuesday, Italians may make a *ponte* (bridge) to the weekend, so that Friday or Monday is taken off as well. Banks, government offices, most shops, museums

*E*ven on closing days,
window-shopping can be a
pleasure.

and galleries are closed on the days listed below.

Shops and offices also close on local feast days honouring a town's patron saint, for example June 24 in Florence is for St John the Baptist.

January 1	*Capodanno* (New Year's Day)
January 6	*Epifania* (Epiphany)
Movable date	*Lunedì di Pasqua* (Easter Monday)
April 25	*Festa della Liberazione* (Liberation Day)
May 1	*Festa del Lavoro* (Labour Day)
August 15	*Ferragosto* (Assumption Day)
November 1	*Ognissanti* (All Saints' Day)
December 8	*L'Immacolata Concezione* (Immaculate Conception)
December 25	*Natale* (Christmas Day)
December 26	*Santo Stefano* (St Stephen's Day)

Time Differences

Italy follows Central European Time (GMT + 1 hour). From the last Sunday in March to the last Sunday in September clocks are put one hour ahead (GMT + 2 hours).

The following is a summer time chart giving the times at various places around the world when it is noon in Florence in summer:

Los Angeles	3am
New York	6am
London	11am
Florence	**noon**

Johannesburg	noon	Australia	61
Sydney	8pm	Austria	43
Auckland	10pm	Belgium	32
		Canada	1
		Eire	35

Communications

France	33
Germany	49
Japan	81

Post Office

Netherlands	31
New Zealand	64
South Africa	27
Spain	34
Switzerland	41
United Kingdom	44
United States	1

The postal service in Italy is more unpredictable than in much of the rest of the world (see OPENING HOURS, page 29). For important messages as opposed to simple holiday greetings, use fax, telex or the telephone. If you expect to receive mail, have it sent to a hotel address rather than the less reliable *poste restante*.

Telephone, Fax and Telex

Italy's telephone system is undergoing extensive modernization, and service, especially in the major cities, has improved considerably. In the process, however, there are constant changes of numbers, so check them carefully. Ask your hotel operator or try directory information (*see* below).

Public telephones are most commonly found in cigarette shops. They are very often just a normal desk set with a coin box attached. Shops or restaurants will let you use their phones to make local calls if you pay in advance.

Remember that phone calls, telex and fax messages from your hotel are charged much higher than the normal rate, but the convenience may make it worthwhile. The public telephone at the post office avoids surcharges, but you may have to book an overseas call up to 24 hours in advance.

To make a direct international call, dial 00 and wait for a change of tone before dialling the country's code, area code and subscriber's number. Here are some country codes:

To telephone Italy from abroad, dial the international access code, followed by 39, area code *without* the initial 0, then the subscriber's number. For the changing conditions concerning reduced charges available at certain times and days of the week for international calls, check with the international operator: dial 15 for European and 170 for intercontinental calls. Dial 12 for local and national enquiries.

What to Read

The choice of books on Tuscany is enormous, not just of history and art books but, most enjoyably, of works of the imagination: novels, poetry and essays. Practically all authors of note who have set foot in Tuscany have felt moved to write about it. Here is a small selection, most of them available in paperback in British and American editions:

History

H Hearder, *Italy, a Short History*.
Ellen MacNamara, *Everyday Life of the Etruscans*.
DP Waley, *The Italian City-Republics*.
JR Hale, *Florence and the Medici*.

Gene Brucker, *Renaissance Florence*.
Niccolò Machiavelli, *The Prince* and *Discourses*.

Art

Howard Hibbard, *Michelangelo*.
JR Hale (ed.), *A Concise Encyclopaedia of the Italian Renaissance*.
Benvenuto Cellini, *Autobiography*.
John Ruskin, *Mornings in Florence*.
Mary McCarthy, *The Stones of Florence*.
Attilio Brilli, *In Search of Piero* (della Francesca).
Kenneth Clark, *Leonardo da Vinci*.
Bernard Berenson, *Italian Painters of the Renaissance*.

Novels, Poetry and Essays

Dante, *The Divine Comedy*.
Boccaccio, *The Decameron*.
EM Forster, *Where Angels Fear To Tread* and *Room with a View*.
Henry James, *Italian Hours*.
DH Lawrence, *Etruscan Places*.
Aldous Huxley, *Along the Road*.
Stendhal, *Rome, Naples, Florence*.
Heinrich Heine, *Italy*.
Charles Dickens, *Pictures From Italy*.

Eating Out

It is the opinion of many a gourmand and not a few slimmer gourmets, too, that Italian cooking is the most enjoyable in the world, and the cuisine of Tuscany is rated by the Italians themselves among the very best of the country's regional variations. Without draining the natural tastes of its fine meats and vegetables, its sauces are savoury, using the region's aromatic herbs and olive oil (most exquisite from Lucca), and only the most judicious use of garlic. As you travel around the region, you will have a chance try the local specialities as well as a whole array of national dishes.

Where to Eat

Only in a few hotels catering specifically for foreign tourists will you get English- or American-style **breakfast**. Otherwise head for a good *caffè* on the piazza and settle, happily, for the local *prima colazione* of superb coffee, *espresso* black or *cappucino* with foaming hot milk (sprinkled in the best establishments with powdered chocolate), and a sweet roll or toast. Italian tea is as anæmic as English coffee, but the hot chocolate is excellent.

Stand-up bars known as *tavola calda* are ideal for those adopting a healthy 'sightseer's diet' of one main meal a day, preferably, with just a snack for **lunch**. They serve sandwiches and hot or cold dishes at the counter (*see also* BARS, page 37). If you want to picnic in the park or out in the country, get your sandwiches made up for you at the *pizzicheria* delicatessen. Ask for *panino ripieno*, a bread roll filled with whatever sausage, cheese or salad you choose from the inviting display at the counter.

For **dinner**, even if you're not overly budget-conscious, it's useful to know that the most elaborate restaurant (*ristorante*), where prices match the real or apparent opulence of the décor, is rarely the best value. Apart from an occasional 'gastronomic temple', the service is too often snooty and obsequious, the cuisine pretentious and mediocre. In a family-run *trattoria* or even a Neapolitan-style *pizzeria* that serves much more than just pizza, the ambience, half the value of an Italian meal, is infinitely more enjoyable and the food has more real character. (Don't expect too much character in the average hotel dining room.)

For more details, consult our listing of HOTELS AND RESTAURANTS, pages 334–345 and remember it's the custom to round off the bill with an extra tip in addition to the service charge.

The first thing that
gourmets will say is that there is
more to an Italian meal than pizza.
The second thing is that pizza has
given fast food a good name.

What to Eat

Besides their local specialities, Tuscan
restaurants serve the classical cuisine of
their honoured rivals in Bologna, Milan
and Naples. Despite the plethora of sauces
for the pasta, the essence of Italian cooking is in its simplicity: freshwater fish
from the mountain streams cooked with
perhaps just a touch of fennel; seafood
from the Mediterranean served marinated
in a hint of lemon, pepper and olive oil,
cold, as an hors d'œuvre. Veal is served in
the simplest of lemon sauces, steaks just
charcoal-grilled, and vegetables sautéed
without elaborate disguise.

Antipasti

Any decent trattoria sets out on a long table
near the entrance a truly painterly display of
its *antipasti* (hors d'œuvre). Get to know the
delicacies by making up your own assort-
ment (*antipasto misto*). Both attractive and
tasty are the cold *peperoni*, red, yellow and
green peppers grilled, skinned and marinated in olive oil and a little lemon juice.
Mushrooms (*funghi*), baby marrows (*zuc-
chini*), aubergines (*melanzane*), artichokes
(*carciofi*) and sliced fennel (*finocchio*) are
also served cold, with a dressing (*pinzimo-
nio*). One of the most refreshing hors d'œuvre is the *mozzarella alla caprese*, slices of
soft white buffalo cheese and tomato sprinkled with fresh basil, olive oil and pepper.

Try tunny or tuna fish (*tonno*) with
white beans and onions (*fagioli e cipolle*).
Mixed seafood hors d'œuvre (*antipasto di
mare*) may include scampi, prawns (*gam-
beri*), mussels (*cozze*), fresh sardines
(*sarde*), but also, chewily delicious squid
(*calamari*) and octopus (*polpi*).

The simple Italian restaurant philosophy of 'What you see is what you get' does wonders for people who might not otherwise imagine ever eating a truly delicious octopus.

Ham from Parma or San Daniele is served paper thin with either melon (*prosciutto con melone*) or, even better, fresh figs (*con fichi*). Most salami is mass-produced in north Italian factories, but watch, too, for the Tuscany's farm-produced sausage (*see* below).

Popular **soups** are mixed vegetable (*minestrone*, a Tuscan speciality), clear soup (*brodo*), and with an egg beaten into it (*stracciatella*).

Pasta

Despite our diet-conscious era, Italian restaurants traditionally serve pasta as an introductory course, not as the main dish. While they won't kill you, even the friendliest restaurant owners will raise a sad eye-brow if you make a whole meal out of a plate of spaghetti. It is said that there are as many different forms of Italian pasta noodles as there are French cheese – some 360 at last count, with new forms being created every year. Each sauce – tomato, cheese, cream, meat or fish – needs its own kind of noodle. In this land of artists, the pasta's form and texture are an essential part of the taste, and pasta manufacturers commission top architects to design new noodle shapes.

Besides spaghetti and macaroni, the worldwide popularity of pasta has familiarized us with *tagliatelle* ribbon noodles, baked *lasagne* with layers of pasta, meat sauce and béchamel, rolled *canelloni*, and stuffed *ravioli*. From there, you launch into the lusty poetry of *tortellini* and *cappelletti* (a Tuscan variation on ravioli), or elliptically curved *linguine*, flat *pappardelle* and *tagliolini*, quill-shaped *penne* and corrugated *rigatoni*. Discover the other 350 shapes for yourself.

There are almost as many sauces. A subtle variation on the ubiquitous *bolognese* meat sauce is made with chopped chicken livers, celery and white wine. Others range from the simplest and spiciest *aglio e olio* (just garlic, olive oil and chilli peppers), *marinara* (tomato), *carbonara* (chopped bacon and eggs), and *pesto* (basil and garlic ground up in olive oil with pine nuts and Parmesan cheese) to *vongole* (clams and tomato) and startling *al nero*, yes, pasta blackened by the ink of the cuttlefish – wonderful. Parmesan is not added to every pasta dish; don't be ashamed to ask if it's appropriate or not.

Main Dish

Among the **meats**, veal (*vitello*) has pride of place. It comes in myriad forms: *osso buco* (stewed veal shinbone), *scaloppine* (veal fillets with lemon), *costoletta* (Milanese-style veal cutlet pan-fried in breadcrumbs), *vitello tonnato* (veal in tunny fish sauce) or *alla fiorentina* (Florentine, with a spinach sauce). The popular *saltimbocca* (literally 'jump in the mouth') is an originally Roman veal-roll with ham, sage and Marsala.

Calf's liver (*fegato*) is served *alla milanese* in breadcrumbs or *alla veneziana*, thinly sliced, sautéed with onions in olive oil. Tuscan beef is the best in Italy, known as *vitellone* 'young beef' rather than veal, and is used in the famous Florentine steak (*see* below). Pork (*maiale*), lamb (*agnello*) and chicken (*pollo*) are also most often just grilled or roasted (*al forno*).

Fish, often displayed at a glass counter with the *antipasti*, are prepared very simply: grilled, steamed or fried. Try the *spigola* (sea bass), *triglia* (red mullet), *pesce spada* (swordfish) or *coda di rospa* (angler fish).

Be careful when ordering the *fritto misto*. It usually means a mixed fry of fish, but can also be a mixed fry of breaded chicken breasts, calf's liver, veal and vegetables!

Cheeses and Dessert

The famous Parmesan (*parmigiano*), far better than the exported product, is eaten by itself, not just grated over soup or pasta. Try, too, the creamy Piedmontese *fontina*, Lombardy blue *gorgonzola*, tangy *provolone* buffalo cheese, *taleggio* from cow's milk or Tuscany's *pecorino* from ewe's milk.

Nothing varies more in quality than the Italian version of trifle, *zuppa inglese* (literally 'English soup'). It may indeed be a thick but sumptuous soup of fruit and cream and cake and Marsala or just a disappointing sweet and gooey slice of cake. Coffee trifle or *tirami sù* ('pull me up') also ranges from the sublime to the sickly. *Zabaglione* of whipped egg yolks, sugar and Marsala should be served warm or sent back.

Easier on the stomach is the fruit: grapes (*uva*), peaches (*pesche*), apricots (*albicocche*) and fresh figs (*fichi*), black or green.

Ice cream is generally much better in an ice-cream parlour (*gelateria*) than in the restaurant.

Tuscan Specialities

Among the most popular **antipasti** are *fagioli toscani con tonno* (Tuscan white beans with tuna/tunny fish), *bruschetti* that make a poem of oven-roasted garlic-bread and *crostini di fegatini* that do the same thing for chopped chicken livers on toast. Cheese and white truffles, *crostini bianchi*, are a speciality of San Gimignano. Anchovies and capers are the basis of the black *crostini neri*. Tuscan **sausage**, from

Siena, Arezzo, Montepulciano, or Florence, is superb, notably the pure pork *salame* or *finocchiona* with fennel seeds, or *salsiccioli secchi*, that are tiny peppery sausages of wild boar.

The favoured **pasta** in Tuscany, served best with a succulent *lepre* sauce (hare in red wine), is flat noodles – *pappardelle* and *tagliolini* rather than rounded spaghetti or macaroni. You will also find *cappelletti* (little hat-shaped ravioli) and spinach *gnocchi*, especially in the Casentino hills of eastern Tuscany.

Those tough winters have encouraged some great **soups**. Tuscany claims the original *minestrone*, distinctive here for its celery (*sedano*) and a little olive oil in place of Parmesan cheese, and *zuppa di fagioli e cavalo nero* (white beans and black cabbage, spiced with garlic and parsley).

The king of **meat** dishes is the *bistecca alla fiorentina*, charcoal-grilled king-sized T-bone steak. However, Tuscany boasts Italy's best **chicken**, either *pollo alla diavola* (straight grilled) or *petti di pollo alla fiorentina* (pan-fried chicken breasts dusted lightly with flour, salt and pepper). **Wild-game**, whether hare, wild boar or venison, is prepared with fragrant herbs and a light tomato sauce. For the robust eater, Tuscan veal tripe (*trippa*) should be eaten chewily *al dente*, never too tender.

Two **fish** specialities are *sarde ripene* (sardines stuffed with cheese, parsley, egg and breadcrumbs) and *anguille in ginocchioni* (Pisan eel-stew).

Mushrooms (*funghi*) are a great local delicacy, notably *ovuli* (small egg-mushrooms) and large boletus, lightly sautéed in local herbs and perfumed with thinly sliced white truffle (*tifola*).

Most Tuscan **cheeses** are of ewe's milk, the best from the *Crete* region south of Siena: tangy *pecorino*, the smoother

Salumi *is not just* salami. *It's any kind of cold meat, like this ham, great with a white* Vernaccia.

creamy *raveggioli* and the famous *ricotta* cottage-cheese.

The best-known **dessert** is the *budino toscano* (Tuscan pudding) made with *ricotta* cheese, almonds, raisins, orange and lemon peel, and vanilla sugar. Otherwise, regional sweets are eaten mostly with a coffee. There is Siena's *panforte nero*, a dark honey-cake rich in almonds and walnuts; *cavalucci* biscuits of honey, nuts and aniseed; and *castagnaccio* made with chestnut-flour, pine nuts and rosemary.

Wines

Besides the world-famous wines of Chianti, with its top-of-the-range Chianti

Classico bearing the proud black-rooster label (*see* THE WINES OF CHIANTI, page 201), Tuscany boasts many more of Italy's finest **red** wines. The Montalcino *Brunello* is so named for the dark red colour produced by its Sangiovese grapes. This powerful wine ages well and complements an equally powerful venison or other roast meat. Montepulciano's *Nobile* is an earthy wine best aged at least two years and drunk with white meat and poultry. If you want to compare Tuscany's reds with their most illustrious rivals, ask in a low voice and appropriately apologetic manner for Piedmont's full-bodied *Barolo*, the fruity *Barbera* or respected *Barbaresca*.

While San Gimignano's *Vernaccia* can age up to five years and is the best regional accompaniment for seafood, most of Tuscany's **white** wines, from Chianti and further south around Pitigliano, are best drunk young, as an apéritif. Otherwise, from just across the Umbrian border, try the fine Orvieto whites or, east of Rome, the light *Frascati*. Another Piedmont product, the sparkling *Asti spumante*, is a highly acceptable alternative to champagne.

As sweet **dessert wines**, try Elba's *Moscato* or *Aleatico*. After-dinner drinks include the anis-flavoured *Sambuca* with a *mosca* coffee-bean (literally a fly) swimming in it or *Grappa* eau-de-vie distilled from grapes.

Bars

There is nothing drowsy about an Italian bar. Its smooth zinc counter, gleaming *espresso* coffee machine and air of brisk efficiency give the place a highly functional air. In Florence or in Chianti hilltowns, people go there in the morning to kick-start the day with a bracing shot of caffeine and a rapidly consumed *cornetto*

(croissant). That's at the counter. At tables further back, locals take it easy, chatting and playing cards.

Prices are cheapest if you follow the Italians' example and drink standing at the bar. In fact, the price list (*listino prezzi*) behind the bar sometimes shows *three* price-rates: bar, inside table and highest outside table.

In busy city centre bars, you must pay for your drinks in advance, specifying your order at the *cassa* (cash-desk). Hand over the receipt (*scontrino*) at the bar and repeat your order, adding a small tip.

Coffee is much more than just *espresso* or *capuccino*. Here is a brief guide:

caffè espresso	a small, strong black coffee in a tiny cup;
ristretto	extra strong;
doppio	double quantity;
lungo	slightly diluted with hot water;
corretto espresso	laced with a shot of spirits, literally 'corrected';
al vetro	in a little glass;
macchiato	with a tiny drop of milk;
caffè latte	milky coffee;
latte macchiato	glass of hot milk with coffee added;
capuccino	served with frothed milk and, ideally, 'dusted' with powdered chocolate;
capuccino freddo	iced coffee in a glass, a summer speciality.

If you want a decaffeinated version of any of the above, ask for *Caffè Hag* (a brand name used in Italy as a generic description).

Tea in an Italian bar is rarely better than a cup of hot water with a separate tea-bag, but there are other refreshing nonalcoholic drinks to try: freshly squeezed orange, lemon or grapefruit (*spremuta di arancia*, *di limone* or *di pompelmo*); or experiment with either a *frullato*, a kind of milkshake made not with ice cream but with chopped fresh fruit and milk or a *granita*, a scoop of crushed ice flavoured with coffee or fruit.

Among the snacks served in the bars, the most common are *pannini* (filled rolls), *tramezzini* (sandwiches) and, in the more chic establishments, Tuscany's famous

crostini (open-faced toast-sandwiches).

Many of the bars also sell bus tickets, postage stamps and cigarettes, and those with a yellow phone sign have a public telephone inside, but you're expected to buy a drink if you use it.

It's just not fair. Even the clouds are prettier in Tuscany – here near Roselle, north of Grosseto.

Light and Colour of Italy's Grandeur Perceived Through a Heady Glass of Chianti

Seeking the quintessence of European civilization, discerning Martians on a fact-finding mission to planet Earth would head straight for Tuscany. Once there, they might never want to go home. Here, man has plunged in and out of civil strife to find in the harmony of his environment a stimulus to paint, to think, but never to lose sight of the importance of good living. Siena's riotous *Palio* horse-race is the perfect antidote to the formidable aesthetics of the Florentines.

Tuscans celebrate the marriage of intellect and fantasy over a glass of wine and a plate of pasta. The magic of the region's ever-changing light has prompted man to shape and colour the landscape. Careful rows of cypresses loom like dark sentinels in the morning mist. Vineyards assert their brilliant green in the midday sun. Olive groves add a silvery shimmer in the late afternoon; and lest people forget a profounder destiny than the carefree serenity of their summer's day, wide expanses of thick forest plunge whole hillsides into

The good ladies of Volterra wonder what the fuss is about; they know Tuscany is the only place to be.

disturbing shadow, deep labyrinths that inspired Dante's Inferno. This is the backdrop for the pink stone buildings of the Tuscans' hilltop towns, for isolated amber or white farmhouses scattered across the rolling plain, and – from the wonderful hilltop vantage point of Fiesole or across the Arno river from the terrace of San Miniato – for the great redbrick dome of Florence's cathedral.

Local Pride

The geographical image of Tuscany may be clear-cut for outsiders, but there is little or no sense of regional unity within its borders. For its inhabitants, the area sweeping from the northerly Apennine mountain range of Emilia-Romagna

down west and south to the Mediterranean is an assembly of independent-minded village or town communes brought together only by geographical accident. This business of town rivalries is a permanent feature throughout the Italian peninsula and nowhere is it more vehement than in Tuscany. This became clear right from the time when the Etruscans needed to unite to resist the Romans: the most they were prepared to do was to form a loosely knit league of the 12 most important towns which could never muster the necessary solidarity to assert their potential strength. It's been the same ever since. The wars of Siena and Florence ended seven centuries ago, but not their hostility. Lucca and Pisa are not and never were good neighbours. Just try asking in the town of Massa how to get to the marble quarries of Carrara, directly adjacent – these communities cannot stand each other.

The last Medicis' title of Grand Duke of Tuscany was always more honorific than honorable. Napoleon's attempt to create the province of 'Etruria' was dismissed as a bad joke. For a dozen years under the Austrian Habsburgs in the 19th century, Tuscany had a unified administration based in Florence, and hated it. Typically, when Lucca, for centuries a fierce adversary of Florence, was asked whether it was prepared to submit to the new kingdom of Italy in 1860, the city fathers reluctantly agreed, observing: 'It is at least better to be Italian than Florentine.'

The cypress, symbol and evergreen guardian of the Tuscan landscape, has made a majestic comeback after years of threatened extinction from traffic pollution.

Even within the towns themselves, the vehemence of the Tuscans' local pride shows up from one quarter to the other. The centuries-old and still passionate rivalries of Siena's 17 neighbourhoods achieve their apotheosis in the grand annual *Palio* horse-race. The competitive spirit is not just a summer phenomenon, it's a year-round affair, and the *Palio* would remain a frenzied contest even if not a single tourist turned up to watch. The same is also true for Arezzo and its annual *Giostra del Saraceno* jousting tournament, Pisa's costumed *Gioca del Ponte* shoving battle on the bridge, or Montepulciano's epic tussle with a giant wine-barrel.

Tuscan individualism finds its most dramatic physical expression in the famous towers dominating the skyline of San Gimignano. They date from the 13th century when each family sought to assert its self-esteem by building a home taller than their neighbours'.

Cradle of the Nation

However reluctant they may be to identify with fellow Tuscans, the people of the region are justly proud of their role in the formation of Italy itself. In a land where there seem to be as many dialects as there are communes, the language of Florence-born Dante, above all in his epic poem, *The Divine Comedy*, was adopted as the national tongue. The Tuscan dialect's pre-eminence was reinforced by the elegant prose of

44

Boccaccio in his *Decameron* as well as the love poetry of Petrarch, to become the most important cement of Italian identity.

Equally pivotal on the national stage, and surely impossible without the almost mystical influence of the region's unique play of light and colour, is the role held by Tuscany's painters, sculptors and architects. Rome, Venice, Bologna and Umbria all claim important parts in the grand story of Italian art, but no other region had such a dominant and wide-ranging position in the

In the late afternoon, the ladies of Castiglione della Pescaia take their babies out for the sacrosanct passeggiata *promenade.*

national pantheon: in painting, Simone Martini in Siena, Giotto and Masaccio in Florence, Piero della Francesco in Arezzo and other great masters of the High Renaissance,

45

Emblematic of its civic pride, the mediæval towers of San Gimignano have created one of the more celebrated skylines in the world.

geniuses. Forget for a moment the cathedrals and museums, Tuscany is also a place where ordinary people delight in just hanging around and doing nothing spectacular, but in the most delightful of surroundings. In that wonderful stretch of land from Florence to Siena that embraces the vineyards of Chianti, the village piazzas of Greve, Radda and Castellina, or further west, in the hilltop towns of Boccaccio's hometown of Certaldo, of proud San Gimignano or ancient Etruscan Volterra, it is enough to just sit at a table with a glass of velvety red wine and dream, perhaps planning an evening meal around superb and simple natural ingredients profiting from the local olive oil and herbs, a savoury pasta, lightly cooked vegetables, straightforward seafood or a Florentine T-bone *bistecca*.

Tuscany has also its Mediterranean coast. At its southern end, sailors and windsurfers make for the peninsula of Monte Argentario and head out from the harbours of Port'Ercole or Porto San Stefano towards the island of Giglio. To the north Elba, the island that couldn't retain Napoleon, provides countless resort beaches for happy holidaymakers. Livorno, known to Britain's 19th-century gentry as the fashionable resort of Leghorn, now concentrates on its original role as Tuscany's principal commercial seaport. Seaside resort activity on a grand scale is to be found further up the coast

such as Botticelli and Leonardo da Vinci; in sculpture, there was the Pisano family of Pisa, Jacopo della Quercia in Siena, and Ghiberti, Donatello and Michelangelo in Florence; and in architecture, Arnolfo di Cambio, Brunelleschi and Michelozzo.

Time off for Wine and Windsurfing

Despite the glories of its past, it would be totally wrong to think of Tuscany only in hushed, reverential terms of its great

Strong winds may whisk you past the island of Elba, but take time out to fish for your supper. With luck, there's a swordfish or red snapper out there waiting just for you.

46

along fine sandy beaches between Viareggio and Forte dei Marmi, both of which are backed by superb pine groves.

For those who want to ease tired bones and muscles, there is also the old-fashioned elegance of health spas like Montecatini Terme or, to the south beyond the great Montepulciano wine-country, Chianciano Terme.

Away from the popular tourist centres, like Florence or Siena, you stand more chance of finding a real bargain at the less-crowded antique fair of Pistoia.

Off the Beaten Track

Modern visitors to Tuscany tend to stay within the region bounded by the *autostrada* that curves around from the coast at Viareggio over to Florence, before heading south towards Rome. However, you should not ignore the many beauties on the other side of this highway. To the north, brave the coolness of the people of Massa and see the spectacular marble quarries at Carrara. Or go hiking in the mountain nature reserves of Garfagnana. In either Pistoia, surrounded by orchards and famous for its great fruit and vegetable markets, or Prato, renowned for its textiles, it's worth going beyond the grace-

less modern suburbs to wander around the handsome *centro storico*.

To the east of the Florence-Rome *autostrada* is the country of the artist Piero della Francesca, rolling hills and plains surrounding Arezzo, Sansepolcro and Monterchi, and the separate elegance of Cortona to the south, each offering a gem of urban charm and rare tranquillity. That, too, is Tuscany.

Not every shrine, not every chapel in Tuscany is a supreme work of art, but even the most modest and anonymous of street altars has its own distinctive charm.

TUSCANY IN NUMBERS

Geography – area 22,989 km² (8,876 sq miles), including Tuscan Archipelago, notably islands of Elba and Giglio, 1,330 km² (513 sq miles). Region bounded on north east by mountain chain of Tuscan-Emilian Apennines and on south west by Mediterranean. Two-thirds of territory covered by hills, the rest by valleys of Chianti and Arno river; only 8.5% plains (mostly reclaimed Maremma marshlands south of Siena).

Arno river flows 241km (150 miles) from Mount Falterona east of Florence to Mediterranean beyond Pisa. Lesser known Ombrone flows south of Siena past Grosseto to coast.

Highest peak: Mount Pisanino, 1945m (6379ft), north east of Carrara.

Population – 3,560,580 (1990).

Capital – Florence (population 413,070).

Major cities – Livorno (171,350), Prato (164,600), Pisa (102,150), Arezzo (91,530), Pistoia (89,970), Grosseto (71,030), Carrara (69,230), Massa (67,570), Siena (58,280).

Government – co-ordinated by regional parliament in Florence. Administration divided into nine provinces, named after major cities, with Massa and Carrara sharing administration of one province. Governing unit most immediately relevant to daily life is the commune of each township.

Economy – chief industries are metal, machine tools and precision instruments in Florence, textiles in Prato, chemicals and fertilizer in Livorno (principal seaport). Elba's iron ore is almost exhausted, but important mainland lead, zinc and coppermines.

Traditional crafts include leather goods, table-linen, lace and porcelain. Agriculture, principally olive oil, Chianti wine, Pistoia fruit and vegetables, cattle-breeding around Grosseto; occupies only 10% of population.

Religion – officially almost 100% Catholic, but enduring rural Marxist tradition would subtract solid atheist minority; small Jewish communities in Florence and Livorno.

Alliance of Merchant Giants and Artistic Genius in Italy's Heartland

Tuscany's story is the tale of its illustrious towns. Merchants, pirates, painters, poets and an occasional pope gave each town its moment in the sun. Only by piecing together the patchwork of their separate destinies is it possible to understand the region's development as a whole. Over the centuries, one or another town came to the fore – Lucca, Pisa, Siena or Florence – but none of them, not even mighty Florence, ever achieved a domination so total as to impose true regional unity. Municipal rivalries made a statecraft of local pride.

The earliest traces of a human presence in Tuscany are a few shards of unbaked pottery found near Pisa, dated around 5500 BC. Over the next couple of thousand years, the ceramics became more sophisticated – lined patterns, glazed and polished black, from kilns near Siena and Pisa. Farmers and herdsmen appeared in the Tuscan hills and valleys during the Bronze Age (1600-1100 BC).

Migrants from central Europe known as Villanovans (from their cemetery excavated

The fortifications at Grosseto show the Medici extending their power throughout Tuscany after emerging victorious from their struggle for the control of Florence.

at Villanova, near Bologna) brought the use of iron down into Tuscany around 1100 BC. All that is known of them is that they cremated their dead, burying the ashes in double-coned urns along with tools, utensils and ornaments, perhaps to accompany the deceased in some form of spiritual afterlife.

The Etruscans

Primitive Villanovan society was superseded by the refined and mysterious civilization of the Etruscans. With a language and culture completely different from any other of Italy's ancient peoples, the Etruscans remain a mystery because nobody knows for sure where they came from. Their name comes from the Latin *Etrusci*, the Greeks calling them *Tyrrhenoi*

An Etruscan warrior from Falterona, a rare sight; the Etruscans preferred trading to fighting.

into Italy over the Alps from northern Europe. Others share the view of Greek historian Herodotus that they came from the island of Lydia in the eastern Mediterranean, driven to Italy by famine. A third group regards them as an indigenous Italian people who just evolved a completely separate civilization. Most recent opinion tends to combine the latter two theories and sees in them a group of gifted native Italians astutely assimilating attractive features brought by Greek immigrants.

Traces of Etruscan society (*see* LIFE WITH THE ETRUSCANS, page 214) survive only in the tombs, the remains of temples and sturdy city walls. What we do know is that their culture began to flourish around 1000 BC and dominated central Italy until the 4th century BC. With rich iron ore deposits on the island of Elba and at Arezzo, and copper from the hills of Tuscany, they prospered from trade with Greek colonists settling in southern Italy in the 8th century BC. They also enjoyed a thriving agriculture of grain, olives and fruit.

Their merchants indulged in a little piracy, a perennial Mediterranean custom, but the Etruscans never mounted anything like a real military expedition. The colonies they set up abroad, in Spain, the Balearic Islands, Corsica and Sardinia, like their alliance with Carthage in north Africa, seemed to be purely commercial enterprises to satisfy the home market in consumer goods rather than any form of expansionist empire.

They founded their main towns, including Volterra (*Velathri* in Etruscan), Fiesole, Arezzo, Cortona (*Cortun*) and Chiusi (*Clevsin*), at the height of their power in the 7th and 6th centuries BC. In most of these towns, you will find signs of the Etruscan presence in ancient fortifications or remains of their sanctuaries.

(whence the name Tyrrhenian Sea for the Mediterranean of Tuscany's west coast).

Since the 19th century, archaeologists have divided into three camps. A few, largely discredited, argue from apparent similarities of town names and other linguistic affinities that the Etruscans came

The towns' league, a loose confederation of a dozen autonomous monarchies, spread down through Rome to Capua and Salerno in southern Italy. They assembled only for religious festivals rather than concerted political action, however, never forming a single Etruscan nation. (Other important places of Etruscan origin out-

The entrance to the Museo dell'Accademia Etrusca in Cortona, one of Italy's more prestigious collections of antiquities including Etruscan bronzes of warriors and animals.

side Tuscany are Tarquinia, the probable head of the confederation, and the Umbrian towns of Perugia and Orvieto.)

With the Etruscans weakened by northern invasions from Gaul in the 4th century BC, Rome broke away from the confederation and gradually asserted its domination over the whole peninsula. The Etruscans quarrelled among themselves and had no real stomach to withstand the rising conqueror. Volterra put up the fiercest fight, holding out until 90 BC. Two years later, the last independent Etruscan aristocratic families pledged allegiance to the Roman state.

Under the Romans

Supreme pragmatists, the Romans did not go around systematically destroying the vanquished Etruscans' towns. They appreciated places like Fiesole, Volterra or Cortona for their strategic hilltop locations. The Romans built their own towns either in the plain, on a river, like the port of Florence (*Florentia*) in 59 BC, or in strategic positions beside one of their new roads, like the military garrison of Pistoia (*Pistoriae*) on the Via Cassia. Arezzo (*Arretium*) was vitally important to the Romans for its iron and the surrounding fertile farmland. In the heart of Tuscany, an isolated hilltop community, a dependency of Volterra, was developed under Augustus as a military colony with the name of *Saena Julia* – Siena.

Pisa, established as a commercial port by Greek settlers before coming under Etruscan control in the 5th century BC, now flourished as the naval base for the Romans' western Mediterranean fleet. They made it the junction of the Via Cassia and the coastal Via Aurelia that continued north into Gaul. The neighbouring

TUSCANY'S ROMAN AMPHITHEATRES

The passage of the barbarians left standing few traces of Rome's colonization of Tuscany, though Florence's Roman foundation can still be seen in the characteristic right-angled grid-plan of the city centre. Otherwise, the tell-tale vestige of Roman rule is the amphitheatre. In Florence itself, the curving streets west of Piazza Santa Croce starting at Via Torta trace the perimeter of the theatre, now covered by medieval housing. At nearby Fiesole, the Roman theatre has been fully excavated in the same area as an Etruscan temple. In Arezzo, the ruins of the amphitheatre have also been uncovered, the auditorium and stage now embraced by the curve of San Bernardino monastery (beside the Archaeology Museum). With its customary good business sense, Lucca has preserved and transformed its amphitheatre into a market, Piazza del Mercato, incorporating Roman brick arches into the construction of the surrounding medieval houses.

Looking over the rooftops of Volterra today, you could be forgiven for not seeing signs of the town's Etruscan past.

town of Lucca (founded by Ligurians from the Italian Riviera region around Genoa) was valuable to Rome for its control of the Italian end of the inland trade-route over the Alps to northern Europe.

When the Roman Empire declined and finally fell in the 5th century AD, Tuscany found itself in the devastating path of the

Volterra was the last of the Etruscan Confederation's 12 great cities to resist Roman conquest. The ruins of its Roman era are still being excavated.

barbarian invasions, in turn Visigoths, Huns and Ostrogoths. They showed little respect for Rome's achievements there, but Pisa was preserved for its strategic value as, what was then, Tuscany's main seaport.

Lombards and Franks

While the Goths and Huns stayed in Tuscany just long enough to kill, rape, plunder and burn as they passed through, the Lombards arrived in the 6th century to set up a kingdom that lasted for over 200 years. From the royal court installed at Pavia, south of Milan, the originally north German *Langobardi* or Long Beards conquered Tuscany and formed a chain of duchies all the way down to the duchy of Benevento south of Naples. To exploit its long-established trade links with northern Europe across the Alps, the Lombards created a duchy at Lucca, making it the capital of Tuscany.

After Charlemagne conquered the Lombard kingdom, he was content to leave the energetic merchants of Lucca in charge of what became in 774 a frontier region of his Frankish empire, the March of Tuscany. Its position as a commercial and military force was strengthened by Count Bonifacio I of Lucca, who died in 823, and especially his son Bonifacio II. His defeat of Arab fleets in the Mediterranean extended Tuscan control to Corsica and Sardinia.

In the 11th century, the Attoni dynasty, ruling from Canossa in northern Italy, made Tuscany the most powerful feudal state in central Italy, with the backing of the Holy Roman (in fact, German) Emperors. However, their most celebrated ruler, Matilda (1076-1115) chose to support Pope Gregory VII against Emperor Henry IV in their fight for control of Italian territories. It was in Matilda's castle that the emperor was obliged publicly to humble himself before the pope. When the feisty lady, known as the Great Countess, donated her lands to the papacy rather than to her family's traditional imperial supporter, she unleashed a conflict that has continued in one form or another to the present day.

Rise of the Communes

Matilda's challenge came at a time when the individual towns of Tuscany were growing richer and stronger, and creating communes to administer their surrounding lands. In this international power-struggle, Tuscan wealth was suddenly up for grabs and the independent-minded communes could side with the forces supporting the pope, who came to be known as the Guelphs, or their enemies backing the emperor, the Ghibellines, or play one off against the other.

For Pisa, Lucca, Siena, Pistoia or Florence, self-interest remained the only criterion. Even within one city, rival clans split off into Guelph or Ghibelline factions. The battles of Guelph and Ghibelline served merely to fuel the natural rivalry that has been the lifeblood of these and all Tuscan towns ever since. In the 20th century, observers have noted in many of Tuscany's communities, both rural and urban, that mayors of the Communist Party and its successor party, the PDS (Partito democratico della sinistra, Democratic Party of the Left) have continued unbroken the Ghibelline tradition, At the same time,Christian Democrats and other right-wing parties have held sway in old Guelph strongholds.

SQUARES OR SWALLOWTAILS

Anybody who claims to understand what the quarrels between Guelphs and Ghibellines were really about has been misinformed. The issues were always too obscure and constantly changing for anyone to have the slightest idea who wanted what, why and how, least of all the Guelphs and Ghibellines themselves.

The name *Guelph* derives from the pro-pope Welf dynasty of Bavarian dukes and *Ghibelline* is believed to be a battle-cry inspired by the pro-emperor German Swabian family by the name of Waiblingen. One historian at a loss to find any other important distinction between the two suggests a good way of remembering which is which lies in the fact that *Guelph* and 'pope' both have one syllable while *Ghibelline* and 'emperor' both have three.

Ideology counted for nothing. It was out of gratitude for Matilda's past material favours that Florence started out in the Guelph camp. That was good enough reason for Pistoia, wary of being swamped by its neighbour, and Siena, the eternal rival, to ally themselves with the Ghibellines. If Pisa and Lucca also supported the Ghibellines, however, it was not because these bitter enemies had suddenly found a common cause, but rather that both had concluded that the emperor was their best bet since he was too far away to interfere in their private affairs. Both were happy to switch sides for the right price.

To confuse things further, in Florence, some feuding families sided with the Ghibellines, and the Guelphs themselves split into camps of Black and White. Perhaps the best way to understand the real significance is to consider the shape of the battlements on Florence's Palazzo Vecchio, stronghold of its communal government. Ghibelline families proclaimed their allegiance with crenellations of simple square blocks atop their walls and towers, while Guelphs built their ramparts with swallowtail blocks. On the Palazzo Vecchio, the Ghibellines erected the square-block main structure and the Guelphs put up the swallowtail tower. You see?

Pisa: the Riches of Sea-power

In the 11th century, Tuscany's most important seaport built a powerful maritime empire rivalling those of Venice and Genoa. Constantly at war with the Arabs, its fleet seized control of Corsica, Sardinia and, in alliance with the Normans, Palermo in Sicily. Other trade-counters were established in Syria, Palestine and Egypt.

Monumental testimony to the wealth amassed by Pisa's medieval empire is provided by the grandiose *Campo dei Miracoli* (Field of Miracles) embracing the Romanesque cathedral, baptistery, Leaning Tower campanile, and completed by the Gothic Camposanto burial grounds. Construction spanned the 200 years of Pisa's golden era. From its victory in Sicily in 1063, Pisa brought back six Arab treasure ships with which it financed the building of the grandiose Romanesque Cathedral, inaugurated 50 years later. Its design draws on many influences from its commerce in the eastern Mediterranean. From its participation in the Crusades in the 11th and 12th centuries, Pisa carried back shiploads of earth from the Holy Land to create the splendid Camposanto cemetery.

This construction boom revived the fortunes of the Carrara marble quarries, that had lain dormant since first being exploited by the Romans in the 2nd century AD, when the site was known as *Luna*. Pisa's spectacular use of the unique purity of Carrara marble, giving the white edifices their luminous, jewel-like quality,

The great cathedral, built by Pisa in the 11th century, inspired the design of Romanesque churches throughout Tuscany. However, the Leaning Tower has not had any imitations.

attracted the attention of sculptors and architects from all over Italy. The master sculptor for the cathedral and baptistery, Nicola Pisano, and later his son, Andrea, were in great demand in Siena, Pistoia, Orvieto and Florence.

In 1284, Pisan superiority came to a grinding halt with its naval defeat by Genoa at the battle of Meloria, a reef just off the coast of Livorno. The empire was dismantled and the city went into slow decline over the next century. Factions of nobles and merchants fought for the dwindling spoils in vicious civil war, frequently invoking the outside help of papal Guelfs or imperial Ghibellines. Subject to frequent periods of foreign government, most notably by the Duke of Milan, Gian Galeazzo Visconti (1396-1405), the town finally, however reluctantly, submitted to Florentine rule in 1406. Among the benefits was the revival of its university (founded in 1343 by Pope Clement VI), its most notable teacher arriving at the end of the 16th century – one Galileo Galilei.

Lucca: Business First

The old Tuscan capital of the Lombards and Franks was smaller than its southern neighbour, Pisa, but was no less independent-minded. Lacking access to the sea, it compensated with imaginative use of land-routes across the Apennines and over the Alps to northern and eastern

European markets. As it was on the path of invading armies from the north, its merchants had learned that the right price paid to the right man was cheaper and safer than armed resistance.

The handsome churches built in Lucca's heyday in the 12th and 13th centuries – the cathedral of San Martino, San Michele and San Frediano – were financed not by overseas conquest and empire but by masterful business skills. Lucca's bankers collected generous interest on loans to crowned heads all over Europe, while enterprising silk merchants struck hard bargains both in the markets of France and Germany, and with the aristocracy of Poland and Hungary.

By the beginning of the 14th century, Lucca had become the most prosperous town in Tuscany after Florence, but like Pisa, the town was rent by civil strife among Guelph and Ghibelline factions, and was governed by a series of military tyrants. The most noteworthy was Castruccio Castracani who expanded Lucca's supremacy in Tuscany to the threshold of Florence until he died of malaria in 1328. The town then fell prey to the constant menace of 'protection' by greedy Genoa, Parma, Verona and, most galling of all, even Pisa, despite this hated neighbour's own declining fortunes. For a brief moment, Lucca had to submit to Florence,

*T*hanks to the guile of the town's businessmen, Lucca's splendid monuments, like the Church of San Michele, have survived all the onslaughts of foreign armies. The merchants just rode out to each new military commander and paid him off to bypass the city.

but such a strong-spirited community soon found the Florentines too domineering. In 1369, the commune finally placed its destiny in the hands of the German emperor, Charles IV, who guaranteed it the status of a republic independent of any Italian power. It was to remain that way until 1847. Business could be resumed.

Siena: Banker to Popes and Emperors

With only the emblem of the she-wolf suckling Romulus and Remus to recall its Roman origins, Siena had remained an obscure outpost of Tuscan politics until the Middle Ages. In the 10th and 11th centuries, civic and religious power was concentrated in the hands of the bishop, who did not hesitate to lead the city's troops into battle. To gain a larger piece of the prospering municipal pie, the nobles formed an alliance with the people against the ecclesiastic authority. In 1147, a government of consuls was formed, but there followed 50 years of civil strife among Siena's squabbling factions – aristocrats against merchants, merchants against workers, and everybody alternately for and against the church.

If the town was nominally pro-emperor Ghibelline because Florence was pro-pope Guelph, that never stopped one interest-group or another calling on the support, financial or military, of the Guelphs' papal forces. In 1159, a son of the local Bandinelli family became Pope Alexander III. The Sienese abandoned the Ghibelline alliance temporarily to support 'their' pope's fight against Emperor Frederick Barbarossa. His agitation culminated in the Lombard League's victory against the German armies at Legnano in 1176, a landmark in the assertion of Italy's national identity. Three years later, he returned to his home town in triumph to consecrate the splendid new cathedral. (England's King Henry II found in Pope Alexander III a stern enemy who forced him to do penance after murdering Thomas Becket, Archbishop of Canterbury.)

Siena's major preoccupation was its growing struggle with Florence for control of the Arno valley and southern and eastern Tuscany. It had seized nearby Poggibonsi in 1156, controlled Montalcino, but had failed to take Montepulciano further south.

In 1199, a *podestà* (magistrate) had to be brought in from outside to settle the local quarrels. Subsequently, a council of 24 citizens forming a delicate balance of nobles and ordinary citizens enabled the merchant classes to assert their ascendancy.

LOAN RANGERS

Beware of the smile on the face of a Sienese bank manager. On the principle that money has neither perfume nor incense, Siena's medieval bankers grew fat lending indifferently to popes and emperors alike. They paid out with the benevolence of saints and reclaimed their loans and handsome interest with a brutality worthy of the wildest west. They had a trick. They had noted the flexible attitude of their Catholic debtors towards lending at interest – notorious backsliders when it came to borrowing, but suddenly piously censorious of the sin of usury when it was time to repay the money. Whenever one of their clients 'turned religious' on them, the Sienese bankers smiled with equal piety and reached into their desk-drawer, not for a gun, but something much worse: a letter which, as part of their deals with the Vatican, they had paid the popes to sign, a letter excommunicating the bad debtor by name and assigning him to eternal damnation in hell. He paid up.

The 13th century saw the bankers of Siena extend their influence throughout Europe and become the dominant financial force in central Italy. Its streets and squares were paved for the first time. Palaces sprang up around the cathedral. Recovering from military defeat by Florence in 1207 and the losses of Poggibonsi and Montalcino in 1225, Siena had become by this time more important in wealth and population than either Paris or London.

Florence was jealous. In 1260, its ambassadors made a characteristically officious declaration to the Siena city council: 'It is our will that your city dismantle its fortifications and that several breaches be opened in the city walls to permit us to enter the town when and where it is our pleasure.' Siena responded by inflicting a resounding defeat on Florence's army at Montaperti some 12km (7 miles) east of those city-walls.

This proved to be a Pyrrhic victory, and the beginning of a long decline. The pope rewarded Florence's unfailing support by excommunicating the whole city of Siena, leaving its bankers without the customary papal protection against their bad debtors (*see* panel, page 62). In 1269, Florence retaliated with ruthless brutality in the devastating battle of Colle Val d'Elsa. Always ready to compromise when profits were at stake, Siena's money men – known by their own citizens as the *popolo grasso*, 'fat people' – replaced the Council of 24 Ghibellines by one of 36 pro-pope Guelphs.

By 1287, municipal government was streamlined to a Council of Nine, still Guelph and happy to make peace with too-mighty Florence. This civil tranquillity permitted a renewed period of prosperity and artistic creation. Giovanni Pisano gave the cathedral its opulent façade, Simone

Martini and the Lorenzetti brothers painted their masterpieces. The imposing Palazzo Pubblico was completed, overlooking the *Campo*, the grand shell-shaped square divided into nine segments to assemble supporters of the municipal government's nine councillors. Behind the Palazzo, as the other pendant of city power, the Piazza del Mercato assembled the vital interests of commerce.

This did not stop the factional strife, of which the frenzied annual *Palio* horse-race was only a sporting sublimation (*see* page 225) once more exploding into violence. The great Buonsignori bank collapsed. The Black Plague of 1348 so decimated the population that there were not enough living to bury the dead. Recovering with difficulty but still reluctant to yield totally to Florence, the town placed its fate in the hands of Gian Galeazzo Visconti, Duke of Milan, from 1399 to 1404. This time of disarray saw the emergence of the celebrated benefactor and spiritual advisor of kings and popes, St Catherine of Siena. Her renown was such that she became patron saint not only for the city but for the whole Italian nation (*see* page 239).

In the 15th century, the town achieved a rare moment of unity under another Sienese pope, Pius II (1458-1463), before submitting to the more or less enlightened despotism of Pandolfo Petrucci (1487-1512) and his successor Alessandro Bicchi, who ruled till 1524. By then, the dominant power in Italy was Emperor Charles V. He installed a Spanish military garrison in Siena. Symbolic of the peace he imposed on the town, a new fortress was built in 1531 largely with masonry from the palace-towers of the town's factious families. An alliance with the French briefly drove out the foreign invaders, but Philip II reaffirmed Spain's authority in a treaty with Henri II of France in 1559. Siena's territory was sold to Florence's Duke Cosimo I de' Medici and the town became a sleepy backwater, revived only by the tourism of the 20th century.

Florence: the Gold Standard

The city's progress in the early Middle Ages was hampered by its allegiance to the pope, who liked to keep a close watch over the affairs of his followers. While the Guelphs of Florence submitted to the authority of Matilda, Countess of Tuscany (*see* page 56), Ghibelline cities like Lucca or Pisa flourished with the status of autonomous communes by allying themselves with the less interfering German emperor.

It was only in the 12th century that Florence established its commune and set about conquering its hinterland. The city's rise to dominance in Tuscany began with victory over Fiesole in 1125 at the end of a two-year war. Florence then proceeded to destroy systematically the feudal domains of hostile barons in the surrounding hills. In 1183, Emperor Frederick Barbarossa was obliged to recognize the commune of the pro-pope Guelphs. However, the destruction of their castles had brought the disgruntled nobles into town. Their new strongholds fomented Ghibelline sympathies within the city walls and promoted the factionalism that was to characterize Florentine history with its constant threat to civil unity.

In the first half of the 13th century, nobles and merchants vied for control of the town's growing wealth. Money rolled in from an astute combination of banking, commerce and manufacturing. Textile production was organized for the first time on a large-scale industrial basis and

Florentine manufacturers challenged the long-established supremacy of Lucca's silk merchants. By 1250, power had shifted from the nobles to the guilds formed by the traders in wool and textiles, grocers, doctors and, above all, the bankers.

In 1252, Florence was the first Italian city to mint its own gold coin, the 'florin' (*fiorino*). Over the next 300 years, Florentine bankers made this unit of currency weighing 3.5 grams (one-eighth of an ounce) the monetary exchange standard for western Europe, the ECU of the Renaissance world.

In a city that was becoming Christianity's financial capital, the churches had to be refashioned to reflect the new prosperity. For Santa Croce, Giotto was commissioned by the Bardi banking family and Peruzzi merchants to paint frescoes in their new chapels, and all the guilds pitched in to ask him to design a campanile for the Cathedral.

Rival clans of merchants and bankers fought for every florin and the frequent outbursts of hostilities are reflected in the civil architecture. The formidable Bargello fortress (now a sculpture museum) was completed in 1261 as the home of the *podestà* magistrate-cum-police chief appointed by the people to defend their interests against the monied oligarchy. Architect Arnolfo da Cambio took time off from building the Cathedral to design the massive Palazzo Vecchio, seat of the *Signorìa* communal government. Its tower was surrounded by those of the equally intimidating bastions of rival factions, often with an overhead bridge to reach the battlements of their allies without having to descend to street level.

Not that these merchant families did much fighting themselves. Business kept them too busy, so they just made a little

extra, in fact a lot extra, and paid mercenaries to fight for them. They found a common cause in consolidating their town's supremacy in Tuscany. After their crushing victory over Siena in 1269, avenging the earlier humiliation at Montaperti, Florentine forces slowly but surely extended the town's domination. They conquered Arezzo-led Ghibelline forces in 1289 at the terrible battle of Campaldino in the Casentino hills of the upper Arno valley east of Florence. Pistoia fell in 1331, Cortona in 1332, Arezzo submitted in 1336, and Montepulciano in 1390. Pisa held out till 1406. Lucca remained infuriatingly aloof.

The Black Plague of 1348 had the same catastrophic effect on Florence as on other Italian cities, but, like the civil strife that drove Dante to give up politics for poetry, it also had a happy literary side effect. To avoid the bubonic contagion, aristocrats fled the city to the isolated safety of their hilltop country villas. The son of a prosperous Florentine merchant banker, though perhaps born in the village of Certaldo where he died, Giovanni Boccaccio (1313-1375) wrote two years after the Plague of just such an assembly in the 100 tales he collected under the title *The Decameron*. For the evolution of the Italian language, Boccaccio's bawdy and elegant account of the Tuscan gentry's manners and attitudes reinforced in prose what Dante had done in poetry.

These genteel preoccupations were light-years away from those of the day-labourers exploited in Florence's woollen mills. Lacking job-security and any of the other protections provided by a guild, the *Ciompi* (named after the clogs they wore in the mill's wash-house) erupted in open revolt in 1378. In the scheme of things, these wool-workers were a kind of sub-proletariat

---

DANTE ALIGHIERI (1265-1321)

Without the imbecilities of Florentine civil war, we could never have rejoiced in that masterpiece of world literature, Dante's *Divine Comedy*. Dante Alighieri was born into a patrician family of Florentine Guelphs, distinguishing himself in the town's cavalry at the battle of Campaldino in 1289. The next year his beloved Beatrice died and he drowned his sorrows in the study of classical philosophy and Provençal poetry.

For five years, 1295 to 1300, he also tried his hand at politics, serving as a town councillor in the Palazzo Vecchio. By then, the Guelphs had split into two, fanatic papist Blacks and more sceptical Whites – which is, of course, not the same as pro-emperor Ghibelline, but what did Dante know, he was just a poet. Disapproving the abuses of power by Pope Boniface VIII, Dante sided with the White Guelph papal sceptics. The Blacks came out on top, confiscated all his property and banished him from Florence.

Forced to travel to Verona, Lucca and Ravenna, he sensed that, in the absence of one unifying monarchy, it was itinerant intellectuals like himself who represented the scattered national identity. On his wanderings, he wrote in the noble Tuscan vernacular that was to become the basis of the national language, *The Divine Comedy*, symbol of Italian nationhood and civilization.

The Beatrice to whom he dedicated his epic poem is believed to be the daughter of a wealthy Florentine family, the Portinari, whom he had first seen when he was just nine years old. After her death, he married another, Gemma Donata, with whom he had three children, but he always idealized Beatrice as the inspiration for all his work. In *The Divine Comedy*, after fellow poet Virgil leads him through the Inferno and Purgatory, Beatrice becomes his guide in Paradise. Not an easy trip: 'Beatrice looked at me with eyes so full of the sparkling of love and so divine that my power, overcome, took flight and, with eyes cast down, I was almost lost.'

> *Beatrice mi guardò con li occhi pieni*
> *di faville d'amor così divini,*
> *che, vinta, mia virtute diè le reni,*
> *e quasi mi perdei con li occhi chini.*

---

in the conflicts that had long been seething between the privileged guilds of lawyers, silk-merchants, bankers and apothecaries, and the minor guilds of butchers and smiths. The *Ciompi* went on the rampage, burning and plundering the merchants' houses. Similarly under-privileged workers who, out of fear for their livelihood, did not join the revolt were attacked by the *Ciompi* as 'traitors who allow us to starve'.

The rebels held sway for a few weeks, the merchants conceded limited guild privileges, but the movement collapsed for lack of solidarity among the humbler guilds. By 1382, the old system was back in force. The *Signorìa* in Palazzo Vecchio was firmly in the hands of an oligarchy of established patrician families – the Albizzi, Ricci, Alberti, Strozzi and Medici.

The Medici Dynasty

Scholars still debate whether the balls (*palle*) on the Medici coat of arms are a play on words as medicinal pills or depict the coins amassed by this most fabulously successful of all Italian banking dynasties.

The merchant family moved into Florence from the nearby Mugello valley in the 13th century. Over 100 years later, Giovanni di Bicci was the first to make his mark financially, but it was his son Cosimo the Elder (1389-1464) who translated the family wealth into the political power that put the Medici name on the world stage.

Other Florentine patricians like the Albizzi waged their struggles for control of the *Signorìa* in the council chambers of the Palazzo Vecchio. The modest but highly intelligent workaholic Cosimo preferred to pull strings behind the scenes from the family home. Ever prudent, he had opposed the Albizzi's impulsive policy of all-out war against Lucca, that had allied with the mighty dukes of Milan in resisting the extension of Florentine power through Tuscany.

In 1433, foisting the blame on Cosimo for their failure to overcome the obstreperous merchants of Lucca, the Albizzi-led oligarchy engineered his imprisonment at the Palazzo Vecchio and then had him banished to Padua. Typically, Cosimo had foreseen the move and transferred all Medici funds out of Florence before they could be confiscated. This enabled him to buy the support of the pope, Venetian troops and, most importantly, the ordinary people of Florence. He returned in triumph a year later to be handed the government of the city – though he preferred not to hold on to the title of *gonfaloniere* (governing magistrate).

His iron-fisted control of Florence and its Tuscan hinterland has prompted modern detractors to see Cosimo as a Mafioso-like Godfather. Kinder observers compare his authority, more often pragmatic than violent, with that of a 20th-century political boss in Boston or Chicago. Where the rulers of Italy's other city-states savagely executed their enemies, Cosimo chose to banish the Albizzi and their aristocratic supporters, some 70 in all. To someone protesting he was stripping Florence of all its leading citizens, he commented: 'Seven or eight yards of scarlet will make a new citizen.' To be on the safe side, he did order the destruction of the towers and other warlike fortifications on the strongholds that menacingly surrounded the Palazzo Vecchio.

The new houses, like the Palazzo Medici designed for Cosimo by Michelozzo (across from the church of San Lorenzo), were still built with massive walls to offer robust defences, but were generally less openly aggressive than before. The more serene era ushered in by Medici government could also be seen on the hills surrounding Florence in the nobles' tranquil country villas, with gardens and vineyards rather than moats and guardhouses.

Significantly, 1434, the year that saw the consolidation of Medici power, was also the year that Brunelleschi built the great dome of Florence cathedral. Renaissance art was getting underway. Masaccio and Masolino had done their revolutionary frescoes for the Brancacci Chapel of Santa Maria del Carmine, the sculptor Ghiberti was at work on the Baptistery doors, and Donatello and Paolo Uccello were also busy (see ART AND ARCHITECTURE IN TUSCANY, pages 80–95).

A great moment of personal pride for Cosimo came with his hosting of a triumphal procession for the princes of the Catholic and Orthodox churches at the Ecumenical Council of 1439, in an albeit abortive effort to reconcile Rome and Constantinople. A year later, the Medici alliance with papal and Venetian armies scored a vital victory over Milanese forces

At the time that the Medicis became top dogs in power, the top sculptor of the Renaissance was undoubtedly Donatello.

Medici supremacy in Tuscany was never total. Lucca's spirited resistance to Florentine authority up to 1847 is epitomized by these 17th-century bastions.

at Anghiari, near Arezzo. The battle that affirmed Florence's supremacy throughout central Italy was the subject of a famous but now disappeared fresco by Leonardo da Vinci for the Palazzo Vecchio.

Lorenzo the Magnificent (1469-1492)

After Cosimo's son, demeaningly known as Piero the Gouty (*il Gottoso*), had weathered a decade of stiff anti-Medici opposition, grandson Lorenzo took over in 1469 to become the most illustrious of all the Medici. In those days, the epithet *Magnifico* might be attributed to any non-royal political leader without implication of real magnificence, but for this grand poet-patron of the Renaissance heyday, it became a title of merited honour.

Lorenzo presided over the artistic achievements of Botticelli, Leonardo da Vinci, Michelangelo, Verrocchio, Ghirlandaio and architect Giuliano da Sangallo. However, his predilection was for scholarship, favouring the company of poets like Angelo Poliziano or philosophers Marsilio Ficino and Pico della Mirandola. (A positive effect of the 1439 Ecumenical Council had been to accelerate the flow

T he Medicis were great patrons of the arts. This Allegory of Spring *by Botticelli was commissioned by Lorenzo.*

> **DON'T MESS WITH A MEDICI**
>
> Tracing their family's noble origins back to the First Crusade in the 11th century, the Pazzi family regarded the Medici as a bunch of vulgar *nouveaux riches*. Egged on by the Archbishop of Pisa and promised the support of Pope Sixtus IV and King Ferrante of Naples, the Pazzi planned to kill Lorenzo and his brother Giuliano de' Medici in Florence Cathedral during Mass. Francesco de' Pazzi and a professional assassin were to take care of Giuliano, but left Lorenzo to a couple of embittered anti-Medici priests. On Sunday morning, 26 April 1478, on the prearranged signal of the sacristy bell heralding Communion, Giuliano was hacked to death, but the clumsy clerics bungled their efforts to run Lorenzo through near the High Altar. With only a light stab wound in the neck, he leapt over the altar rail and escaped through the sacristy. His poet friend Angelo Poliziano saved him by slamming shut the heavy bronze doors before the other assassins could reach him.
>
> Lorenzo's revenge was merciless. Over 300 people suspected of links with the conspirators were executed, including Francesco de' Pazzi and Archbishop Salviati of Pisa, both hanged naked from windows of the Palazzo Vecchio. Poet Poliziano wrote an account of the plot and its aftermath in Latin verse. Leonardo da Vinci went over to the Palazzo Vecchio with his sketchbook to make meticulous anatomical drawings and notes for costume colours of one of the tortured victims.

W hether governed by the authoritarian Medici or more democratically minded republicans, Renaissance Florence stood fast against all its foes and Michelangelo's statue of David was its defiant symbol.

into Italy of texts of classical Greek philosophers.) It was Lorenzo who revived the University of Pisa. For the Florentines, he made a public library of the family's great Biblioteca Laurenziana (founded by Cosimo, but named after St Laurence, not Lorenzo himself). Both the Vasari portrait at the Uffizi and the Verrocchio bust in Washington's National Gallery show him to have been ugly, but with a certain delicate sensuality, a wide mouth, big nose and resolute jutting chin.

Unlike grandfather Cosimo, Lorenzo readily used violence against opponents. In 1472, he sent mercenaries to smash the town of Volterra in a dispute over local deposits of alum (a mineral vital to Florence's textile-dyeing industry). Six years later, Lorenzo ordered hundreds executed after the Pazzi family failed in a plot to assassinate him – but did kill his brother Giuliano.

After the abortive plot, the Pazzi family's backers, Pope Sixtus IV and the King of Naples, declared all-out war on Lorenzo with an army of mercenaries. It was led by Federico da Montefeltro, the broken-nosed Duke of Urbino made famous by Piero della Francesca's wonderful portrait in the Uffizi. His troops advanced through the Chianti valley, took Radda and Castellina and would probably have conquered Florence if they had not stopped for the prolonged period of a winter truce. This time, Lorenzo chose not to fight but engaged in a prudent, perhaps even courageous, piece of diplomacy by travelling to negotiate peace personally with the King of Naples.

Lorenzo's talents did not extend to banking. At his death in 1492, the Medici business was in ruins. His son Piero lacked his strength of character and left Florence vulnerable to the rabble-rousing preaching of a fanatical Dominican monk.

Republican Interlude

Near the Palazzo Vecchio is a round plaque set in the piazza pavement to mark the spot where Girolamo Savonarola (1452-1498) experienced his greatest triumph and excruciating end. Son of a distinguished doctor of Ferrara, the Dominican monk arrived in Florence in 1482 to launch his campaign against the vices of the pagan Renaissance and the sins of the pope, the clergy and the aristocracy. His fiery sermons prophesied calamities that would regenerate the Church. This rearguard action of the Middle Ages won for Savonarola a fanatical popular following, including many born-again Christian artists like Botticelli and the young Michelangelo, and even the respected philosopher, Pico della Mirandola. After nine years of preaching, Savonarola was made prior of the San Marco monastery.

Charles VIII of France invaded Italy in 1494, a landmark year that effectively ended any semblance of real Italian political autonomy until national independence four centuries later. Savonarola called on the French king to take Florence and help him reform the church by ousting Pope Alexander VI. The French army stayed in the city only long enough to replenish its war-chest from Florentine coffers before continuing down to Naples. Piero de' Medici had already fled the city and Savonarola championed a Florentine Republic. This offered more representative government, but for the next four years functioned as a theocratic dictatorship in which Savonarola was proclaimed Jesus King of Florence.

The Dominican preacher converted libertines and whores and banned traditional festivities and public games; bawdy carnival songs were replaced by hymns;

Jewish money-changers were banished and replaced by Catholic pawnbrokers. Though vice and licentiousness were indeed rife, the good monk installed an equally vicious totalitarian system of police surveillance to root them out. Servants denounced masters, children denounced their parents.

On 7 February 1497, at the Piazza della Signorìa, Savonarola staged his Bonfire of the Vanities. In a state of religious frenzy, the town's aristocracy cast their jewels, mirrors, cosmetics, silks and satins onto the fire. Musicians burned their instruments. Botticelli and Andrea della Robbia tossed their paintings and sculpture into the flames. Pursuing the time-honoured custom of tyrannies throughout history, books of Boccaccio and Petrarch were used for kindling. (Almost as influential as Dante in the development of Italian poetry, Petrarch wrote most of his offending love lyrics in French exile. His family had been banished from Florence in the same Black-White Guelph conflicts that drove Dante out of town.)

Pope Alexander VI, sick of being the prime target of the friar's attacks, excommunicated him, but he continued preaching. The pope summoned the city to surrender him to Rome or risk being 'interdicted' as a whole community. This threat to Florentine property holdings, such as banks and lands, on papal territories lost him the support of influential citizens. A Franciscan monk challenged him to prove the divine protection to which he laid claim by facing the ordeal of fire. When he weaseled out by getting one of his Dominican assistants to take his place, saying 'I reserve myself for a greater task', the city elders decided they had had enough and threw him into jail. Just one look at the torture-rack and he confessed to whatever they asked.

On 22 May 1498, at the same spot where he had burned Botticelli's paintings, Savonarola was hanged on a gibbet and in turn burned to ashes that were scattered in the Arno river.

With the republic, the Florentines had developed a taste for democracy and representative government. This was symbolized in Michelangelo's proud statue of *David* erected outside the Palazzo Vecchio. Government was placed in the hands of a series of executive committees re-

---

OLD NICK

Niccolò Machiavelli (1469-1527) wrote his masterworks *The Prince* and *Discourses* in the retirement enforced on him, after 1512, for being too closely identified with his discredited former master, Piero Soderini. Hoping to win their favour, the wily but not wily enough diplomat dedicated his books to the Medici. If they had listened to his advice instead of jailing and torturing him, they might have held on to real power a lot longer.

The terrifying world depicted in his writings gained him such a diabolical reputation that in 17th-century England his was the widely accepted alternative name for the devil. In fact, what old Nick analysed was less a theory for an ideal state and perfect prince than the real state as he had observed it, with its actual strengths and weaknesses, along with the successful prince best able to exploit them.

Even though no prince himself, he might have avoided a life of pain and disappointment if he had followed his own advice: 'As a prince must be able to act just like a beast, he should learn from both the fox and the lion; because the lion does not defend himself against traps, and the fox does not defend himself against wolves. So one has to be a fox in order to recognize traps, and a lion to frighten off wolves.'

71

sponsible for commerce, war and other public affairs, and coordinated under the rotating chairmanship of what was intended to be a merely titular *gonfaloniere*. However, political infighting weakened this system and the old oligarchy reasserted its claims, with a powerful *gonfaloniere* elected for life.

From 1502, the patrician Piero Soderini held the position for ten years, during which time one of the chief diplomats in his chancery was Niccolò Machiavelli. The secretary for the Committee for War had his work cut out chasing around Europe trying to drum up support for a pro-French policy that was proving increasingly unpopular back home in Florence.

Before his death, Lorenzo had left an inspired time-bomb that was to engineer a Medici comeback. What he didn't know about banks, he made up for with knowledge about church politics. He had had his son Giovanni made a cardinal. In 1512, Pope Julius II got the Medici cardinal to rally Florentine forces against the French, drive Soderini out and bring the Medici back to power. The deal was consolidated the following year when the cardinal became pope, as Leo X (1513-1521). He immediately commissioned Michelangelo to build the monumental Medici chapel in the church of San Lorenzo. Leo's cousin Giulio, illegitimate son of Lorenzo's assassinated brother, ruled Florence as archbishop, then cardinal. He in turn became pope as Clement VII (1523-34). He, too, was a great patron of the arts, benevolently encouraging the bravura of Florentine sculptor-goldsmith Benvenuto Cellini, but also Michelangelo's design genius for the new family library at San Lorenzo.

In 1527, when Clement had to flee as the German Emperor's troops mutinied and plundered Rome, the Medici were also driven out of power in Florence – replaced again by a short-lived republic. After the pope's reconciliation with the Habsburg emperor three years later, the Medici were restored by popular acclaim in front of the Palazzo Vecchio.

Dukes of Tuscany

Depending on the good graces of Charles V and his Habsburg armies, Medici power after 1530 had to forsake the subtleties it had known under Cosimo the Elder and Lorenzo the Magnificent. The old sober authority wielded by discreet behind-the-scenes manipulation gave way to the more conventional ostentatious court pomp favoured by other Italian city-states.

Alessandro de' Medici was installed with the double titles of Duke of Tuscany and 'Lord of the Florentine Republic'. Presented in public as the illegitimate son of Lorenzo, Duke of Urbino, he was reputed in fact to have been fathered by Pope Clement VII when he was still a cardinal dallying either with a Moorish slave from Naples or a Roman peasant woman. The republican idea was quickly dropped and Alessandro proved such a tyrant to his subjects that he had to give up the family home to take refuge in the better-guarded Palazzo Vecchio. In his not-so-private life, he was a man of extravagant bisexual habits, preferably conducted in transvestite costume in the company of his cousin Lorenzaccio. He ended up stabbed to death in bed – by Lorenzaccio – while awaiting a promised rendezvous with a married lady. (The sordid affair was transformed into a famous romantic tragedy by French poet-dramatist Alfred de Musset.)

The death was hushed up for a few days so that another Medici could be safely enthroned before any new republican aspirations could take hold. A descendant of

Cosimo the Elder's brother, Cosimo I de' Medici became Duke of Tuscany (1537-1569) and later *Grand* Duke of Tuscany (1569-1574). He proved a proud ruler whose business-like methods might have appealed to his revered namesake, but he lacked the imaginative vision of Lorenzo the Magnificent. This was mirrored in the calibre of the artists working at his court, sculptors Giambologna and Cellini, and painters Pontormo and Bronzino, who achieved moments of brilliance but never true genius. The duke's most prolific artist was Arezzo-born Giorgio Vasari, in the end best remembered for his masterful writing as art historian of the Renaissance. He himself was a Renaissance man only in the sheer breadth of his activities as a workmanlike painter, sculptor and architect.

Making a clean break with his Medici ancestors and the Florentine republic, Duke Cosimo crossed the Arno river to take over the grand but rather forbidding Palazzo Pitti as the official residence, brightening it up in the style of the day with an elegant new inner courtyard. His courtiers also chose more ornate, less austerely feudal palazzi.

GOING TO WORK

Duke Cosimo I ran the duchy of Tuscany like a business, but he still had the security problems of a Renaissance prince. He asked Giorgio Vasari to build new offices (*Uffizi*) to house the duchy's expanding bureaucracy (and now, of course, Italy's finest art collection). To get there each morning without having to confront potentially hostile crowds of workers, he had Vasari also build him a closed corridor from his home in the Pitti Palace, over the shops on the Ponte Vecchio bridge and directly into the Uffizi. An extension led to the neighbouring Palazzo Vecchio, where the duke received official visitors.

The heroic equestrian statue that his son Ferdinando erected in his honour on the Piazza della Signoria epitomizes Duke Cosimo's expansive goals for Tuscany. To compete with other Italian states like Genoa or Venice, Cosimo wanted to promote Tuscany as a sea-power. Pisa had been conquered in 1406, but with its harbour silting up he decided in 1571 to expand Livorno as the duchy's major seaport, linked to the Arno river by a new canal. Another monument on the Piazza della Signoria, Cosimo's dreadfully pompous Neptune fountain, was a symbol of Florence's new maritime ambitions.

Over the next century, Cosimo and his successors strengthened defences with a network of fortresses, the Basso and Belvedere for Florence and others in Siena, Arezzo, Livorno and the island of Elba. (At the same time, Lucca pointedly asserted its independence by building its own splendid system of fortifications.) Notorious malarial marshlands were dried up and reclaimed for farming in the Maremma south west of Siena, the lowlands around Pisa and the Valdichiana south of Arezzo. In science, Galileo Galilei was studying and teaching in his home town of Pisa, and in Padua, Siena and Florence. His findings in astronomy earned him international fame and the post of court mathematician and philosopher to the Grand Duke of Tuscany – until the church condemned his, to them preposterous, insistence that the earth revolved around the sun.

In the 17th and 18th centuries, Tuscany became little more than a pawn in the international intrigues of the European super-powers, France, Spain and Austria. The Medici presided over a court that preferred to withdraw to its country villas and enjoy the fruits of its estates and vine-

Those little square windows on Ponte Vecchio mark the Vasari Corridor – ostensibly to protect Duke Cosimo I from the smell of the bridge's butchershops, but in fact to evade popular protest.

yards, leading a life not so very different from that of the modern bourgeois tourist.

The last decadent flicker of the once proud dynasty was Grand Duke Gian Gastone (1671-1737). He gambled and drank away the remaining florins of the Medici fortune in the brothels and gaming-houses of Prague and Paris, his court in

Florence teeming with some 400 *ruspanti* (toy-boys). Homosexuality would have posed no problem if only he had fathered an heir, but he could not bring himself even to touch his repulsively ugly wife Anna Maria. He died in his bed in the Pitti Palace, with no one to clean his sheets.

Habsburg Dominion to Independence

In 1737, the Habsburgs annexed Tuscany to their Austrian empire, placing its administration under the Vienna-based François, Duke of Lorraine, future husband of Maria Theresa von Habsburg. At the end of the century, the region was invaded by the French Revolutionary Army, 'liberated' by the Austrians and then reconquered by Napoleon Bonaparte. He created the kingdom of 'Etruria', which pleased some progressives with its modern ideas of government, but displeased many more with its irreligious ideology and heavy taxes.

After the Congress of Vienna of 1814, the Habsburgs came back, but prudently preserved most of the French legislation. In the 1840s, Tuscany called in pioneering Scottish engineer Robert Stephenson to build its first railway line from Florence to nearby Pistoia, and out to the coast at Pisa and Livorno. On the Mediterranean, the new taste for seaside resorts was promoted at Viareggio and Forte dei Marmi.

In 1847, after nearly 500 years of autonomy, Lucca was at last placed, grumbling bitterly, under Florentine administration. From the French experience, the people of Tuscany had inherited a new sense of national identity and Florence became the cultural capital of the *Risorgimento* independence movement. The works of Dante, Boccaccio and Petrarch gave the Tuscan dialect pride of place as the Italian national language.

In 1861, the Palazzo Vecchio briefly housed the first parliament of the new kingdom of Italy, with King Vittorio Emanuele residing at the Pitti Palace. A nice turn of the

Napoleon would have preferred to forget Tuscany. Instead of enjoying the beauties of Florence or Siena, he had to kick his heels on the island of Elba as a prelude to his last hurrah at Waterloo.

wheel was achieved by putting Tuscany's regional government in the Palazzo Medici.

Florence's landmark monuments were either restored, like the Bargello, or at last completed, with unequal success, like the controversial façade of the cathedral and the Neo-Gothic campanile for the church of Santa Croce. Other 'improvements' were close to catastrophic, such as the razing of the old medieval market and ghetto to make way for the pompous Piazza della Repubblica.

In the 20th century, Italian nationalism turned sour after World War I and succumbed to the totalitarian temptation of Mussolini's fascism. In Tuscany's local politics, towns divided into fascist and partisan anti-fascist factions along time-honoured Guelph and Ghibelline lines. In Florence in 1943, this took the form of vicious street-fighting between conservative, largely Catholic interests and left-wing partisans.

*F*lorence's Stazione *Centrale, which was built in 1936, is one of the few attractive architectural achievements of the Mussolini era.*

As World War II drew to an end, the Germans abandoned Florence to the approaching Allied armies in August 1944, but only after blowing up four of the five bridges. The oldest, Ponte Vecchio, was spared (*see* RIVER OF TROUBLE, page 148). The bridges were rebuilt, with the same spirit that followed the devastating floods of the Arno river in November 1966 and the Mafia bomb that ripped through the Uffizi Gallery in 1993. Italy's national genius is too deeply rooted in Tuscany to be crushed by natural or man-made disasters. It has eternity on its side.

HISTORICAL LANDMARKS

5500 BC	Earliest traces of human settlement near Pisa.
1600 BC	Bronze Age farming in Tuscan hills.
1100 BC	Central European Villanovans bring iron to Tuscany.

The Etruscans

1000 BC	Etruscan civilization takes over.
8th century BC	Trade with Greek colonists from southern Italy.
7th-6th centuries BC	Towns founded at Volterra, Fiesole, Arezzo, Cortona and Chiusi.
4th century BC	Rome breaks with Etruscan confederation, begins conquest of central Italy.
90 BC	Volterra last Etruscan town to fall to Rome.

Romans and Lombards

59 BC	Florence founded as Roman port on Arno river.
5th century AD	Roman Tuscany plundered by Goths and Huns.
6th century	Lombard duchy established at Lucca.
774	Charlemagne makes Lucca capital of Tuscany.
9th century	Lucca fleet seizes Corsica and Sardinia from Arabs.
1076-1115	Countess Matilda sides with pope against German emperor, launching Guelph-Ghibelline conflict.

Heyday of City-States

11th-12th centuries	Pisa builds maritime empire.
1125	Florence conquers Fiesole.
1147	Siena forms government of consuls, first mention of *Palio* horse-race.
1173	Leaning Tower of Pisa begun.
1183	Emperor Frederick Barbarossa grants Florence communal status.
12th-13th centuries	Lucca's merchants make it most prosperous town in Tuscany.
1252	Florence's florin is first gold coin minted by Italian city; becomes standard for Europe.
1259	Siena cathedral built.
1260	Siena at height of its power defeats Florentine forces at Montaperti.
1269	Florence crushes Siena at Colle Val d'Elsa.
1284	Genoa's victory at Meloria ends Pisa's supremacy at sea.

Rise of Florence

1287	Siena Council of Nine settles for submissive peace with Florence.
1294	Florence cathedral begun (completed 1887).
1300	Dante exiled from Florence, begins *Divine Comedy*.
1328	Death of military leader Castruccio Castracani foils Lucca's conquest of Florence.
1348	Black Plague decimates populations throughout Tuscany.
1350	Boccaccio writes *Decameron*.
1369	Lucca pledges allegiance to German emperor, and gains 500 years of independence from Florence.

| 1378-1382 | *Ciompi* revolt of Florentine wool-workers, crushed by merchant guilds, reinstalling tough oligarchy. |
| 1406 | Florence conquers Pisa. |

The Medici Dynasty

1434–1464	Cosimo the Elder wields power in Florence from behind the scenes.
1434	Brunelleschi completes Florence cathedral dome.
1439	Florence hosts Ecumenical Council of Roman and Orthodox churches.
1440	Victory over Arezzo at Anghiari asserts Florentine power throughout central Italy.
1469-1492	Lorenzo the Magnificent presides over Renaissance's golden era.
1478	Pazzi assassination plot fails; Lorenzo executes 300 in brutal reprisals.

Florentine Republic

1494	Republic declared after Piero de' Medici flees city; preacher Savonarola welcomes Charles VIII's French army as saviours.
1497	Boccaccio burns paintings on Savonarola's Bonfire of Vanities.
1498	Florentines burn Savonarola.
1502-1512	Republic under patrician Soderini, assisted by Machiavelli.

Return of Medici

1513-1521	Medici pope Leo X restores family power.
1523-1534	Second Medici pope Clement VII; Michelangelo working on San Lorenzo chapel and library.
1530	Habsburgs give Medici duchy of Tuscany.
1537	Alessandro assassinated by cousin Lorenzaccio.
1537-1574	Cosimo I de' Medici, Duke (from 1569 Grand Duke) of Tuscany.
1564-1642	Galileo watches earth revolve around sun, but pretends it doesn't.
1571	Livorno replaces silted up Pisa as main Tuscan seaport.
1737	Grand Duke Gian Gastone ends Medici dynasty.

From Habsburgs to Independence

1737	Habsburgs annex Tuscany to Austrian empire.
1799-1814	Napoleon Bonaparte invades, after briefly being ousted by Austrians, creates French-ruled kingdom of 'Etruria'.
1814	Congress of Vienna reinstates Austrians.
1840s	First railways link Florence to Pistoia, Pisa and Livorno.
1847	Lucca at last submits to Florentine administration.
1861	Florence's Palazzo Vecchio briefly houses parliament for new kingdom of Italy.

The Twentieth Century

1944	Germans blow up Florentine bridges.
1966	Arno river ruins Florence art treasures in devastating floods.
1992	Galileo rehabilitated by Vatican.
1993	Mafia bomb rips through Uffizi Gallery.
1994	Pisa halts decline of Leaning Tower.

Art and Architecture in Tuscany

At once charming and inspiring, the leitmotiv of art in Tuscany has always been the dual presence of a decorative, often playful sensuality and a more formal, but by no means passionless, taste for dignity and discipline. This was as true of the Etruscans and Romans as it was to be for the painters of Siena, the sculptors of Pisa and the Renaissance masters of Florence.

Antiquity

Villanovan Ceramics
The primitive pottery of Tuscany's earliest known settlers, the Villanovan émigrés from Central Europe, offers (in the prehistoric collection of Florence's Archaeology Museum) a poignant glimpse of their hankering for the good life in a hand-to-mouth existence. Decorated at best with simple geometric patterns – wavy lines or swastikas – the deep red or dark brown sheen of the pottery (1100 BC) is an imitation of the precious bronze they could afford only for their war-helmets – the most handsome things they have left us.

Etruscan Art
After the frugal culture of the Villanovans, life was easier for the Etruscans and it shows in their more opulent art, from the 8th century BC onwards. It is in large part the Etruscans' taste for the exotic that has prompted many historians to seek their origins in Asia rather than Europe (see LIFE WITH THE ETRUSCANS, page 214). Certainly, their extravagant design often seems distinctly 'oriental' compared with their Greek contemporaries or the Romans that followed them.

*F*lorence's Museum of Archaeology is a good place to begin for serious students of Tuscany's ancient origins before going out to tackle the Etruscan and Roman sites themselves.

Practically the only architecture the Etruscans have bequeathed us, apart from a few remnants of city walls and totally ruined sanctuaries, is in their cemeteries. There, they create a stylized dwelling for the afterlife, like the Egyptians but infinitely more simple (for example, Vetulonia, near Grosseto). Topped by a tumulus mound, the tomb is often just a modest rectangular chamber with a double sloping ceiling divided by a long cylindrical beam. Around the deceased's sarcophagus, the frescoes and other decoration, utensils and ornaments reproduce the ambience of the earthly existence rather than provide the whole wherewithal to continue a life into eternity. It is here that we sense the Etruscans' attachment to the pleasure-principle.

The tomb treasure displayed in the museums of Florence, Volterra, Siena, Arezzo, Chiusi and Cortona reveals the superb art of the goldsmith: jewellery and ornaments in granulated patterns, delicately chased or decorated with fine engraving and lacy filigree. Ivory from Ethiopia and Egypt is treated with equal refinement, carved for statuettes, plaques for funerary caskets, and handles for mirrors. Etruscan bronze, much in demand around the Mediterranean, is used for handsome household vessels, statuettes and jewellery.

In ceramics, the fine black bucchero pottery achieves sophisticated imitations of precious metals. In the 8th and 7th centuries BC, Etruscan art was influenced by contact and trade with the Greeks, particularly by the products of Corinth and Athens. However, the motifs on vases and jewellery are more akin to what was to be found in Anatolia, Phoenicia or further east: weird monsters, sphinxes, griffins, furies, often in delightful scenes with humans eaten alive. These grotesques are the product of a fertile imagination, all naturally assimilated, without the artifice of mere imitation that characterizes so many Greek attempts at exotica. By the 6th century BC, Greek cultural imperialism had overpowered Etruscan creativity, at least in ceramics, and Tuscany was flooded with cheap imitations of mass-produced Corinthian or Attic vases.

In painting, richly coloured frescoes, particularly from Chiusi, are less important for what they tell us about Etruscan art than about the Greek painting styles it imitates in the 5th century BC (of which nothing remains in Greece itself).

Sculpture digests Greek influences without sacrificing Etruscan originality and individualism. The monumental lion-like Bellerophon Chimera, one of the great bronze statues of all antiquity (5th century BC, Florence), is astonishing in its energy. The earliest bronze death-masks or portraits painted on coffin lids reveal something of the personality of the deceased. In later stone sculptures covering the sarcophagus, the deceased man is frequently shown reclining with his spouse, as if attending a banquet with the gods. Unabashed realism remains the objective, as with the Obese Etruscan (2nd century BC) at the Florence museum, seeking neither the Greeks' idealized beauty nor gratuitous ugliness. On the Larthia Seianti sarcophagus, the lady is vividly shown rising on one elbow as if greeting an unexpected guest.

The Romans

For Rome, Tuscany was a secondary colonial outpost, never a major artistic centre, though its hills did offer a big challenge to the Romans' road-building skills. Fiesole has the most substantial relics of Roman architecture, with an amphitheatre seating 3000 spectators and, also of the 1st century BC, a temple incorporating elements of an earlier Etruscan sanctuary. A good example of brick arches can be seen in the nearby public baths built under Emperor Hadrian in the 1st century AD. Roman sculpture found in the area does not evolve beyond its Greek origins.

The Middle Ages

Romanesque Architecture

With Pisa enjoying its heyday from the 11th to 13th centuries as a maritime republic independent of Florence, Tuscany developed two separate traditions in Romanesque architecture. Pisa's cathedral (begun 1063) set a dominant style with its façade of tiered arcades above three porches. Designed with decorative elements that architect **Buscheto** (c.1050-c.1110) had gathered on his visits to Arab, Byzantine, Armenian and other monuments in the eastern Mediterranean, its exterior is like a monumental reliquary for the treasures brought back from the Crusades.

Pisa's combination of cathedral with baptistery, the free-standing Leaning Tower campanile and the Campo Santo burial-ground launched the Italian taste for architectural 'stage sets'. The theatrical aspect is particularly evident in the Massa Marittima cathedral hoisted on a podium, while the ornate arcaded façade is echoed in the cathedrals of Lucca and Pistoia, and as far away as the Pieve di Santa Maria church in Arezzo.

In characteristic Florentine manner, the Basilica of San Miniato (largely 12th century), with its geometrically patterned façade of green and white marble, is more concerned with harmony of colour and clarity of line than with the intricate sculptural delicacies of Pisan design. Indeed, Florence's classical pictorial framework for a simple Lombard Romanesque structure has prompted many to consider San Miniato 'proto-Renaissance'. In fact, it is the cathedral's

baptistery, frequently overlooked architecturally because of its celebrated bronze doors, that is considered the true jewel of Florentine Romanesque for the sheer purity of its geometric forms and even more effective combination of white Carrara and green Prato marble.

Outside any Italian tradition is Sant'Antimo Abbey (12th-century, south of Montalcino), significant for its exquisite cluster of limestone apsidal chapels inspired perhaps by Cluny monks from French Burgundy.

Asserting the emerging pride of the communes, civic building largely within the Romanesque spirit includes the famous towers of San Gimignano and the town hall at Massa Marittima.

Painting Before the Renaissance
Tuscan painters injected a new native vigour and nervous tension into the languid beauties of Byzantine style that had for centuries dominated Italian art. Florence-born **Coppo di Marcovaldo** (1225-1275) renewed the Byzantine repertoire with intense emotion, as in his convulsed *Crucifixion* at San Gimignano. The style of **Cimabue** (1240-1302) is more gentle than his nickname meaning 'dehorner of oxen' (real name Cenni di Pepo). His humanizing of Byzantine formalism in the *Madonna Enthroned* (*Maestà*) in the Uffizi, Florence, and *Crucifixion* (Santa Croce Museum, Florence) makes him an undoubted precursor – some would say creator' of Giotto.

The Church of Santa Maria backing onto Piazza Grande in Arezzo shows just how far the Pisan architectural styles stretched across the region.

Duccio di Buoninsegna (1255-1318), veritable founder of the Siena school of painting, creates well within the severe Byzantine tradition while adding the elegance and sensitivity that have ever since characterized the art of his city. Besides his *Madonna Enthroned* (*Maestà*) in the Siena cathedral-museum and the *Rucellai Madonna* in the Uffizi, a *Crucifixion*, recently restored, has been conclusively identified in Grosseto's church of San Francesco.

It is **Giotto** (1267-1337) who achieves the vital breakthrough in psychological and physical realism, giving bodies a new density, a new depth to space. As scholars continue to dispute his paternity of the Assisi frescoes, we can unhesitatingly admire in Florence his *Madonna d'Ognissanti* at the Uffizi, and the Bardi and Peruzzi Chapel frescoes in the church of Santa Croce. Giotto's new realism can even be seen in Andrea Pisano's panels carved from the master's drawings for Florence cathedral's campanile. His most notable pupils both painted frescoes in Santa Croce: **Taddeo Gaddi** (active 1325-1366), whose subdued elegance can be admired in the Baroncelli Chapel; and **Maso di Banco** (active 1336-1350), who uses intense colour with a fine plastic sense in his St Sylvester cycle in the second Bardi Chapel.

Simone Martini (1284-1344) emphasizes the Siena school's taste for highly ornate elegance, bordering on the opulent, in his *Madonna Enthroned* (*Maestà*), in the town's Palazzo Pubblico, and masterful altarpieces – *St Catherine* in Pisa's San Matteo museum and an *Annunciation* in the Uffizi. He set the standard for what became known as the decorative International Gothic style, that he spread throughout Europe

While remaining deeply religious, Giotto anticipated – with works like this Deposizione – *new psychological insights of Renaissance humanism.*

when working with the French kings of Naples and at the court of the popes exiled in Avignon. Brothers **Pietro** and **Ambrogio Lorenzetti** (active 1305-1347) are unique in the scope of detail with which they depict life in Siena and the surrounding countryside, both allegorical and realistic, in the Palazzo Pubblico's *Good Government* and *Bad Government* and landscapes in the Siena Pinacoteca.

Bernardo Daddi (1280-1348), a Florentine who spent time in Siena, combines Giotto's massive treatment of bodies and drapery with the Lorenzetti brothers' use of high colour and rich detail, notably in a *Madonna* triptych in the Uffizi.

Sculpture in the 13th and 14th Centuries

The energy of Pisan enterprise is perfectly expressed in the work of **Nicola Pisano** (1210-1278), justly considered the founder of modern sculpture. Like the anonymous sculptors of the Lucca cathedral façade and long before the masters of Renaissance, he drew on ancient Roman and Greek models of soldiers and mythical heroes for his saints and patriarchs. The graphic, tightly packed scenes on his pulpit for the Pisa baptistery clearly take their inspiration from the marble panels of Etruscan and Roman sarcophagi. The monumental pulpit also makes a transition from the Romanesque motifs of lions supporting the pillars to the Gothic form of the pulpit's arches. His pulpit for Siena cathedral anticipates Giotto's painting in the sculpture's psychological expressiveness.

Giovanni Pisano (1248-1314) carried his father's art to greater heights. Also a student of ancient models – Greek, Roman and Byzantine – he collaborated with Nicola on the Siena cathedral pulpit before striking out on his own. He brought great turbulent energy to his ambitious sculpture for the façade of Siena cathedral and pulpits in Pistoia, Prato and Massa Marittima, as well as the cathedral pulpit at Pisa. His Sienese disciple **Tino da Camaino** (active 1285-1337) was more formal in his carvings for the tombs of Cardinal Petroni in Siena and Cardinal Orso in Florence.

Andrea Pisano (active 1290-1348, originally Andrea da Pontedera and no relative of Nicola and Giovanni) gave eloquent sculptural form to the new humanism of Giotto. Over and above the fine panels he carved for the master's Florence campanile, he deserves recognition for his magnificent bronze doors for the baptistery. His beautifully observed scenes of craftsmen and scientists show an acute sense of life too often overshadowed by the more celebrated work of Ghiberti on the other doors.

Gothic Architecture

With civic government increasingly taking the upper hand over the church from the late 13th into the 14th century, secular building takes a prominent place in Tuscany's Gothic design. Florence seated its government in the solid fortress of the Palazzo Vecchio (1298). As designed by Arnolfo di Cambio (c.1240-1302), it offers adversaries a massive front, bristling with battlements, a menacing tower and minimum space for windows. The equally formidable Bargello residence of the police-chief was easily adapted for use as a prison (now a sculpture museum). With the elegance of its slender tower, Siena's Palazzo Pubblico (1297) is less severe, less aggressively 'masculine'. Imposing a harmonious design on its private palazzi, the Sienese Campo establishes the pattern for city squares in southern Tuscany – Volterra, Arezzo and Montepulciano.

The greatest of Tuscany's Gothic churches is Siena cathedral (1284). Even with its statuary, Siena cathedral's grand polychrome marble façade designed by **Giovanni Pisano** remains firmly in the Italian pictorial tradition, employing less of the purely architectural effects of French or German Gothic. Similarly, in Florence's Santa Maria Novella (1279), built by a group of Dominican monks, and the Franciscans' Santa Croce (1294), designed by Arnolfo da Cambio, Tuscan builders were just not interested in imitating north European Gothic's elaborate lofty stone cages. Instead they replaced walls with spacious arcades crowned by monumental stained glass windows; what Italians wanted was plenty of good wall space for side-aisle paintings and chapel frescoes.

Florentine priorities are clear in the Orsanmichele (1357) oratory, Gothic in its triple-mullioned windows but first and foremost a timeless showcase for the city's sculptors. Also the Loggia dei Lanzi (1382) has a Gothic rib-vaulted ceiling,

but the great rounded arches look forward to the Renaissance. It, too, became a sculpture-gallery. Unfortunately, Florence's cathedral is a hodgepodge victim of civic procrastination (begun 1294 by Arnolfo da Cambio but completed only in 1887), though Giotto's campanile remains for many art-historians Italy's finest single Gothic monument.

Renaissance Sculpture

The 15th Century
It may sound crude, but the astounding explosion of sculptural genius in Florence at the beginning of the 15th

From an original design by Giotto, the Campanile of Florence's cathedral developed into a joint effort of the city's sculptural talents (opposite).

Siena Cathedral is the finest of Tuscan Gothic churches. It has little in common with the Gothic tradition north of the Alps (below).

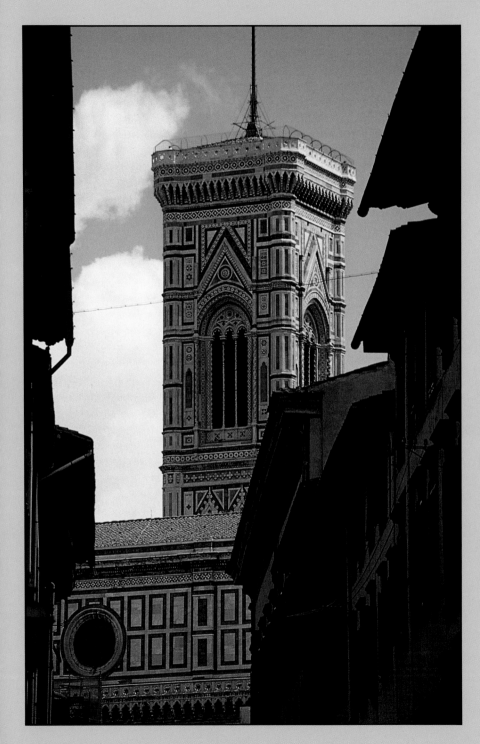

SANT E PATER· BARTOLOMEE · ORA·PRONOBIS

century is due in no small part to the money made available for it by the city's wealthy merchants. The baptistery competition that they announced in 1401 for designing two bronze doors to go with that of Andrea Pisano attracted such masters as Brunelleschi, Ghiberti and Jacopo della Quercia. The winner, **Lorenzo Ghiberti** (1378-1455), could afford to take Donatello and Uccello as his assistants and work on the doors for the next 20 years. His work in bronze, on the doors and in niche statues for the Orsanmichele oratory, display the finesse of the goldsmith and the more heroic sweep of classical antiquity.

Despite the genius of Ghiberti, the greatest of early Renaissance sculptors was **Donatello** (1388-1466), who combined an innate grace and elegance with supreme technical skills and versatility. His repertory is inexhaustible: the anguish of his marble *Abraham and Isaac*

Glazed terracottas of Luca della Robbia, like this one for the church of Santa Croce in Florence, had great popular appeal and his family turned their production into a veritable industry.

and wooden *Mary Magdalene* in the cathedral museum, the androgynous naked impudence of his bronze *David* in the Bargello, the impeccable design of the bronze pulpit in San Lorenzo or the bronze panels for the Siena baptistery.

Originally a goldsmith by trade, **Andrea del Verrocchio** (1435-1488) proved a worthy successor to Donatello in bronze sculpture, his masterpiece being the *Christ and St Thomas* group for the Orsanmichele. In the Bargello is his *David*, a more than honourable counterpart to Donatello's, and inside the Palazzo Vecchio a delightful *Cherub with a Dolphin*. He is important also for having trained Leonardo da Vinci in his workshop and strongly influencing the work of Michelangelo.

Another goldsmith, **Lucca della Robbia** (1400-1482), achieved consummate mastery in polychrome glazed terracotta sculpture. Fine examples are his *Resurrection* and *Ascension* in Florence cathedral and some of the panels on Giotto's campanile, all infused with a tranquil spirituality. The workshop achieved enormous popularity under his son **Andrea** (1435-1525).

The 16th Century
One of the supreme Renaissance masters of architecture, painting and poetry, it was as sculptor that **Michelangelo Buonarroti** (1475-1564) wanted to be remembered. He took the achievements of his Florentine predecessors to new heights of spiritual and heroic grandeur, for which he felt the marble of Carrara was the only appropriate medium. Though much of his work was executed for the popes in Rome, most of the sculpture is to be seen in his native Florence, the city which formed his genius. In the Accademia gallery are the original of his *David* (1504), classical symbol of the Florentine Republic, and four struggling *Slaves* (1534) intended for the tomb of Pope Julius II. For the Medici Chapel in San Lorenzo, he sculpted the monumental tombs of Giuliano and Lorenzo, Duke of Urbino, with the allegorical figures of *Day, Night, Dawn* and *Dusk.*

Benvenuto Cellini (1500-1571) is more famous for his *Autobiography* than for his equally splendid skills as a sculptor and goldsmith. It is the superb

If Benvenuto Cellini's creative genius could not match that of Michelangelo, his gravity-defying bronze statue of Perseus *would at least prove his virtuoso audacity knew no limits.*

technique of the latter that we see in the tour de force of his *Perseus* in the Loggia dei Lanzi, Florence. Among his works in the Bargello, his bravura is most evident in the magnificent bronze bust of *Duke Cosimo I.*

Giambologna (1529-1628) was born in Flanders under the name of Jean Boulogne, but he made his reputation as virtuoso court-sculptor to the Medici. Like Cellini, he possessed a dazzling technique in all media – bronze, marble or terracotta – and learned everything from Michelangelo except the expression of deep feeling. His marble Rape of the Sabine in the Loggia dei Lanzi and bronze Mercury in the Bargello are brilliant, but nothing more.

Painting: Early Renaissance

If Giotto prepared the ground, it is **Masaccio** (1401-1428) who makes the quantum leap into the visual and psychological world of Renaissance painting, seen by art historians as the veritable dawn of art's modern era. In Florence, he draws on Donatello's work for the sculptural quality of his figures and on architect Brunelleschi for innovative geometric relationships, deepening perspectives and heightening drama with a unique source of light. But it is his own personal vision that brings such powerful individual emotion to his frescoes for the Brancacci Chapel of Santa Maria del Carmine, painted with his greatly underestimated master and Brancacci collaborator, **Masolino** (1383-1440). The new naturalism appears with great strength in Masaccio's *Trinity* for Santa Maria Novella and another collaboration with Masolino, their *Madonna and St Anne* (Uffizi). Masolino also painted important frescoes in Santo Stefano, Empoli.

Siena's finest painter of the era, **Sassetta** (1392-1450), in many ways builds a bridge between the decorative International Gothic spirit of Simone Martini and the more formal Renaissance art of Florence, where the gentler Masolino touched him more than the uncompromising Masaccio. His work can be seen in Siena's Pinacoteca (*Last Supper*) and Palazzo Chigi (*Epiphany*), and in Pienza.

Domenico Ghirlandaio (1449-1494) produces less intense but still admirably individualized narrative frescoes, such as the *Last Supper* in the Ognissanti refectory in Florence and a vivid portrait gallery of his Tornabuoni patrons in the Santa Maria Novella frescoes of the Madonna's life.

An exquisite lyrical quality tinged with as much melancholy as joy earned **Sandro Botticelli** (1445-1510) his outstanding popularity among Renaissance

painters. Aristocratically light and subtle in line, and gentle in colour, he also possessed a strong sense of a painting's architecture and perspective. He worked for the Medici and included them in his *Adoration of the Magi*. It was they who commissioned his *Birth of Venus* and *Allegory of Spring* (all in the Uffizi).

Amid the progressive secularization of Renaissance art, even when treating religious themes, **Fra Angelico** (1400-1455) – *Beato*, 'blessed' to the Italians –

asserts a profound spirituality. His *Annunciation* in the Museo di San Marco, Florence, may be the most famous icon of western Christian art – Cortona's Diocese Museum offers another fine version. Admirable examples of his subtle perspectives and purity of colour and form at San Marco monastery are a *Deposition From the Cross* in the Hospice and a *Crucifixion* in the Capitular Hall.

Fra Filippo Lippi (1406-1469) was a gifted but reluctant monk with none of

Luckily, unlike some other sensuous works by Botticelli, The Birth of Venus *was not tossed onto Savonarola's Bonfire of the Vanities.*

the *Beato* Angelico's spiritual vocation. His religious paintings built a bridge between the simple, humanistic sobriety of Masaccio and a lighter, more colourful and complex nature, close in spirit to the elegance of Donatello's sculpture and heralding the work of Botticelli. Outstanding are a *Coronation of the Madonna* in the Uffizi, an *Annunciation* in San Lorenzo and *John the Baptist* and *St Stephen* frescoes in Prato cathedral. **Domenico Veneziano** (1400-61) drew on both Fra Angelico and Filippo Lippi for his use of light and delicate colour, notably in his Uffizi *Madonna*.

Born in Borgo Sansepolcro in eastern Tuscany, **Piero della Francesca** (c.-1420-1492) is a towering force among painters of his age, his intelligence and subtle aesthetics presenting a quintessence of the Renaissance spirit. Despite his apprenticeship with Domenico Veneziano, he stands outside the Florentine mainstream. Piero's work achieves a timeless purity by combining an exquisite sense of colour with meticulously calculated geometric perspectives to place the human being amid buildings or landscape. An aura of ineffable mystery surrounds his Arezzo *True Cross* frescoes, the grandiose *Resurrection* at Sansepolcro and *Pregnant Madonna* at Monterchi, but also his cool portraits of *Federico da Montefeltro* and his wife *Battista Sforza* in the Uffizi.

As Ghiberti's apprentice, **Paolo Uccello** (1397-1475) contributed his skills as a perspectivist to the bronze doors of the Florence Baptistery. Criticism for being more preoccupied with visual theory than artistic imagination ignores the surrealistic poetry of his celebrated *Battle of San Romano* triptych (dispersed among the Uffizi, the London National Gallery and Paris Louvre) and the lesser known *Universal Flood* at Santa Maria Novella.

Painting: High Renaissance

The first decade of the 16th century was a miraculous moment in Italian art, indeed in the history of mankind, bringing together in one city Leonardo da Vinci, Michelangelo and Raphael. This was no gathering of friends – Michelangelo could not stand either of his two rivals – just a concentration in Florence of the age's greatest artistic geniuses. **Leonardo da Vinci** (1452-1519) said: 'A painter is not admirable unless he is universal' – easy to say for a man interested in mathematics, geography, geology, botany, zoology, engineering, aviation, optics, astronomy, town planning, music, athletics, sculpture and a little painting on the side. However, it is only this universality that can begin to explain the man capable of giving his paintings their rich expression of complex composition and subtle intellectual and emotional ambiguities. His celebrated *sfumato* softening of contour light and shade is just the veil to that mystery. Only three of his works remain in Tuscany, all in the Uffizi: an unbearably beautiful angel upstaging his master Verrocchio's *Baptism of Christ*, a wondrous *Annunciation* and the great unfinished *Adoration of Magi*. (Complete the picture with trips to the Louvre and the national galleries of London and Washington.)

With the sheer *terribilità* of his personality, **Michelangelo** brought to his painting an incomparable heroic dimension in the classical tradition. His earliest painting is the very sculptural *Holy Family* in the Uffizi. After sketching the works of Giotto and Masaccio, he learned something of fresco technique with Ghirlandaio, but a great mural commissioned by the city government for the Palazzo Vecchio was interrupted by a call to Rome by Pope Julius II. Florence's loss was the Sistine Chapel's gain.

After these two giants, the gentleness of **Raphael** (1483-1520) prompts many to dismiss him as a sentimental painter of pretty Madonnas. Certainly this most accessible of Renaissance artists suffers among scholarly critics for his great popularity. The more delicate side

The bicycle Leonardo da Vinci designed but never built (above). With a contrariness enchanting to engineers but infuriating to art historians, Leonardo often cared more about paddlewheels for irrigation than frescoes for eternity (below).

of his art may be traced to his Umbrian origins, but the years he spent in Florence, from 1504 to 1508, added a stronger note after his studies of Leonardo and Michelangelo. Beside the *Goldfinch Madonna* in the Uffizi, we can see the acute psychological observation he brought to portraits – *Agnolo Doni* and *The Veiled Lady* in the Pitti Palace and *Pope Leon X* in the Uffizi.

Andrea del Sarto (1486-1531) and **Fra Bartolommeo** (1472-1517) are both accomplished exponents of the tender suggestiveness of much High Renaissance art, often infused with variations on Leonardo's *sfumato*.

Forming a bridge between Renaissance and Baroque, the often over-sophisticated Mannerists, painting more for effect than honest emotion, coincided with Florence's transformation into a duchy. **Pontormo** (1494-1556) displayed perfect technique in his skilful elongations and distortions of the human body, notably in his astonishing *Descent from the Cross* in the church of Santa Felicità. **Agnolo Bronzino** (1503-1572) was court painter to Duke Cosimo I, especially his wife Eleonora. His portraits in the Uffizi have an icy refinement that probably only unconsciously expose the artificiality of aristocratic life.

Siena, emerging momentarily from its slumber to honour an almost surreal deformation of the decorative painting of its golden era, produced two notable Mannerists: **Domenico Beccafumi** (1486-1551) and **Sodoma** (1477-1549), a follower, though never a disciple, of Leonardo, and much more heterosexual than his nickname suggests.

Renaissance Architecture

Though imperial Rome's stability and poise were the keynotes of Renaissance design, it was in 15th-century Florence, not in the ancient capital, that these qualities were first to be found. They appear enhanced by a new elegance in the work of **Filippo Brunelleschi** (1377-1446). His Foundlings' Hospital in Florence (*Spedali degli Innocenti*, designed in 1419) epitomizes the spirit with its graceful arcades of slender columns with Andrea della Robbia's handsome roundels decorating the abutments. Florence cathedral's grandiose dome is considered Brunelleschi's masterpiece, but the full serenity of his work is perhaps best appreciated in Santa Croce's Pazzi Chapel (1429). He also provided the initial designs for Santo Spirito and the Pitti Palace.

Florence's great architectural theorist and town planner is **Leon Battista Alberti** (1404-1472). His ideas of seeking a balance between utility and ornament come to fruition in his harmonious design for the Palazzo Rucellai (1446), breaking with the mediæval concept of fortified redoubt. **Bernardo Rossellino** (1409-1464) faithfully executed Alberti's plans for the Rucellai palace and followed his town-planning concepts for Pius II in the rebuilding of the pope's home town of Pienza.

Though allowing themselves a little decorative light relief in their inner courtyards, Florence's other Renaissance palaces still choose formidable fortress-like façades. The dominant model is the Palazzo Medici of **Michelozzo** (1396-1472). He also designed the imposing Palazzo Pubblico for Montepulciano. Later, Lorenzo the Magnificent studied Alberti's theories to evolve a gentler style for the Medici country residences. He hired **Giuliano Sangallo** (1443-1516), whose masterpiece is the Villa Medici at Poggio a Caiano (1485). His best-known religious building is Santa Maria delle Carceri, the first Renaissance church built on a Greek cross plan, with a Brunelleschi-inspired interior. An important collaborator was **Cronaca** (Simone del Pollaiolo, 1457-1508) whose best independent work was done for Santo

Spirito sacristy, the Palazzo Vecchio and Palazzo Strozzi.

As power shifted to Rome, High Renaissance design took on ever more grandiose dimensions in an extravagant architectural equivalent of Mannerist painting and sculpture. Before leaving for good, **Michelangelo** offered Florence two highly stylized designs, but on a more intimate plane, for San Lorenzo's Medici Chapel and Laurentian Library (*Biblioteca Laurenziana*, 1524).

As an all-round Renaissance Man – painter, architect, thinker and writer – **Giorgio Vasari** (1511-1574) had everything it took to make him a worthy successor to Leonardo da Vinci, everything except genius. As it was, apart from his history of the Renaissance itself, he is best remembered as architect of the Uffizi and the corridor linking it across the Ponte Vecchio to the Pitti Palace.

Bartolommeo Ammannati (1511-1592), sculptor of the dreadful Neptune fountain in front of the Palazzo Vecchio, won more respect with his design of a handsome courtyard for the Pitti Palace and the Santa Trinità bridge (rebuilt after its destruction by the Germans in 1944).

Tuscan Art after the Renaissance

As the Baroque movement triumphed in Rome, Naples and Turin, Tuscany became an artistic backwater. For a rare but noteworthy example of Baroque architecture in Florence, see the church of San Gaetano (Via Tornabuoni), the work of **Gherardo Silvani** (1579-1673). On one of its altars is a *Martyrdom of St Laurence* by Tuscany's best-known painter of the period, **Pietro da Cortona** (1596-1669). Making his career mainly in Rome as a prince of High Baroque painting, Cortona worked briefly in Florence in the 1640s. His allegorical frescoes in the Pitti Palace extol the virtues of the Medici dukes with themes of *Venus, Apollo, Mars, Jupiter* and *Saturn.* The Pitti's Boboli Gardens, laid out by **Bernardo Buontalenti** (1536-1608), offer an ornate setting for Baroque fountains and statuary.

Tuscan painters briefly recaptured national and European attention with the 19th-century movement of the *Macchiaioli*, so called because of their *macchia* or 'blob' technique exploiting the effect of individual touches of paint. The group, meeting at Florence's Café Michelangelo, were active from 1855 to 1865, rebelled against the official Academic style stifling artistic creativity, and were in some ways precursors of the French Impressionists. Major exponents were **Telemaco Signorini** (1835-1901), **Silvestro Lega** (1826-1895) and the Livorno-born **Giovanni Fattori** (1825-1908), all well represented at Florence's Gallery of Modern Art and the Livorno municipal museum. Cortona-born **Gino Severini** (1883-1966) was a leader of the Futurist movement that flirted for a moment with Fascism, but he was later attracted by Cubist and other non-representational painting.

In 1870, **Giuseppe Mengoni** (1829-1877) designed the Mercato Centrale (Central Market, Florence) as a bold structure in iron, glass and masonry similar to the celebrated Galeria Vittorio Emanuele he created for his home town of Milan.

Most important of Tuscany's 20th-century architects is **Giovanni Michelucci** (1891-1991). Born in Pistoia, he designed Florence's Santa Maria Novella railway station (1936) in an international style that represented a rare act of resistance to the dominant bombast of Fascism. Its bold form pays tribute to the rationalist designs of Le Corbusier and Bauhaus functionalism, while using marble cladding in homage to local classical tradition.

Just the Essentials

The problem with Tuscany is its embarrassment of riches. It needs a lifetime to do it justice. We suggest here a list of sightseeing landmarks for the first-time visitor who wants to have seen at least the most important places.

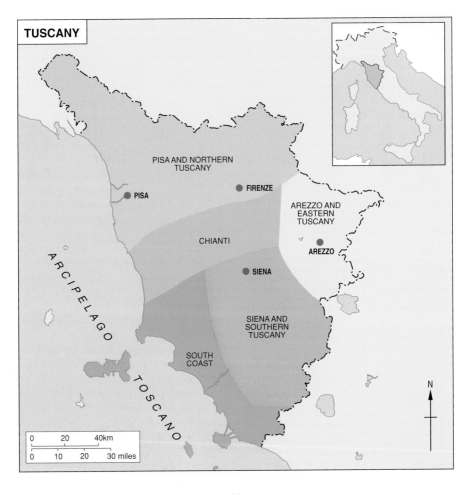

Florence

Piazza del Duomo: baptistery's bronze doors, cathedral's Brunelleschi dome and Giotto campanile

Palazzo Vecchio: city hall, centre of civic pride

Uffizi: Renaissance's greatest museum for Giotto, Masaccio, Botticelli

Accademia: original of Michelangelo's *David*

Bargello: sculpture museum for Donatello, Michelangelo, Cellini

San Marco: monastery-museum of Fra Angelico frescoes

Santa Croce: Brunelleschi's Pazzi Chapel

Ponte Vecchio: jewellery market on oldest bridge

Via Tornabuoni: luxury shopping street

Pitti: palace museum of High Renaissance painting, Boboli Gardens

Santa Maria del Carmine: Masaccio frescoes in Brancacci Chapel

Day Trip: Fiesole's hilltop villas and gardens

Pisa and Northern Tuscany

Pisa: Cathedral, Leaning Tower and Baptistery – 'Field of Miracles' unique architectural ensemble, with Niccola and Giovanni Pisano pulpits

Viareggio: celebrated beach resort

Carrara: spectacular marble quarries for Michelangelo

Lucca: beautifully preserved ramparts and mediæval monuments

Prato: Cathedral's Donatello pulpit and Filippo Lippi frescoes

South Coast

Argentario: Porto Ercole, chic sailing resort

Maremma: Nature park with Talamone fishing village

Castiglione della Pescaia: popular family resort

Punta Ala: exclusively fashionable resort

Elba: Napoleon's island exile; best resorts at Marina di Campo, Biodola and Marciana.

Chianti and the Tuscan Hills

Via Chiantigiana: vineyard-route for Chianti Classico in Radda, Gaiole and 'châteaux' of Meleto and Brolio

Certaldo: home of Boccaccio

San Gimignano: famous mediæval towers

Volterra: Etruscan bastion

Siena and Southern Tuscany

Siena:

—Campo: golden piazza, scene of *Palio* horse-race

—Palazzo Pubblico: museum's frescoes of Lorenzetti brothers, Simone Martini

—Via di Città: Gothic and Renaissance palazzi

—Duomo: Gothic cathedral with Pisano sculptures and pulpit, baptistery

—Cathedral Museum: Jacopo della Quercia, Duccio and Donatello

—Pinacoteca: Siennese school, Duccio, Simone Martini, Lorenzetti brothers

Montalcino: charming wine-town with nearby San Antimo abbey-church

Pienza: unique Renaissance city planning

Montepulciano: mellow wine-town with Renaissance church of San Biagio

Monte Amiata: mountain summer and winter resorts, ruined castles

Arezzo and Eastern Tuscany

Arezzo:

—Church of San Francesco: Piero della Francesca's *True Cross* frescoes

—Piazza Grande: historic centre, scene of summer jousting tournament

—Pieve di Santa Maria: exquisite Romanesque parish church

Casentino: forested hills of upper Arno valley

Poppi: pretty porticoed town

Romena: romantically situated castle and Romanesque church

Camaldoli: dense forest refuge for hermitage and monastery

La Verna: hilltop abbey where Francis of Assisi received stigmata

Sansepolcro: home-town of Piero della Francesca, masterpieces in museum

Cortona: splendid Etruscan hill-town with mediæval and Renaissance monuments

Going Places with Something Special in Mind

People come to Tuscany with a multitude of personal interests, hobbies, and even obsessions. It can be a good idea to plan your itineraries to cater for your own particular tastes. Track down the works and landmarks of a great artist or scientist, seek out historical battlefields, or find the most beautiful gardens, villas or palaces, and the most popular pageants. Here are our suggestions.

Brunelleschi in Florence

Tuscany's greatest architect mastered his fiery temperament to embellish the city with some of its most harmonious creations.

1 DUOMO
His landmark cathedral dome earned him the unique privilege of a tombstone inside the church.

*E*very town has something worth seeing – in Grosseto it's the charming Piazza del Duomo. To investigate the rest of the sights, consult our LEISURE ROUTES.

2 SAN LORENZO
Consummate Renaissance design for Medici church, especially the Old Sacristy.

3 SPEDALE DEGLI INNOCENTI
Colonnaded Foundlings' Hospital on a gracefully conceived piazza.

4 SANTA CROCE
His masterpiece here is the Pazzi Chapel; inside the church is one of his rare sculptures, a monumental *Crucifixion*.

5 BARGELLO MUSEUM
Whatever architecture's gain, we see sculpture's loss in his violent *Abraham Sacrificing Isaac*, his losing but magnificent entry for the baptistery bronze-door competition.

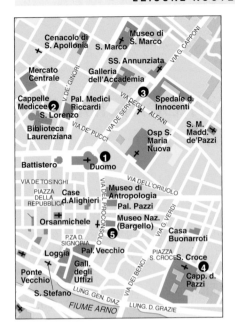

The Beatitude of Fra Angelico

Simple, luminous piety shines through the work of the Dominican monk, avoiding mawkish sentiment through honesty.

1 FLORENCE

San Marco monastery-museum contains his greatest frescoes, notably *Annunciation* and *Jesus Mocked*.

2 FIESOLE

San Domenico, Fra Angelico's first monastery, *Madonna and Saints* in church, *Crucifixion* in chapter house.

3 CORTONA

Major works in the Museo Diocesano.

*W*onderful Brunelleschi buildings in Florence (above), the works of Fra Angelico (1-3, below) and in the footsteps of Dante (4-7, below).

Dante in Florence and in Exile

Trace the turbulent life of the politician turned poet, sublime witness of man's passage through hell, purgatory and paradise.

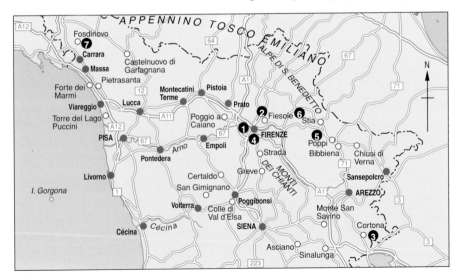

4 FLORENCE
His house on Via Dante Alighieri, Palazzo Vecchio where he served as councillor, and his tomb in the church of Santa Croce.

5 CAMPALDINO
Battlefield outside Poppi (eastern Tuscany) where he distinguished himself in the Florentine cavalry against the forces of Arezzo.

6 ROMENA
Guidi counts' *Castello* where Dante took refuge after his banishment in 1300.

7 FOSDINOVA
Near Carrara, Malaspina lords' beautiful castle where exiled poet wrote part of *Divine Comedy*.

Michelangelo in his Home Town

A walking tour of Florence gives you the scope of the Renaissance giant's genius, in sculpture, architecture and one painting. A trip out of town will take you to his birthplace.

1 GALLERIA DELL'ACCADEMIA
The original of his great *David* statue, but also his *St Matthew* and *Slaves*.

2 SAN LORENZO
For his architecture in the Laurentian Library (*Biblioteca Lorenziana*) and sculpture of Medici tombs in New Sacristy.

*W*alk around Florence to catch a glimpse of the man that was Michelangelo.

3 BARGELLO MUSEUM
Among other major sculptures, extraordinary *Drunken Bacchus*, but also Daniele da Volterra's bust of the master himself.

4 PIAZZA DELLA SIGNORIA
To see *David* copy, at least for its original placement.

5 UFFIZI MUSEUM
Holy Family tondo, Florence's only Michelangelo painting.

6 SANTA CROCE
Michelangelo's tomb which he, alas, did not design himself.

7 CASA BUONARROTI
Memorabilia in the house in which he installed his family.

CAPRESE MICHELANGELO
Birthplace in eastern Tuscany.

101

Donatello, Prince of Sculptors

Compared with the almost relentless titanic emotion of Michelangelo, the range of Donatello's art seems more broadly human – lyrical, joyous, passionate, tragic.

Outside Florence

1 PRATO CATHEDRAL
Bas-reliefs for exterior pulpit (originals in Cathedral Museum).

*D*onatello's brilliance outside Florence.

2 PISA
San Matteo Museum, bronze bust of *St Rossore.*

3 SIENA
Bronze reliefs and statues in baptistery and Cathedral Museum.

In Florence

1 SANTA CROCE
Magnificent bronze *Annunciation* and naturalistic *Crucifixion* in wood.

*D*onatello in Florence (1-5) and where to see Giotto (6-9).

2 BARGELLO MUSEUM
Two versions of *David*, in bronze and marble, and Orsanmichele originals.

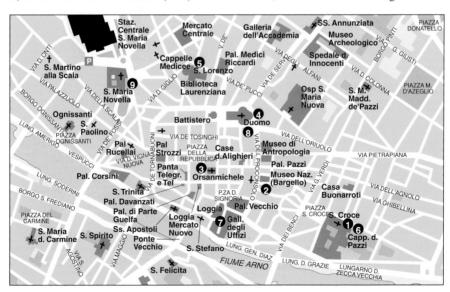

3 ORSANMICHELE
Good copies of heroic *St Mark* and *St George* let you gauge impact *in situ*.

4 MUSEO DELL'OPERE DEL DUOMO
In Cathedral Museum, *Mary Magdalen* from baptistery, *Prophet Habbakuk* and *Abraham Sacrificing Isaac*.

5 SAN LORENZO
Two bronze pulpits, and wall medallions for Brunelleschi's Old Sacristy.

Giotto, Father of the Renaissance

Some of the finest work of the man who took painting out of its Middle Ages with an acute new sense of humanity can be seen in Florence.

6 SANTA CROCE
Two sets of frescoes: *St Francis* in Bardi Chapel, *John the Evangelist* and *John the Baptist* in Peruzzi Chapel.

7 UFFIZI MUSEUM
New spirit apparent in *Madonna Enthroned* and *Madonna* triptych.

8 DUOMO
Campanile demonstrates his skill as an architect.

9 SANTA MARIA NOVELLA
Compare his *Crucifixion* in the sacristy with Brunelleschi's more idealized version in Gondi Chapel.

VICCHIO
House of his birth outside Florence, on Sieve river; now a Giotto research-centre.

The Wilds of Tuscany

Beyond the tailored vineyards, orchards, rows of cypresses and olive groves, the Tuscan countryside also has vast tracts of dense forest and rugged mountains now protected in nature reserves.

1 CASENTINO
National park encompassing spectacular Camaldoli forest and source of Arno river on Mount Falterona.

2 MAREMMA
South coast nature park reclaimed from marshes combines Mediterranean *macchia* heathland with pine and oak forest.

3 ELBA
Wilderness on Monte Capanne, Elba's highest peak.

4 GARFAGNANA
Two nature reserves for hiking or horse-riding in Apuan Alps or Apennines.

Wine Tours

Tasting or buying wine is an added delight – or prime goal, depending on your inclination – of any tour of Tuscany. Most vineyards organize sales and tasting on the property, but other wines can be found in major distribution centres, often in an attractive old *enoteca* (wine cellar).

Chianti
Follow the Via Chiantigiana's road-sign of the black rooster (*Gallo Nero*) denoting the top-of-the-range Chianti Classico.

5 GREVE
Important distribution centre, autumn

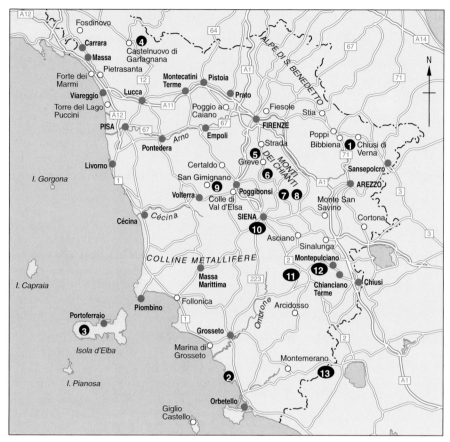

wine fair, with several good vineyards to visit in the vicinity.

6 RADDA
Capital of Chianti League since 1415, visit *Piccolo Museo del Chianti* and excellent surrounding vineyards.

7 GAIOLE
Major wine-tasting centre, near top-rated vineyard of Castello di Meleto.

8 BROLIO
Most prestigious of Chianti Classico vineyards with Bordeaux-style château (good olive oil, too).

*P*laces *for nature lovers in Tuscany (1-4), and for the discerning palate, the best places for wine-tasting (5-13).*

Southern Tuscany
There are other good wines, both red and white, to be found outside the strictly defined borders of the Chianti Classico region.

9 SAN GIMIGNANO
Famous not only for its mediæval towers but for its first-class white *Vernaccia*.

104

10 SIENA
National Wine Library and good place to buy.

11 MONTALCINO
In charming walled city, taste heady red Brunello in its 14th-century castle *enoteca*.

12 MONTEPULCIANO
Renowned red Vino Nobile di Montepulciano served from attractive old wine-cellars.

13 PITIGLIANO
Dramatic rocky setting for dry white wines akin to vintages of neighbouring Umbria.

Country Villas

To escape the city's summer heat, the Tuscan aristocracy built airy hilltop residences, preparing the way for Surrey stockbrokers and Bavarian beer magnates. Not all of these are for rent which is perhaps just as well.

1 POGGIO A CAIANO
This 15th-century Medici villa was built by Giuliano da Sangallo for Lorenzo the Magnificent.

2 ARTIMINO
Just down the road from Poggio a Caiano, Duke Ferdinando I built his villa 100 years later.

3 FIESOLE
Peep in at splendid private villas along Via di San Domenico. Cosimo the Elder's Villa Medici, built by Michelozzo, can be glimpsed along Via Vecchia Fiesolana.

Country villas of the Tuscan aristocracy.

4 GREVE
South west of town, Villa Vignamaggio perhaps housed Mona Lisa, but certainly hosted Kenneth Branagh's 1993 film of *Much Ado About Nothing*.

5 LUCCA
Hills outside Lucca abound in merchants' villas: Mansi at Segromigno, Torrigiani at Camigliano, and Reale di Marlia.

6 VIAREGGIO
Villa Puccini, opera composer's home at Torre del Lago.

Romanesque Churches

Tuscany had two distinct styles in the design of churches from the 11th to 13th century, with the Pisan influence proving stronger than the Florentine. Observant travellers will notice many fine examples on their journeys throughout the region.

1 PISA
The finely sculpted arcades of the cathedral's façade set the patterns for churches throughout Tuscany.

2 LUCCA

The church of San Michele in Foro subtly varies the colour and carving of its façade's arcades.

3 PISTOIA

Proximity to Florence did not keep it from using Pisa as the model for its Duomo San Zeno.

4 FLORENCE

In San Miniato's superb green and white marble façade, line and colour prevail over sculptural effects, but the baptistery is more purely Romanesque.

5 EMPOLI

Collegiata di Sant'Andrea is rare instance following Florentine example of San Miniato.

6 MASSA MARITTIMA

Duomo adds Gothic arcade to essential Pisan Romanesque design.

7 AREZZO

Even this far away, the Pisan influence is evident in Pieve di Santa Maria.

Gothic Churches

The more painterly Italians did not take easily to the soaring aspirations of northern European Gothic cathedrals. Tuscan Gothic is more serene.

8 SIENA

The cathedral, with lofty façade designed and sculpted by Giovanni Pisano, is the supreme example of Tuscan Gothic.

A feast of mediæval architecture: Romanesque churches (1-7), Gothic churches (8-10) and Gothic town halls (11-16).

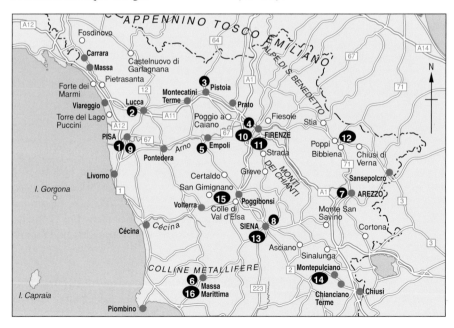

9 PISA
Santa Maria della Spina is more classically Gothic in line, but not so much a church as a monumental reliquary jewel casket in stone.

10 FLORENCE
Santa Maria Novella and Santa Croce are more interested in providing wall space for their art works than height to elevate their worshippers.

Gothic Town Halls

In the Middle Ages, the civic pride of Tuscan communes is proclaimed in their town halls, with Florence leading the way.

11 FLORENCE
Palazzo Vecchio is the great fortress model asserting the citizens' rights against church and aristocracy.

12 POPPI
Working on this little town's Palazzo Pretorio in eastern Tuscany, architect Arnolfo da Cambio may have developed his ideas for Florence's Palazzo Vecchio.

13 SIENA
Palazzo Pubblico is a more ornate variation on the assertive Florentine fortress.

14 MONTEPULCIANO
Comparisons between its Palazzo Comunale and the Palazzo Vecchio were reinforced by the Medici takeover.

T hree Renaissance palaces of the Medici in Florence, setting the style in the Middle Ages.

15 SAN GIMIGNANO
Of the remaining dozen or so towers, that of the municipal Palazzo del Populo is the tallest in town.

16 MASSA MARITTIMA
Massive Palazzo Comunale proudly proclaims the citizens' prosperity in mining heyday.

Renaissance Palaces

In the 15th- and 16th-century transition from defensive fortress to aristocratic residence, Medici Florence set the tone.

In Florence

1 PALAZZO MEDICI-RICCIARDI
The prototype: architect Michelozzo chose rough-hewn ashlar stone for the façade of Godfather's stronghold.

2 PALAZZO RUCELLAI
Classical purity of line in this design of Leon Battista Alberti, completed by Bernardo Rossellino.

3 PALAZZO STROZZI
Handsomest of the city's palaces, with little museum telling its story.

Southern Tuscany

Town palaces outside Florence were influenced by either the expansion of Medici political power or the urbanism of Siena's Pope Pius II.

4 SIENA

Palazzo Piccolomini, now housing ancient state archives, has a Michelozzo-style ashlar façade designed by Bernardo Rossellino.

5 PIENZA

In the city centre designed for Pope Pius II, Rossellino has added to the Palazzo Piccolomini a hanging garden overlooking the valley.

6 MONTEPULCIANO

Main street Via di Gracciano del Corso lined with grand palazzi.

Renaissance Churches

After elaborately sculpted Romanesque and Gothic monumentality, the Renaissance churches seek a simple harmony of line and form.

7 FLORENCE

Outstanding examples: Brunelleschi's Pazzi Chapel for Santa Croce and Michelangelo's Medici Chapel for San Lorenzo.

*P*innacles of Renaissance architecture reached in palaces (4-6) and churches (7-10). For something different, visit an antique pharmacy (11-18).

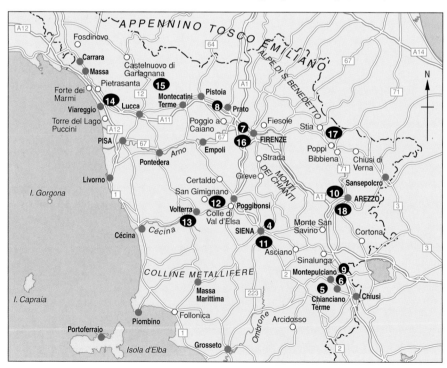

8 PRATO
Santa Maria delle Carceri designed by Giuliano da Sangallo, favourite architect of Lorenzo the Magnificent.

9 MONTEPULCIANO
San Biagio on a hillside below town, by Antonio da Sangallo the Elder.

10 AREZZO
Santissima Annunziata built by Sangallo family while working on Medici fortress.

Antique Pharmacies

Hypochondriacs and perfectly normal people find unending fascination in the mortars and pestles, stone jars and bottles of blue, green and amber glass to be found in pharmacies all over Tuscany, often attached to monasteries and hospitals.

11 SIENA
The *Quattro Cantoni*, Via San Pietro 4, is in an 18th-century building; *Farmacia del Campo* is 17th-century.

12 SAN GIMIGNANO
Attached to Ospedale di Santa Fina, founded in 1507.

13 VOLTERRA
Near the ramparts, *All Insegna della Porta all'Arco* dates back to the 15th century.

14 VIAREGGIO
Only dating from 1870, but the graceful *Farmacia Inglese*, Corso Garibaldi 27, specializes in English complaints.

15 BAGNI DI LUCCA
In Garfagnana, *Antica Farmacia Betti*, Viale Umberto, has cured the aches and

pains of Romantic poets since the 18th century, notably Byron, Shelley and Heinrich Heine.

16 FLORENCE
San Marco's, since 1436 at Via Cavour 146; Santa Maria Novella's, open to the public at Via della Scala 16 since 1612, but much older; and *Farmacia del Cinghiale* on Mercato Nuovo since 1752.

17 CAMALDOLI
Herbal cures at 16th-century pharmacy attached to hermitage.

18 AREZZO
Neo-Classical *Farmacia del Cervo*, Piazza San Francesco since 1830.

Masaccio's Brief Moment of Greatness

His death at 26 deprived European painting of one of its most powerful geniuses. His short path through Florence is all too easy to follow, but essential for a full understanding of Renaissance Art.

1 SANTA MARIA DEL CARMINE
The matchless *Creation* frescoes in the Brancacci Chapel, magnificently restored.

2 UFFIZI MUSEUM
A poignant *Madonna and Child with St Anne*, painted with his master, Masolino.

3 SANTA MARIA NOVELLA
Monumental fresco of *Trinity*.

PISA: SAN MATTEO MUSEUM
One panel, *St Paul*, of a dispersed polyptych.

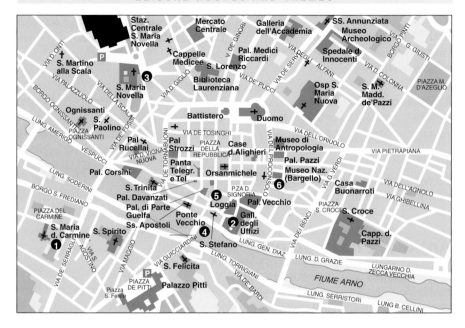

T he magic of Masaccio
(1-3) and the brilliance of Cellini (4-6) in Florence.

Benvenuto Cellini, Virtuoso

The brilliant goldsmith led a stormy life throughout Italy, but left his mark as a sculptor in his native Florence.

4 PONTE VECCHIO
A 19th-century sculpture portrays Cellini, this far from saintly patron saint of goldsmiths on the bridge.

5 LOGGIA DEI LANZI
Tour de force *Perseus* holding head of Medusa.

6 BARGELLO
Heroic bust of his patron, Duke Cosimo I.

The Etruscans

Archaeologists are steadily increasing our knowledge of the mysterious founders of Tuscany's noble civilization.

1 FLORENCE
The Museo Archeologico assembles much of Tuscany's finest Etruscan art.

2 FIESOLE
Remains of the ancient settlement's temple and ramparts.

3 VOLTERRA
Leading town of Etruscan Confederation, with important Guarnacci Museum, and ancient city-gate.

4 POPULONIA
Necropolis of ancient iron port.

5 VETULONIA
Mining town's tombs from 7th century BC.

110

6 CHIUSI
Key town in Confederation, major museum, underground galleries, extensive necropolis.

7 CORTONA
Handsome hill-town retains significant vestiges of Etruscan walls.

To the Stars and Back with Galileo

When he was not defending his truth – and freedom – in Rome, the scientist pursued his studies in Pisa and Florence.

8 PISA
In Duomo, he tested theory of oscillation (but did *not* test gravity from Leaning Tower). Near his old university, Domus Galileana, Via Santa Maria 26, is an astrophysical research centre.

9 FLORENCE
In Uffizi, splendid portrait by Justus Sustermans; in Science History Museum, his telescopes.

10 ARCETRI
Villa Gioiello, Via Pian de'Giullari 42, on the southern outskirts of Florence, where Galileo spent the end of his life under house arrest.

*F*ragments of the ancient Etruscan civilization (1-7), and a glimpse of Galileo, famous now, but mistrusted by his Catholic fathers (8-10).

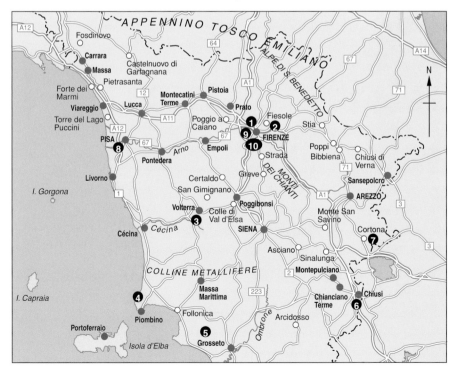

Costumed Pageants

Tuscany attracts thousands of summer visitors to its Renaissance tournaments, of which Siena's *Palio* is only the most famous.

1 SIENA
The *Palio* horse race and banner twirling on the Campo provide a frenzied outlet for neighbourhood rivalries.

2 MONTEPULCIANO
In super-strenuous *Bravio delle Botti*, wine-town's toughs push huge barrels up steep winding Via di Gracciano del Corso.

3 AREZZO
Piazza Grande is the handsome setting for the *Giostro del Saraceno*, a jousting tournament on horseback.

4 SANSEPOLCRO
Crossbow contest, *Palio della Balestra*, held on Piazza Torre di Berta, pits the town against arch-rival Gubbio from nearby Umbria.

5 FLORENCE
The Florentines play *Calcio* football in Renaissance costume, Nikes, Reeboks and Adidas.

6 PISA
Push-of-War *Gioca del Ponte* across the Ponte di Mezzo between strongmen from the town's north- and south-bank districts.

For colour, spectacle and excitement, try one of Tuscany's costumed pageants.

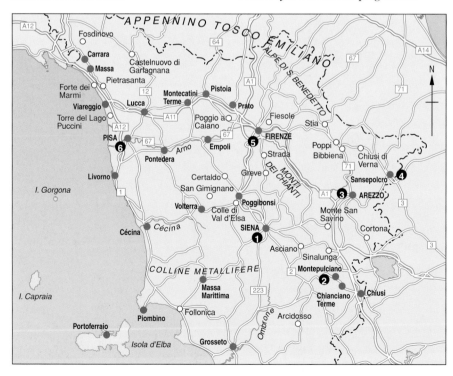

The Medici in Florence

Bankers, dukes and popes, rarely has one family left such a mark on the town and country in which they wielded their power.

1 PALAZZO MEDICI-RICCARDI

Palace built for Cosimo the Elder: Gozzoli fresco of *Journey of the Magi to Bethlehem* portrays Medici family in kings' retinue; Luca Giordano portrays dukes in Baroque *Apotheosis of the Medici*.

2 SAN LORENZO

Family church: statue of Alessandro, father of Duke Cosimo I on piazza, Michelangelo sculpted family tombs in Medici Chapel.

3 DUOMO

Sacristy, where Lorenzo the Magnificent escaped assassination in Pazzi conspiracy.

4 PALAZZO VECCHIO

Transformed from grim fortress into richly frescoed palace under Duke Cosimo I; duke's equestrian statue in piazza.

5 UFFIZI MUSEUM

Originally family offices built by Vasari.

6 PONTE VECCHIO

Vasari Corridor to take Medici dukes from Uffizi to Pitti Palace across the river.

7 PITTI PALACE

Ducal residence, Medici art collection includes portraits of Lorenzo the Magnificent and other family members; Boboli Gardens for court's 'private' parties.

8 FORTE BELVEDERE

Medici dukes' fortress in new get-tough military policy.

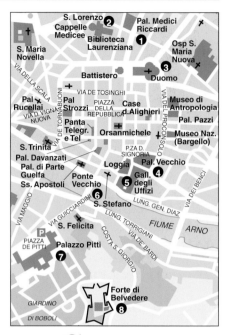

Get a taste for the power of the Medici in Florence.

Music Festivals

Summer classical music concerts held in the open air, often in ornate palazzi.

1 FLORENCE

In Teatro Comunale, *Maggio Musicale*, literally 'Musical May', in fact lasts from May to July.

2 LUCCA

Home of Boccherini and Puccini holds open-air concerts in gardens by city walls.

3 SIENA

Summer open-air recitals of Accademia Musicale Chigiana in courtyard of Palazzo Chigi-Saraceni, Via di Città.

4 MONTEPULCIANO
Renaissance music at Palazzo Tarugi.

*M*usic in the open air, amid Renaissance palaces.

5 AREZZO
Choral festival, *Concorso Polifonico*, held in Teatro Petrarca.

*T*he rise and fall of Savonarola in Florence.

Savonarola, Vanities' Pyromaniac

The fanatical Dominican friar's theocratical dictatorship threw out the Medici and proclaimed Jesus King of Florence.

1 SAN MARCO
The monk's cell is still there, but more reassuring are Fra Angelico's frescoes.

2 PIAZZA DEL DUOMO
The brilliant preacher attracted such huge crowds that a wooden amphitheatre was built on the cathedral square.

3 PIAZZA DELLA SIGNORIA
Plaque marks the spot where artworks and jewellery burned on Savonarola's Bonfire of Vanities and where, after execution, his body was also burned.

Nicola and Giovanni Pisano

Father and son, Pisa's master sculptors of the 13th and early 14th centuries, were as important in the evolution of their art as Giotto and later Masaccio were in painting.

1 PISA
Father and son worked together on baptistery façade sculpture, but the pulpit is Nicola's masterpiece. Son Giovanni carved pulpit for Duomo.

2 SIENA
Giovanni designed Duomo façade (originals of sculpture in Cathedral Museum), while Nicola carved the pulpit.

3 PISTOIA
Giovanni gave city its masterpiece: the marble pulpit in church of Sant'Andrea.

Gardens of Tuscany

The region's gardens are a delight, landscaped for the villas, formal in the geometric style of the Italian Renaissance, or botanical, containing thousands of varieties of Mediterranean plant.

4 FLORENCE
Boboli Gardens on a hillside behind the Pitti Palace; grottoes, nymphs, fountains and love-temples among the trees.

5 FIESOLE
Public gardens by church of San

Sculptures of the Pisano family (1-3), a feast of gardens (4-12) and finding the unassuming Piero della Francesca (13-16).

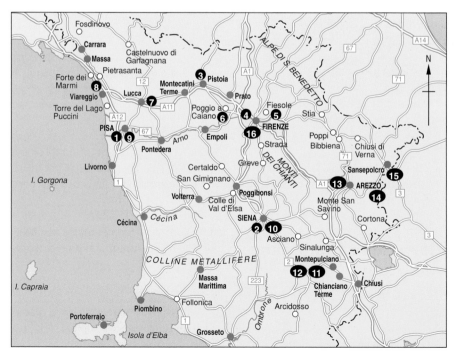

Francesco and secluded villa gardens all along Via Vecchia Fiesolana.

6 POGGIO A CAIANO
Spacious walled garden for Medici villa.

7 LUCCA
Near ramparts, botanical garden with American sequoia, Chinese ginkgo and cedar of Lebanon nearly 200 years old.

8 VIAREGGIO
Giardini d'Azeglio surrounded by pine groves; pay homage to English poet Shelley.

9 PISA
Botanical gardens run by the university since 16th century; trees from Asia, Africa and the Americas.

10 SIENA
Hillside botanical gardens founded in 18th century; 50,000 specimens from Tuscany, and cacti, orchids and tropical plants.

11 SAN QUIRICO D'ORCIA
Leonini Gardens, 16th-century Italian Renaissance style, hedges in geometric patterns on slope overlooking Orcia valley.

12 PIENZA
Palazzo Piccolomini's hanging gardens of evergreen hedges and trees in Italian Renaissance style.

Piero della Francesca, Man Apart

Impossible to classify with the more obvious 'stars' of the Renaissance, the hypnotic Piero made his reputation slowly, away from the bustle of Florence, Rome or Venice, in his home town of Sansepolcro.

13 AREZZO
The *True Cross* fresco cycle turns naive legend into noble poetry.

14 MONTERCHI
Poignant unique portrayal of Mary pregnant, *Madonna del Parte*.

15 SANSEPOLCRO
In hometown Museo Civico, his *Resurrection* and *Madonna of the Misericordia* among greatest paintings in Italy.

16 FLORENCE
Uffizi's cool, bewitching portraits of *Federico da Montefeltro* and wife *Battista Sforza*.

Tuscany's Historic Industries

Since the Etruscans grew rich on iron ore, the region's industries have been as much rooted in centuries-old tradition as its painting, sculpture and architecture.

1 ELBA
Medici dukes' 'iron port' of Portoferraio, picturesque mining village of Capoliveri, and Rio Marina, still an active ore port.

2 MASSA MARITTIMA
Mining Museum with Europe's first Mining Code, 13th century, to protect workers.

3 CARRARA
Ancient Roman marble quarries reactivated for Renaissance sculpture, still productive; marble museum.

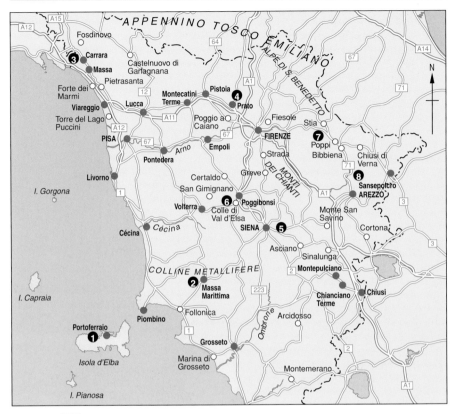

*T*uscany's traditional industries (1-4) and a sample of ancient battles (5-8).

4 PRATO

International textile centre since Middle Ages, Cloth Museum (*Museo del Tessuto*).

Battlefields

Tuscany's stormy history has known more civil war than foreign invasion, most spectacularly involving Florence's rise to dominance.

5 MONTAPERTI

Close enough east of Siena to be visible from palace watchtowers, memorable Sienese victory over Florence in 1260.

6 COLLE DI VAL D'ELSA

Scene of Florence's brutal revenge over Siena in 1269.

7 CAMPALDINO

Momentous Florentine defeat of Arezzo forces near Poppi in Casentino hills in 1289, when Dante served in cavalry.

8 ANGHIARI

Florentine victory in 1440 over Milanese invaders near Sansepolcro; subject of famous lost Leonardo da Vinci fresco.

117

Renaissance Treasures and the Surprises of the Hinterland

Florence, or *Firenze* if you are Italian, nestles at the heart of the Arno valley where the river turns its back on the Apennines and heads for the Mediterranean. The location made Tuscany's capital a natural arbiter of taste between Rome to the south and the influences of the north. With a quotient of geniuses in those blessed decades of the Renaissance comparable only to that of Athens in classical Greece, the town presents a splendid showcase for their achievements.

The great patrician city divides conveniently into its four historical quarters or parishes, each named after a principal church: **San Giovanni** (the name of the baptistery church that originally served as the town's cathedral), **Santa Croce**, **Santa Maria Novella** and **Santo Spirito**. We have accordingly drawn up four itineraries that make a circuit of each quarter's palazzi, churches, museums and other monuments. To avoid cultural overdose

The cupola ceiling of Florence's baptistery is decorated with a multitude of 13th-century mosaics. The Biblical scenes follow designs by Cimabue and Coppo di Marcovaldo.

(*see* STENDHAL'S SYNDROME, page 122), we also indicate in each quarter points of interest (gardens, cafés, food-markets, artisans' workshops and shopping streets) for a change of pace or relaxation.

At any season of the year, like its grilled T-bone steak, the famous *bistecca alla fiorentina*, the city can be completely ruined if 'overdone'. After a morning's sightseeing, sensible people desert the squares and sidewalk cafés and head for the hills, if only the shady parkland on the heights south of the Arno river.

This is good advice at the best of times. In summer, it becomes an imperative. The magical golden light over the Arno creates a wonderful ambience for the town's monuments, but in July and August the river basin turns into a torrid cauldron. Take a leaf out of the book of the aristocrats of

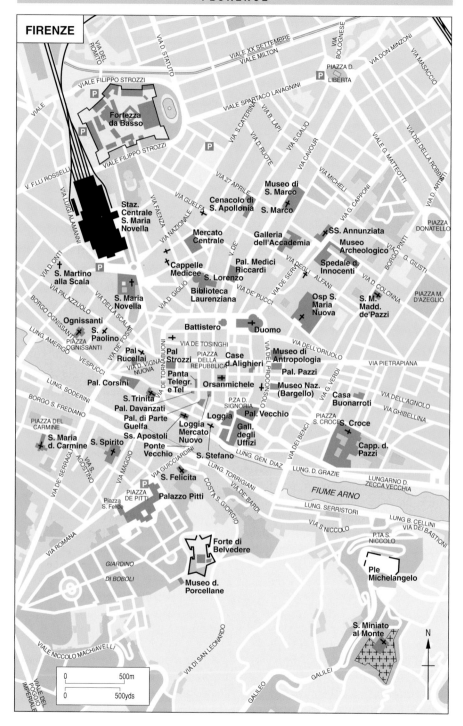

FIRENZE

old – Medici, Guelphs and Ghibellines, English duchesses and rich American art-collectors – who divided their time between Florence itself and the surrounding hilltop towns where they had their country villas. The closest of these is Fiesole, charming in itself and with the wonderful added asset of its dream-like panorama over Florence. For that first view, many romantics arriving in Tuscany make a point of driving up to Fiesole even *before* going into the city.

Time Plans

The city's three main poles of attraction, the sacred at the **Duomo** (cathedral), the secular at the **Palazzo Vecchio** city hall and the purely commercial on **Ponte Vecchio** bridge, serve as useful starting-points for our itineraries. The Ponte Vecchio doubles for the walk to Santa Maria Novella and for the sights south of the river (best tackled at least in part by car or taxi). Those who do not have the time (or the inclination) to make a systematic exploration of the whole city in all four quarters can make up their own itineraries from this list of the principal sights:

1. San Giovanni: Duomo to San Marco
- **Duomo**, as the cathedral is universally known, with baptistery, campanile, cathedral museum: works of Donatello, Andrea Pisano;
- **Palazzo Medici-Riccardi**, city Godfather's stronghold;
- **San Lorenzo**, Medici church: Michelangelo chapel and library;
- **San Marco**, Dominican convent museum: Fra Angelico frescoes, Savonarola's quarters;
- **Galleria dell'Accademia**: Michelangelo's sculpture, the original of *David*;

- **Museo Archeologico**: Etruscan, Greek and Egyptian treasures.

2. Santa Croce: Piazza della Signorìa to Santa Croce
- **Orsanmichele** oratory: Verrocchio, Donatello and Ghiberti sculpture;
- **Bargello**, sculpture museum: Donatello, Michelangelo and Cellini;
- **Palazzo Vecchio**, city hall on Piazza della Signorìa: Cellini sculpture in Loggia dei Lanzi;
- **Uffizi** museum, Renaissance masterpieces: Giotto, Masaccio, Botticelli, Michelangelo, Dürer, Cranach, Raphael and Titian;
- **Santa Croce** basilica: Machiavelli, Michelangelo and Galileo tombs, Giotto frescoes, Pazzi Chapel.

3. Santa Maria Novella: Ponte Vecchio to Ognissanti
- **Ponte Vecchio**, jewellery shops on city's oldest bridge;
- **Mercato Nuovo**, street-market;
- **Lungarni,** Arno embankment road;
- **Palazzo Strozzi** on Via Tornabuoni luxury shopping street;
- **Ognissanti** church: Ghirlandaio frescoes; Excelsior hotel bar.
- **Santa Maria Novella** church: Giotto, Masaccio and Brunelleschi;

4. Santo Spirito: South of the Arno
- **Viale and Piazzale Michelangelo:** hillside views of city;
- **San Miniato**, Romanesque masterpiece, 13th-century pulpit;
- **Pitti Palace**, Medici's ducal residence, High Renaissance collection: Raphael, Titian, Rubens, and Modern Art Gallery;
- **Boboli Gardens**: Baroque fountains, porcelain museum;

- **Santo Spirito**, gem of Renaissance churches;
- **Santa Maria del Carmine**: Brancacci Chapel's Masaccio frescoes.

5. Excursions
- **Fiesole**, hilltop town: villas, gardens, Etruscan-Roman remains;
- **Certosa del Galuzzo**, charterhouse amid the olives;
- **Poggio a Caiano**, Renaissance Medici villa in walled gardens: side-trip to **Villa dell'Artimino**.

Here are some suggested programmes:
One day: Duomo, Palazzo Vecchio, Uffizi, Ponte Vecchio, shopping on Via Tornabuoni, Boboli Gardens and Santa Maria del Carmine.
Two days: take it easier and add San Lorenzo, San Marco, Excelsior hotel bar, Santa Croce and Bargello.
Three days or more: add any or all of the rest, broken up with an afternoon at Fiesole or another day-trip.

From Duomo to San Marco

The Duomo (cathedral) area that constitutes the sacred core of Florence in fact embraces two adjacent squares, Piazza San Giovanni and Piazza del Duomo. Together, they take in the baptistery dedicated to John the Baptist (*San Giovanni*), the soaring campanile, the Duomo and the cathedral museum (*Museo dell'Opere del Duomo*).

*A*mbitious plans for the Duomo ran out of funds and it had to wait till 1887 for the marble facing to be completed.

Loggia del Bigallo

On the corner of Via de'Calzaiuoli and Piazza San Giovanni, this little 14th-century arcade gives a great ensemble view of baptistery and Duomo. In the Middle Ages, the strategically situated loggia was where the charitable Company of Misericordia put abandoned children on display for three days before they were allotted to foster parents. From their headquarters across the street, the black-caped fraternity still operates an ambulance and other services for the poor.

Inside the Loggia, a small **museum** (when it is open) displays a fine *Madonna and Child* triptych (1333) by Bernardo Daddi, a disciple of Giotto. A fresco attributed to his workshop, *Madonna della Misericordia* (1342) is interesting principally for its representation of mediæval Florence, in which can clearly be seen the baptistery and Duomo, still in the course of construction.

The Baptistery

Architectural purists consider the baptistery (*battistero*) much more important than the admittedly spectacular Duomo. From the 9th to 11th century, in its function as a church, the baptistery served as the town's cathedral. Whatever one may think, the specifically baptistery-church to which it reverted in the 12th century remains for many the most beautiful Romanesque building in Florence. The harmony of its geometric forms and glorious combination of white Carrara and green Prato marble provide a perfect setting for those jewels that are the **bronze-panelled doors** of Andrea Pisano and Lorenzo Ghiberti. The sculpture covering the period from 1330 to 1452 makes a magnificent leap from sober Gothic dignity to the graceful élan of the Renaissance.

The Italian phenomenon of having a large baptistery-church separate from the cathedral derives from the custom of holding collective baptisms just twice a year, attracting huge crowds and needing several doors to admit them all. Always conscious of the big occasion, Florence's merchants parlayed this into a masterpiece, commissioning the greatest sculptors to do the job.

A true architectural and sculptural treasure, the Romanesque baptistery beside the cathedral is an exquisite jewel casket.

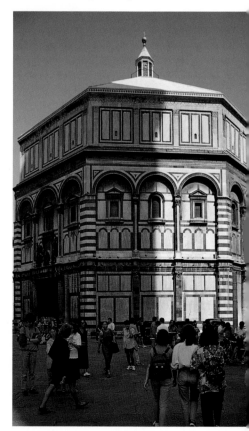

124

The octagonal Baptistery of San Giovanni has three doors facing due south, north and east, with the west, directly facing the cathedral, closed off for the apse and altar inside.

South Doors

It is best to take the doors chronologically, first Pisano, then Ghiberti. Approaching from the Via de'Calzaiuoli, start on the baptistery's south side, facing the Loggia del Bigallo.

Andrea Pisano worked for six years on the bronze door-panels, from 1330 to 1336, while collaborating with Giotto on the campanile (*see* below). Twenty panels illustrate the life of John the Baptist. In the lower registers are eight allegories of the cardinal virtues. The panels read like the pages of a book – for worshippers mostly illiterate, they *were* a book – from the upper left to lower right on each of the two doors. It is worth seeking out at least the best two groups of panels:

First, on the left-hand door, from the top, third row right: *John as a Boy in the Desert*, a scene that inspired dozens of Florentine painters; immediately below, *Preaching to the Pharisees* and *Annunciation of Jesus*; below that, *Baptism of the Disciples* and *Baptism of Jesus*.

At the same level on the second, right-hand door, third row: *Dance of Salomé* and *Beheading of John the Baptist*; below that, *Presentation of John's Head* and *Salomé Carries Head to Herod*.

North Doors

To preserve the chronology, continue left, round to the north. This was the first of Lorenzo Ghiberti's two sets of baptistery doors. His contract stipulated that he must deliver three panels a year, could use all the collaborators he liked, he chose Donatello and Uccello, but must do the trees, faces and hair himself. In fact, the 28 panels, 20 on the life of Jesus and eight on the Church fathers and writers of the Gospels, took him over 20 years (1403-24), but nobody complained.

In these doors, the panels' story, from the Annunciation to Mary to the Descent

---

ALL OR NOTHING AT ALL

In 1401, the Florentine merchants, at the height of their prosperity, announced a grand competition to decorate the baptistery doors in bronze. The subject for the trial panel was to be *Abraham's Sacrifice of Isaac*. Seven artists entered, including Brunelleschi, hesitating for his career was between architect and sculptor, Jacopo della Quercia, the great Sienese artist, and Ghiberti. Brunelleschi's competition entry, full of dramatic violence and energy, showing a fanatical Abraham who looked as if he was murdering rather than just sacrificing his son, was too revolutionary for the conservative Florentines. Ghiberti's winning panel was more in keeping with the dignified Gothic spirit appreciated by these refined merchants. (These two competing entries can be seen and compared at the Bargello Museum, *see* page 144.)

Artist and Renaissance historian Giorgio Vasari tells that when Brunelleschi saw Ghiberti's entry, he withdrew from the contest in comradely respect for a piece of superior work. His account, however, was some 150 years after the event. More plausible is the account of Antonio Manetti, a contemporary, that the merchants had proposed a collaboration between the two great artists, but that was more than Brunelleschi's ego could bear. He refused to share the prize and gave up sculpture to concentrate on architecture. From this defeat came, in Florence alone, the cathedral dome, the church of San Lorenzo and the Pazzi Chapel.

---

of the Holy Ghost, reads from the lower half upwards, in pairs. This is the convention of stained-glass windows. The scenes show a freer naturalism than Pisano's. Especially interesting are two panels on the right-hand door, fourth and fifth from the top: *Jesus Walking on the Water* and *Jesus in Dispute with the Rabbis*. The door-frame is also particularly beautiful; above the left-hand door, the head in the middle is Ghiberti's self-portrait.

East Doors

The merchants were so happy with the artist's work on the North Doors that they immediately commissioned another pair for the East Doors, in gilded bronze, and this became Ghiberti's masterpiece, dubbed by Michelangelo the 'Gate of Paradise'. Ghiberti devoted the rest of his life to it (1425-1452), dying just three years after it was completed.

Liberated from a certain constraint evident in the first commission, Ghiberti let himself go on this one, combining the skills of goldsmith and sculptor. His intricate painterly compositions drew on the experiments of his pupils Donatello and Uccello. They depict ten scenes from the Old Testament, all worth 'reading', from top left: *Adam and Eve* and *Cain and Abel*; *Noah's Ark* and *Abraham and Isaac*; *Jacob and Esau* and *Joseph and his Brothers*; *Moses on Mount Sinai* and

Joshua at Jericho; *David and Goliath* and *Solomon and Sheba*.

The panels are framed by statuettes of prophets, female oracles and contemporary portraits. Another Ghiberti self-portrait can be found at the bottom right-hand corner of the *Jacob and Esau* panel.

Inside the Baptistery

The Roman Corinthian columns of the interior led some Renaissance artists to

Ghiberti's bronze panel for the baptistery's east doors shows Jacob getting his father's blessing, after he had bought it from brother Esau for a bowl of lentil soup.

imagine that the baptistery itself was a work of classical antiquity. The Biblical scenes of the cupola are 13th-century **mosaics** in late Byzantine style, executing designs by various Tuscan masters such as Cimabue and Coppo di Marcovaldo. On the far left side from the entrance is Donatello's **tomb of John XXIII** (the antipope unsuccessfully promoted by Cosimo the Elder), with allegorical figures on the pedestal by Michelozzo.

Duomo

Exterior

Yes, the façade is a dazzling sight, all that white Carrara and green Prato marble with the touches of Siena red. But if the Duomo lacks the grace of the baptistery and would without its dome be much less impressive than Siena cathedral, it is largely because the marble facing and bronze doors are such a heavy-handed afterthought. The

late 19th-century Neo-Gothic pastiche (by Emilio de Fabris) creates a certain homogeneity but lacks the inspiration of the church's first builders.

Already renowned for his work in Orvieto, Perugia and Rome, architect Arnolfo di Cambio was commissioned by the city council in 1294 with a *carte blanche* he could not refuse: 'to prepare models and designs for the renewal of (the cathedral) with the highest and most prodigious magnificence so that the industry and power of men could not invent or ever be able to attempt anything more vast and more beautiful.' The council liked his initial work enough to exempt him from all taxes in 1300, but he died two years later before completing his task.

Construction dragged on through the 14th century, in the hands of such masters as Giotto, more interested in his campanile, and Andrea Pisano. By 1368, the church had taken on its final shape – minus the dome completed in 1434. The façade was demolished in 1587 and replaced exactly 300 years later.

Other than the campanile and dome, the most important feature of the cathedral's exterior is around the north side (left as you face the entrance), the **Porta della Mandorla**. Up in the gable, this monumental porch has Nanni di Bianco's finely sculpted *Assumption of the Madonna* in an almond-shaped frame (*mandorla*).

Campanile

The wonderfully ornate five-tiered bell-tower adds a playful note to a cathedral square highly charged with holy dignity. The green, white and red marble are used to magnificent effect.

Giotto was appointed chief architect (*capomastro*) for the whole cathedral in 1334, but he had only three years to live and concentrated all his energies on the campanile. His designs were used for Andrea Pisano's sculpted panels around the base. After Giotto's death, Pisano added the niches for statues on the next level and Francesco Talenti (designer of the Loggia dei Lanzi, *see* page 136) completed the three upper storeys with mullioned windows. Giotto's original plan for a spire was abandoned in favour of a simple square cornice and balustrade.

The originals of the bas-reliefs and statues are in the cathedral museum (*Museo dell'Opera del Duomo, see* page 131), but the copies give a good idea of the work: around the base, Pisano's hexagonal

panels of Adam, Eve and Noah, and ancient Greek scholars at work. The panels on the side facing the church, allegories of *Logic*, *Music*, *Geometry* and the like, are by Luca della Robbia. The sculptures of prophets and female oracles in the higher tiers are by Donatello and Nanni di Bartolo.

The Dome

Among the great innovations of Renaissance art, Brunelleschi's crowning achievement for the Duomo does for architecture what Donatello's work performs for sculpture and Masaccio's frescoes for painting. Before starting work on a dome for St Peter's in Rome, Michelangelo is

At rooftop level, two masters of Italian civilization salute each other, Giotto with his campanile and Brunelleschi with his dome.

said to have observed of Brunelleschi's work: 'I'll give her a bigger sister, but will she be as beautiful?' With its deep red herringbone brickwork and eight white stone ribs curving to a marble lantern at the top, the cathedral's grandiose dome supplanted the tower of the Palazzo Vecchio as

THE SECRET

When Thomas Edison said that 'Genius is one per cent inspiration and 99 per cent perspiration', Filippo Brunelleschi would not have given him an argument. (He saved his arguments for Florence's city fathers.) They asked him to design their cathedral dome in 1402. His response was to leave town and spend the next three years in Rome for a minute study of all the ancient Roman buildings, every last one of them, measuring and analysing their structure and function. He ended up with the Pantheon, which gave him the final idea for his dome.

He returned to Florence but told nobody of his plans. He proposed only to build the pillars to support the drum that would elevate the dome. Without letting the city fathers know what the dome itself would look like, he went off again to Rome. They ran after him and pleaded for him to divulge his ideas. Clearly still nettled by the baptistery competition (*see* ALL OR NOTHING AT ALL, page 125), Brunelleschi suggested the council should launch another one for the dome. Competitors should design a dome with a diameter of 46m (150ft) at the base to be raised without a wooden frame to support the vault during construction. 'That's impossible,' they said. 'Show us how it could be done, give us a model.'

He built a model 7m (22ft) high, but kept it concealed. Distrustful of this prima donna, the council had the gall to invite him to take on Ghiberti as an assistant. Brunelleschi exploded and would have smashed his model to smithereens if his pals Donatello and Luca della Robbia had not held him back. They suggested he feign illness and propose to the council that Ghiberti do it alone. Ghiberti, of course, could not manage it. With the field cleared of all rivals, Brunelleschi unveiled the wooden model which gave rise to the dome you see today.

Florence's identifying landmark, visible not only all over the city but also far beyond in the Tuscan hills.

Completed in 1434, it measures 45.5m (149ft) in diameter. It is worth climbing to the top, 463 steps in comfortable stages (entrance inside the church in the north aisle, left as you enter). The climb reveals glimpses of the surrounding city, different views of the cathedral's interior and fascinating closeups of the dome's structure. Brunelleschi's original wooden model is displayed in the cathedral museum.

Inside the Duomo

The cathedral's interior is cool and somewhat forbidding, but is worth a tour. In the second and third bays on the north aisle are two fine, statue-like equestrian frescoes of mercenaries serving the Florentine state in the 14th and 15th centuries: *Niccolò da Tolentino*, vividly painted by Andrea del Castagno, and Paolo Uccello's **portrait of Sir John Hawkwood** (unpronounceable for Italians, so known as Giovanni Acuto). After brilliant performances in the 100 Years' War in France, the English knight obtained what modern-day footballers would call an 'independent transfer' to Florence as a *condottiere*. His 'fee' included tax-exemption, state funeral and cathedral monument.

At the east end of the church, below the high altar, is Ghiberti's finely modelled **bronze shrine**. To the left, in the north sacristy, is a Luca della Robbia *Resurrection* in glazed **terracotta relief**. The bronze doors, behind which Lorenzo the Magnificent hid to escape assassination in 1478 (see DON'T MESS WITH A MEDICI, page 68), are also the work of della Robbia.

In the south aisle (right of the entrance), stairs lead down to excavations of an earlier church on this site, Santa Reparata. At the bottom of the stairs, found in 1972 and protected behind a grille, is the unadorned **tombstone of Brunelleschi**, the only citizen honoured with burial in the cathedral.

Museo dell'Opera del Duomo

The cathedral museum (Piazza del Duomo 9, at the rear of the church) includes in its collections original panels of the baptistery's bronze doors and Donatello's sculptures for the upper niches of the campanile, along with many of the Duomo's finest works of art. Two rooms on the ground floor are devoted to Brunelleschi, notably wooden models of the dome and lantern, as well as some of the original ropes and pulleys, wheels, capstans and other equipment used in the construction.

Michelangelo's *Pietà* of the dead Jesus in his mother's arms, an unfinished sculpture done in his latter years, portrays a tragic agony rather than the pathos of his earlier treatment of the subject in St Peter's in Rome. Michelangelo originally conceived the group for his own tomb and represented himself in the figure of Nicodemus. Flaws in the marble so enraged him that he hurled a hammer at it, destroying a part that had to be restored. The rather insipid Mary Magdalen was added by a pupil.

Altogether more powerful in its anguish and sorrow is **Donatello's *Mary Magdalen***, originally standing in the Baptistery. Two other Donatello statues, the prophet *Habakkuk* and *Abraham Sacrificing Isaac* have the searing individuality of portraits from life.

On a decidedly cheerful note, two splendid **choir galleries** show merry boys and girls singing, dancing and playing musical instruments, stone carvings by Luca della Robbia and Donatello that once graced the doorways of the Duomo's sacristies.

Palazzo Medici-Riccardi

Something of the might of the Medici family can still be sensed in their massive 15th-century palace, north west of the cathedral. It is now Florence's prefecture (Riccardi was a marquis who purchased it in 1659). The façade, at street level forbidding with its rough ashlar stone and defiant grill windows, smooths out more decoratively in the upper storeys in a design by Michelozzo that became a prototype for the city's Renaissance palaces. The ground floor originally had an open loggia at the corner for the family banking business.

The charming atrium-style arcaded courtyard is more hospitable. Beyond it, you may like to rest a moment in the quiet little 17th-century **garden** of orange trees before visiting the palace's upstairs **family chapel** to see Benozzo Gozzoli's majestic fresco of the *Journey of the Magi to Bethlehem* (1460). Against an enchanting Tuscan landscape, it portrays the Medici clan led by the white-clad Lorenzo the Magnificent in what is in fact an allegory commemorating the processions of Greek patriarchs at the Ecumenical Council of 1439 (*see* HISTORY, page 66) and again in 1459 to meet Pope Pius II. In the gallery leading to the Riccardi library, a prodigious Baroque ceiling fresco by Luca Giordano rounds off the family saga with *The Apotheosis of the Medici* (1683).

Beside fruit and vegetables, the **street market** on Piazza San Lorenzo sells leather goods hand-made in workshops on back streets nearby.

San Lorenzo Church

Across the square from their palazzo, the Medici family church was designed by Brunelleschi and adorned by the great Renaissance masters. Funds ran out before Michelangelo's planned façade could embellish the austere barn-like exterior. Inside are **two pulpits** (1465) with bronze reliefs by Donatello: the *Crucifixion* and *Passion of Jesus* (left aisle), and *Martyrdom of St Lorenzo* and *Resurrection* (right aisle). Set in the floor in front of the high altar, Verrocchio's round marble *tondo* carved with the Medici family arms stands over the crypt containing the tomb of Cosimo the Elder. Brunelleschi is at his most elegant in the **Old Sacristy** at the end of the left transept, decorated with four Donatello wall medallions.

Medici Chapels

Adjoining the church but with a separate entrance (Piazza Madonna degli Aldobrandini) are the *Cappelle Medicee*, monuments to the splendour and decadence of the dynasty. Designed by a son of Duke Cosimo I, the octagonal **Princes' Chapel** (*Cappella dei Principi*) is a piece of 17th-century Baroque bombast. For this almost Mussolinian anachronism in oppressive

dark marble, the altar was not completed, appropriately enough, until 1939.

At the end of a corridor, the summit of Medici power is better celebrated in Michelangelo's superb **New Sacristy**, conceived as a pendant to Brunelleschi's sacristy in the church. Lorenzo the Magnificent and his assassinated brother Giuliano lie in simple tombs beneath the sculptor's *Madonna and Child*, flanked by lesser artists' statues of the family saints, Cosmas and Damian. Michelangelo's greatest work here is reserved for two minor members of the family: Lorenzo's third son, the Duke of Nemours, portrayed

The extravagant Baroque cupola over the Princes' Chapel was built when the Medici had given up behind-the-scenes discretion for up-front pomp and circumstance.

as an alert warrior above two allegorical figures of *Night* and *Day*; and Lorenzo's grandson, the Duke of Urbino, seen as a more pensive Roman soldier above two figures of *Twilight* and *Dawn*.

Laurentian Library

To the left of the church entrance, the handsome *Biblioteca Laurenziana* offers a charmed moment of peace. The library was built by Giorgio Vasari and Bartolommeo Ammannati to designs by Michelangelo. It houses a priceless collection of books and manuscripts begun by Cosimo the Elder, including the famous 5th-century *Virgil codex*. Michelangelo also designed the inlaid wooden desks used to display the manuscripts.

Refectory of Sant'Apollonia

For a view of Andrea del Castagno's monumental but controversial *Last Supper* fresco (1450), you must ring the doorbell to gain entrance to the monastery's refectory (*cenacolo*), at the corner of Via XXVII Aprile and Via San Gallo. In this traditional theme for the monks' dining room, there is no mistaking which of the Apostles is Judas. The only one without a halo, he sits dark and alone opposite Jesus. The overall tone here and in a nearby *Crucifixion* is one of raw sculptural power rather than painterly grace.

IN THE TEETH OF DEATH

Apollonia was a 4th-century Christian saint martyrized in Alexandria for refusing to make sacrifices to pagan gods. She was duly sacrificed, in particularly savage manner, by having all her teeth pulled out before being burned to death. Naturally enough, she became the patron saint of dentists.

San Marco Monastery

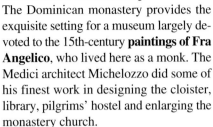

The Dominican monastery provides the exquisite setting for a museum largely devoted to the 15th-century **paintings of Fra Angelico**, who lived here as a monk. The Medici architect Michelozzo did some of his finest work in designing the cloister, library, pilgrims' hostel and enlarging the monastery church.

Off the **cloister**, with its ancient cedar tree, are some of Fra Angelico's best paintings, notably a *Descent from the Cross* altarpiece from the church of Santa Trinità and miniatures of the life of Jesus. In the small **refectory** is a stately Ghirlandaio mural of the *Last Supper*. In the monks' cells upstairs, the **frescoes** of the man Italians call *Beato* (Blessed) Angelico were intended to be inspirational rather than decorative. His celebrated *Annunciation* faces the top of the stairs (compare the simpler version in cell 3). Other outstanding works include the mystic *Transfiguration* in cell 6 and *Jesus Mocked* in cell 7.

The **Prior's Quarters** in the second dormitory (cells 12, 13 and 14) were the home of fire-and-brimstone preacher Girolamo Savonarola from 1481 until his death in 1498 (*see* HISTORY, pages 70-1). You can see some of his belongings, a portrait painted by his fellow-monk Fra Bartolommeo (present in the monastery at the time of Savonarola's arrest), and the picture of his burning at the stake.

Chiostro dello Scalzo

North of San Marco at Via Cavour 69 (ring the bell for access), the *Scalzo* ('barefooted') confraternity's cloister is decorated with striking **frescoes** (1514-1526) by Andrea del Sarto. Scenes from the life of John the Baptist are treated in various tones of monochrome with some of the spontaneity of drawings.

Galleria dell'Accademia

The museum (Via Ricasoli 60) is conceived primarily for students of Florentine painting from the 13th to the 16th century, serving as an important adjunct to the Uffizi (*see* pages 139-41). But it is a single work of art that draws most visitors here: Michelangelo's great **David**. Completed in 1504 when Michelangelo was 29, the statue depicts the hero in repose, but infused with all the energy needed to hurl that stone at Goliath. The gallery's collection of other works by Michelangelo includes four unfinished *Slaves*, originally intended to form part of a monumental tomb for Pope Julius II. Even incomplete, each writhing figure is a fascinating revelation of how Michelangelo releases their power from the marble.

Among the more important paintings are a Botticelli *Madonna,* an *Adoration of Jesus* by Lorenzo di Credi, two works by Filippino Lippi and Fra Bartolommeo's *Enthroned Madonna.*

Piazza Santissima Annunziata

Brunelleschi made of the square a consummate piece of Renaissance urban planning and a pioneering example of the piazza as stage-set. He designed the graceful colonnade of nine arches for the **Spedale degli Innocenti**, hospital for foundlings, symbolized by the charming little babes in Andrea della Robbia's roundels above the arches. Michelozzo's later **Santissima Annunziata church**, together with the 17th-century fountains and equestrian statue of Grand Duke Ferdinando, preserve the harmonies of the master's overall design. In the little **cloister** leading to the church, see Andrea del Sarto's frescoes of the *Birth of Mary* and *Arrival of the Magi* (to the right of the church entrance).

Museo Archeologico

Adjoining the foundlings' hospital, the archaeological museum (Via della Colonna 36) houses one of Italy's most important collections of Egyptian, Greek and Etruscan antiquities. Among the highlights: the Greek *François Vase* (6th century BC), discovered perfectly intact in southern Tuscany in 1845, dropped and smashed in 1900, and beautifully restored; two remarkable Etruscan bronzes, the *Chimera* (5th century BC) and *Arringatore* (orator, 1st century BC); and an Egyptian granite sculpture (14th century BC) of a divine cow giving milk to a pharaoh.

Piazza della Signorìa to Santa Croce

The thoroughfare linking the cathedral to the secular heart of the city at Piazza della Signorìa is flanked by one after another elegant shoe shop maintaining the tradition of the street's mediæval name, **Via dei Calzaiuoli** (stocking and shoe-makers).

Orsanmichele

If the tall rectangular block looks more like a grain silo than the church it is supposed to be, that is because it was once both. Florentines always liked combining faith and business. The present building stands on the site of an 8th-century oratory church, San Michele in Orto (St Michael in the [market]-garden) known popularly as Or'-San-Michele. In the 14th century, the old church was replaced by a grain and cereals market and a loggia to provide the merchants with a shelter and place of worship. The loggia's arches were subsequently closed in to form today's triple-mullioned windows with upper floors added to store grain and city archives.

More importantly, each pillar overlooking the street was assigned to one of the town's guilds to be decorated with **statues** of their patron saints by Florence's greatest talents. Most of the originals are now sheltered in the Bargello, but a tour of this veritable gallery of Late Gothic and Renaissance sculpture also affords an amusing sense of the importance and self-importance of Florence's powerful guilds.

On the Via dei Calzaiuoli side (coming from the Duomo): Giambologna's *St Luke* (1601), writer of the gospel truth and so patron saint of Florence's Judges and Notaries; Verrocchio's *Doubting Thomas* (1484), the saint who, before accepting the resurrected Jesus, wanted tangible evidence, a natural for the Trade Tribunal; **Lorenzo Ghiberti's** *John the Baptist* (1416), patron saint of the Cloth Merchants' guild (despite John's ascetic taste for coarse untreated camel's hair).

Turning right on Via dei Lamberti, the first three niches – the Silk Weavers' *St John the Evangelist*, the Doctors' and Pharmacists' *Madonna and Child* and the Furriers' *St James* – have little artistic interest, but the fourth, **Donatello's** *St Mark* (1413), one of the first statues erected here (for the Linen Manufacturers), is a landmark in the transformation of Christian saint into Renaissance hero.

Turn right again, on Via dell'Arte della Lana (Wool Weavers' Street). After Nanni di Bianco's *St Eligius* (1415) shoeing and exorcising a horse possessed by the Devil, for the Blacksmiths' guild, come two masterpieces in the second and third niches: **Ghiberti's** *St Stephen* (1428), the first Christian martyr, for the wealthy Wool Manufacturers; and **Ghiberti's** *St Matthew* (1420), tax-collector in the Bible and so patron of Money-changers.

Complete the tour turning right on Via Orsanmichele to a bronze copy of Donatello's *St George* marble original (14-16) for the guild of Armourers – cool, tough warrior at ease but poised for action, slaying the dragon in a *bas relief* below; then **Nanni di Bianco's** *Four Crowned Saints* (1408), his masterpiece for the guild of Smiths, Carpenters and Masons – the saints are four Christian artists martyred for refusing to sculpt a pagan deity for the Roman emperor, Diocletian; in the third niche is Donatello's marble *St Peter* (1413) for the Butchers, though the apostle was a fisherman, and Nanni di Bianco's *St Philip* for the Shoe-makers (1410).

Inside the oratory is Andrea Orcagna's admirable 14th-century Gothic marble **tabernacle altar**. For a great view back at the baptistery and Duomo, take the entrance on Via dell'Arte della Lana to go upstairs to the old granaries.

Piazza della Signorìa

This is Florence's civic centre. In a town where the church nearly always played second fiddle to city hall, this much more than the Piazza del Duomo was where the action was. The square still bustles in all seasons, not least because it leads to the richest of Italy's art museums, the Uffizi. The piazza was a market place in prehistoric times and the Romans had their public baths here.

The square is not at all square. The irregular shape is what was left when a group of palaces were razed to the ground in the Guelph-Ghibelline civil war in the 13th century (*see* HISTORY, page 56). Florentine town-palaces were all built like fortresses with heavy grilled windows to fend off attackers, many of them with drawbridges and battlements. The vacuum left by the losers' palaces was filled in part by the fortress-palace to top them all, the city hall (*Palazzo della Signorìa*, now *Palazzo Vecchio*).

It was the place for public executions, most notoriously for the Pazzi conspirators in 1478 after assassinating Giuliano de'Medici, Lorenzo's brother (*see* DON'T MESS WITH A MEDICI, page 68). It was here also that preacher Savonarola held his Bonfire of the Vanities in 1497, only to be burned himself on the same spot a year later, marked by a commemorative stone near the fountain (*see* HISTORY, page 71).

Loggia dei Lanzi

On the south side of the square, the loggia was built in 1382 to shelter the formal inauguration of city governors and other public ceremonies. The original idea was that this open arcade of three arches would give such government proceedings a semblance of democracy. In the 16th century, the authoritarian Duke Cosimo I de'Medici put a stop to such nonsense by turning it into a guardhouse for his Swiss-German halberdiers – *Landknechte*, a word garbled by Florentines into *Lanzi*. As Machiavelli frequently complained, few Florentines cared to dirty their hands by doing their own soldiering. Always great snobs, they preferred leaving it to foreigners like the *Schwytzertütsch*, Spaniards, Lombards, Neapolitans and such, who seemed actually to enjoy it.

Later dukes turned the loggia into the grand sculpture gallery it is today. At the rear are six ancient Roman statues, heavily restored, of vestal virgins, priestesses and patrician matrons. Of the other six sculptures, guarded by a couple of marble lions (left, Renaissance; right, ancient Roman), only two are of real artistic value. On the right, in front of an uninteresting *Hercules*, is **Giambologna's** *Rape of the Sabines* (1583), a heroically muscular study of a soldier claiming his sexual spoils from the vanquished enemy.

On the left, **Benvenuto Cellini's** *Perseus* brandishing the severed head of Medea is for many the splendid braggart's masterpiece. In one inspired moment, Cellini has combined the legendary technical wizardry he loved to show off as a goldsmith with undoubted sculptural beauty. It is a sheer *tour de force* to have

---

HOT HEAD

Benvenuto Cellini's *Perseus* was executed in a state of delirium. For the bronze, Cellini had installed at his home a special forge. The struggle to keep the furnace fire going and stop it burning the house down sent him to bed with a fever. Assistants had to watch the fire, melt down the copper and bronze to achieve the proper fusion and warn their master of the critical moment for the casting. Facing a shortage of cheap metal (copper, tin, etc.) to 'bind' the bronze, the despairing smiths left the forge to tell their master that all was lost.

With the fire burning a hole in the roof and rain threatening to extinguish the furnace in the middle of the night, the fever-racked Cellini stumbled down to the forge. From the kitchen, he gathered up all the metal utensils, pots, pans, dishes, knives and spoons and threw them into the cauldron with the bronze. Two hours before dawn, he achieved the desired fusion, poured it into the *Perseus* mould and went back to bed, his fever cured.

But his troubles were not over. The duke's wife, Eleonora of Toledo, loved his little pedestal statuettes so much that she asked to keep them for her country villa: 'they'll risk being spoilt down in the piazza'. Fuming inwardly, the artist said nothing and the next day soldered them firmly to the pedestal. The art custodians of Florence have now decided Eleonora was right, replaced them with copies and put Cellini's originals in the Bargello.

---

cast this bronze in perfect balance with the head of Medea held aloft so far from the main mass of the statue. It was commissioned by Duke Cosimo I in 1545 but took nine long, brutally exhausting years to complete. The statue's pedestal is decorated with superb figures of *Jupiter, Mercury, Minerva* and *Danaë*, who was the mother of Perseus.

In a piazza that is a veritable sculpture garden, more statuary graces the orator's platform along the city hall's sober façade. A weathered copy of **Michelangelo's** *David* occupies the spot directly beneath the palazzo tower where the original was set in 1504 by the Florentine Republic as a symbol of the city's fiercely defended independence. Standing against a hostile world of cruel Philistines, Florentines loved to identify with the beauty and courage of the poetic giant-killer, a constant subject for the city's sculptors.

As a sadly clumsy counterpart, to the right is Baccio Bandinelli's *Hercules and Cacus*. Over to the left are two Donatello copies, the *Marzocco*, Florence's heraldic lion, and a bronze of *Judith and Holofernes*. The latter sculpture was originally commissioned for a fountain in a Medici palace garden, but Savonarola, the city's virtual dictator of the time, ordered it brought here as an example of virtue punishing licentiousness. In fact, Donatello's Judith looks decidedly bored by the whole business.

Jutting out from the corner of the Palazzo Vecchio is Bartolommeo Ammannati's **Neptune Fountain**, a ghastly white marble monstrosity commissioned by Duke Cosimo I. The God of the Seas stands naked in his chariot celebrating the new Florentine fleet that the duke had built in the 1540s.

Out in the piazza, the duke has his own bronze **Equestrian Statue** (1594). The grand but somewhat mannered and pompous monument by Giambologna (Flemish name Jean Boulogne) highlights the change in the Medicis from a dynasty of subtle and usually discreet bankers to a more pushy, ostentatious titled aristocracy flexing its military muscle. It was commissioned by Cosimo's son Ferdinando after the duke's death.

BIG NOSE

Michelangelo's first rule with his patrons: humour them. At the unveiling of his *David* in front of the Palazzo Vecchio, Piero Soderini, the city *gonfaloniere* (governor), came to express his admiration, but also to play the connoisseur by making a little criticism. The nose, he decided, was too big. Michelangelo immediately climbed a ladder with hammer and chisel, apparently to correct the defect. In fact, he just went through the motions without touching the nose. To make it look more realistic, he let drop some marble dust he had sneaked from his pocket, glancing anxiously down at his critic for approval. 'Bravo!' said Soderini when Michelangelo came back down, 'That's perfect. You have given him life.'

Palazzo Vecchio

The great Gothic civic fortress, originally known like the piazza as the Palazzo della Signorìa, was begun in 1299 by Arnolfo di Cambio, who was also working on the Duomo. It was designed to provide council halls, a communal dining room and private apartments for the city elders, the *Signorìa*, when they met for two months each year to discuss affairs of the city-state. An unambiguous image of civic authority, the Palazzo had the tallest tower in town, with its upper storey used for a guard to keep a daily watch for enemies. The steeple is crowned by a bronze ball and the *Marzocco*, city emblem of a lion holding a lily. From the 14th to the 18th

*F*ew of the world's municipal buildings so aptly express the personality of their city as Florence's cool, dignified, faintly aloof Palazzo Vecchio.

abandoned it, however, for the Palazzo Pitti across the river, and made the Uffizi his business headquarters. Henceforth, the Palazzo della Signorìa became known as the Palazzo Vecchio.

Upstairs, the **Salone del Cinquecento** was built in 1495 for Savonarola's short-lived Republican Council before serving as Duke Cosimo's throne room and, three centuries later, the chamber of Italy's first national parliament. The décor celebrates Florentine power – Vasari's frescoes of victories over Siena and Pisa, and Michelangelo's *Victory* statue, designed originally for Pope Julius II's tomb and recycled here to honour the Grand Duke of Tuscany.

On the second floor, the **Sala dei Gigli** (Hall of the Lilies) is brilliantly decorated in blues and golds with Ghirlandaio frescoes of Roman and early Christian history. It adjoins the **Chancery** (*cancelleria*) where Niccolò Machiavelli served as secretary to the Florentine Republic (*see* OLD NICK, page 71). Santi di Tito's portrait of the young diplomat-philosopher has little of the calculating pragmatism popularly attributed to the author of *The Prince*. Any lingering cynicism is dispelled altogether by the original of Verrocchio's cuddly cherub.

Opposite the Palazzo Vecchio, before tackling the Uffizi museum, you may like to try an equally cherished institution, the **Café Rivoire** (Via Vacchereccia), renowned for serving a great capuccino or the best hot chocolate in Italy.

centuries, a couple of live lions were kept in cages at the palazzo.

In the 15th century, when real power shifted to the Medici and to their family palace, the Palazzo was 'demilitarized' by architect Michelozzo with some graceful Renaissance touches visible in the arcades and windows of the inner courtyard. The porphyry fountain by Francesco del Tadda is decorated by a copy of Verrocchio's delightful bronze *Cherub with a Dolphin* (original inside the palace). This plus the ornate stucco and frescoes were added for a Medici wedding in 1565 when Duke Cosimo I commissioned Vasari to convert the edifice to a ducal palace. He soon

MR NICE GUY

Duke Cosimo I was a cunning prince, prudish family man but totally vicious. When planning to assassinate his arch enemy Piero Strozzi, he tested the efficiency of sample poisons by feeding them first to convicts in the Bargello prison. His court artist (and chronicler) Giorgio Vasari sheds interesting light on the duke, known for brutally punishing the slightest hint of lechery among his courtiers. One hot afternoon while Vasari was up on a scaffolding painting a ceiling-fresco for the Medici private apartments in the remodelled palace, Cosimo's daughter Isabella came in to take a siesta on the couch below. A few minutes later, she was followed by Duke Cosimo. Vasari was startled by the girl's screams as her father proceeded to tear off her clothes. The artist hid behind his tarpaulins until it was all over. 'I didn't feel like painting any more that day,' Vasari noted later.

The Uffizi

The grandiose museum of Italian and European painting stretches in a long U-shape from the Palazzo Vecchio down to the Arno river and back. Duke Cosimo had Vasari design it in 1560 as a series of government offices (*uffizi*, hence the name), a mint for the city's florin and workshops for the Medici's craftsmen.

That makes for a lot of museum, but a great one that it would be sad to renounce through visual fatigue. We will not burden you with guilt by telling you 'not to miss' this or to 'be sure' to see that, but just signal some of what is really worth seeing. See all or only half a dozen, stop for an occasional peek out of the window over the Arno river and the Ponte Vecchio bridge. Be sure to rendezvous later at the museum's **roof-garden café** above the Loggia dei Lanzi.

Particularly since the heroic repair work following the bomb destruction of 1993, constant reorganization makes it hazardous to specify room numbers, but the paintings are exhibited chronologically from the 13th to the 18th century. To place the artists in historical perspective, *see* ART AND ARCHITECTURE IN TUSCANY, pages 80-95. Following largely the same method, here are some of the highlights: **Giotto** breathes a warm humanity into his *Madonna Enthroned* (1300) that distinguishes it from the more formal treatment of the subject by **Cimabue** and **Duccio di Buoninsegna** in the same room, both 15 years earlier. See also Giotto's *Madonna* polyptych.

Simone Martini depicts in his *Annunciation* (1333) a young Mary shying away from archangel Gabriel, expressing the characteristic elegance and poetry of his Siena school.

Paolo Uccello is dream-like, almost surrealist in his obsession with his (largely unsolved) problems of perspective and merry-go-round horses in his *Battle of San Romano* (1456).

Piero della Francesca brings his own form of heightened reality to the cool, dignified portraits of *Federico da Montefeltro*, Duke of Urbino, and his wife *Battista Sforza* (1465), portrayed against their Umbrian landscape.

Filippo Lippi, the maverick monk, shows himself a true Renaissance master of light and perspective in his *Coronation of the Madonna* (1447) and *Madonna with Child and Two Angels* (1460).

Sandro Botticelli, inextricably linked to his native Florence, favourite of the Medici, has a gallery practically all to himself. His graceful *Primavera* ('Spring', 1478) and the almost too famous but undyingly delightful *Birth of Venus*

Try to imagine what the Uffizi was like when its corridors echoed to the steps not of a solitary tourist but of Medici managers hurrying to their offices.

achieve an enchanting mixture of sensuality and purity.

Leonardo da Vinci produced, in his workshop contribution to Andrea Verrocchio's *Baptism of Christ* (1470), his earliest identified work: the background landscape and the angel on the left, beautiful enough to reduce his companion angel to wide-eyed jealousy and persuade Verrocchio to give up painting for sculpture. Leonardo's *Annunciation* of a few years later already shows his characteristic gentle tone and feeling for precise detail. The *Adoration of the Magi*, left unfinished by his departure for Milan

(1481), reveals his revolutionary power of psychological observation.

Giovanni Bellini is represented by a mystic *Holy Allegory* (1490) in which we can appreciate the typical Venetian serenity even without understanding all its symbols.

Michelangelo has only one painting in the Uffizi, his *Holy Family* roundel (1504) from the same year as his *David* and decidedly sculptural in the group's solid plastic qualities.

Raphael may not share Michelangelo's strength and torment or Leonardo's complexity, but earns his place as the third of Italy's three High Renaissance giants with his own powers of clarity and restraint, eminently present in his *Madonna of the Goldfinch* (1506) and a revealing *Self-Portrait*.

Titian has a superbly sensual *Venus of Urbino* (1538), less Greek goddess than the prince's mistress she probably was, and an equally disturbing *Flora* (1515).

Parmigianino achieves another kind of

THE TRIBUNA

The grand octagonal *Tribuna* gallery was conceived in 1585 by Bernardo Buontalenti as a separate showcase within the Uffizi to display the most prized private treasures in the Medici collection. With its mother-of-pearl inlaid ceiling and ornate floor of polychrome *pietre dure* stone paving, the room itself is a work of art. It epitomizes the last splash of extravagance of the Medici dynasty. On the lovely octagonal table, 16 years in the making, is the famous *Medici Venus*, a 1st-century BC marble copy of a work done 300 years earlier by the great Praxiteles. Around the walls are 16th-century portraits of the Medici family by their court painter, Agnolo Bronzino. The height of his Mannerist art is achieved in the opulent portrait of Duke Cosimo's wife, Eleonora of Toledo, and their chubby baby son.

eroticism in his almost kinky but undeniably graceful *Madonna with the Long Neck* (1534). Those bizarre long fingers are an exquisite expression of the sophisticated Mannerism that followed the High Renaissance.

Caravaggio is happily ambiguous in his treatment of the half-naked peasant youth posing as *Bacchus* (1589) beside a bowl of over-ripe fruit; and brings a powerful realism to his *Abraham and Isaac* (1603).

Flemish, Dutch and German paintings here are few but are of the highest quality: compared with Caravaggio, there is nothing complicated about the robust sexiness of **Rubens'** *Bacchanale*, though he is also capable of great tenderness in the portrait of his wife, *Isabella Brandt* (1620); **Rembrandt** is wonderfully contemplative in his *Old Rabbi* (1658) and other portraits. Also displayed for comparison with their Italian contemporaries are: *Portrait of a Man* (late

15th century) by **Hans Memling**; *Deposition in the Tomb* (1450) by **Rogier van der Weyden**; a splendid *Portrait of his Father* (1490) by **Albrecht Dürer**; *Adam and Eve* (1528) by **Lucas Cranach**; and *Richard Southwell* by **Hans Holbein**.

Vasari Corridor

The *Corridoio Vasariano* linking the Uffizi via the Ponte Vecchio to the Pitti Palace is usually open only to guided tours arranged by prior appointment with the museum's administrative offices. It presents a gallery of artists' self-portraits that include Rubens, Rembrandt, Van Dyck, Velazquez, Joshua Reynolds, Delacroix and Ingres.

Science History Museum

The *Museo di Storia della Scienza* (Piazza dei Giudici 1, in the Palazzo Castellano down by the river) offers change of pace from all that fine art. The collection of scientific instruments gives pride of place to **Galileo's telescopes**, lenses, prisms, compass and his (pickled) middle finger, and finds a place for a Thomas Edison phonograph.

Santa Croce Church

East of the Uffizi, this church was built at the end of the 13th century by Arnolfo da Cambio, taking time off from building the Duomo and Palazzo Vecchio. The Neo-Gothic marble façade, a three-tiered affair preceded by a forecourt raised on stairs, was added in 1863, in apparent emulation of the great Gothic cathedrals of Siena and Orvieto.

Designed like Piazza Santa Croce to receive huge congregations for its itinerant preachers, the church's interior corresponds to the Florentine Gothic desire for space and breadth rather than north

European Gothic's taste for lofty verticality. Santa Croce is revered by Florentines as the last resting place of many great Italians. Michelangelo, Galileo, Machiavelli, Ghiberti and composer Rossini are all buried here. Though these great men were not necessarily honoured with monuments equal in quality to their talents, French novelist Stendhal was moved to comment: 'One must admit that few churches are distinguished with such honourable tombs. It makes one feel like being buried.'

Over in the right aisle, second bay, **Michelangelo's tomb** was designed by Vasari, a worthy but unspectacular effort with allegorical statues of *Painting, Sculpture* and *Architecture* mourning beneath a bust of the artist (aged 89 when he died). Michelangelo wanted the tomb surmounted by the *Pietà* now in the cathedral museum (*see* page 131), but the Florentines nearly did not even get his body; they had to smuggle it out of Rome hidden in a bale of sacking. For Dante, the nearby ugly 19th-century cenotaph (rather than the monument Michelangelo himself had begged in vain to create) must suffice, as Ravenna, his burial place, refuses to part with his remains.

The **pulpit** (1480) is a remarkable piece of sculpture by Benedetto da Maiano, with five *bas-reliefs* depicting scenes from the life of St Francis.

In the right aisle's sixth bay (beyond Machiavelli's graceless 18th-century

The church of Santa Croce serves as a pantheon for some of Italy's finest heroes of the arts and sciences. Unfortunately, their funeral monuments do not always do justice to their greatness.

FUN AND GAMES

Despite their solemn reputation, Florentines do occasionally take time off from work and worship. Piazza Santa Croce was designed in the 13th century for the devout masses who gathered to hear the open-air sermons of Franciscan monks. However, by the 15th century it attracted less pious crowds to its games and tournaments, including young aristocrats like Giuliano de'Medici, brother of Lorenzo, who scored a famous victory in 1469. It was here in Renaissance times that the Florentines first played their version of football, *calcio*, even continuing to play on the piazza when the rest of the town was engulfed in one of its periodic civil wars in 1529. Extending from the rear of Piazza Santa Croce, Via Torta curves around to embrace the form of the ancient Roman amphitheatre, showing that the neighbourhood's leisure and sporting association goes back to antiquity.

funereal monument) is **Donatello's** *Annunciation* **tabernacle** (1435), a masterpiece of gentle elegance set in gilded stone.

The finest of the church's sculptural works is Bernardo Rossellino's **tomb of Leonardi Bruni** (1451). The great Renaissance humanist's monument is infused with the spirit of classical antiquity in which only a discreet Madonna and Child above the reclining scholar betrays any note of Christianity. With this, Rossellino, who went on to lay out the town centre of Pienza for Pope Pius II (*see* page 217), set the style and standard for Renaissance monumental tombs (not observed by the feeble pastiche for Rossini).

In the transept immediately to the right of the apse, two chapels have some important **Giotto frescoes** in which the pathos manages to shine through the heavily restored painting: *St Francis* in the

Bardi Chapel, and *St John the Evangelist* and *St John the Baptist* in the adjacent Peruzzi Chapel. Over in the left transept in a second chapel of the Bardi family, Donatello's wooden **Crucifixion** (1425) makes an affective naturalistic contrast to the Renaissance idealism of the time.

Pazzi Chapel

At the back of the cloister of Santa Croce's Franciscan monastery adjoining the church, Brunelleschi's design is a radiant gem of Renaissance grace. Its spaciousness is enhanced by geometric patterns of dark stone against whitewashed walls. The master's ego controlled the décor. Brunelleschi preferred Luca della Robbia's subdued glazed terracotta roundels to the too-competitive wall medallions he had let Donatello do for the Old Sacristy of San Lorenzo. In fact, while most scholars accept that della Robbia executed the blue-and-white wall-roundels of the seated Apostles, the larger polychrome roundels of the four Evangelists are attributed to Brunelleschi himself.

Church Museum of Santa Croce

Housed in the monks' refectory, the museum displays Cimabue's 13th-century *Crucifixion,* rescued and painstakingly restored from its apparent ruin in the town's 1966 flood. Other notable works include

Taddeo Gaddi's fine *Last Supper* (1350) and Donatello's *St Louis of Toulouse* (1418) brought here from the Orsanmichele oratory.

Look out, too, behind the church sacristy, for the **leather workshops** installed in what were once the monks' cells.

Bargello Sculpture Museum

The ominous 13th-century fortress (Via del Proconsole 4) was the stronghold of

These narcissistic ladies in the Bargello courtyard are blithely oblivious to the building's dark origins. Before it became a museum to the glory of Michelangelo, Donatello and company, it was a nasty prison for enemies of the republic.

Florence's mediæval Police Chief (*Bargello*) and subsequently a very unpleasant prison, before becoming the National Museum of Sculpture. Its old armoury is now the **Michelangelo Hall**, greeting you with a sad-looking bust of the master by his friend Daniele da Volterra. Michelangelo's works here include a bust of *Brutus*, a marble roundel of the *Madonna and Child*, and an early *Drunken Bacchus* (1497). Compare Sansovino's more decorous *Bacchus* of 20 years later – but then Sansovino was himself more decorous than Michelangelo. Among the **Cellini bronzes** is an imposing bust of his master, *Duke Cosimo I.*

The **General Council Hall** is dominated by the work of Donatello: his vigorous *St George* (originally at the Orsanmichele, *see* page 135); two statues of *David*, doubting in marble, naked and restless in bronze; and the stone *Marzocco* lion city

emblem from the Palazzo Vecchio. You can also see the two *Abraham and Isaac* bronze panels submitted for the baptistery doors competition by Brunelleschi, the loser, and Ghiberti, the winner (*see* ALL OR NOTHING AT ALL, page 125). On the second floor is a Verrocchio *David*, for which his 19-year-old pupil Leonardo da Vinci is believed to have been the model.

Badia Fiorentina

Opposite the Bargello is the 'Florentine Abbey', a Benedictine church, part Romanesque, part Gothic, with graceful, slender bell tower. On the left as you enter the church is an ethereal *Madonna Appearing to St Bernard* (1485) by Filippino Lippi, talented son of Filippo Lippi and his mistress Lucrezia Buti.

Casa Buonarroti

The home that bachelor Michelangelo bought for his closest relatives is at Via Ghibellina 70. Decorated by 17th-century artists with paintings commemorating his long life, it exhibits letters, drawings and portraits of the great man. Most important are two of his own sculptured reliefs, from

his youth: the *Madonna of the Steps* done before he was 16, and a tumultuous *Battle of the Centaurs*, dating from about the same time but astonishingly different.

Around Sant'Ambrogio

In the Santa Croce quarter's northern neighbourhood, the **church of Sant'Ambrogio** is of interest principally for its finely carved 15th-century **tabernacle** by Mino da Fiesole and as the burial place of Andrea Verrocchio. The nearby **fruit and vegetable market** is a colourful meeting-place for the locals, with a **flea market** on

Piazza dei Ciompi, a few minutes' walk to the west. At Via Farini 4 is the town's 19th-century **synagogue** (*Tempio Israelitico*), a bizarre architectural mishmash in marble with Byzantine and Islamic onion domes.

Santa Maria Maddalena dei Pazzi

Just north of the synagogue, this Benedictine monastery church (entrance Borgo Pinti 58) is a Renaissance design by Giuliano da Sangallo, with a fine chapel (*capella maggiore*) added by Ciro Ferri. Its principal art treasure is a superb **Perugino Crucifixion** (1496) in the chapter house.

Ponte Vecchio to Ognissanti

The quarter of Santa Maria Novella extends from the river-front shops on the *Lungarni* (Arno embankments) to the main railway station. It has its share of fine churches but is distinctive principally for its handsome palazzi, market and shopping streets. The itinerary begins at one of the world's most famous bridges.

Ponte Vecchio

A bridge has spanned the river here since Roman times, but the present structure

The synagogue rises above the Santa Croce quarter. Jewish scholars played a significant role here during the Renaissance. From Elijah del Medigo, the great humanist Pico della Mirandola learned the mysteries of Kabbalistic philosophy.

RIVER OF TROUBLE

Since EM Forster's famous novel about love in Florence, people continue to ask for a 'room with a view' of the Arno, but there is nothing very romantic about its muddy green waters. In fact, in the 20th century, the river has been nothing but trouble. To slow the Allied advance in August 1944, the Germans systematically blew up four of the town's five bridges: the Ponte alle Grazie, built in 1237, Ponte alla Carraia (1218), Ponte Santa Trinità (1570) and the Ponte della Vittoria (1920). Only the venerable Ponte Vecchio was spared, but even then, in case the enemy planned to drive vehicles across this ancient foot-bridge, they blocked approaches by destroying houses at either end (including the home of Machiavelli).

On 4 November 1966, the river burst its banks and flooded the city, destroying and damaging over 1,000 paintings and sculptures, as well as countless books and manuscripts in the libraries. In places like the Bargello's Michelangelo Hall (*see* page 145), you can see wall marks registering the flood level: 3m (10ft) and more above ground level. Never fear, the 60s were the golden Age of Aquarius (the Water-Carrier!), and from all over the world, the flower children's art-loving brothers and sisters, dubbed Angels of Mud, poured into the city to help with the rescue operation, spearheaded by Florence's own proud citizenry.

dates from 1345 and was the town's only bridge still standing in 1945. The boutiques with their back rooms overhanging the river were built from the 16th to the 19th centuries. Duke Cosimo did not like the smell of the bridge's original butcher shops and had them replaced by the goldsmiths and jewellers whose descendants offer you their high-quality (and high-priced) wares today.

In the middle of the bridge is Rafaello Romanelli's modern **bust of Benvenuto Cellini** (1900). The hugely gifted lecher and liar was practically a patron 'saint' to the bridge's goldsmiths.

A row of windows above the bridge's shops (visible on the right side as you face the Uffizi), are part of the **Vasari Corridor** that Duke Cosimo I's architect designed to link the Medici's residence in the Pitti Palace to the family business headquarters in the Uffizi. It saved the duke having to test his public popularity down in the street when he went to work each day. Decorated with works of art to make the walk more pleasant, the corridor was perhaps the world's first true 'art-gallery' (*see* page 141).

Mercato Nuovo

Leaving the Ponte Vecchio behind you and the Piazza della Signorìa to your right, the colourful Straw Market – 'new' only in name – dominates Via Calimala, street of the drapers' guild in the heart of mediæval Florence. The 16th-century loggia, with its fountain where people stroke for luck the snout of a bronze wild boar known as the *Porcellino*, may seem a little grand for a mere straw market, but it was originally designed for the local gold- and silk-merchants. Today, you can buy a straw hat against the Tuscan sun and a basket to carry off the cheap and not so cheap jewellery, leather goods and lace embroidery.

(The vast Piazza della Repubblica nearby is universally condemned for the graceless style in which it replaced in 1885 the city's picturesque mediæval neighbourhood around the Old Market, on the site of the ancient Roman Forum.)

Palazzo Davanzati

West on Via Porta Rossa, this characteristic 14th-century town-palace had its stern, fortress-like exterior lightened

A painter milks the tourist trade on the Ponte Vecchio.

Rare moment: the Piazza della Repubblica with no traffic jam.

200 years later by the open gallery replacing its rooftop battlements. At ground level, the rings are still there for tethering horses and on upper storeys to hold torches and lanterns for festive occasions. Inside, the home of a wealthy family of wool merchants has been transformed into a **museum** of Florentine domestic life in mediæval and Renaissance times (*Museo dell'Antica Casa Fiorentina*). The furniture, utensils and ceramics are at their most attractive in the **Sala dei Pappagalli** (Hall of the Parrots) with its *trompe l'oeil* parrot-patterned tapestries frescoed like draped curtains on the walls.

Palazzo Strozzi

The city's most elegant shops continue the centuries-old tradition of **Via Tornabuoni** for aristocratic luxury, accented by some of the city's grandest Renaissance palaces. North of Piazza Santa Trinità, the design by Benedetto da Maiano and Cronaca for Filippo Strozzi at the end of the 15th century is the handsomest of them all. The majestic harmony of the palazzo's four solid ashlar stone façades, each with a single arched door at the centre, made it a natural choice as headquarters of the National Institute for Renaissance Studies (*Istituto Nazionale di Studi del Rinascimento*). The porticoed **courtyard** (entrance Piazza Strozzi) offers a wonderful haven of tranquillity. A neatly organized **museum** traces the palazzo's history – in their heyday, the Strozzi were second only to the Medici. Back on the street, notice the intricate **wrought-iron lanterns** by the much sought-after and expensive craftsman Niccolò Grosso, known as *Caparra* (Mr Down Payment) who coined the philosophy later attributed to Hollywood: 'If you want something for nothing, you get what you paid for.'

Piazza Santa Trinità

Back at the southern end of Via Tornabuoni, the square offers an intriguing juxtaposition of Italian styles. In the centre is the **Colonna della Justizia** (Column of Justice), with its allegorical porphyry statue atop an ancient granite monolith brought here in the 16th century from the Roman Baths of Caracalla. On the south side of the square is the 13th-century **Palazzo Spini-Ferroni**, an austere mediæval fortress providing a paradoxical setting for the super-sophisticated Ferragamo shoe-emporium it houses today. It is in stark contrast to the Baroque façade of the church across the square.

Santa Trinità Church

The Baroque façade by Bernardo Buontalenti has been added to an originally Cistercian church, that retains a sober late 14th-century Gothic interior. In the Sassetti Chapel (far right of the high altar) are the **Ghirlandaio frescoes** of St Francis that, with the *Adoration of the Shepherds* on the chapel altar, are considered his greatest work (1486). In the right aisle, fourth chapel, are important **frescoes** (1425) by the Sienese artist, Lorenzo Monaco.

Santi Apostoli

Lovers of unadorned Romanesque architecture will want to take a short side-trip along Borgo Santi Apostoli to this 11th-century basilica on Piazza Limbo. Its noble simplicity made it a prototype for the Florentine Romanesque churches that followed. A Latin inscription to the left of the entrance proclaims the church's legendary foundation by Charlemagne. It backs onto what were the town's Roman baths, from which it took Corinthian columns for the first two columns in the nave, using them as models for the rest of the church. In the left aisle, a fragmentary early 15th-century fresco removed from the façade has been beautifully restored in the form of its *sinopia* (preparatory drawing), depicting a *Madonna and Child*, by Paolo Schiavo.

The Lungarni

The Arno's broad embankments were built in the 19th century to protect the city from flooding – more or less. When in force, regulations to reduce traffic make a river-front promenade a pleasant proposition. Bartolommeo Ammannati's **Ponte Santa Trinità**, destroyed in 1944, has been rebuilt with its original 16th-century masonry scooped from the bottom of the river, including Pietro Francavilla's statues of the *Four Seasons* on the parapets. While the Ponte Vecchio's quaintness makes it the sentimental favourite of foreign visitors, the Florentines themselves prefer the Ponte Santa Trinità for its beautifully restored elegance – with the bonus of a great view of the Ponte Vecchio itself.

Past the 17th-century Palazzo Masetti (housing the British Consulate), take a look at the grand **Palazzo Corsini**. Started in

---

WHO DUNNIT?

Unable to believe that the man who perpetrated the Neptune Fountain on Piazza della Signorìa (*see* page 137) could possibly have designed the exceptional curves of the Ponte Santa Trinità's three beautiful arches, the Florentine restorers remain convinced Ammannati was working from a design by Michelangelo. In *The Stones of Florence*, Mary MacCarthy performs a delicious piece of detective work by finding the same curve in only one other place – the Medici Chapel at San Lorenzo, the sarcophagus covers for the tombs of Lorenzo and Giuliano de'Medici, sculpted by Michelangelo.

1648, but completed only in 1765, this elongated High Baroque residence in which the Corsini family still lives boasts Florence's finest remaining private art-collection, with works by Raphael, Filippino Lippi, Luca Signorelli and Pontormo. Admission to the **museum** is by appointment only, at the palace's rear entrance, Via Parione 11.

Palazzo Rucellai

Back from the river on Via della Vigna Nuova, this classic Renaissance palace was designed by the great 15th-century architect and theorist, Leon Battista Alberti, and completed in 1451 by his gifted disciple, Bernardo Rossellino. The building's three tiers, square-windowed at ground level, gracefully mullioned for the upper stories, present an object lesson in classical proportions. Ever the humanist eager to relate his buildings to their urban environment, Alberti designed the stone benches between the palace doors, where waiting clients of the Rucellai merchants could talk business and arrange marriages.

Piazza Ognissanti

Take time out from your sightseeing with a restful drink in the plush Neo-Renaissance bar of the Excelsior Hotel, even – or particularly – if you are not staying there. The décor is overdone, but the service is as close to impeccable as such a haughty establishment can muster. Opposite the hotel, in the imposing Palazzo Lenzi, is the French Institute.

Ognissanti Church

At the rear of the square, the church dedicated to All Saints is 13th-century, with a Baroque façade by Matteo Nigetti added in 1637. When the Franciscans took it over in the 15th century, the church was in large part financed by bankers of the Vespucci family, including Amerigo. Inside, the navigator who was to give his name to the American continent is depicted above the family altar (right aisle, 2nd bay) as a young man in **Ghirlandaio's** *Madonna of Mercy* (1470), kneeling immediately to the left of Mary. Further along this right aisle is **Botticelli's** *St Augustine in his Study* (1481), a striking portrait of the Christian philosopher at work. Botticelli is buried in a chapel at the end of the right transept. Ghirlandaio has painted a contemplative *St Jerome* in the left aisle.

In the Franciscan's cloister (accessible from the square through a door next to the church), visit the **refectory** to see Ghirlandaio's charming *Last Supper*. Scholars are certain that the fresco executed in 1480, two years before Leonardo da Vinci left Florence, influenced the master's monumental treatment of the same subject for the Dominican friars of Milan.

Santa Maria Novella

The finest of Florence's monastic churches was built in its present form by the Dominicans in the 13th and 14th centuries with Leon Battista Alberti's graceful white and green marble façade completed in 1470. The church is rich in art treasures, but its most prized, indeed one of the city's greatest frescoes, is the **Masaccio** *Trinity* (1426), left aisle, third bay. Within the frame of the picture, its donors, Judge Lorenzo Lenzi and his wife, kneel stoically as Mary and St John stand on either side of the crucified Jesus upheld by his Father, while the white dove of the Holy Spirit hovers between them. The ensemble forms an inspiring triangle under the coffered ceiling of a Renaissance chapel that integrates brilliantly the geometric principles established by Brunelleschi. At the base of the fresco,

offered as a lesson of universal destiny, is a skeleton (perhaps one of the donors) lying on a sarcophagus with the Italian inscription: 'I was once that which you are and what I am, you will also be.'

The Filippo Strozzi Chapel (right of the altar) is decorated with Filippino Lippi's **frescoes** of St Philip and St John, rich in colour and anecdotal detail: notice in the monumental *Exorcism of Demons in the Temple of Mars* three bystanders holding their nose at the smell.

The **Ghirlandaio frescoes** of the lives of the Madonna and St John, for the chancel behind the altar, kept the master's workshop busy from 1485 to 1490. The pupils probably included teenage apprentice Michelangelo, picking up fresco technique for his work 20 years later on the ceiling in the Vatican's Sistine Chapel.

In the Gondi chapel (left of the high altar), the **Brunelleschi** *Crucifixion* (1410), one of his few sculptures, brings to the human body a characteristically idealized strength and harmony. This treatment may appear too formal when compared with Donatello's more personalized *Crucifixion* in Santa Croce, which Brunelleschi is said to have dismissed as too 'peasant-like' (*see* page 141). Of another age, at once austere and serene is the **Giotto** *Crucifixion* (1290) in the Sacristy (left transept).

Through an entrance to the left of the church, escape the bustle of the piazza in the Dominicans' 14th-century **cloister** (*Chiostro Verde*), with Paolo Uccello's frescoes of *Universal Flood* in the refectory.

*T*he 'piazzale' on which the artist is working is named after Michelangelo, but that's where the connection ends.

Stazione Centrale

North of Santa Maria Novella, spare a moment to look at the simple, clean-lined architecture of Florence's main railway station that shares the name of the monastery. It was built in 1936 at the height of Mussolini's power, but somehow defies the prevailing inflated neoclassicist pretentions of the Fascist regime. For your day-trips out of town (*see* EXCURSIONS page 157), take note of the various bus-stops around the station.

One short bus-trip from near the station, N°4, will take you north to the bizarre **Museo Stibbert** (Via Stibbert 26), created by 19th-century English businessman Frederick Stibbert. It houses an astounding collection of 50,000 items – sculptures, porcelain, tapestries, paintings, but most importantly antique European and Asiatic **arms and armour**. Prize exhibits include the armour of Giovanni delle Bande Nere, rare *condottiere* among the Medici, and the uniform worn by Napoleon when crowned King of Italy.

South of the Arno

The Santo Spirito quarter, popularly known as *Oltr'arno* (literally 'other side of the Arno') covers the whole of the city's south bank. Most of the sights are in the area west of the Pitti Palace and can be tackled on foot, in easy stages. The Boboli Gardens behind the palace are a good place to park the kids if they don't feel like sightseeing. To the east, the hillside route along the winding Viale dei Colli is best handled by car or N°13 bus from Santa Maria Novella railway station via the Duomo. This takes you to Piazzale Michelangelo and the church of San Miniato, with a side-trip to Forte di Belvedere, all up on the heights overlooking the city.

Since its wholesale destruction in 1944, the area immediately beyond Ponte Vecchio along Via Guicciardini has been only partially restored, alternating shops and popular dwellings with patrician palazzi.

Santa Felicita

Set back on a little piazza to the left off Via Guicciardini, this church is one of the oldest foundations in the city (5th century), built over an ancient Christian cemetery. Its present appearance dates from 1736, when it was the court church of the Grand Dukes of Tuscany. Notice above the arch to the left of the façade the continuation of the Vasari Corridor on its way from the Uffizi to the Pitti Palace. Inside, to the left of the entrance, the Capponi Chapel designed by Brunelleschi in 1425 possesses on its altar an astounding masterpiece of Mannerist art: **Pontormo's** *Descent from the Cross* (1528). Amid the bizarre, contorted figures of those mourning or bearing Jesus from his crucifixion, there is no trace of the cross itself.

Pitti Palace

In the 16th century, the dukes of Tuscany made the quarter south of the Arno an aristocratic preserve where the Medici held court. Today, their palace is a popular museum and the gardens of their private festivities are a public park.

The palace's dauntingly ponderous façade belies the ornate and colourful interior. Anything was preferable to the incorrigibly austere Palazzo Vecchio from which Eleonora of Toledo was determined to escape when persuading Duke Cosimo to acquire the palace from the Pitti merchant family in 1549. Subsequently, the palace served in turn as the vacation home of the Habsburgs and, in the 1860s, official residence for the royal household of a newly united Italy.

Pitti Gallery

The palace museums take you into the rich world of the Medici, much as they left it. The *Galleria Palatina* is quite simply,

quite opulently, the family art collection. As such, the paintings are displayed just as the dukes themselves hung them, two-, three- and four-high, by personal preference rather than in any historical sequence. Like any collection of family pictures, there is a preponderance of portraits, although here the aunts and uncles tend to be princesses and cardinals. Besides, the Medicis' taste and means did permit a considerable number of masterpieces.

The richly decorated halls are named after the themes of their Baroque ceiling frescoes: Venus, Hercules, Prometheus, and so on. Painted by **Pietro da Cortona**

Art in the Pitti Palace quite explicitly glorifies the Medici dynasty: allegorical paintings celebrating their virtues and heroic portraits flattering their ancestors.

and his workshop for Ferdinando II between 1641 and 1665, the allegorical cycle illustrates the idealized education of the Medici prince.

Titian displays his masterly use of colour and light in *The Concert* (1513) and a monumental *Pietro Aretino* (1545) in the *Sala di Venere* (Venus); and disquieting psychology in his portrait of *The Englishman* and the bare-breasted *Magdalen* (both 1540) in the *Sala di Apollo.*

Rubens shows his clear personal preference with Venus restraining Mars in his vivid *Consequences of War* (1638) and portrays himself on the far left of his *Four Philosophers* (1602) in the *Sala di Marte* (Mars).

Raphael is well represented by a stately *Veiled Woman* (1516) in the *Sala di Giove* (Jupiter) and a hauntingly beautiful tondo, *Madonna of the Chair* (1515) in the *Sala di Saturno* (Saturn). In the same hall, *Maddalena Doni* (1506) clearly deliberately imitates the pose of Leonardo da Vinci's *Mona Lisa* painted a couple of years earlier.

Caravaggio contributes a typically disturbing canvas, an ugly *Sleeping Cupid* (1608), a late work with more intimations of death than slumber, in the *Sala dell'Educazione di Giove* (Jupiter's Education).

Upstairs, the **Modern Art Gallery** (*Galleria d'Arte Moderna*) is devoted to 19th- and 20th-century Italian art. Most interesting are the *Macchiaioli* school of Tuscan pre-Impressionists, in particular **Telemaco Signorini**, **Silvestro Lega** and **Giovanni Fattori** (*see* ART AND ARCHITECTURE IN TUSCANY, pages 80-95). Rebelling against the academic art amply represented here, their work seeks a new freedom to parallel the political liberation of the *Risorgimento*. Most important among 20th-century artists here are Futurist **Gino Severino** and Surrealist **Giorgio di Chirico**.

Pitti's other Museums

Left of the main Pitti entrance, the **Silverware Museum** (*Museo degli Argenti*) has 16 profusely ornamented rooms of family treasures, silver, jewels, 16th- and 17th-century amber and ivory, crystal and porcelain, and Baroque furniture. The **Carriage Museum** (*Museo delle Carrozze*), in a wing on the far right of the palace, and the **Ducal Apartments** (*Appartamenti Monumentali*), upstairs, right of the main entrance, reveal an opulent, truly palatial life that the Pitti's dour exterior might never let you suspect. The Florentines had never been ostentatious, and in this sense, the Pitti's luxury exposes the era of the Medici dukes as a 'betrayal' of what had previously been the city's true character.

Boboli Gardens

Another time-out for relaxation, this time in the shade of the holm oaks, pines and cypresses of the fanciful palace gardens. Laid out to the specifications of Duke Cosimo's wife, Eleonora of Toledo, they provided a hillside setting for the court's playtime, games, open-air banquets and theatrical spectacles performed high above the city of commoners on the other bank of the Arno. To the modern eye, they form a Renaissance and Baroque theme-park dotted with loggias, cool fountains, grottoes with artificial stalactites, myriad statues of gods and nymphs – and a Viennese coffee-house added by the Habsburgs in 1775.

Directly behind the palace, the **Amphitheatre**, shaped like a Roman circus, was the scene of the Medicis' most extravagant fêtes and masked balls. In the middle of the nearby **Pond of Neptune** (*Vivaio del Nettuno*), the burly sea god wields his trident in petrified parody of one of the Boboli's gardeners. Look out, too, for the **Fountain of Bacchus**, tucked

Sansovino. To the left of the nave, Giuliano da Sangallo's elegant **sacristy** (1492) is entirely in keeping with the spirit of Brunelleschi's design.

Across the church's tree-shaded piazza, popular for its pleasant market, is the **Cenacolo di Santo Spirito**, formerly the monastery's refectory. Inside are Andrea Orcagna's 14th-century frescoes of the *Last Supper* and a *Crucifixion*.

Santa Maria del Carmine

The church is an essential stop on any artistic pilgrimage to Florence. The edifice itself is an unprepossessing reconstruction since the devastating fire of 1771, but in the right transept, the **Brancacci Chapel** survived intact. It is here, magnificently restored at the end of the 1980s, that the great **Masaccio-Masolino frescoes** recount the Creation story from Genesis and the life of St Peter, a work that revolutionized Renaissance painting (*see* ART AND ARCHITECTURE IN TUSCANY, pages 80-95). Masaccio died at 27, after only five years of known activity (1423-1428), but long enough to affirm a technique and psychological power that has overshadowed the contribution of his mild-mannered friend and master, Masolino. To appreciate the subtlety of their psychological and spiritual range, compare Masolino's gentle and harmonious Adam and Eve in his *Original Sin* (chapel entrance, upper right) with Masaccio's despairing figures in the *Expulsion from the Garden*

away in a corner of the gardens to the left of the entrance arch in the palace's rear courtyard. The statue is of Duke Cosimo's pot-bellied court jester, Pietro Barbino, seated naked on a turtle.

Santo Spirito

After the somewhat raucous extravagance of the Pitti palace, the 15th-century church that gives its name to the south-bank parish is an edifice of tranquil dignity. Though the unadorned whitewashed façade of 1700 does not follow the spirit of the original design, the church in its interior remains a major work of Brunelleschi, asserting a superb spatial clarity with the greystone Corinthian colonnade of the nave. In the right transept is a strikingly theatrical *Madonna Enthroned* (1490) by Filippino Lippi. In the left transept, see the handsome **Corbinelli Chapel**, designed architecturally and sculpted in white marble by Andrea

of Eden (chapel entrance, upper left). Florence's greatest artists, with Michelangelo at their head, came to sketch Masaccio's trail-blazing use of light and visual depth as instruments of emotional impact. This is particularly striking in the broad sweep of *St Peter Paying the Tribute Money* (chapel wall, upper left).

The chapel frescoes were completed in the 1480s by Filippino Lippi, who painted the side walls' lower panels. His honourable efforts, the fruit of a solid apprenticeship in the workshop of Botticelli, would anywhere else be hailed as remarkable. Here, their elegance seems almost frivolous.

Viale dei Colli

This meandering route offers a wonderful panoramic view of the city. To take in the skyline dominated by the cathedral dome, stop off at **Piazzale Michelangelo** (with a monument that includes another copy of his *David*).

San Miniato al Monte

Up the hill above the *piazzale*, this largely 12th-century Romanesque church has a beautiful façade of green and white marble. An extra touch of colour is added above the central gabled window by a 13th-century polychrome mosaic of Jesus enthroned between Mary and St Miniato (the first Christian martyr of Florence). Inside, in the elevated presbytery preceding the choir, an elegant marble **pulpit** is more architectural than the more familiar Pisan style of elaborately sculpted pulpits. In a chapel off the nave to the left, see the monumental marble **tomb of the Cardinal of Portugal** (1461) by Antonio Rossolino. His two beautiful genuflecting angels on the sarcophagus had a considerable influence on Michelangelo.

Forte di Belvedere

Continuing from San Miniato west along Viale Galileo, turn right on Via di San Leonardo to the fortress built in 1595 for Duke Ferdinando I by Bernardo Buontalenti. In the middle of the star-shaped fortifications, the *palazzino* is used today for temporary exhibitions. From its terrace and the bastions of the ramparts, you get a great view across the city to the Tuscan hills beyond.

Excursions around Florence

Outside the months of high summer when it is better to get out of the city anyway, Florence has a great choice of day-trips to surrounding Tuscan towns. For those who prefer to save their driving for longer trips, we have confined ourselves to just three which, for those not driving, can be easily handled by bus from the Santa Maria Novella station or the Duomo. Destinations further afield, like Prato, Empoli, Vinci and Pistoia, all accessible by car but with the disadvantage of time-consuming exits and returns through Florence's heavy urban traffic, are included in the next chapter, PISA AND NORTHERN TUSCANY.

Fiesole

Just 8km (5 miles) north east of Florence, starting out from Viale Alessandro Volta (or 30 minutes on the N°7 bus from the Duomo), the road winds up a wooded hillside, revealing at each bend ever-changing views over Fiesole's gardens and villas to the monuments of the great city below.

Stop just south of the town at **San Domenico di Fiesole** to see its 15th-century monastery church. There are two important works by Fra Angelico, a

If you hesitate about a trip out to Fiesole, take a look at that landscape viewed from the Boboli Gardens (previous pages).

Madonna and Saints (1428) in the church's first chapel to the left, and a *Crucifixion* in the monastery's Chapter House. Off to the west along Via Badia dei Rochettini is the pretty marble-façaded church of **Badia Fiesolana**, originally the town's Romanesque cathedral and redesigned by Brunelleschi in the 1450s.

In the 14th century, taking a leaf out of the book of the wily Etruscans, the monks of San Francesco perched their cloister on the breezy top of the Fiesole hill.

The town's centre is Piazza Mino da Fiesole, built over the Etrusco-Roman Forum and site of a pleasant **open-air market**. On the north side of the piazza, the austere **cathedral**, Romanesque in origin but deformed by its 19th-century restoration, is chiefly distinguished by the crenellated belltower (1213) which serves as Fiesole's landmark when viewed from Florence.

Of the ancient stronghold's **Etruscan ruins**, you can see fragments of the citywalls and the infrastructure of a temple (3rd century BC) in the **archaeological site** beyond the cathedral. The later Roman remains are more extensive, including an amphitheatre for 2,500 spectators (still in use), a temple and an arcade of the public baths. A small **museum** displays Etruscan funerary urns and architectural fragments.

Fiesole's greatest treasure is its own magical **view** over the Arno valley and Florence. From the west side of the piazza, beside the Bishop's Palace (*palazzo vescovile*), climb the steep and narrow Via

San Francesco to a first viewing-terrace and past the ancient **basilica of Sant' Alessandro**, many times restored since its 6th-century foundation. At the top of the hill, where the Etruscans had their acropolis, are the 14th-century monastery and **church of San Francesco**, with its altar-painting by the eccentric Piero di Cosimo. The **public gardens** are a perfect place to have a picnic to go with the view.

Hikers and drivers favour the winding old side-road, **Via Vecchia Fiesolana** running south west of town past glimpses of more handsome old villas, half-hidden among the cypresses and olive trees.

Certosa del Galluzzo

In a charming hillside setting of olive trees, the Carthusian monastery (charterhouse) is situated 5km (3 miles) south of Florence from Piazza Romana on the Siena road, or 20 minutes on the N°36 or 37 bus from Santa Maria Novella Station. The *Certosa* was founded in 1341 and rebuilt in

Renaissance style from the 15th to the 17th century. Monks conduct guided tours of the church, chapter house, *Chiostro Grande* (great cloister), monastic cells and the 14th-century Gothic **Palazzo degli Studi**. The prized works of this picture-gallery are a series of five frescoes by Pontormo devoted to the *Passion of Jesus.*

Poggio a Caiano

Lorenzo the Magnificent's grand country palace is a 30-minute drive west along highway 66 or on the COPIT (Pistoia-based) bus from Santa Maria Novella station. Set in handsome walled gardens, the masterly Renaissance residence was designed in 1484 by Lorenzo's favourite architect, Giuliano da Sangallo. Beyond the monumental porticoed terrace, pass through the spacious neoclassical vestibule decorated under subsequent Austrian and French occupants to the **main hall** (*grande salone*). Here, Andrea del Sarto, Francabigio and above all Pontormo painted **frescoes** (1521) depicting in allegorical form the carefree rustic life to which the aristocrats aspired in their country villa.

If you, too, rediscover here a taste for the country life, continue from Poggia a Caiano another 7km (4 miles) south to Duke Ferdinando I's gleaming white **Villa dell'Artimino** – 20 minutes by the rural CAP (Prato-based) bus. Set among woods and olive groves with its own forest of fanciful chimneys on the roof, the residence was designed in 1594 by Bernardo Buontalenti. It houses in its basement an interesting **archaeological museum** of Etruscan and Roman antiquities found in the vicinity. Artimino itself is an attractive village surrounded by mediæval walls, with a Romanesque church and Etruscan necropolis.

From Leaning Tower to Lazing on the Beach, and Inland to Leonardo's Birthplace

That piece of inspired architectural magic that encompasses Pisa's Cathedral, Baptistery and Leaning Tower campanile has left an indelible mark on northern Tuscany. For all their independent spirit, Lucca and Pistoia were both inspired by the creative heyday of the Pisa maritime republic. For their marble façades, they had only to turn to the nearby quarries of Carrara. From the 19th century, Tuscan and foreign holiday-makers discovered the delights of seaside resorts like Viareggio and the health resort of Montecatini Terme.

By its celebrity, Pisa presents a natural focus for your tour of northern Tuscany, but you will find good hotels all along the route. Choose any one of them as an alternative base for your excursions. We propose three itineraries:

1. Pisa – an extended visit:
- **Piazza del Duomo** embracing cathedral, baptistery and Leaning Tower;
- Renaissance **Piazza dei Cavalieri** and **San Matteo Museum**;

Pisa's Leaning Tower is an icon that defies analysis almost as much as it defies gravity. Perhaps, at once beautiful and funny, it is just a comment on the exquisite fallibility of man.

- monuments on the Arno: **Ponte di Mezzo** and the Gothic **Santa Maria della Spina**.

2. The Coast:
- begin at the cosmopolitan old port-town of **Livorno**;
- head north to the popular seaside resort of **Viareggio** and the more genteel **Forte dei Marmi**;
- it's then back from the sea to the 'marble country' of **Pietrasanta**, **Massa** and the mountain quarries of **Carrara**.

3. The Hinterland – heading north east:
- **Lucca**, eternally independent with its handsome ramparts and mediæval monuments;
- next stop **Montecatini Terme**, a spa with old-fashioned bourgeois elegance;

PISA AND NORTH-WEST TUSCANY

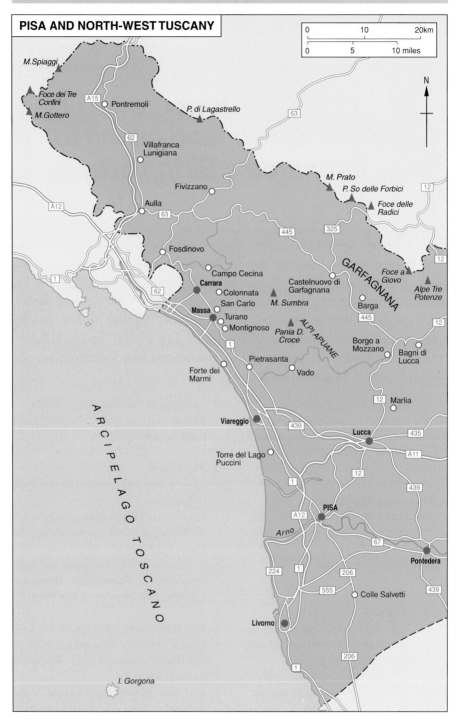

0   10   20km
0   5   10 miles

N

M.Spiaggi

Foce dei Tre Confini
M.Gottero
A15
Pontremoli
P. di Lagastrello
63

62
Villafranca Lunigiana

Fivizzano
M. Prato
P. So delle Forbici
12
Foce delle Radici

A12
Aulla
63
445   325

Fosdinovo

GARGAGNANA

Campo Cecina
Carrara
Castelnuovo di Garfagnana
Foce a Giovo
62
Colonnata
Alpe Tre Potenze
Massa
San Carlo
M. Sumbra
Barga
Turano
1
Montignoso
Pania D. Croce
445
12
ALPI APUANE

Borgo a Mozzano
Bagni di Lucca
Pietrasanta
Forte dei Marmi
Vado

Marlia
12

Viareggio
439
Lucca
435

Torre del Lago Puccini
A11

12
439

1
PISA
A12
Arno
67
224   1   206
Pontedera

555
Colle Salvetti
439

206

Livorno

ARCIPELAGO TOSCANO

1

I. Gorgona

- **Pistoia**, important both for its fine churches and delicious fruit and vegetables;
- **Prato**, beyond its textile factories, has a handsome *centro storico*, not least of all for the imperial castle and the cathedral's Donatello pulpit and Filippo Lippi frescoes;
- make a pilgrimage to **Vinci**, charming birthplace of the great Leonardo, with excellent science museum;
- finally to **Empoli**, with interesting art museum, Masolino frescoes at Santo Stefano and famous glass factories.

Pisa

The Leaning Tower is an eloquent allegory of the town itself. For centuries, it has threatened total collapse, but somehow it has survived and even thrived. In the mediæval heyday of Pisa's maritime empire (*see* HISTORY, page 57), the riches of trade and plunder of war financed the building of that radiant white marble complex of religious edifices, unique jewels of Romanesque and Gothic architecture. The town's decline began with defeat by Genoa, followed by imposed submission to Florence, and was hastened with the silting up of its port at the Arno estuary and replacement by Livorno just down the coast as Tuscany's chief outlet for sea trade.

In an unprepossessing setting of coastal plain, the invasions and wars of the succeeding centuries left unscathed those early acquired treasures. As a magnet for tourism, they are as important to the town's economy as the textile, metal and pharmaceutical industries (whose monuments are somewhat less attractive). Luckily, after alarming signs of accelerated tilt caused it to be closed in the early 1990s,

> **GOOD NEIGHBOURS**
>
> The centuries-old neighbourly hostility between Tuscan towns is proverbial, but no place attracts it in more virulent form than Pisa. Ever since Livorno took over from Pisa in the 16th century as Tuscany's principal seaport, the mutual scorn has seethed and often broken out in open violence. With its university and grandiose monuments, Pisa nurtures an image of scholarship and high culture, looking down on the crass materialism it sees in Livorno's port trade. With something less than scholarly refinement, Pisa-based paratroopers go down to Livorno to hammer out the message in regular brawls with the port-town's equally tough dock-workers.
>
> To the north, the good people of Lucca still repeat a saying that dates back to the days of the Black Plague: *'Meglio avere un morto in casa che un Pisano all'uscio'* – 'Better to have a dead man in the house than a Pisan at the front-door.' To which the Pisans still reply: *'Che Dio ti accontente'* – 'May God fulfil your wish.'

the tipsy Leaning Tower has been stabilized and is once more being opened to the public, at least for the lower levels.

Piazza del Duomo

Justly known as the *Campo dei Miracoli* (Field of Miracles), the piazza's assembly of buildings conquers the flat, ungrateful landscape with serene, other-worldly harmony. The accomplishment of three centuries, from the 11th to the 13th, celebrates the whole cycle of life. At birth, a good Pisan Catholic can be admitted to the Church at the baptistery, take communion and the vows of marriage in the Duomo, proclaim the good news from the Leaning Tower and find final rest in the monumental cemetery of the Campo Santo.

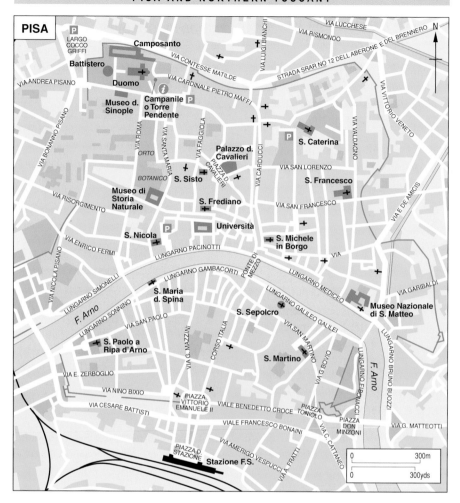

The Duomo

Exterior

The cathedral was built from 1063 to 1118 in triumphant commemoration of Pisa's victory over the Arabs in Sicily. With oriental and Byzantine decorative elements reflecting the spread of the Pisan Republic's interests overseas, its four-tiered arcaded **façade** over three porches is a supreme achievement of grace and delicacy. Architect Buscheto did not hesitate to inscribe on his sarcophagus in Latin (inserted in the far left arch) 'This marble church has no equal'. His design was partially modified in the 12th century by Rainaldo, who duly placed his own personal inscription, just a signature, slightly to the right above the central arch.

The Madonna at the top of the façade is by Andrea Pisano (sculptor of the Florence baptistery's earliest set of bronze doors), and is flanked by angels from the workshop of Giovanni Pisano. After a fire in 1595, the cathedral's bronze doors were recast by pupils of Giambologna.

*F*lat as it is, the landscape beyond Pisa shares with the rest of Tuscany that magic light of dawn.

At the rear, immediately to the right of the apse in the south transept facing the Leaning Tower, the bronze doors (1180) of the **San Ranieri portal** are a fine work by Bonanno Pisano, incorporating Byzantine and Norman Romanesque elements acquired from his time spent at Monreale, Sicily.

Inside the Duomo

The 11th-century pillars in classical Roman style give the interior a noble simplicity. In the north aisle (to the left, facing the high altar), Giovanni Pisano's early 14th-century **marble pulpit** has superbly sculpted reliefs dramatically illustrating scenes from the Old and New Testaments and the *Last Judgment*.

On the entrance-columns to the **choir** are 15th-century paintings of four saints by Andrea del Sarto, the most important being *St Agnes*, over to the right. Another work commissioned after the 1595 fire is the bronze *Crucifix* (1603) at the **high altar** by Giambologna. Beyond the choir in the vault of the **apse** is a mosaic of *Jesus the Redeemer* (1302) by Cimabue.

Leaning Tower

Work started on the duomo's campanile in 1173, led by Diotisalvo, architect of the baptistery. Already by the time the third storey was reached, unstable subsoil had caused the structure to begin to list, halting construction for a century. Completed in 1301, the tower has continued to tilt ever since, despite constant attempts by architects, engineers and geologists, if not to put the thing straight – souvenir-sellers could not sell *straight* towers – at least to keep it still.

Today, with the help of bolstering soil and cement in the foundations and steel

167

Galileo Galilei (1564-1642)

The story that Pisa-born Galileo tested the velocity of falling weights from the Leaning Tower is apocryphal – his scientific problems began where they ended, in the Catholic church. When he was 19, he had a hard time paying attention during Mass in the cathedral. He found himself watching a heavy bronze lamp swinging from the ceiling and began timing its oscillations against his pulse beats to work out the theory that the timing of a pendulum remains the same however wide the swing. Exactly 50 years later, in a Dominican convent in Rome, he had to kneel in the white shirt of penitence to hear the Holy Tribunal of the Inquisition declare:

Galileo's tomb in Florence.

'The proposition that the Sun is the centre of the Universe and does not move from its place is absurd and false philosophically and formally heretical, because it is expressly contrary to the Holy Scripture. The proposition that the Earth is not the centre of the Universe and immovable but that it moves, and also with a daily motion, is equally absurd and false philosophically...'

But how was he to deny the evidence of his own eyes? After switching from medical studies at Pisa University to mathematics and astronomy, he had developed the first astronomical telescope in 1610, based on an invention by an obscure Dutch optician. It enabled him to test the solar system theories of Copernicus. Galileo was the first to observe the distinction between planets (revolving around the Sun) and stars (fixed), the Moon's similar configuration to the Earth's, and Jupiter's four moons.

He 'converted' Jesuit astronomers in Rome to the idea that the Earth moved around the Sun, but in 1616 this Copernicanism was formally prohibited. Despite attempts to convince the pope and cardinals with his telescope that Copernicanism was compatible with the Bible, Galileo was ordered to stop teaching it. After composing a *Dialogue* to show the scientific validity of Copernicus while acquiescing in the pope's theological dogma, he was brought to trial in 1633 and forced to abjure his theories. What he then muttered under his breath, '*E pur si muove*' ('Nevertheless, it does move'), was long believed to be a legend invented in the 18th century, but the phrase has been found inscribed on a Galileo portrait dated 1640, two years before his death.

Galileo was sentenced to lifelong house arrest near Florence (and he was rehabilitated by the Vatican only in 1992) The heavens' great observer ended his days in total blindness, dying coincidentally on the very day that his great English successor, Isaac Newton was born.

cables around the tower-base and lower tiers, the Leaning Tower (*Torre Pendente*) has stopped its teeter, some 5m (16ft) out of true. Upright, it would be 55m (180ft) high. Sadly, it may never again be possible to climb all the way to the top for the view over the Campo dei Miracoli and across the city to the Mediterranean.

Beyond its structural oddity, spare a moment to take in the beauty of the tower – topped by a blind-arched belfry, six colonnaded tiers in perfect harmony with the façade of the duomo, from which it appears to be standing back to admire.

The Baptistery

Beside the angular cathedral, the beautiful circular *Battistero*, with the generous curve of its cupola topped by a statue of John the Baptist, adds to the ensemble a certain maternal quality. Like Buscheto's duomo, there is a faintly oriental flavour to the design of Diotisalvi, also architect of the Leaning Tower. Begun in 1152, construction was interrupted in the 13th century until Nicola and Giovanni Pisano took over the work, adding the Gothic decoration to the upper tiers and the sculpture of Biblical figures around the doorway.

Inside, Nicola Pisano's hexagonal **marble pulpit** (1260) is his own masterpiece and for many the greatest accomplishment of Pisan sculpture. His carving of Old and New Testament themes has clear links to French Gothic sculpture, but also artfully draws on models from Etruscan and Roman sarcophagi using motifs from Greek antiquity – witness a Herculean Daniel and portrayals of Mary inspired by heads of Juno and Phaedra. Notice, too, a fine 13th-century **baptismal font** of white marble with mosaic inlay. Arabic design, from Palestine or Sicily, is reflected in the baptistery's inlaid marble

pavement and bands of black and white marble around the walls.

Campo Santo

The cloistered cemetery of the *Campo Santo* (Holy Field) is laid out on earth reputedly brought to Pisa from Palestine by Lanfranc, Italian-born Archbishop of Canterbury. Its Gothic design, by Giovanni di Simone in 1278, is in the form of an elongated three-aisle basilica with its nave open to the skies. The 14th-century marble **tabernacle** in the wall facing the duomo has a *Madonna and Child* and other figures sculpted by pupils of Giovanni Pisano. In a chapel (*Cappella Ligo degli Ammannati*) along the cloister's opposite north wall, remarkable **frescoes** by Andrea Orcagna, Benozzo Gozzoli and Taddeo Gaddeo, badly damaged by 1944 bombardment, were detached to undergo extensive restoration and are displayed in a separate gallery. Most impressive is an anonymous fresco of the *Triumph of Death* (1360) showing how commoner and aristocrat share the same destiny.

From the 14th century, the cemetery also served as an 'exhibition hall' for Roman sculpture and finely carved sarcophagi, some of them re-used for the burial of prominent Pisan citizens. At the west end of the cemetery is a particularly fine oval sarcophagus bearing the figures of two Roman citizens in toga from the 3rd century AD and used again by a Pisan merchant over one thousand years later – pagan stone sanctified by the soil of the Holy Land.

Museo dell'Opera del Duomo

The cathedral museum, in the Chapter House behind the Leaning Tower, assembles sculpture and other treasures from the baptistery, Campo Santo and the cathedral itself. Highlight of the collection is a

The Campo Santo's cloister wall encloses a cemetery of sacred earth from Palestine.

Giovanni Pisano *Madonna and Child* (1209), carved in ivory as part of the cathedral high altar before the 1595 fire. Also remarkable is an 11th-century Islamic **bronze griffin**, part of the Pisan fleet's war booty in wars against the Arabs.

Towards the Arno

Before visiting the rest of the town, take time off for a stroll through the **Botanical Gardens** (*Orto Botanico*) due south of the duomo. It has been run by the university since the end of the 16th century, and displays many handsome specimens of trees from Asia, Africa and the Americas.

Piazza dei Cavalieri

East of the gardens, this is one of Giorgio Vasari's prouder architectural achievements, a bold Renaissance square, on which he also designed the campanile for the **church of Santo Stefano**. Also on the square, behind Francavilla's statue of Duke Cosimo I, is Vasari's redesigned façade for the **Palazzo dei Cavalieri**. It is now Pisa University's prestigious *Scuola Normale Superiore* (founded by Napoleon in 1810 on the model of Paris's *Ecole normale supérieure*).

San Matteo Museum

Besides its fine examples of Pisan Romanesque and Gothic sculpture, this former Benedictine monastery down by the river boasts a remarkably eclectic collection. It includes Simone Martini's gentle *Madonna and Child*, Gentile da Fabriano's *Madonna of Humility,* a splendid Donatello gilded bronze bust of *St Rossore* and, most importantly, **Masaccio's *St Paul*** (1426). This is one panel of a monumental polyptych Masaccio was commissioned to do for a Carmelite church in Pisa while still working on the Brancacci Chapel in Florence (*see* page 156). It has since been cut up into some 11 known pieces exhibited variously in London, which possesses the central *Madonna and Child* panel, Berlin, Naples and Malibu, California (with four other pieces missing).

The little riverside **church of San Matteo** is an originally Romanesque construction, as can be seen in the charming arcading that directly faces the Arno, with the west façade and interior reconstructed in admirable Baroque style after a fire in the 17th century. The ceiling fresco of *The Glory of St Matthew* is by two Pisan painters, Francesco and Giuseppe Melani.

South of the Arno

The best view of the river is from its oldest bridge, **Ponte di Mezzo**, rebuilt after World War II. It is the venue for Pisa's *Gioca del Ponte*, a colourful Renaissance pageant held each year on the last Sunday in June. Dating back to the 15th century, the two halves of the city, from the north and south banks, join in a parade of several hundred costumed citizens. Their roughest, toughest champions participate in the climactic 'Push-of-War', cheered on by thousands of supporters on the river banks as they try to shove a heavy cart across the bridge.

Santa Maria della Spina

Just west of the Solferino bridge, this delicate white-stone Gothic church stands like a bejewelled ivory casket or reliquary on the south bank. Built from 1230 to 1323, it takes its name from a treasured thorn (*spina*) from Jesus's crown of thorns, brought back by a Pisan merchant from Palestine. The most decorative flank of the church faces away from the river, a series of Gothic tabernacles with porticoed niches sheltering statues of Jesus the Redeemer and the Apostles, sculpted by the workshop of Giovanni Pisano. Further west along the river is the handsome 13th-century Romanesque church of San Paolo a Ripa d'Arno.

*T*he Ponte di Mezzo is a modern reconstruction of Pisa's oldest bridge. Literally the 'Bridge of the Middle', it has long been the scene of the fierce historic rivalry between the city neighbourhoods north and south of the river (following pages).

The thorn that gives the church its name, Santa Maria della Spina, is said to have come from Jesus's Crown of Thorns. But there are enough other such thorns around the Christian world to make crowns for all the Apostles, too.

The Coast: Livorno to Carrara

Business, leisure and art join hands along northern Tuscany's coast. Cosmopolitan Livorno is Italy's largest seaport for the modern container trade. The beach resorts north of Pisa form part of Tuscany's

Versilian Riviera. Inland, sculptors (and undertakers) select the world's finest marble at Carrara.

Livorno

Ever since its 16th-century edict of religious and political tolerance by Duke Ferdinando I, the city has attracted ethnic groups from all over Italy and Europe: Jews escaping the Spanish (and Italian) Inquisition, Greek refugees from the Ottoman Empire, French Provençal Protestants and even English Catholics. (The latter gave it the name of 'Leghorn', by which it was known to British travellers of the 19th century.)

Given its importance to Tuscany's sea trade, it was a natural choice in pioneering the development of the railway and has two fine monuments of station architecture to show for it: the now disused neoclassical 19th-century **Stazione San Marco**, on the north side of the city centre, and the fine Art Nouveau **Stazione Centrale**, welcoming passengers from Pisa (and Florence) on the east side of town. On the Piazza Dante in front of the station, a genteel old resort hotel shows some of the style that graced the town in the early 1900s.

The harbour provides a natural moat for Livorno's Fortezza Vecchia, designed by Antonio da Sangallo and incorporating Roman fortifications.

Before going downtown, romantics might prefer to visit the sea promenade along **Viale Italia**, where more of the grand late 19th-century resort hotels recall that golden age known throughout Europe as the *Belle Epoque*.

On Piazza Michele near the fishing harbour, the **Monumento dei Quattro Mori** is Livorno's most celebrated sculpture. It was intended to honour Duke Ferdinando I, but his stilted statue by Giovanni Bandini (1595) yields pride of place, and the monument's modern name, to Pietro Tacca's four striking bronze Moorish slaves, completed 30 years later.

Bombardment in World War II badly damaged the city centre on and immediately surrounding **Piazza Grande**. The valiantly reconstructed late 16th-century **Duomo**, preceded by an elegant Doric-columned portico (following a design of the British architect Inigo Jones), has a hard time resisting the ugly modern construction around it.

A system of canals, *Fosse Reale* (Royal Moats), inevitably gave the 17th-century neighbourhood the name of **Venezia Nuova** (New Venice). Most interesting of its surviving monuments is the moated **Fortezza Nuova** (1590), designed like Florence's Forte Belvedere by Bernardo Buontalenti and now serving as a pleasant public park.

The town's Jewish community, still one of the most important in Italy, gathers at the **synagogue**, a new building replacing one destroyed in 1944 (Via del Tempio, south of the relentlessly modern Via Grande). The British contingent is long gone, but some of their most venerable representatives are buried in the **British cemetery** (entrance Via Giuseppe Verdi), including 18th-century Scottish novelist, Tobias Smollett.

South of Venezia Nuova, just beyond the canal, the **Mercatino** on Piazza XX

Settembre continues a tradition since the town's liberation at the end of World War II of selling ever-popular US Army surplus and other American goods; Camp Darby is a nearby US Army base.

The small **Museo Civico** (municipal museum, Piazza Matteotti 19) is housed in the Villa Fabbricotti. It is chiefly important for its collection of 24 paintings and over 300 drawings and etchings by Livorno-born Giovanni Fattori, a leader of the 19th-century *Macchiaioli* school (*see* ART AND ARCHITECTURE IN TUSCANY, pages 80-95). Its Renaissance paintings (on permanent loan from the Uffizi) include Fra Angelico's remarkable *Jesus with Crown of Thorns*.

Viareggio

The town is laid out in an elongated gridwork pattern along the almost perfectly straight sea shore, with shady parks of umbrella pines just inland. It got into its stride as perhaps the most popular of all Italian beach resorts when the nation was achieving its unity in the 1860s. This was when the sporting British were introducing to Mediterranean folk on their various rivieras the bizarre idea of swimming in the sea and lying on the beach. However, it was Napoleon Bonaparte's flighty and stunningly beautiful sister Paolina who had first made Viareggio fashionable by building a holiday villa there in 1820 (*see* ELBA, page 286).

Today, it continues to stage what is perhaps Italy's most boisterous Mardi Gras **Carnival** (February to March), with gigantic grotesquely masked floats satirizing contemporary political life.

The long **promenade** is lined with palm trees and first-class modern hotels directly on the sea front. The establishments of old-fashioned elegance in the Art

Whenever the beach at Viareggio gets too crowded, head for the cool of the Carrara marble quarries looming there in the background.

In the heat of the day, Viareggio's Esplanade is deserted. Things grow much more lively for the early evening passeggiata.

The Pineta di Ponente, Viareggio, is ideal for a picnic for the kids, a siesta for the grandparents, and romantic trysts for the generation in between.

PEACE FOR THE POET

The death of Percy Bysshe Shelley (1792-1822) was turned by his poet friends into a grand Romantic happening. His body and that of his sailor friend, Lieutenant Williams, were washed ashore after their boat, sailing north from Livorno, had sunk off the coast of Viareggio. Fellow writers Lord Byron and Leigh Hunt, and their companion-adventurer, Edward John Trelawny, prepared a funeral on the beach worthy of a Greek tragic hero. Trelawny cast aromatic oil and spices on Shelley's funeral pyre and his ashes were carried down to Rome to be buried in the English Cemetery. His heart was preserved to be buried with his wife Mary, author of *Frankenstein*, in a churchyard in Bournemouth.

Nouveau style of the late 19th and Art Deco style of the early 20th century are to be found just back from the sea front, notably on Viale Michelangelo Buonarroti and its prolongation, Viale Foscolo. This avenue borders the beautiful pinewoods of **Pineta di Ponente** (Pine Grove of the Setting Sun). South east of the yachting harbour is the **Pineta di Levante** (Pine Grove of the Rising Sun). Viale Foscolo divides the Giardini d'Azeglio (Azeglio Gardens) from **Piazza Shelley** where a monument to the English poet commemorates his drowning near Viareggio in 1822.

Music-lovers may like to make the pilgrimage 6km (4 miles) south of town to Torre del Lago, famous for its **Villa Puccini** where the composer of *La Bohème* and *Madame Butterfly* spent the last years of his life. The house is now a museum of his memorabilia and Giacomo Puccini (1858-1924) is buried in a chapel there, with his wife and son.

Forte dei Marmi

As its name suggests, this was once a centre for shipping marble from the inland quarries, but it is now the most fashionable of the Versilian Riviera's coastal resorts. Directly north of Viareggio, it is the favourite of the Florentine bourgeoisie, staying in elegant villas or cozy hotels hidden behind exotic trees and shrubs. The beaches are less crowded and the discothèques more sophisticated.

Pietrasanta

A pleasant inland excursion from the beach resorts, this attractive little town is a major centre of the region's marble industry and associated bronze foundries. On the outskirts are several handsomely designed factories dating back to the 1900s. In the centre, the **Duomo**, built in the 13th and 14th centuries, serves as a veritable showcase for the town's masons and sculptors in white marble. Local craftsmen fashioned the admirable Gothic **rose window** on the façade, and in the largely Renaissance and Baroque interior marble altars, a fine 16th-century **pulpit** and the **choir stalls**, also in marble, by Lorenzo Stagi. Charmingly located amid olive trees is the hillside **Rocca da Sala**, a fortress built in 1324 by Lucca's military governor, Castruccio Castracano, and now sheltering a 15th-century palace.

Massa

Fief of the Malaspina lords from the 15th to the 18th century, the predominantly modern town shares with Carrara the status of capital of the coastal province. The family's huge Baroque **Palazzo Cybo Malaspina** dominates the city centre. Their monumental tombs are equally prominent in the Baroque interior of the nearby **Duomo**, marred by a pompous 20th-century marble façade. Climb up to the impressive hilltop **Rocca**, the Malaspinas' grand mediæval fortress

protecting a handsome Renaissance palace. The effort is repaid with a great view over the town and Mediterranean.

Carrara

The town lies at the centre of unrivalled marble resources that provided the raw material of Italy's greatest achievements, the monuments of the Roman Empire and of the Renaissance. The town is still full of sculptors and the marble-paved **Piazza Alberica**, surrounded by grand 17th-century palazzi, is the scene of a summer sculpture competition that gives contestants 14 days to produce a masterpiece.

*A*t Carrara, apprentice *sculptors imitate the Renaissance and ancient Greek classics. Proportions may be wrong, but the effort is honourable.*

The **Duomo**, naturally enough of finest white marble, was started in the 11th and completed in the 14th century. It has a Pisan-style façade with a superb Gothic rose window. Entrance is on the south (right) side through a stately Romanesque portal. The fountain near the cathedral entrance is decorated by a 16th-century **statue of Andrea Doria**, the Genoese statesman who controlled the Massa-Carrara duchy. It is an unfinished work of Florentine sculptor Baccio Bandinelli, who suffered all his life from the strain of competing with Michelangelo.

South of the cathedral, the **Accademia di Belle Arte** (Academy of Fine Arts) is installed in the Malaspina Palace, and houses behind its 17th-century façade a museum of Roman marble sculpture and reliefs from the Carrara quarries (entrance by prior request).

The **Museo Civico del Marmo** (Municipal Marble Museum), on the southern edge of town on Viale XX Settembre, is devoted to the history of the ancient art of quarrying marble. Its exhibits include some 300 different kinds of marble from Italy and all over the world.

The Carrara Quarries

The quarries are situated in valleys east of Carrara in the Apuan Alps that slope down towards the Mediterranean. If you do not take the bus (from Via del Cavatore), be ready for a hair-raising winding drive,

---

ONLY THE BEST

In 1516, imagine the 41-year-old Michelangelo scrambling around in the mountains among the sheer ravines of white marble. He had been coming here since he was 22, when he picked out the perfect piece for his *Pietà* in the Vatican. Now, happy as a monkey, he was hunting down gigantic blocks with which to complete his monumental tomb for Pope Julius II. Thereafter, his Medici masters, always ready to save a florin when possible, obliged him to exploit their own, inferior quarries at nearby Pietrasanta – 'I have been hoodwinked,' the sculptor wrote to a friend.

What Michelangelo wanted was the stuff that the quarriers of Carrara classify as *Statuario* – only their purest white was fit for statuary. Other categories, established according to quality and colour, include: *Bianco chiaro*, a 'clear white', nice enough for decorative purposes; *Bardiglio chiaro*, light grey-blue, or *Bardiglio cupo*, dark blue; *Paonazzo*, yellowish; and the popular *Cipollino*, green and white streaked, literally 'like a spring onion'.

The ancient method of quarrying was by ramming dampened wooden wedges into natural crevices in the marble and soaking the wood continually with water until the wedges swelled and broke the marble into a block. Much more strenuous was the process of cutting with two men working handsaws lubricated with water and sand. They progressed at a rate of 5cm (7 inches) a day. By the end of the 19th century, steel wire speeded things up and diamond-wire has raised the rate to 20cm (22 inches) an hour.

In the cool mountain setting of Carrara, the palm trees come as something of a surprise. This one stands outside part of an older, heavily restored castle housing the Accademia di Belle Arte.

sometimes hemmed in behind huge marble-freight lorries. On and off, the quarries have been worked for at least 2000 years, and 300 of them are still producing half a million tons of marble a year. The marble that Michelangelo chose for his *Moses* and *Pietà* is now hewn for replicas at casino-

That is not snow in the Apuan Alps behind Carrara. It is the marble of the famous quarries from which Michelangelo painstakingly chose the ideal block for his work (previous pages).

hotels in Las Vegas and tombstones in Los Angeles' Forest Lawn cemetery.

The most accessible of the main quarries are: **Fantiscritti**, 6km (4 miles) from Carrara at an altitude of 450m (1476ft), with the bonus of an explanatory museum; **Colonnata**, 8km (5 miles), offering a particularly good closeup view of operations; and for those continuing north, the captivating mountain landscapes leading to **Campo Cécina**, 21km (13 miles) from Carrara and 1350m (4428ft) above sea level.

Back on the Carrara road (highway 446), make a side-trip north west to the magnificently located mediæval **Castello di Fosdinova**. Here in the early 14th century, the local feudal lord, Malaspina della Lunigiana, played host to the exiled Dante (*see* DANTE ALIGHIERI, page 65) who was acting as itinerant ambassador and also found time to write part of his *Divine Comedy* here.

The Hinterland: Lucca-Pistoia-Empoli

The towns between the Arno valley and the Apennines have lived more or less in the shadow of Florence, more in the case of Prato and Pistoia, less for the headstrong people of Lucca. All have retained a *centro storico* with many splendid monuments. For a bracing change of pace, go hiking or

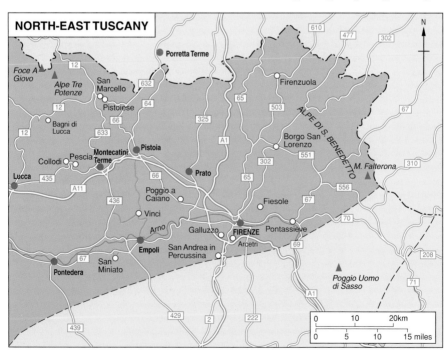

NORTH-EAST TUSCANY

horse-riding in the Garfagnano's nature reserves in the mountains north of Lucca.

both born here – and hosts a series of music festivals throughout the summer.

Lucca

The sights of this town can be comfortably visited in one day, but the seductive tranquillity within its old ramparts is such that people end up staying for weeks. Peace of mind has always been a priority here. During the stormy 15th and 16th centuries, Lucca's prosperous silk merchants preserved the peace by intercepting advancing enemy armies and paying them to bypass the town. It has been particularly rich in musicians – most notably, Luigi Boccherini and Giacomo Puccini were

The Ramparts

To begin – or end – your tour of the city's sights, take a walk along the beautifully preserved 16th-century fortifications. Among the most formidable city walls in all of Tuscany, 12m (39ft) high and as much as 30m (98ft) thick at the base, they were solid enough to assert Lucca's defiance of potential enemies, though never a shot was fired there in anger. The complete walk, **Passeggiata delle Mure**, is just over 4km (2 miles). Above the grassy moats, a perfect setting for the summer music

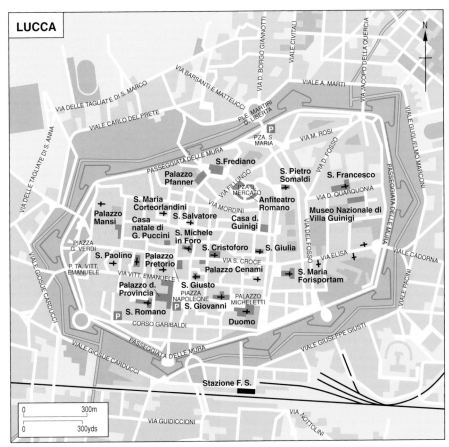

185

festivities, the 11 **bastions** have been planted with trees and provide a delightful park from which to view the city's monuments. On the south-east side, the **San Regolo bastion** is a children's playground. It also provides convenient access to the **Botanical Gardens** (*Giardino Botanico*), including a fine American sequoia, Chinese ginkgo and a cedar of Lebanon planted at the time of the gardens' creation in 1820. The **San Pietro bastion** at the ramparts' north-east corner offers a fine view across to the Apuan Alps.

Duomo San Martino

Ever assertive of its individuality, Lucca chooses for its fine 14th-century cathedral a striking asymmetry with which the Lombard crenellated campanile modifies the Pisan-style arcaded façade. The full effect of the polychrome marble façade is somewhat cramped by encroaching houses, but notice over the north porch two sculptures attributed to Nicola Pisano, the *Descent from the Cross* and the *Adoration of the Magi*.

Inside, to the right, is a 12th-century equestrian sculpture of *St Martin and the Beggar*, with a distinctly ancient Roman flavour to it. In the north (left) transept is the **tomb of Ilaria del Carretto** (1406), a major work of Sienese sculptor Jacopo della Quercia. Nearby is his **John the Baptist**, a giant statue from the cathedral's exterior.

San Martino's most venerated art-treasure, half-way down the left aisle, is the mediæval **Volto Santo** (Holy Face), a miracle-working wooden crucifix housed in a specially built octagonal marble shrine (*Tempietto*, 1484). The 11th- or 12th-century sacred effigy was carved from a cedar of Lebanon with, according to legend, the angelic assistance of Nicodemus (the Pharisee friendly to Jesus).

San Michele in Foro

North west of San Martino, this beautiful example of Pisan Romanesque stands less encumbered than the cathedral on the site of the old Roman Forum, still the centre of town. The arcaded façade varies the patterns of its columns: sculpted, striped, scrolled,

The noble, lofty façade of Lucca's church of San Michele in Foro brings a more vertical thrust to the elegant Romanesque inspiration from the neighbouring masters of Pisa.

PUCCINI'S BIRTHPLACE

In the tortuous maze of streets west of San Michele in Foro is the first home of Giacomo Puccini, composer of some of opera's best loved arias, like *Mimi* from *Madame Butterfly* or *Che gelida mano* ('Your tiny hand is frozen') from *La Bohème*. The house where he was born in 1858, off the Via di Poggio at Corte San Lorenzo 9, is a now a museum of his mementoes, including the piano on which he composed *Turandot*. He studied piano and organ in Lucca before going off to seek fame and fortune at La Scala in Milan.

*T*he Madonna and Child *on this altar in the north aisle of San Michele in Foro is by Rafaello da Montelupo (1522), with a Baroque frame added later.*

chevroned, in pink, green, black or white marble. With a pair of binoculars, you can spot up on the third tier of arches (3rd and 4th from the right) the heads of *Risorgimento* heroes Garibaldi and Cavour, carved here during a 19th-century restoration. Inside, on the first altar to the right, is a charming enamelled terracotta *Madonna and Child* by Andrea della Robbia. In the north (left) transept is a noteworthy painting of four saints, by Filippino Lippi.

Via Fillungo and Via Guinigi

Over to the east of Piazza San Michele, you can recapture something of the heyday of Lucca's mediæval and Renaissance silk merchants (*see* HISTORY, page 59) among the towering houses of Via Fillungo, now a prestigious address for elegant shops. Notice the ancient public clock on the tall thin **Torre dell'Ore** (Tower of the Hours).

Via Fillungo leads north to the delightful shop-lined **Piazza del Mercato** which traces the elliptical outline of the 2nd-century **Roman amphitheatre**, some of its ancient brick arches still incorporated in the piazza's houses.

To the south east, on Via Guinigi, named after an important merchant family, notice the **Guinigi houses**, two handsome 14th-century Gothic brick mansions standing opposite each other. Beside them, on the Via Sant'Andea, is the curious **Torre Guinigi**, 41m (134ft) high. From its little roof-garden of holm oaks, you get a fine view of the city and the Apuan Alps beyond.

San Frediano

Just north west of Piazza del Mercato, the church façade has a dazzling gold 13th-century (but much restored) **mosaic** of *Christ's Ascension and the Apostles*. Inside (4th chapel on the left aisle) is the

The original church of San Frediano is one of Lucca's oldest, dating back to the 6th century under the Lombards. It was completely rebuilt in the 13th century.

Trenta family altar (1422) with superb reliefs of the Madonna and saints sculpted in marble by Jacopo della Quercia.

Pinacoteca Nazionale

Housed in the 17th-century Palazzo Mansi over on the west side of the city centre (Via Galli Tassi 43), the museum assembles Italian art principally from the 16th to the 18th century. Among Florentine works are Pontormo's *Portrait of a Youth* (believed to be the ill-fated Alessandro de'Medici) and Bronzino portraits of *Duke Cosimo I* in armour and *Duke Ferdinando I*. The late Sienese school is represented by Beccafumi's *Scipio* and Sodoma's *Christ Bearing the Cross*. From Venice are works by Jacopo Bassano, *Adoration of the Shepherds*; Tintoretto, *St Mark Freeing the Slaves*; and Veronese (in poor condition), *St Peter the Hermit*.

Lucca's Country Villas

Like their Florentine counterparts, Lucca's most prosperous citizens built villas in the surrounding countryside, many of them set in large parks open to the public. Most notable are the 16th-century **Villa Mansi** at Segromigno, with Muzio Oddi's elaborate Baroque façade added in the following century; the equally extravagant **Villa Torrigiani** at Camigliano; and the **Villa Reale di Marlia**, country retreat of Napoleon's sister Elisa Baciocchi, who ruled Lucca for him from 1805 to 1814.

Garfagnana

Take time off from sightseeing to do a little hiking, horse-riding or just plain deep breathing in one or other of northern Tuscany's two secluded nature reserves in the mountain region known as the Garfagnana. The countryside north of Lucca on either side of the Serchio river is quite untypical of the accepted view of Tuscany's landscape. It offers dramatic crags in the Apuan Alps to the west, cool green forests in the Apennines to the east.

A first stop for poetic romantics (or unromantics with muscle pains) is the health spa of **Bagni di Lucca**, 27km (16 miles) from Lucca, just west of the Serchio river. England's Byron and Shelley, France's Lamartine and Germany's Heinrich Heine all took the sulphur and saline waters here. It can claim Europe's oldest licensed gambling casino (1837). Further up the Serchio valley, **Barga** has a charming old hilltop village (less charmingly modern at the bottom) with a picturesque Romanesque cathedral of local white stone (*alberese*).

Castelnuovo di Garfagnana, at the confluence of the Serchio and Turrite rivers, is the region's 'capital', 47km (29 miles) from Lucca. It is here, at the *Comunità Montana della Garfagnana*, that you will find maps, hiking trails and information for horse-riding for the two nature reserves.

Parco delle Alpe Apuani takes in the area west toward the Mediterranean, including the marble quarries behind Carrara (*see* page 181). Its rugged mountains include Tuscany's highest peak – Mount Pisanino, 1945m (6379ft). Up on the crags, you may spot mountain goats, and in the woods, deer and wild boar.

Parco dell'Orecchiella is east of the valley in the Apennines, a more gentle

landscape of green meadows, with forests of fir and beech trees.

Montecatini Terme

Italy's most elegant spa town is good for the liver, digestion and respiratory ailments. It is also popular with film-makers. Federico Fellini shot part of his *8½* here and Nikhita Mikhalkov his period film *Otschi Tschornie* (Dark Eyes). You will find many a white-suited Marcello Mastroianni look-alike strolling around the **Parco delle Terme** in search of a lonely dowager. Patients taking the waters can

choose between the extravagant Grecian colonnade of the **Tettuccio** or the Art Nouveau **Excelsior**. Mudbathers head for the neoclassical **Terme Leopoldini**. The town's most venerable Belle Epoque monument, the **Grand Hotel e la Pace**, is home from home to dukes, begums and Agnellis. Its orchids are overpowering.

Collodi

A short excursion 13km (8 miles) west of Montecatini, the hillside village is famous for the 18th-century **Gardens of Villa Garzoni** and the children's theme park,

The Greco-Roman colonnade surrounding the Tettuccio basin gives the Montecatini Terme health spa an appropriate atmosphere of antiquity, prompting many guests to wrap themselves in tunics or towel-togas.

Parco di Pinocchio. Journalist Carlo Collodi, creator (in 1881) of the lovable long-nosed lying puppet, took the name of his mother's birthplace.

Pistoia

Fight your way through the charmless crowded modern suburbs towards the more spacious nobility of the *centro storico* around the **Piazza del Duomo**, with its nearby fruit and vegetable markets supplied daily with the fresh produce of the commune's celebrated orchards and market-gardens.

Duomo San Zeno

The arcaded Pisan-Romanesque cathedral is dominated by a massive campanile that was probably the town's mediæval watchtower before the upper arcades and belfry were added. In the arch over the church façade's porch is Andrea della Robbia's enamelled terracotta *Madonna and the Angels*. Inside, on the south (right) aisle wall is a *Crucifixion* (1274) by Coppo di Marcovaldo and his son Salerno. Just beyond, in a chapel off this aisle, is the cathedral's great treasure, the grandiose silver **Dossale di San Jacopo** (Altar of St James). Its 628 bas-relief figures from the Bible were wrought by Tuscan artists from the 13th to the 15th century. Their number is believed to have included Brunelleschi, architect of Florence cathedral's great dome. In the Chapel of the Sacrament in the far northeast corner (left of the high altar) is a carved relief attributed to Verrocchio and a painting of the *Madonna Enthroned* (1485) by Lorenzo Credi.

Baptistery

Across the square, the lovely 14th-century octagonal Gothic sanctuary in green and white marble was designed by Andrea Pisano. The sculpture over the entrance, notably a Madonna in the tympanum, was the work of other Pisan artists. Inside, see the polychrome marble **baptismal font** (1226).

Two Palazzi

The cathedral square also has two imposing Gothic civic buildings of the 13th and 14th centuries: next to the baptistery, the **Palazzo Pretorio**, with its handsome courtyard decorated with the magistrates' coats of arms; and beside the Duomo, the **Palazzo del Comune**. The latter houses the **Museo Civico** (municipal museum), that includes 16th- and 17th-century paintings by Lorenzo di Credi, Carlo Saraceni and José de Ribera, and a room devoted to the work of the important Pistoia-born 20th-century architect Giovanni Michelucci (see ART AND ARCHITECTURE IN TUSCANY, pages 80-95).

Sant'Andrea

North west of Piazza del Duomo, the modest little 12th-century church can claim Pistoia's most important work of art: the **Giovanni Pisano's pulpit**, superbly carved in 1301 to rival and even surpass his work in Pisa and Siena. His characteristically emotional sculpture becomes harrowingly realistic in the *Massacre of the Innocents*. A little light relief (at least for us) is provided by the comic grimace of the caryatid straining to hold up one of the pulpit's pillars on the nape of his neck. On the north wall behind the pulpit, in a 15th-century tabernacle, is a **wooden crucifixion** attributed to Giovanni Pisano.

San Giovanni Fuorcivitas

Along its north wall facing Via Cavour (south of the Duomo), this fine Romanesque church has distinctive blind arcading in black and white marble on either side of the entrance. (The name *fuorcivitas*, 'outside the city', dates back to the church's 8th-century foundation when this area was beyond the city walls.) Inside, switch on the light to the right of the door to see the remarkable **pulpit** carved in 1270 by

Guglielmo da Pisa, a pupil of Nicola Pisano. On the north wall to the left of the high altar is **Taddeo Gaddi's polyptych** (1355), a delicate study by the Giotto pupil of the *Madonna and Child* flanked by 12 saints.

Prato

Half-way between Florence and Pistoia, the town has been prospering from the manufacture of textiles since the Middle Ages, and still produces more wool than any other city in the world.

For the devout, Prato's other claim to fame is as the home of a legendary relic, the Holy Girdle, traditionally given by Mary to Doubting Thomas on her ascension to heaven. The Holy Girdle is housed in the cathedral, **Duomo di Santo Stefano**. Five times a year, the relic is displayed from the **Pulpit of the Holy Girdle** that projects from the right-hand side of the cathedral's green and white-striped façade. The 15th-century pulpit was designed by Michelozzo, the Medici architect, its balustrade beautifully carved with reliefs by Donatello. The originals are now displayed in the **Museo dell'Opera del Duomo** (cathedral museum) on the north (left) side of the church. Inside the cathedral, the choir is decorated by **Fra Filippo Lippi frescoes** (1464), scenes from the lives of John the Baptist and St Stephen that are considered the renegade monk's masterpiece.

The **Galleria Comunale** (housed in the Gothic Palazzo Pretorio, Piazza del Comune) exhibits other notable works by Filippo Lippi and his son Filippino, born in Prato, as well as a 14th-century polyptych by Bernard Daddi narrating the story of the Holy Girdle.

East of the Piazza del Comune, off the Via Cairoli, **Santa Maria delle Carceri** is a masterpiece among Renaissance churches. This late 15th-century work of

Giuliano da Sangallo, favourite architect of Lorenzo the Magnificent, includes in its interior some splendid **enamelled terracottas** by Andrea della Robbia.

Vinci

Some 10km (6 miles) north of Empoli on the southern slopes of Monte Albano, Leonardo da Vinci's first home celebrates its most famous son with a fascinating **museum** (*Museo Vinciano*) housed in the severe 13th-century Castello dei Conti Guidi. It displays nearly 100 models built from his sketches of scientific inventions and machines for flying, bridge-building and machine-tools, as well as facsimiles of preparatory drawings for his great paintings. Upstairs is a library (*Biblioteca Leonardiana*) for studying the great man's manuscripts and other prints and documents. The village **church of Santa Croce** has the **baptismal font** believed to be used for little Leonardo. Up the mountain slope covered in olive groves, in the hamlet of **Anchiana**, is the house in which the baby genius is actually said to have seen the first light of day.

Empoli

The airy town that has recovered well from its World War II bombing is known for its glass manufacture, as it developed the famous green-glass bottles in protective basket-weave for Chianti wine. Its **glassworks** can be visited on Piazza Gramsci and Piazza Guido Guerra.

The Romanesque church, **Collegiata di Sant'Andrea**, has an attractive façade of green and white marble in the style of Florence's San Miniato. Its marble porch is 16th-century. Since the war, most of its art treasures are housed in the excellent modern **Museo della Collegiata** to the right of the church. A highlight is the marvellously

---

THE RELUCTANT MONK

Prato was the town where the monk, Fra Filippi Lippo, found happiness in the arms of a nun, Lucrezia Butti. As a 15-year-old, Filippo had not much wanted to enter the Carmelite order, but for an orphan in 1421 the monks of Santa Maria del Carmine in Florence offered him his best chance of food and shelter. More importantly, he could watch the great Masaccio at work and learn to paint his own frescoes to complete the decoration of the Brancacci Chapel (*see* page 156). But ten years of monastic life were enough. With Lucrezia he had two children, Filippino, who followed in his father's artistic footsteps, and Alessandra. Lucrezia served as model for many of his Madonnas. In his painting, he showed more taste for the ornate style of Fra Angelico (his rich colour without the purity) than for the harsher psychology of Masaccio. He added a personal warmth anticipating the poetic sensuality that burst forth in the work of Botticelli.

---

restored *Pietà* **fresco** (1425) by Masolino, master and collaborator of Masaccio for the Brancacci Chapel frescoes. Other works include a marble font (1447) by Bernardo Rossellino, Lorenzo Monaco's *Madonna of Humility* (1404) and, in the cloister, enamelled terracottas by Andrea della Robbia and his workshop.

The nearby 14th-century church of **Santo Stefano degli Agostiniani** is worth a visit, even if only fragments of its important **Masolini frescoes** have survived the revolutionary destruction of 1792. Painstaking work has restored fresco fragments or at least the *sinopie* preparatory drawings on which frescoes were painted for *The Legend of the True Cross*, along the south (right) aisle, and a *Madonna and Child* in the south transept.

Sunny Vineyards and Silvery Olive Groves Surround Etruscan and Mediæval Hill Towns

The Tuscany of the popular imagination is best epitomized by the sunny southern-oriented slopes of the Chianti country between Florence and Siena. With an eye to the main chance, the region's tourist offices' cheerful signposts guide the visitor along back roads from vineyard to vineyard. In addition, between wine-tastings and gourmet restaurants, there are the cultural delights of San Gimignano's towers, the Etruscan town of Volterra and Boccaccio's home-town of Certaldo. *Alla salute!*

For the sake of convenience, our itineraries are drawn up for visitors approaching the region from the north, from Florence. Starting out on Florence's southern outskirts along the Siena road from Piazza Romana, two separate routes are possible. Each bypassing the traffic hazard of the so-called *Superstrada* that heads straight down to Siena (*see* page 219), one itinerary is more specifically wine-oriented to the south east, the other more 'cultural' to the south west.

*B*eyond the vineyards, *where San Gimignano produces its fine dry white Vernaccia, loom the proud towers, civic and private, erected by the town's feudal lords.*

To do proper justice to the region, both itineraries should be attempted. Car-drivers can work out their own network combining the two. Bus-travellers starting out from Santa Maria Novella Station can use the Florence-based SITA country buses that serve each of the following routes:

1. **Via Chiantigiana**: vineyard route starting out from market-town of **Impruneta** then travelling south east to:
   • **Greve**; wine-distribution centre;
   • **Panzano**; fortified hill town;
   • **Radda**, **Gaiole**, noble **Brolio** and **Castellina**; *Chianti Classico* centres.

2. **Towards San Gimignano**:
   • from hilltop **San Casciano** with fine art-museum;
   • via **Certaldo**; Boccaccio's home;

- to famous towers of **San Gimignano**, Etruscan bastion of **Volterra** and fortified **Colle di Val d'Elsa**.

Via Chiantigiana

From Florence, make an early-morning start, so as to visit vineyards in the morning, enjoy a good lunch and spare time for an afternoon siesta. In any case, have an abstemious backup driver, so that wine-tasting remains a pleasure and not a hazard. With a few side-trips down winding country lanes, the wine-route signposted with Chianti Classico's coveted *gallo nero* (black rooster) is principally along southbound highway N°222. Several wine festivals make the October and November grape harvest, *la vendemmia*, the liveliest, most colourful time. The best known are at Greve and Impruneta, just south of Florence. But tasting – and buying at the vineyard or in the wine-towns – goes on all year round (*see* WINES OF CHIANTI, page 201).

YOU CAN'T GO HOME AGAIN

Like the land of the Lotus-Eaters in Homer's *Odyssey* or Cloud-Cuckoo-Land in Aristophanes' *Birds*, the Chianti region is high-risk territory for visitors who have a job to maintain and a family to feed. All nationalities are vulnerable, but in particular, many a British or German tourist has rented a villa here for a couple of weeks – or just driven through on a motoring holiday – and ended up staying the rest of his or her life. Side by side with British colonizers of 'Chiantishire', the more sophisticated wing of the German Social Democratic Party (SPD) has made this part of Tuscany a sort of summer party-headquarters. For their mind-boggling talent in cooking pasta *al dente*, a few Italians are also tolerated.

Impruneta

Just south of the Bologna to Rome Autostrada, 13km (8 miles) from Florence's city centre, the wine-route starts off from this farming village. It is famous for the fine clay supplied to the Della Robbia terracotta

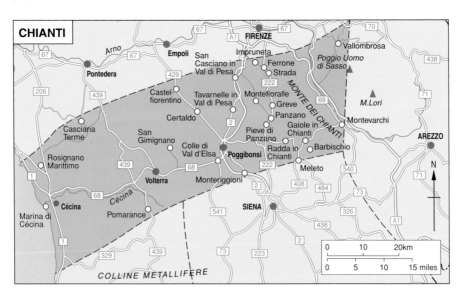

196

workshops of the Renaissance and for modern ceramics: pottery, statuary and decorative tiles. Impruneta's big **autumn fair** in mid-October is devoted to cattle, horses and regional produce, with plenty of Chianti to wash down the meats and cheeses.

The church of **Santa Maria dell'Impruneta**, Romanesque in origin but now largely Baroque, displays the town's local product beyond the choir: Luca della Robbia's superb enamelled terracotta decoration for two Renaissance chapels designed by Michelozzi, *della Croce* and *della Madonna*.

Greve

Beyond Impruneta, the route to Greve forks south along the Greve river through some of the first Chianti vineyards or east through pretty wooded hills to join the broader highway N°222 passing through the village of **Strada**, with its little Romanesque church of San Cristofano. Greve is one of Chianti's major wine-distribution centres, an excellent base for exploring the surrounding vineyards and for buying a selection of wines at the end of the tour. It hold its annual **wine fair** in late September. (Unless you already have a specific wine in mind, price differences you may notice between the town's wine-shops and on-the-spot vineyard sales are small considering the advantage of comparing the region's different labels here in one place.)

Greve has the rural charm of a market town, its activity concentrated around the arcaded **Piazza Verrazzano**. New Yorkers will be the first to appreciate the square's monument to Giovanni da Verrazzano, the local boy who 'discovered' New York Bay. In fact, Americans tracing their nation's roots should feel right at

*I*n the vineyards of Greve, the machinery is state-of-the-art, but the fine wine labelled Chianti Classico gives us the same mellow glow as of old.

A MAN AND A BRIDGE

Giovanni da Verrazzano (1480-1527) was born in Greve but worked for the French – like Columbus, seeking trade passages to Asia. In 1524, he sailed up the coast from North Carolina to Maine, entering on the way what is now New York Bay, probably the first European to do so. Two or three years later he was killed by natives while exploring the West Indies. Since 1964, his name (with one 'z' less) graces the bridge spanning New York Bay between Brooklyn and Staten Island, the longest suspension bridge in the United States.

home here. The elliptically shaped fortified village of **Montefioralle**, just up the hill east of Greve, was the feudal redoubt of the Vespucci family of navigator Amerigo, who gave his name to the whole continent. Its church of Santo Stefano boasts a Gothic triptych by Bicci di Lorenzo.

Among the vineyards surrounding Greve to the south east is the beautifully located **Vignamaggio**, with a hilltop villa in which Leonardo da Vinci's most celebrated model, Mona Lisa, is said to have had her country home. More recently, it served as the location for Kenneth Branagh's film of Shakespeare's *Much Ado About Nothing*.

Panzano

Participating in their own modest but spirited way in the national sport of communal rivalries, the people of this fortress town look down, in all senses, on nearby Greve. With homes built along the top of a ridge commanding a magnificent view of the countryside, they pride themselves on a more refined style of life than their mercantile neighbours. Panzano's mediæval castle, left in ruins by the fights

between Papal and Medici forces in the 15th century, has been restored as a handsome residence favoured by eccentric art historians. On the outskirts is the town's Romanesque parish church, **Pieve di Panzano**, dedicated to San Leolino, with an imposing 16th-century porch.

Castellina

Before tackling an enchanting branch of the wine-route further east to Radda (*see* below), continue down the main Siena road to this typical ancient Etruscan fortified hill town, 578m (1895ft) above sea-

level. Its massive mediæval castle and ramparts with 15th-century town gate, can be seen to emerge from dense woodland, vineyards and olive groves, with a spectacular view over three valleys, the Pesa to the north, Arbia to the east and Elsa to the west. One of the finest vantage points for the westward view is at the **Etruscan burial vaults** on Monte Calvario at the northern edge of town. Jewellery, sculpture and ceramics found in the four tombs, from the 4th century BC, are on display in the archaeological museums of Florence and Chiusi.

Radda

Double back from Castellina to drive across the lovely rolling hills east of the N°222 to the town that was made capital of the Chianti League (*Lega del Chianti*) in 1415 as a Florentine outpost. It was a

Etruscans built their towns like Castellina on isolated hilltops, whereas the Romans preferred valleys for easier access to their roads.

major objective in the 1478 campaign led by the Duke of Urbino's Papal forces against Lorenzo the Magnificent (*see* HIS-TORY, page 67). The façade of its **Palazzo Comunale** is decorated with the coats of arms of the ruling families, and with a 15th-century fresco by Florentine artists of the *Madonna and Child* flanked by John the Baptist and St Christopher. Wine-making techniques and the history of the region's vineyards are displayed in the **Piccolo Museo del Chianti**.

Some 6km (3 miles) east of Radda, surrounded by a forest of pines and oaks, **Badia di Coltibuono**, a 12th-century greystone monastery traces its origin to a Benedictine hermitage founded in 770. It was rebuilt from the ruin left by the Papal troops and is now converted to a luxury restaurant and wine-cellar.

Gaiole

This is a favourite wine-tasting centre, so before getting back into your car, take a walk along the beautiful green **Barbischio valley** east of town. You will pass castle ruins, an old flour-mill that belonged to the abbots of Coltibuono and a massive stone spinning-mill (*Filandra*) once used both for wool and silk.

Castello di Meleto, barely 3km (2 miles) south of Gaiole, is a fortified wine-grower's castle (comparable to a Bordeaux château) with elegant round towers and a handsome Renaissance courtyard. Its vineyards produce a top-rated *Chianti Classico*. Talk the owners into showing you the charming little 18th-century theatre.

Castello di Brolio, 8km (5 miles) off to the east of Meleto, is the home of one of Chianti's most celebrated wines (*see* WINES OF CHIANTI, page 201), in addition to its most refined olives and oil. Vine-

yards and olive groves have been cultivated here since the 9th century and the Ricasoli family's property constantly coveted throughout the communal struggles of mediæval and Renaissance times. The Neo-Gothic castle you see today is largely a reconstruction of 1860, but despite its modern mosaic, the 14th-century chapel is worth a visit for the family tombs and a Gothic polyptych by Ugolino di Nerio.

Towards San Gimignano

This itinerary follows for the most part highway N°2 from Florence's Porta Romana. It avoids the dreaded Florence to Siena *superstrada* to cut across the western boundary of Chianti country to the mediæval bastion of San Gimignano, and proposes a side-trip to Volterra.

On the way down to your first stop at San Casciano, take a side-road to the right to pass through the picturesque little village of **Sant'Andrea in Percussina**. Here, after his exile from Florence in 1512, Niccolò Machiavelli holed up in its old inn (*Albergaccio*), marked by a plaque, to write his masterwork, *The Prince*. Staying on N°2, you pass the **American Cemetery**, last resting place for over 4000 American soldiers who fell in the Italian campaign in World War II.

San Casciano in Val di Pesa

This fortified hilltown, 17km (11 miles) south of Florence, commands a superb view of Chianti country south to the Pesa valley. The **ramparts** built in 1355 were reinforced by Duke Cosimo I in the 15th century. Its main church, the **Collegiata**, rebuilt in 1793, has a noteworthy 15th-century Florentine fresco of *Madonna and*

The Wines of Chianti

The familiar image of Chianti wine, almost a folklore icon, is of its chubby green-glass bottle, traditionally manufactured in Empoli, in protective basket-weave with jolly red and green labels. As the wine grew more and more popular, mass-production shamelessly imitated the basket-weave in straw-coloured plastic, too ugly even for the worst pizzeria's candlesticks. These days, respect for upmarket Chianti has increased, the best being bottled in high-shouldered Bordeaux-style bottles with either elegant black and gold or austere white labels.

Fighting for Quality

Wine has been produced in Tuscany since Etruscan times, but Chianti's vine-yards were especially prized, and a major bone of contention in the Middle Ages between Florence and Siena. It was a logical step in Florentine ascendancy over Tuscany to create in 1415 the Lega del Chianti (Chianti League), uniting the wine-growing estates with Radda as their capital. The prestigious Castello di Brolio of the Ricasoli family was accordingly a natural target of the 1478 military campaign that followed the Pazzi conspiracy.

Question: do they use white grapes for white wine and black grapes for red? Answer: no, they use black grapes for both, but the skins are kept for the red and are removed for the white wine.

CHIANTI CLASSICO REGION

The ruined castle was rebuilt, and in 1716 the Duke of Tuscany promulgated one of the first label-protection laws to safeguard Brolio and other top Chianti wines against fly-by-night counterfeiters. England's Duke of Norfolk was among Brolio's prominent early 18th-century customers.

Leaving the Dance

Like Italy itself, Chianti wine went into eclipse at the end of the 18th century, but revived with the Risorgimento. Bettino Ricasoli was a chief promoter of both. The man who was to become one of united Italy's first prime ministers in the 1860s had earlier revived the fortunes of his Brolio vineyards.

It all happened because of love, jealous love. Ricasoli was a deeply religious, highly serious fellow known rather derisively to his friends as the Iron Baron (Barone di Ferro). Newly-wed, he took his bride, Anna Bonnacorsi, to a winter ball in Florence, where a young man danced with her a little too closely. He cut in to whisper: 'We must leave, my dear' and took her out to his waiting carriage. Abandoning their Florence home, Bettino and Anna drove through the night and the snow to the isolated family residence at Castello di Brolio, where no Ricasoli had lived for years.

The Iron Baron rebuilt the manor as a permanent home and replanted the vineyards, experimenting with different varieties and new combinations of grapes. The formula that he finally hit upon, Brolio vintage 1841, the fruit of 20 years of research, was registered at a wine congress in 1847. It became the standard for what we know as today's best Chianti and Bettino's own Brolio Ricasoli remains one of its most prestigious labels.

The Making of a Chianti

There is Chianti and Chianti:
Table Red is served in the basket-bottles or open carafes, a perfectly respectable but, as the wine-waiters say, unpretentious new wine tickling the palate with the faintest of sparkles. The method of vinification or governo is to set aside 10 per cent of the harvested grapes, unpressed, to be dried on straw racks. At the end of November, this part with its concentrated juice is crushed, fermented and then added to the rest of the Chianti grapes. It is kept in closed vats till the spring, when it is ready for your pasta or pizza.
Chianti Classico is a label granted only to the region's highest quality wines, distinguished by the proud black rooster (gallo nero) that decorated the military banner of the 15th-century Chianti League. Connoisseurs esteem the wine's firm, well-balanced, full-bodied character and fine bouquet, all improving with age. By and large as first

202

developed by Bettino Ricasoli, Chianti Classico blends 70-75 per cent San Giovese black grapes, for the wine's essential wild fruity quality, and 5-10 per cent Canaiolo, also black, with 5-10 per cent Malvasia and 5-10 per cent Trebbiano, both white. Traditionally, the vines grow at relatively high altitudes on dry, arid slopes, usually surrounded by olive groves.

The principal Chianti Classico centres are Greve, Radda, Castellino and Gaiole, with vineyards covering 10,000 hectares (24,700 acres), of which only 7000 hectares (17,300 acres) are specifically registered with the European Community.

Non-Classico wines that price somewhere between the common-or-garden table reds and the upmarket labels in-

Wine casks are most often made of oak. Traditionalists insist that these are still better than modern stainless steel vats for the oxidation and other natural chemical processes that will produce the characteristic bouquet.

clude, in descending order of quality, Rufino and Montalbino, Colli Fiorentini, Colli Pisani, and – close to rot-gut – Colli Sienese and Colli Aretini, often mixed with anonymous wines from elsewhere in Italy.

A modest Chianti white, from the Trebbiano grape, is gold in colour, dry in taste, fine for a casual spaghetti alle vongole (spaghetti in clam-sauce) or seafood pizza.

Child with John the Baptist and St Stephen over the baptismal font. In the **church of the Misericordia** is Simone Martini's *Crucifixion* (1325). The new **Museo d'Arte Sacra** (Museum of Sacred Art, now occupying the converted church *del Suffragio*, Via Roma 31) displays works by Coppa di Marcovaldo and Ambrogio Lorenzetti.

Certaldo

The home of Boccaccio, 22km (14 miles) south west of San Casciano, is proclaimed in the lower town's main square and car park by the marble statue (1879) of the great 14th-century author of *The Decameron*. Much more attractive is the mediæval **upper town** bordering the Via Boccaccio. At N°18, you can visit the

tower-house with loggia that served as **Boccaccio's home**. It is now a museum and research centre for students of his writings.

In the same street, in the 13th-century brick-façaded church of **Santi Michele e Iacopo**, the writer's tomb (20th century) is in the nave, with his bust (1503) by Giovanni Francesco Rudici on the north wall. Left of the church entrance is a 14th-century fresco by a Sienese painter.

The fortified **Palazzo Pretorio** (magistrates' palace), rebuilt in the 15th century, bears the Florentine governors' coats of arms, carved in stone or modelled in glazed terracotta. In the inner courtyard are the dungeons, courtroom and chapel with a fresco by Benozzo Gozzoli of *Doubting Thomas*. Go up to the garden

---

GIOVANNI BOCCACCIO (1313-75)

His most celebrated work, *The Decameron*, has earned Boccaccio a one-sided reputation as a writer of bawdy tales. In fact, he was throughout his life a serious scholar and pioneer in humanist thought, championing translations of Homer, the poetry of his friend Petrarch and wider publication for the revered works of Dante. Not that he would have renounced the lighter side shining through his work that many consider the foundation of the modern novel. Voltaire praised *The Decameron* as 'the prime model in prose of precision, purity of style and narrative naturalism,' and Chaucer borrowed from Boccaccio, not vice versa.

The Decameron presents 100 stories told by seven women and three young men at their country refuge, isolated from the Black Plague ravaging Florence in 1348. After describing the plague itself in gruesome detail, Boccaccio paints a psychologically acute picture of 14th-century people who appear cowardly or noble, sensual or ridiculous, cruel or tender, ladies, gentlemen and not so gentle ladies and downright ruffians, and a horrendous bunch of degenerate churchman. He made a major advance over the artifices of the courtly poetry of his age by placing woman on an equal footing with man – and even when superior, never on a pedestal. Love is resolutely physical, not ethereal.

It remains uncertain whether Boccaccio, son of a merchant banker, was born in Florence or in the family's country home at Certaldo, but he is no longer believed to be the illegitimate child of a Frenchwoman in Paris. At any rate, he seems to have acquired his taste for observing the human condition hanging around the brilliant court of the King of Naples, while studying banking and law. In Naples, his own love affair with the king's daughter provided the raw material for early romances in prose and verse. Triumphs, disappointments and the cuckoldry of other unfortunates in Naples and Florence fed the licentious character of his *Decameron*. Ultimate disillusionment turned him into a vicious woman-hater in his satirical *Corbaccio*.

In the 1370s he returned in poverty to his hometown of Certaldo and ended his life with public readings of Dante's *Divine Comedy*.

---

terrace for the fine view across the Val d'Elsa to San Gimignano.

San Gimignano

On the 13km (8 miles) of road meandering south from Certaldo, one of the most wondrous sights in all Europe emerges on the horizon – the haunting silhouette of Tuscany's mediæval Manhattan. That skyline bristling with rectangular towers and the lovingly preserved *centro storico* make this the most magical of hill-towns.

During the Middle Ages, San Gimignano was Florence's most advanced fortified outpost in its wars against Siena. The town prospered and its leading citizens vied with one another by building ever more vertiginous towers. The rivalry continued until there were more than 70 of these symbols of power and prestige. When Siena fell under Florentine domination, San Gimignano lost its strategic importance, went into slow decline, with less need for towers from which to pour boiling-hot pitch and rocks on passing foes. Many of the towers crumbled and fell or were torn down, and the town itself was frozen in time, remote enough from the main trade route to retain its mediæval aspect.

Today, a dozen of the towers, most of them 13th-century, remain to justify the

San Gimignano's defences are a vestige of days when it was of vital strategic importance in Florence's rivalry with Siena.

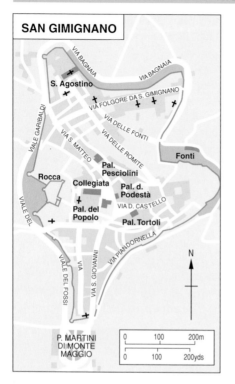

SAN GIMIGNANO

centuries-old name of *San Gimignano delle Belle Torri* ('San Gimignano of the Beautiful Towers'), their lovely travertine stone blushing pink or gleaming gold in the morning or afternoon sun.

Park your car at the south end of town and walk through the **Porta San Giovanni** to plunge immediately into its mediæval atmosphere along the narrow Via San Giovanni with a first view of the towers ahead in the main square. On the right, the Romanesque church of San Francesco is now a wine-shop giving pride of place to the local white *Vernaccia*. Strong and dry, it is a notch above the rival white wines of Chianti, but not all connoisseurs are convinced that it is quite as terrific as Michelangelo suggested, when he said it 'kisses, licks, bites, thrusts and stings'.

*T*he walk through San Gimignano's Porta San Giovanni is a moment of magic, as the mediæval townscape is revealed on the narrow street ahead

*P*erhaps a trophy bagged by the wine-merchant himself, the boar's head dangles a sample of the tangy salami that goes so well with the local wine.

Piazza della Cisterna

The town's most important towers are clustered around two adjacent squares of its historic centre. From Via San Giovanni, the *Arco dei Becci* archway leads to this first, triangular piazza, brick-paved in herringbone pattern and named after its 13th-century travertine well – **Cisterna**. In Tuscany's arid hill country, such a freshwater well was vitally important, and this one also gives its name to the fashionable hotel and restaurant housed in the nearby Palazzo Salvestrini, with a splendid view over the surrounding countryside. West (left) of the archway are the dual towers of the Ardinghelli family and at the far end the Devil's Tower (*Torre del Diavolo*), diabolically elevated a few feet while the owner was away on a journey.

Piazza del Duomo

The centre of San Gimignano's civic and religious power is dominated by the massive **Palazzo del Populo**, its *Torre Grossa* (Great Tower) the tallest in town, rising 54m (177ft) from a staircase beside the church. It houses today the **Museo Civico** (Municipal Museum). Among its most important works are: an emotionally gripping *Crucifixion* by Coppa di Marcovaldo, probably painted after his capture by the Sienese army at the battle of Montaperti of 1260; two Madonnas (1460s) by Benozzo Gozzoli; and an *Enthroned Madonna* (1512) by Pinturicchio. Taddeo

Like the clock at London's Victoria Station or the Eiffel Tower in Paris, the well on San Gimignano's Piazza della Cisterna has become a landmark rendezvous for travellers through Tuscany.

di Bartolo tells in a charming polyptych the story of Saint Gimignano, the Bishop of Modena who, among other miracles, saved the town – anachronistically imagined as already a veritable forest of towers – from Attila the Hun in 450.

The 12th-century Romanesque **Collegiata** was deprived of its cathedral (*duomo*) status when the town lost its bishop, but not of its many art treasures. In its interior, immediately left of the entrance against the west wall are two **wooden sculptures** (1421) of *Arcangelo Gabriele* and *Maria Annunziata* elegantly carved by the Sienese master, Jacopo della Quercia, and painted five years later by Martino di Bartolomeo. More violent in their impact are **Taddeo di Bartolo's frescoes** of the *Last Judgment* (1393), also on the west wall, with the damned in Hell to the left and the blessedly saved in Paradise to the right. Taddeo's master, Bartolo di Fredi, painted the **Old Testament frescoes** (1367) along the north (left) aisle. The **New Testament frescoes** (mid 14th-century) on the south (right) aisle are attributed to Barna da Siena, the master's last work: he fell off the scaffolding and died from his injuries.

At the end of this south aisle, the **Santa Fina Chapel** is devoted to the town's other saint. St Fina died in 1253 at the age of 15 and was rewarded – truly a miracle in the light of her stunningly uneventful life as an invalid – with violets bursting into bloom on her coffin and on the city towers. With the Florentine painter's customary penchant for the chic and decorative, **Ghirlandaio's frescoes** (1475) narrate the legend but are more interested in offering us a series of sophisticated social portraits. In the funeral scene, the man behind the bishop is Ghirlandaio himself.

Rocca

Behind the Collegiata, make a separate trip up the tower amid the ruins of this 14th-century citadel, now part of a public park. It offers a magnificent view of the surrounding countryside with its glistening olives, dark cypresses and neatly terraced Vernaccia vineyards.

Volterra

Perched high in the rugged hills 50km (30 miles) west of San Gimignano, this fortified town exerts an austere but powerful charm among the buff-stone mediæval edifices safeguarding its illustrious history as an ancient Etruscan stronghold.

Ramparts

Signs of the Etruscans abound from the massive lower structure of the city walls to the three carved stone heads of Etruscan deities set into the 4th-century BC **Porta all'Arco**, the town's western entrance gate. The Romans finally crushed Volterra's stubborn resistance as the last Etruscan holdout in 90 BC, and evidence of the conquerors' presence can be found south of the Porta all'Arco in the vast **Parco Archeologico** just inside the city walls. On the east side of town, a **Roman theatre** with handsome Corinthian columns, subject to ongoing excavations, is being prepared for public visits.

Piazza dei Priori

Its sober harmony makes this one of Italy's finest mediæval squares. Its jewel is the **Palazzo dei Priori** (1208), oldest of Tuscany's town halls, with mullioned windows and two-tiered tower, each tier with formidable battlements. Opposite is the triple-arched **Palazzo Pretorio** with its soaring crenellated *Torre del Podesta*, dungeon of Volterra's mediæval police headquarters.

Piazza San Giovanni

Behind the Pisan-style but bare façade of the 12th-century **duomo** is an interior worth visiting for some remarkable works of art. Most noteworthy are a poignant *Deposition* (1228) carved in polychrome wood probably by a Pisan sculptor, in a chapel off the south (right) transept; and flanking the high altar, two

There's many a surprise in the arid country to the south-west of Volterra. Here, rising from the wheat fields, the formidable ruins of a mediæval fortress.

The outside might look bare, but the interior of Volterra's duomo holds some beautiful works of art.

15th-century angels on Gothic columns sculpted by Mino da Fiesole, who also fashioned the altar's tabernacle.

The octagonal 13th-century **baptistery**, partially clad in green and white marble, has in its interior a **font** with bas-reliefs sculpted in 1502 by Andrea Sansovino. The stoup (basin for holy water) was originally an Etruscan memorial stone.

The Museums

The most important of the town's art collections is to be found at the **Etruscan Guarnacci Museum** (Via Don Minzoni 15). Founded in the 18th century, it boasts one of Italy's finest collections of Etruscan art. It includes stone tomb sculpture, alabaster and terracotta funeral urns, ceramics and jewellery dating back to the 7th century BC. One gaunt bronze statue, *Ombra della Sera* (Shadow of the Evening), is an uncanny 2000-year-old precursor of a modern Giacometti.

The town's small **art gallery** (*Pinacoteca*, Via dei Sarti 1) is housed in the elegant Palazzo Minucci-Solaini, a design attributed to Antonio da Sangallo the Elder, architect of Montepulciano's San Biagio. Of particular interest is Rosso Fiorentino's *Deposition* (1521), a masterpiece of the bizarre juxtaposition of acrobatic forms characteristic of Mannerist art. Other artists represented here include Taddeo di Bartolo, Luca Signorelli and Ghirlandaio.

Colle di Val d'Elsa

Some 14km (8 miles) east of San Gimignano, the modern lower town, *Colle Bassa*, can be rapidly by-passed for an exploration of the older, much more attractive upper town, **Colle Alta**, fortified on its horseshoe-shaped hill. The town was long a pawn in the mediæval power struggle between Siena and Florence, cul-

*T*his splendid bastion was added to Colle di Val d'Elsa's mediæval fortifications in the 16th century.

minating in a brutal Florentine victory in 1269 (*see* HISTORY, page 62).

The ramparts date from the 12th century, but the formidable main gate and bastions of **Porta Nuova** are an early 16th-century addition attributed to Giuliano da Sangallo, architect of the Medici villa at Poggio a Caiano. Beyond the gate,

the road leads up to the elegant Renaissance **Palazzo Campana** designed by Baccio d'Agnolo, more Roman than Tuscan in its sunny serenity. Its archway leads across a bridge to what is the heart of the old town. The picturesque **Via del Castello** is lined with mediæval tower-houses and palazzi of the 15th and 16th centuries. **Palazzo Pretorio** houses a small **archaeological museum** of Etruscan finds from nearby Monteriggioni. At the end of the street is the 13th-century tower-house, birthplace of architect Arnolfo da Cambio (c.1240-1302), who went off to build Florence's Palazzo Vecchio and cathedral.

KEEPING YOUR HEAD HIGH

Provenzano Salvani, victorious Ghibelline commander at Siena's famous victory over Florence at Montaperti in 1260 was worried by the 'return bout' looming nine years later at Colle di Val d'Elsa. Camped below the walls of the Florentine-held town, he massed an army of 1400 cavalry and 8000 infantry – a huge force for the times. In a pep talk to the troops, he said the Devil had assured him in a dream that at the end of the battle, 'Your head will be the highest on the battlefield.' He was right. Florentine forces routed the Sienese in a surprise attack and paraded Provenzano Salvani's severed head around the battlefield.

Life with the Etruscans

The little knowledge we have of the Etruscans, from the testimony of their art, shows they were clearly a lot more fun than the earnest empire-building Romans. Some historians have interpreted as prudish jealousy the fact that, apart from disparaging remarks about their loose living, the Romans had remarkably little to tell us about them.

From the meagre archaeological evidence, we know that at the pinnacle of society during the Etruscan heyday of the 7th and 6th centuries BC was a king who seems to have functioned as high priest. The symbol of power, the *fasces* bundle of rods, was taken over by the Romans for their magistrates and later by Mussolini for his Fascists. The priesthood was the exclusive preserve of a landed aristocracy otherwise given over to leisure rather than anything resembling work. The coastal merchant classes provided what little muscle was needed, in the form of piracy to boost their trade figures. They clearly made a reputation at this, as Greek mythology relates that the god Dinoysos was kidnapped by Etruscan pirates. The underclass provided the artists, craftsmen and peasantry, certainly submissive but not oppressed serfs or slaves.

The Language
With no signs of literature, whether poetry, drama or political speeches, only religious inscriptions on the tombs and pottery give any guidance to the Etruscans' language. From about the 7th century BC, the Etruscans had adopted

Outside the museums and a few overgrown tombs, only a few stones like these ancient fortifications at Volterra testify to the presence of the Etruscans in the region to which they gave their name.

The frescoes in Etruscan tombs carried into the after life the pastimes of the living. Here, the elegance of the prancing horses matches anything you might see at the Spanish riding School in Vienna.

This funeral urn combines the Greek theme of a winged Pegasus with a little monster at the base that is characteristic of Oriental mythology

the Greek alphabet of their trading partners in southern Italy.

The Etruscan language was written almost always from right to left, like Hebrew and Arabic (but in a few cases alternating with lines written from left to right in a system known as *boustrophedon*, like the furrows ploughed by oxen turning in their field). It has no recognizable links to the Indo-European languages or any other known linguistic family.

The writings offer insights into liturgy and the names of gods, but nothing about social or political organization. Scholars suggest that one modern vestige of the Etruscan language is the Tuscan H for C that you will hear in words like *casa* (house).

215

Good Living

In the absence of abundant literary sources, the works of art found in the tombs (sculpture, frescoes, sarcophagi and ceramics) speak with considerable eloquence of the Etruscans' taste for the good things of life. They traded their iron and copper for luxury goods from Greece and the Orient (jewellery, gold, silver, ivory, ornaments and perfume). They enjoyed rich crops of grain and did not wait for the Greeks to teach them the nourishing value of olives or the joys of the grape. It was the Etruscans, before the Romans, who deserve our everlasting gratitude for showing those talented fellows from Gaul how to make wine.

Etruscan men and women clearly enjoyed an easygoing intimate relationship. Greeks and Romans scarcely, if ever, depicted in their art such moments of tenderness and affection as this.

Though their houses seemed to be simple structures of reed or wood, their artistic creations were a rich cosmopolitan mixture of eastern Mediterranean and Oriental styles. For their funereal urns, they developed a distinctive form of black *bucchero* pottery. They were especially skilful in working bronze. Their goldsmiths were esteemed throughout the ancient world for the superb delicacy of their art, intricately granulated for fine detail in brooches, ear-rings and necklaces, using the surplus for dentistry.

In those deadly serious days of world conquest, the Romans were scornful of the Etruscans' propensity for private and public pleasure. Versatile in their use of the wheel, they introduced the chariot to Italy, but, characteristically, for racing at their hippodromes rather than for use in battle. They enjoyed banquets, gambling, dancing, and music to accompany every pursuit, whether boxing, baking bread or even whipping a slave. They were held to be inordinately sensual, making hetero- and homosexual love in public.

The Place of Women

What bothered the macho Greeks and Romans most was the prominent status accorded to Etruscan women. Unlike their early Roman counterparts, Etruscan women might be property owners. At dinner, they actually reclined beside their men. Greek historian Theopompus snorted: 'They dine not just with their husbands, but with any man present; and they toast to anyone they want to.'

A tomb engraving shows a man and a woman wrestling and the man isn't winning. Another depicts a woman telling her male opponent in a table game: 'I'm going to beat you.' He replies: 'I believe you are.' Such equality was unheard of in the ancient world.

Italian women had to wait till the 20th century to regain even a few of the privileges accorded Etruscan women, such as this one, reclining majestically on her sarcophagus.

The tenderness of husband and wife is a frequent theme of Etruscan sculpture, as is the seated mother and child, perhaps inspired by the Egyptian goddess Isis and precursor of the Christian Madonna rarely to be found in Roman art.

Religion

The Etruscans were fatalists, accepting their destinies as foretold by *haruspices*, soothsayers who read the future in the livers of sheep, or by interpreters of chance occurrences of lightning. The liver, like the heavens, was divided into 16 regions, each ruled by a separate deity. (At the time of Julius Caesar's assassination, the importance attached to the many supernatural phenomena noted and interpreted by soothsayers is said to be of Etruscan origin.)

To beseech the intervention of a particular god for a specific health disorder, the Etruscans brought to their shrines *ex voto* miniature terracotta arms, legs and livers (like the French to this day, they attributed many of their problems to a crisis of the liver). Model genitals, breasts and uteri were also deposited to enhance fertility or perhaps fend off venereal disease.

Prolonged prosperity and easy living were not without anguish. By the 5th century BC their religion turned away from its themes of light and celestial serenity to adopt sombre Greek concepts of a diabolical underworld that became more prevalent the more they went into political decline. Fatalistically, they saw the Roman conquest as inevitable. Priests interpreted unusual swarms of insects as signs that it was the 'last Etruscan century'. It was the last century BC.

Mellow Town in a Russet Glow with More Good Wine in the Southern Hills

Many travellers with a lifelong attachment to Tuscany make a happy marriage of reason with Florence, but for a passionate love affair they turn to Siena. Warm colour and resilient forms triumph over cool and orderly line. Feeling always runs high in the home of the frenzied *Palio* horserace. To the south, the hills abandon the greenery of Chianti to a bewitching, almost lunar landscape, often best defined in colour by the 'burnt sienna' of the painter's palette.

Much more than Florence, Siena is a town to hang out in. Ideally, to get the measure of it, it is worth devoting three, four or even more days, not just to seeing its sights, but to drinking in its atmosphere, sitting around its secluded courtyards and piazzas, and whiling away an hour or two in a terraced restaurant overlooking the hills and valleys roundabout.

Besides the itineraries for Siena itself, both inside the town and a couple of day-trips, we propose two longer programmes for southern Tuscany. The first can also be tackled on day-trips from Siena itself. The other, further south, is more comfortably managed from a hotel in one of the many resorts *en route*.

*T*he fantino *(jockey) and his page in Renaissance costume savour a moment of quiet before the Siena* Palio *horse-race begins. The horse is just hoping he will come out of it in one piece.*

1. Siena:
(a) From Campo to Duomo:
- take in the **Palazzo Pubblico**, with its **museum** overlooking the piazza where the *Palio* is staged;
- visit the noble **palazzi** along **Via di Città**;
- end at the great Gothic **Duomo** with **baptistery** and **cathedral museum**.
(b) Pinacoteca:
- superb **art museum** of greatest Sienese painters.
(c) Away from the Campo:
- explore town's neighbourhoods;

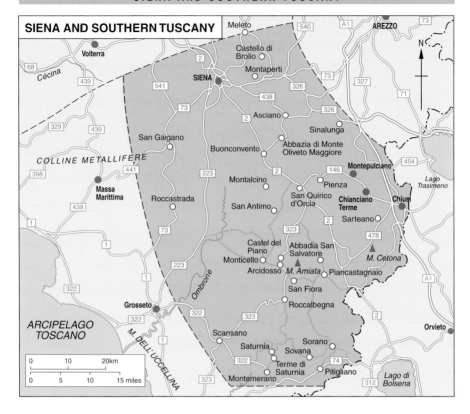

SIENA AND SOUTHERN TUSCANY

- **Palazzo Piccolomini**;
- churches **Santa Maria dei Servi**, **Sant'Agostino**, **San Niccolò al Carmine**, and sanctuary-home of **St Catherine of Siena**, the church of **San Domenico**.

(d) Day-trips:
- **Monteriggioni**, fairytale fortified town;
- **Abbadia Isola**, nearby abbey-church;
- **San Galgano**, outstanding Cistercian monastery.

2. South to Montepulciano – over the clay hills south of Siena (*Crete Sienese*) via:
- **Asciano**, mediæval ramparts around Romanesque church;
- **Monte Oliveto Maggiore**, Benedictine abbey;
- **Montalcino**, charming wine town and

nearby **Sant' Antimo**, Romanesque abbey-church;
- **Pienza**, jewel of Renaissance town-planning;
- **Montepulciano**, elegant wine town: **San Biagio** church, Antonio da Sangallo's Renaissance masterpiece;
- **Chianciano Terme**, health spa.

3. Around Monte Amiata – picturesque extinct volcano amid dense forests:
- **Abbadia San Salvatore**, mountainside resort, mediæval town with monastery;
- **Arcidosso** holiday resort;
- **Roccalbegna**, castle ruin on Monte Labbro;
- **Saturnia**, chic health spa;
- **Sovana**, tiny village with castle and cathedral;

220

- **Pitigliano**, mediæval houses on spectacular rocky foundation, Etruscan ramparts.

Siena

A city of rich russet browns and ochres, Siena is as bewitchingly feminine as greystone Florence is imposing in its masculinity. Contrasts with its old rival to the north are striking and inevitable. Whereas the nucleus of Florence was built to a strict Roman city plan, Siena has all the haphazard organic forms of the Tuscan hilltown, in this case embracing the forked ridge of not one but three hilltops.

Similarly, while Florentine art developed its formidable intellectual and emotional power, the tone of Sienese painting – Simone Martini, the Lorenzettis, even the later Mannerist Domenico Beccafumi and Sodoma – remained gentle and delicate, bathed in the hazy light and colour of its surrounding countryside.

PARK AND WALK

With its narrow, often steeply sloping streets, Siena quite deliberately and quite sensibly makes it illegal to take your car into the city centre, but good alternative parking is provided, notably on the north-west periphery around the municipal stadium (*Stadio Comunale*). On the south-east corner of town, at *Due Ponti* and *Coroncina*, parking is free with frequent mini-bus shuttles into the city centre. If you are staying in the *centro storico*, you may be allowed to drive in once with your bags, but thereafter ask your hotel how to get a permit from the police (*Vigili Urbani*) if you need to come in again.

Seemingly clustered one on top of the other, the houses of Siena climb the three hills that meet at the Campo. This is not a town for driving through, just walking – slowly.

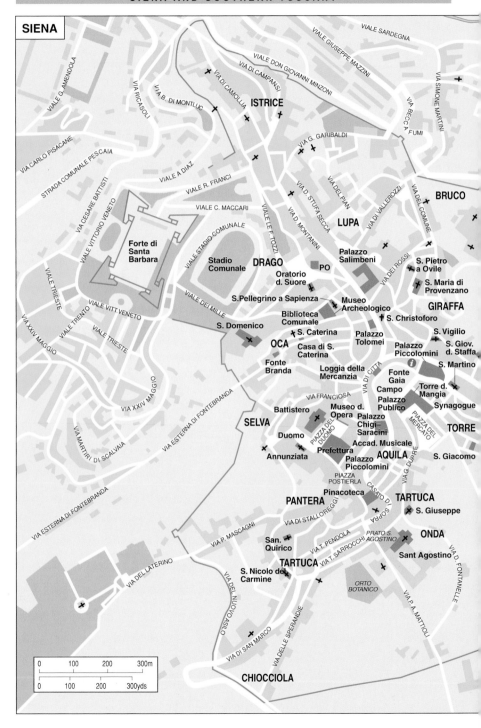

That is not to say that the town lacks vigour. No longer directed at conquering foreign markets, it expresses itself in intense neighbourhood rivalries that achieve their paroxysm in the summer *Palio* tournament.

From Campo to Duomo

Siena's virtual exit from Italian political life after being incorporated by the Medici dukes into the duchy of Tuscany in 1559 was a blessing for the integrity of its *centro storico*. Being a backwater preserved from destruction the Gothic and Renaissance monuments between the civic centre of the Piazza del Campo and the chief religious focus of the Duomo. Few city walks in Italy are so unencumbered by jarring modernism.

Piazza del Campo

A deficiency of the English language makes us call this place a 'square' when in fact there is not a right angle to be seen. Never designed on any town-planner's drawing-board, the Campo embraces the hill-and-valley landscape in the form of a wonderful swooping scallop shell. It lies at the crux of Siena's Y-shaped topography, at the junction of three hills.

The Campo was the site of the ancient Roman forum and has ever since been the amphitheatre of the city's historical, social and political events, with the towering Palazzo Pubblico as its backdrop. It is here that the people rallied and rioted, followed their leaders or hanged them, celebrated victories, mourned catastrophes, and stage to this day the grandest pageant of them all, the *Palio* horse-race.

It was politics that determined the form of the piazza as it was laid out in the 14th century. You will notice that the herringbone pattern of its redbrick paving is

For his Fonte Gaia (this is a 19th-century replica), sculptor Jacopo della Quercia had a hard time getting city elders to pay up. They promised 2,000 florins but for three years paid only 120. It took them another seven years to cough up the rest and get their fountain.

divided by rows of white stone into nine segments. This was where the political forces lined up for the nine city elders ruling the town (*see* HISTORY, page 62).

At the rear of the Campo, the rectangular white marble fountain, **Fonte Gaia**, was designed in 1409 by sculptor Jacopo della Quercia. The originals of his carved reliefs have been moved upstairs to the museum in the Palazzo Pubblico, replaced here by 19th-century replicas of the biblical scenes and allegories of Christian virtues.

The Palio

Siena's world-famous horse-race, known by its full name as the *Corsa del Palio,* is held on the Campo every 2 July and 16 August, both invariably very hot days. The first recorded race was back in 1147, but it took its present form in Renaissance costume in the 15th century.

A great tourist attraction but by no means staged *for* the tourists, the Palio is a hotly contested local affair that would be a huge crowd event even if a single tourist did not turn up. The excitement derives from the centuries-old, all-year-round rivalries among the city's 17 neighbourhoods.

Each neighbourhood or *contrada* has its own headquarters, oratory chapel and museum displaying past glories. The *contrada* derives its name from the emblem and flag: *Aquila* (Eagle), *Chiocciola* (Snail), *Onda* (Sea-wave), *Pantera* (Panther), *Selva* (Forest), *Tartuca* (Tortoise), *Civetta* (Owl), *Leocorno* (Unicorn), *Valdimontone* (Mountain Goat), *Nicchio*

(Scallop Shell), *Torre* (Tower), *Bruco* (Caterpillar), *Drago* (Dragon), *Giraffa* (Giraffe), *Istrice* (Porcupine), *Lupa* (She-Wolf) and *Oca* (Goose).

For the race, only ten of the 17 *contrade* can compete, chosen each year by a complex rotating system. Race-day is preceded by weeks of feasts and rehearsals. Informal games are played in the streets. People parade through the neighbourhoods, beating drums and raucously ridiculing their rivals. Traditionally, *Istrice* and *Lupa* cannot stand each other, *Tartuca* loathes *Chiocciola* and *Oca* despises *Torre*, all with an intense hatred born often of long-forgotten insults.

Although the 2 July race commemorates the Feast of the Visitation (when

Though only ten of the 17 neighbourhoods compete in the race, they all participate in the Sbandierata parade of banners. These standard-bearers represent Chiocciola *(Snail) from the city's south-west corner.*

Mary visited her cousin Elizabeth, pregnant with John the Baptist) and 16 August the day after the Assumption (when Mary rose to heaven), the elaborate ritual is more pagan than Christian. Many historians think the Palio derives its true origins from the Etruscans. The *contrada* banquets on the eve of the race would have some of the solemnity of the Last Supper, if it were not for the amount of wine drunk and the fact that horse (*barbero*) and jockey (*fantino*) occupy the place of honour.

The horse is groomed in his stable with a lamp-lit effigy of the neighbourhood patron saint hanging over his feed-box. On the afternoon of the race,

Given the frenzy of the Palio's neighbourhood rivalry, it's hard enough at the best of times to keep your cool. Imagine what it must be like under this solid steel armourplating in the middle of August.

the horse and his jockey are led to the *contrada* church to be blessed by the priest, again watched over by the local patron saint.

Festivities begin with a parade in Renaissance costume around the Campo by representatives of all the neighbourhoods, followed by a spectacular flag-throwing display (*Sbandierata*) which boggles the mind of the nimblest British drum-major or American majorette. Then, the ten horses and jockeys, riding bareback in modern livery with the *contrada* colours, emerge from the inner courtyard of the Palazzo Pubblico.

The track is strewn with gravel but otherwise is as treacherous as a steeple chase, with horses frequently hurtling into the mattress-cushioned walls. The winning horse is the first past the post after three laps – with or without its jockey.

Despite all the priests and patron saints, the Palio race is as holy as a Las Vegas casino. The only piece of fair play is the choice of horses, done by drawing lots three days before the race.

Then, since there can only be one winner, neighbourhood leaders make pre-race alliances to fix the outcome. Even if *Tartuca* cannot win, it will do all it can to stop *Chiocciola*, and so on. Practically anything goes, you can whip your opponents' jockey, block his horse to let another through, accept all bribes. Jockeys often make secret deals, against the interests of their own neighbourhood, if the money is good enough. In the days preceding the race, teenagers are assigned to sleep in the same room as the jockey to make sure he does not receive any night-time visitors bringing a payoff. There is nearly always a fix, and the gamblers are just betting on what the fix is and whether it will work.

Race-day tension is such that the most fanatic supporters cannot even bear to watch and prefer to stay away from the Campo, praying in the neighbourhood church. People may intermarry from different neighbourhoods, but as race-day approaches, the wife

After the parade of horses and standard-bearers, there is a long wait before the Palio race gets underway. The jockey who draws the right to signal the start may opt for a tactical delay of several hours.

goes back to live with her parents until the Palio is over. Appetites for food and sex noticeably diminish before the race and increase afterwards, at least in the neighbourhoods of the winners and their allies. Post-Palio suicides and murders are not infrequent, but usually hushed up.

Some people are never happy, however. The owner of a winning horse in a horrendously close finish welcomed the jockey by slapping him in the face. 'Why'd you do that?' said the jockey. 'I won!'

'What about the fright you gave me?' replied the owner, 'Who's going to pay me for that?'

Palazzo Pubblico

The headquarters of communal government (city hall) is a classical piece of Tuscan Gothic civic architecture, softened by Siena's natural taste for the decorative. Built 1297-1310, it has all the accoutrements of a fortress – battlements, turrets and guards' lookout on the belltower – but its façade cannot resist curving to fit the contours of the Campo. Neither the airy arcade nor the elegant triple-mullioned windows for the council chambers would have resisted the first whiff of gunpowder. (The mullioned windows became a building specification for all edifices on the Campo.) To appreciate the painterly impact of that warm, russet, brick façade, look at it over a late-afternoon coffee from the Campo's shady side (next to the tourist office).

For all its lofty dignity, this Palazzo Pubblico has none of the macho pretensions associated with Florence's aggressive grey ashlar Palazzo Vecchio. Even the **Torre del Mangia**, a tower 102m (334ft) high topped by a white limestone belfry, is straight out of a fairytale castle (Disney people have borrowed the plans). There are 503 steps to the observation deck, but the view over Siena to nearby orchards, the Tuscan hills and vineyards of Chianti, makes it all worthwhile. (*Mangia* is the abbreviated nickname of the first bellringer, *Mangiaguadagni*, literally 'Money-Glutton').

In the late afternoon sun, the grace and colour of Siena's Palazzo Pubblico and soaring Mangia tower contrast sharply with the cool grey Palazzo Vecchio in Florence. The difference between the two towns is right there.

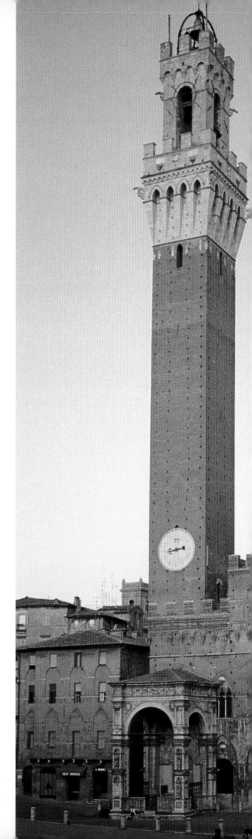

The chapel *(Capella di Piazza)* at the foot of the tower was built to commemorate deliverance from the Black Plague of 1348. Originally just a square canopy of four pillars with a flat roof, it acquired its Renaissance arcade later. For some, this white marble projection breaks the harmony of the redbrick piazza, but others like the contrasting platform it provides for the tower. Before entering the palazzo, peek into its little **inner courtyard** (*Cortile del Podestà*) for a striking view up at the Torre del Mangia from behind.

Museo Civico

Over the ground floor's modern town hall offices, the upper chambers, frescoed by the city's foremost artists, have been transformed into a magnificent municipal museum. The principal art treasures are to be found in four council chambers:

Sala di Balia: frescoes (1407) by Spinello Aretino illustrate events in the life of Sienese Pope Alexander III (*see* HISTORY, page 61), the most striking being the *Venetian Fleet Defeats Emperor Frederick Barbarossa*.

Sala del Concistorio: ceiling frescoes (1535) by Domenico Beccafumi in high Mannerist style celebrate the ancient republican virtues, most notably *Patriotism*, *Justice* and *Concord* in the large central octagonal and circular panels.

Sala del Mappamondo: only a circular outline remains of the chamber's map of the Sienese state, painted here by Ambrogio Lorenzetti to trace the city's international banking interests. Still very much visible is **Simone Martini's Madonna Enthroned** (*Maestà*, 1315), a stately Madonna enthroned beneath a canopy with her celestial court. On the opposite wall is the grand but controversial fresco, also attributed to Simone

Martini, of **Guidoriccio da Fogliano**, Siena's heroic *condottiere* riding to victory at Montemassi. In the nicely detailed Tuscan landscape, notice the little Chianti vineyard in the military encampment.

TRANSALANTIC TROUBLE-MAKERS

To understand the scandal, you must appreciate that the great 14th-century painter Simone Martini, master of delicate colour and supple line, is as important to Siena as Michelangelo is to Florence. Nonetheless, according to claims published in the authoritative *Burlington Magazine* in 1986, two American scholars, Gordon Moran and Michael Mallory, dared to discover anachronisms and other discrepancies in the Palazzo Pubblico's exquisite *Guidoriccio da Fogliano* fresco. These suggested not only was the fresco, apparently commissioned in 1330, *not* by Simone Martini but that it could not have been painted in the 14th century. Zigzagging ramparts in the fortress behind the *condottiere*, they said, were first designed – to repel canon-fire – in the 15th century. Another fresco discovered partly *beneath* this one (depicting the south Tuscan town of Arcidosso) was, they argued, painted *after* the 1330 commission attributed to Simone Martini.

Moran and Mallory went as far as to claim, since no mention of the fresco had been found until 1785, that the painting was a clever 18th-century *forgery*. They had overstepped the mark. Italian art experts found a mention of the fresco in 1525 and promptly dismissed all the American arguments as preposterous. The mayor of Siena accused Gordon Moran of being a CIA agent. The Americans counter-attacked by accusing Siena art-scholar Professor Piero Torriti of effacing incriminating evidence during a restoration. It is still a very nice picture.

Sala della Pace (Hall of Peace) was the council chamber of the Nine Patricians who ruled mediæval Siena. The full force of the town's civic pride strikes home in **Ambrogio Lorenzetti's frescoes** (1339) that cover three walls of the room. One fresco, badly damaged, is devoted to an allegory of *Bad Government*, a gloomy portrait of *Tyranny*, the horned monster surrounded by *Greed*, *Pride* and *Vainglory*, bat-winged *Fraud* and boar-headed *Fury*. The other two walls are given over to Siena's own enlightened *Good Government*. The work depicting the *Effects of Good Government* (on the entrance wall) is full of fascinating detail of mediæval town life: roof-builders, shoe shop, school, outdoor tavern, ladies dancing in the street, while beyond the city-walls, hunters ride out to the surrounding countryside.

For another fine view of the city, take the stairs to the second floor **Loggia** where you can also see the battered remnants of Jacopo della Quercia's 15th-century carvings for the Fonte Gaia city fountain down in the Piazza del Campo.

Loggia della Mercanzia

Outside the centre exit from the Piazza del Campo, this arcaded loggia stands at the intersection, *Croce del Travaglio* ('Labour Crossroads'), of the mediæval town's three main streets: Via Banchi di Sopra, Via Banchi di Sotto and Via di Città. It was the meeting place of a commercial tribunal so widely respected for its impartiality that foreign companies brought their disputes here for arbitration, a kind of precursor of today's international court at The Hague.

In the niches of the Renaissance arcade, the five 15th-century statues are dull portrayals of Christian saints. More interesting, beneath the portico, are the two marble benches sculpted with figures of Roman antiquity and Christian allegory.

Via di Città

With the Campo behind you, turn left on this street of palazzi to discover the grandeur of the town's mediæval merchant aristocracy. Peep in at whatever courtyard is left open to the public gaze and you will sense what good living was really like for Europe's greatest bankers and financiers in the 14th and 15th centuries.

On the left side of the street (N°89), the redbrick 14th-century Gothic **Palazzo Chigi-Saracini** fortress-palace has a lovely concave curving façade. The battlements are pure ornament, never serving in any battle, though the tower did provide a lookout to report on the progress of the town's great victory over Florence in the

THE CHIGI FAMILY

The grand palazzi of Siena serve to remind us that the Medici were far from being Tuscany's only important banking family. In the 15th century, despite Cosimo de'Medici's subsequent reputation, Agostini Chigi was the most powerful banker in Italy, creditor to the kings of Europe and Pope Julius II, with branches in Antwerp, Lyon, London, Constantinople, Alexandria and Cairo. He was a great patron of the arts, notably sponsoring Raphael and Giulio Romano.

The Chigi-Saracini provided a heroine in Dante's *Purgatory* – Sapia, who loved to make fun of her Sienese compatriots for their frivolous vanity (celebrated by a bas-relief carving in the palazzo's lobby). The family also boasted two popes: Julius III (1550-55) and Alexander VII (1655-67). Alexander (originally Fabio Chigi) is best remembered for having Bernini build the colonnade for St Peter's in Rome; and also the Chigi Chapel in Siena Cathedral.

eastern hills at Montaperti in 1260. Behind the triple-mullioned windows is the Music Academy founded in 1932 by the last scion of the great Chigi family, Count Guido Chigi-Saracini. In the summer, the palazzo stages chamber music concerts and exhibitions of the family's art collection, which includes two of the small number of works by Sassetta, a superb *Epiphany* and *St Martin.*

The Renaissance **Palazzo Piccolomini delle Papesse** (N°128) is more soberly Florentine in style, like Michelozzo's palace for the Medici, but lightened by ornate Gothic windows in the upper storeys. Seat of the Banca d'Italia now, it was built in 1460 by Caterina Piccolomini, sister of Pope Pius II. The bantering nickname (*Papesse*: 'female popes') is derived from Pius II's generosity to the ladies of his Piccolomini family (*see* Pious Pius, page 247).

Piazza di Postierla

At the end of Via di Città, the piazza has two interesting monuments: the mediæval **Forteguerre**, a tower-house similar to those of San Gimignano; and a 15th-century **marble column** topped by the town's emblem of a legendary she-wolf suckling two little boys who became the founding fathers of the city, Aschius and Senius. To assert an ancient link between Siena and Rome, the emblem echoes the ancient imperial capital's foundation-legend, Siena's boys being the sons of Romulus, and raised in the same way as their father. Notice, too, the lovely wrought-iron standard-bearing post.

Palazzo Capitano del Popolo

Turn right on the Via del Capitano past the formidable 13th-century Gothic residence of the people's representative against the all-powerful merchant aristocracy. It was later attributed to the town's military commander, but ended up in the hands of the Piccolomini (and today the Monte dei Paschi bank). Take a look inside the courtyard with its sculpture of the people's lion at the foot of a handsome staircase.

Piazza del Duomo

As you come into the cathedral square, on your right is the police prefecture, housed in a late 16th-century palazzo, and on your left, the Santa Maria della Scala Hospital. (Plans are afoot to convert its buildings into the city's principal cultural centre, including the transfer of the Pinacoteca Nazionale.) Beyond it is the oratory-chapel of Santa Caterina della Notte, where the amazing St Catherine of Siena came to pray after late-night shifts looking after victims of the bubonic plague (visits by request at the archbishop's office).

Duomo: the Exterior

Construction on this earliest of the great Tuscan Gothic cathedrals was begun in the 13th century by monks commissioned from the Abbey of San Galgano (*see* page 241). By 1284, Giovanni Pisano was working on the façade, while his father Nicola was busy inside the Duomo carving its great marble pulpit.

The cathedral is an eloquent monument to Siena's overweening expansionist

Siena Cathedral is the most ambitious project undertaken by Giovanni Pisano. It was a rare opportunity to combine his skills of sculptor and architect.

ambitions and its inexorable decline. It had been decided in 1317 to extend the choir out over the slope at the end of the church with an apse standing above what is now the baptistery. But this was not enough. Twenty years later, the city fathers decided to branch out with a colossal transept that was to be a whole new cathedral, the Duomo Nuovo. Unfortunately, this had to be abandoned after the Black Plague of 1348, which wiped out 65,000 inhabitants of Siena (80% of the population) and a rebellion against the Council of Nine in city hall. The shell of the Duomo Nuovo, adjacent to the south (right) side of the Duomo proper, now serves as a museum for the cathedral's more vulnerable art treasures.

Flanked by two columns bearing the town's **she-wolf emblem**, the raised platform presents the cathedral like a sumptuous banquet. Some find the polychrome **façade** ostentatious, but this may be chiefly due to the garish Venetian mosaics added to upper gables in 1877. The black-and-white marble bands of the façade are the heraldic colours of the municipality that wanted to immortalize its part in commissioning the church. Architectural buffs reared on French and German cathedrals find that the general horizontal impact of these stripes clashes with their notion of soaring Gothic. Siena's champions argue, however, that the town is more eager to please the eye than elevate the spirit. The effect here is monumental without being too overwhelming. The façade's essential nobility is enhanced by **Giovanni Pisano's statues** of prophets, philosophers and patriarchs over his three intricately carved portals (originals in the cathedral museum). Pisano's work here preceded Giotto's paintings in expressing intense emotions in human forms.

Notice the **campanile** rising from the transept with each tier boldly increasing its number of windows from one to six. At the foot of the tower, Donatello's *Madonna and Child* bas-relief presents a remarkably tough-looking mother (again, original in cathedral museum).

Duomo: the Interior

The interior continues the municipality's proud motif of black-and-white bands of marble with dramatic effect. **Inlaid marble paving** covers the floor with 56 pictures of biblical and allegorical themes created over two centuries (1370-1550) by some 40 artists, chief among them

234

Domenico Beccafumi, Pinturicchio and Domenico di Bartolo.

Off the left aisle is the early 16th-century **Piccolomini Library**, vividly decorated by **Pinturicchio's frescoes** of the energetic life of Enea Silvio de'Piccolomini, poet, diplomat, scholar and ultimately pope, as Pius II (*see* PIOUS PIUS, page 247). The frescoes were commissioned in 1495, some 30 years after the pope's death, by his nephew, Cardinal Francesco Piccolomini. He himself became pope, Pius III, but lasted only ten days.

In the north (left) transept is **Nicola Pisano's pulpit** (1268), a magnificent octagonal structure carved with help from son Giovanni and Arnolfo di Cambio. Among the fantastic detail of the New Testament scenes, notice the damned being eaten alive in the *Last Judgment*. Over in the south (right) transept, is a splendid but disturbing Baroque monument, **Bernini's Chigi Chapel**, commissioned in 1659 by Pope Alexander VII, a Chigi by birth. Flanking the entrance, the Roman master's statues of an ecstatic *St Jerome* and sensual *Mary Magdalen* both seem tinged with madness. Bernini also designed the cathedral's monumental organ.

The Baptistery

Saving till last the cathedral museum (*Museo dell'Opera del Duomo*), pass through the Duomo Nuovo doorway and down the stairs running alongside the

It is in the interior that the cathedral achieves its vertical effect, but even here there is little attempt to exploit the full potential of Gothic vaulting in the northern European manner.

cathedral choir. At this lower level, due to the sloping terrain, the baptistery was conceived almost as a crypt. Although unfinished by Domenico di Agostino in 1355, most noticeable in the space left for a huge rose window, its façade is considered a more purely conceived piece of Gothic architecture than that of the Cathedral itself. Inside is a noble 15th-century **baptismal font** designed by Jacopo della Quercia. It is topped by his statue of John the Baptist, while Lorenzo Ghiberti and Donatello contributed some of the bronze reliefs and statues.

Cathedral Museum

Quite apart from the masterpieces of sculpture and painting in its collection, the *Museo dell'Opera del Duomo* is well worth a visit to get an idea of what the huge new cathedral would have looked like if its entire structure had been completed according to the original plans. Beyond the façade and marble arcades of the nave, which now embrace the Piazza Jacopo della Quercia, the museum occupies what would have been the new church's south aisle. On the ground floor, it displays the originals of **Giovanni Pisano's statues** for the Duomo façade, with strangely distorted poses because they were meant to be seen from below. Also here are a *Madonna and Child* bas-relief by Jacopo della Quercia and Donatello's campanile tondo. Upstairs, **Duccio di Buoninsegna's *Madonna Enthroned*** (*Maestà*, 1308) is a gigantic painting from the cathedral's high altar, its two sides (originally back to back) depicting the *Madonna and Child* and the *Story of the Passion*. Other works on upper floors include Pietro Lorenzetti's *Birth of the Madonna* and a newly restored wooden *Crucifixion* by Giovanni Pisano.

Pinacoteca Nazionale

The great museum of Sienese painting housed in the Palazzo Buonsignore (Via San Pietro 29) south of Via di Città offers an 'itinerary' all to itself. Stroll an hour or two through the enchanted Sienese landscape of a gentler light, a richer colour, a more tender ambience than can be seen in the dominant Florentine school of Tuscan painting. In contrast, the palazzo itself is a sober late Gothic edifice built at the end of the 14th century, offering a cool tranquillity around the hexagonal well of its arcaded courtyard.

The more or less chronological arrangement of the paintings will be conserved if and when the collections are transferred to a new site on the Piazza del Duomo (*see* page 232). Beginning on the palace's second floor, roughly in order of their current exhibition, these are the highlights:

Guido da Siena, 13th-century, one of the oldest paintings on canvas, sets Siena's decorative tone with scenes from the life of Jesus, *Transfiguration* (revealing his divinity to the disciples), *Entry into Jerusalem* and *Resurrection of Lazarus*;

Duccio di Buoninsegna, *Madonna of the Franciscans* (1290), fluid line with gracefully posed right hand above three adoring monks;

Bartolo di Fredi, *Adoration of the Magi* (1380) admirable for its bold, warm colour;

Simone Martini, *St Agostino Novello* (1324) polyptych, solemn central figure of Sienese monk contrasts with almost humorous realism of saint's four miracles in side-panels; and exquisite fragment of *Madonna and Child* recently rescued from beneath a 16th-century painting;

Pietro Lorenzetti, *Crucifixion with Madonna, St John and Mary Magdalen* (1326), tragedy poignantly understated, and *Madonna with Child* (1329),

Carmelite altar-painting, pained anticipation of future suffering;

Ambrogio Lorenzetti, *Annunciation* (1344) portrays Mary's intense commitment to her destiny; and charmingly maternal *Madonna and Child* (1335) with Jesus's arm around mother's neck;

Taddeo di Bartolo, *Crucifixion* (1420), translucent treatment of Jesus's body;

Giovanni di Paolo, *Last Judgment: Heaven and Hell* (1460) imposes Sienese preference for ceremonial fantasy over contemporary Renaissance realism;

Sassetta, *Pala dell'Arte della Lana* (polyptych for wool-merchants' guild altar-painting, 1426) skilfully combines Siena's decorative International Gothic with Florentine influence in architectural elements and perspective of *Last Supper*; fine landscape detail in *St Anthony Beaten by Devils*;

Francesco di Giorgio Martini, almost languid *Madonna and Child* (1472) beside angel with heavy-lidded eyes; and *Birth of Jesus*, craggy landscape and antique Roman columns in keeping with 15th-century classicism;

Mannerists: Domenico Beccafumi, *Trinity* triptych (1513), characteristically unreal, even surreal light for God the Father holding up crucified Jesus; similarly, in *St Catherine Receiving Stigmata* (1515), flanked by classical High Renaissance figures of Benedict and Jerome, saint is bathed in dazzling light of her miracle; even more weird, *Birth of Mary* (1540), theatrically posed female figures become splashes of violent colour;

Sodoma, *Christ on the Column* fresco (1511), impressive sculptural torso portrays powerful stoical martyr; *Deposition from Cross* (1510), virtuoso arrangement around Jesus of figures in miraculously acrobatic balance.

The small collection of non-Sienese art includes an **Albrecht Dürer**, *St Jerome*; and two Venetians: **Lorenzo Lotto**, *Birth of Jesus*, and **Paris Bordone**, *Annunciation*.

Away from the Campo

The city spreads out from the Campo along the three ridges of its unique hilltop formation, each with a street giving its name not to a quarter, but to a 'third' (*terza*): **San Martino**, east, to the church of Santa Maria dei Servi; **Città**, west, including the central area between the Campo and the Duomo (*see above*, page 223); and **Camollia**, north, including the neighbourhood of St Catherine.

San Martino District

East of the Palazzo Pubblico, Via Rinaldini leads out of the Campo to the **Palazzo Piccolomini**, an imposing Florentine-style Renaissance building designed by Bernardo Rossellino (Via Banchi di Sotto 52). As part of its precious collection of ancient state archives, the delightful **Museo delle Tavolette Dipinti** (Museum of Painted Miniatures) exhibits pictures to embellish the covers of the municipality's account-books (*biccherne*), by some of the town's greatest painters: Ambrogio Lorenzetti, Taddeo di Bartolo, Francesco di Giorgio Martino and Domenico Beccafumi.

At the south-east corner of San Martino district, on Piazza Alessandro Manzoni, is the Romanesque-Gothic church of **Santa Maria dei Servi**, left with an unadorned brickwork façade and campanile. It is worth a visit for its airy interior with finely sculpted pillar-capitals and, in the second chapel in the right aisle, **Coppo di Marcovaldo's** *Madonna del Bordone* (1261). It was painted in the first year of his Sienese captivity after fighting on the losing Florentine side in the battle of Montaperti.

On the way back towards the Campo, just off the Via di Salicotto, is the 18th-century neoclassical **synagogue**, centre of Siena's old ghetto that clustered around what is now a **food-market** on the Piazza del Mercato.

Città District

From the Pinacoteca Nazionale, Via San Pietro leads south towards the 13th-century church of **Sant'Agostino**. The terrace offers a fine view across the city and surrounding orchards. The church interior (currently under restoration) boasts a Perugino *Crucifixion* and works by Ambrogio Lorenzetti, Sodoma and Francesco di Giorgio Martini.

At Prato di Sant'Agostino 4, the **Accademia dei Fisiocritici**, a natural science academy founded in 1691, is now a museum of birds, reptiles and other Tuscan

---

PRAYING FOR VICTORY

Dotted all over Siena are the oratory chapels where *Palio* contestants and supporters come to pray for victory, not just before the race, but all year round. Some of them have interesting art work, most of it being 16th- and 17th-century. Sunday morning is the surest time to find them open, but inquire at the tourist office for other opening hours.

Near the church of Sant'Agostino, on the north side of the Prato, Via Sant'Agata leads east to the **San Giuseppe** oratory chapel of the *Onda* (Sea-wave) *contrada*. It has a simple but stately 17th-century façade. Two others are: **San Rocco**, north of the Campo on Via di Vallerozzi, for *Lupa,* with its She-wolf in bronze on an ancient column outside the chapel and Rutilio Mannetti's fine 17th-century paintings inside; and the 13th-century **Santi Vincenzo e Anastasio**, one of the oldest and prettiest, also north of the Campo, on Via Giuseppe Garibaldi, for *Istrice* (Porcupine).

---

fauna, a collection of mushrooms meticulously modelled in terracotta, and intriguing geological specimens, minerals, crystals and meteorite fragments.

Hugging a steep slope to the west (Via Pier Andrea Matteoli 4), the **Botanical Gardens** founded in the 18th century nurture 50,000 specimens from Tuscany alone, as well as cacti, orchids and other tropical plants from Africa and the Americas.

At the south-western tip of the old town, on Pian dei Mantellini, are the 14th-century Carmelite convent and church of **San Niccolò al Carmine**, dominated by a soaring campanile. Inside, in the middle of the south (right) aisle, beautifully restored, is Domenico Beccafumi's otherworldly *St Michael Slaying the Dragon* (1528).

Camollia District

Even if you are not a devout believer, it is worth visiting **St Catherine of Siena's neighbourhood** – around Via Santa Caterina – to observe the fascinating phenomenon of her cult and the artworks, some good, most atrocious, that it has produced.

On the narrow street, Viocolo del Tiraolo, the **home** of the nation's patron saint has been transformed since the 15th century into a sprawling **sanctuary** (*Santuario Cateriniano*) of four chapels. Over the entrance is the inscription *Sponsae Kristi Catherinae domus* ('Home of Catherine, Bride of Christ').

In the **Oratorio della Cucina** (Kitchen Chapel), above elegant Renaissance prayer-stalls, 14 syrupy pictures (16th- to 19th-century) tell the saint's story. Built on the family vegetable garden, the **Oratorio del Crocifisso** (Crucifix Chapel), houses over its altar the precious 13th-century wooden cross from Pisa before which the saint said she received the stigmata of Jesus. The **Oratoria della Camera** (Chapel of Catherine's Chalber), where she prayed and received visitors, is drenched with the sentimentality of its late 19th-century frescoes. The sanctuary's best artworks are to be found in the **Oratorio della Tintoria** (Chapel of the Dyer's Shop), where Catherine's father worked. Here you will find a fine 15th-century polychrome wooden statue of the saint and five angels painted by Sodoma.

Downhill to the west of the shrine, at the end of Via Santa Caterina, is the **Fonte Branda**, a most ancient and cherished freshwater spring, its fountain roofed with attractive redbrick Gothic vaulting in 1248.

For a more genuine sense of Catherine's life, take Via della Sapienza up to the formidable fortress-like church of **San Domenico**. In this largely 14th-century Gothic edifice, the saint came regularly to pray and experienced many of her visions. At the west end, in the *Capella delle Volte* (Vaulted Chapel) is her only known **authentic portrait**, a fresco of 1414 painted by Andrea Vanni, observing her in a state

ST CATHERINE OF SIENA (1347-80)

This highly strung nun, who made St Teresa of Avila look like Mary Poppins, is a patron saint for the whole of Italy. The daughter of a prosperous Siena dyer, Giacomo Benincasa, she was born in 1347, just one year before the Black Plague broke out. At six, she had her first vision and decided to go and live in the desert. She got as far as some barren rock south of Siena, fell asleep and was brought home by her father.

With 24 other children to feed, Giacomo decided to marry her off when she was 12, and started to dress her nicely and do up her hair to attract a suitor. Catherine found this disgusting and protested to the neighbourhood priest. He absolved her of what she considered sinful vanity, but much too easily for her liking. She contracted an apparently psychosomatic case of smallpox to make herself really ugly and at 16 joined the Dominican order.

In plague-ridden Siena, steeled by self-flagellation and exalted by recurrent visions of Jesus, Mary and the saints, she tended the sick and poor with terrifying vehemence. She took particular pleasure in looking after wretched Niccolò Tuldo, who was tormented with fear about being condemned to death for some minor offence. Catherine calmed him down with prayer and prepared him to face his destiny, accompanying him in cheerful mood to the scaffold. There, she lovingly undid Niccolò's shirt for the executioner's axe, and in a state of ecstasy, caught his severed head in her lap. She told her mother in a letter: 'When the corpse was taken away, my soul bathed in a delightful peace and I derived such joy from the perfume of this blood that I did not want to let anyone remove what had splattered on my clothes.'

This was the lady who conducted a vigorous correspondence with the spiritual leaders of the day (unable to write, she dictated literally hundreds of letters) and became a highly active papal diplomat. In 1375, she received on her body the five stigmata of the Crucifixion while at prayer in a chapel in Pisa. The wounds were transmitted by rays of heavenly light, strangely similar to those customarily depicted at the time in the popular paintings of St Francis of Assisi, but in her case not visible to others than herself until after her death. The invisible stigmata inspired her to go to Avignon and bring the exiled Pope Gregory XI back to Rome, ending the Great Schism. She declared that the aggressive energies wasted in this dispute would be better used in a new crusade against the Moslems. The Vatican canonized her in 1939.

of ecstasy. It was in this chapel that she donned the habit of a Dominican nun. Further along the south (right) wall, the mon-

Interior of the church of San Domenico. Like almost all Dominican churches, this one was conveniently built on the outskirts of town to catch the attention of pilgrims before they spotted the churches of rival orders in the city centre.

umental **St Catherine's Chapel** is decorated with Sodoma's frescoes, the most celebrated being to the left of the altar, *The Swooning of St Catherine*. In the altar's marble niche (1466) is a Renaissance reliquary containing **Catherine's head**.

To end the walk on a more down-to-earth note, wander down the Viale dei Mille past the city stadium to the vast, sprawling **Forte di Santa Barbara**, built for Duke Cosimo I in 1560. In the vaults of the Medici fortress, you can inspect, taste and buy a wide selection of Chianti and other wines the **Enoteca Italiana** (Italian Wine Cellars).

Day-trips from Siena

For these excursions within easy reach of Siena, plan a picnic with provisions from the food-market on Piazza del Mercato behind the Palazzo Pubblico – and wine from the Medici fortress's Enoteca Italiana.

Osservanza Monastery

Really just a half-day trip 3.5km (2 miles) on Via Simone Martini, north east of town through the Porte Ovile, the attractive 15th-century **basilica** of this Franciscan monastery was badly bombed in World War II but beautifully restored in 1949. Among the notable works inside are: Andrea della Robbia's enamelled terracotta *Coronation of the Madonna*, second chapel in the north (left) aisle; *Madonna with St Ambrose and St Jerome* (1436) by the Maestro dell'Osservanza, an anonymous gifted pupil of Sassetta, fourth chapel in the south (right) aisle; and in the sacristy to the right of the choir, a remarkable *Pietà* group of polychrome terracotta figures (1497) by Giacomo Cozzarelli, probable architect of the church.

Monteriggioni

Some 15km (9 miles) north on highway N°2, the exquisite little mediæval hilltown has miraculously kept intact its ring of 13th-century fortifications with 14 rectangular bastions, the stuff dreams are made of. Surrounded only by vineyards and olive groves, the towers are as striking today as when Dante compared them in his *Inferno* (canto XXXI, verse 41) to the mythical giants petrified by Jupiter in their battle with the gods.

Just 3km (2 miles) west is **Abbadia Isola**, a 12th-century Cistercian abbey-church with a fine Taddeo di Bartolo fresco in its south (right) aisle and handsomely carved baptismal font (1419).

To quote Dante: 'as on the circle of its walls, Monteriggioni is crowned with towers...'

San Galgano

A longer trip south west of Siena, 34km (21 miles) along the winding road towards Massa Marittima, the splendid **Cistercian abbey** is well worth the journey, both for the lovely countryside and its architecture. The main French Gothic abbey-church (begun 1224) has lost its roof, which collapsed after a corrupt abbot sold off the leading in the 16th century. The beautiful

remaining shell, with lofty Gothic arches, grassed-over nave and gaping windows open to the heavens, is one of the most spectacular ruins in Italy.

The **Chapel of San Galgano**, above the abbey on Monte Siepi, is in the main a round structure built in alternating bands of red brick and white stone or travertine. Inside are **frescoes** by Ambrogio Lorenzetti and his workshop depicting the *Annunciation*, the *Madonna Enthroned* and scenes from the life of St Galgano. Galgano was a mediæval knight who abandoned, for the Christian faith, a violent plan to elope with a lady denied him by her parents. His sword is planted in a stone in the middle of the chapel.

South to Montepulciano

We discover south east of Siena an eerily beautiful landscape from another planet. The familiar greenery of vineyards and forests in the Chianti country gives way to broad stretches of arid hillocks known as *le Crete* – 'crests' of clay dramatically eroded by wind and rain that turn gullies of sand into ravines. Occasionally outlined by a solitary row of cypresses, the mounds that change with the light from silvery grey in the morning to buff and then deep amber in the afternoon are familiar from the pictures of Giovanni di Paolo, Bartolo di Fredi and Ambrogio Lorenzetti. The

241

If you risk overdosing on too much Tuscan greenery, take a walk across these weird, other-worldly hills around Monte Amiata.

desolate aspect left by a parched summer or bitterly cold winter has prompted literary travellers to see *le Crete* as the inspiration for Dante's *Inferno*.

Asciano

Turn south off the Arezzo highway onto road N°438 for what is a mediæval 'oasis' in the *Crete* desert, 26km (16 miles) from Siena. The hill-town looks over the Ombrone valley from 14th-century ramparts. In the main square is the Romanesque **Collegiata Sant'Agata** with slender arcaded façade, octagonal dome and a crenellated campanile. Left of the church, the **Museo di Arte Sacra** has a good

collection of Sienese artists: Taddeo di Bartolo, Ambrogio Lorenzetti (*St Michael*), Giovanni di Paolo and the Maestro dell' Osservanza (*Birth of Mary*). The **Museo Archeologico**, Corso Matteotti, has a small Etruscan collection from the nearby necropolis of Poggio Pinci.

Monte Oliveto Maggiore

Set dramatically on a long outcropping of rock 9km (6 miles) south of Asciano, the Benedictine monastery is the object of pilgrimages as much for the walks it offers in a delightful **cypress park** as for its art treasures.

In the arcades of the **Great Cloister**, the life of St Benedict is recounted in a famous but often stilted series of frescoes (1498-1508) by Luca Signorelli (born in Cortona), along the west wall, and Sodoma, from Siena, along the other three walls. At the entrance to the **church**, Sodoma has painted a more admired *Christ on the Column*. Inside the church

are an impressive set of inlaid wooden **choir stalls** (1503) by Fra Giovanni da Verona. Besides the bookshop and restaurant, the monks run an important laboratory for restoring illuminated manuscripts.

Buonconvento

Nine kilometres (5 miles) west of the monastery is the old Siena to Rome highway N°2, in many parts following the ancient Roman *Via Cassia* that linked the imperial capital with northern Italy and territories across the Alps. Straddling the road, the attractive little town of Buonconvento shelters behind remarkable brick fortifications. The battlemented **Palazzo Pretorio** adds to the formidable image of what was once a major bastion in Siena's mediæval line of defences. Opposite the 18th-century church of Santi Pietro and Paolo, the **Museo d'Arte Sacra** (Via Soccini 17) has an important collection of Sienese paintings from the 13th to the 17th century.

Montalcino

Set amid olive groves and vineyards 14km (8 miles) south of Buonconvento, this is one of the most charming fortified hill-towns in southern Tuscany. Its heady Brunello red wine is much admired among connoisseurs, and priced accordingly, but it tastes wonderful on a terrace in the main town square – in fact triangular – **Piazza del Popolo**, looking across to the imposing clock-tower of the 14th-century **Palazzo dei Priori** and a good-looking brick-and-stone arched **loggia**. On the right of the piazza, as you face the palazzo, is a café with attractive 1900s furnishings.

The town's 14th-century fortress, **la Rocca**, has massive ramparts added by Duke Cosimo I and provides a grand view of the surrounding countryside. In the Middle Ages, when the town was under attack, the main keep protected the gentry and nobility, while the rest of the populace huddled under makeshift canvas shelters between the keep and these outer walls. In today's more peaceful times, the keep's ground floor is an *Enoteca* (wine cellar) for tasting, and buying, the local wine.

The **Museo Civico** (Via Ricasoli 29) is presently housed in the Episcopal Palace but it is to be extended to the cloister of the adjacent church of Sant'Agostino. Its most important works are: a 13th-century polychrome *Madonna del Carmine* from the nearby Romanesque church of Sant'Antimo (*see* below); Bartolo di Fredi's *Coronation of the Madonna* triptych (1388), and his rather emotionally harsh *Descent from the Cross* (1380); and a Sodoma *Crucifixion*.

Sant'Antimo

The beautiful little 12th-century Benedictine abbey-church has a place apart in Tuscan Romanesque architecture. Clearly influenced, if not actually built, by the Cluny monks of French Burgundy, its honey-coloured stone, framed by two cypress sentinels, stands out in the fields, olive groves and thickets of holm oak 10km (6 miles) south of Montalcino. Tradition attributes the abbey's foundation to Charlemagne in 781, after his army was delivered from a plague. The church itself was begun in 1118.

Its distinctive feature among Tuscany's Romanesque churches is the cluster of **domed chapels** forming the apse at the rear of the church. These mark the interior's French-style ambulatory, with beneath it a 9th-century **crypt** visible through a small window at the base of one of the chapels. The four-tier, four-square **campanile** is of clearly north Italian Lombard inspiration. The church exterior has an intriguing set of **stone carvings**, notably two animals joined at the head on the entrance portal, griffins and eagles over the portal on the south (right) flank, with an intricately carved door frame that suggests Islamic influence, and animal heads on the apse, one impudently sticking its tongue out.

Inside the church, notice the remarkable **sculpted capitals** on the columns, most of them with fine geometric or floral patterns typical of French Romanesque sculpture. The most important, attributed to a French artist from Toulouse, is a vigorous *Daniel in the Lion's Den* (second on the right of the entrance) in which the beasts tear each other apart but leave Daniel unscathed. Over the high altar is an admirable 12th-century wooden *Crucifixion*, probably of Burgundian origin. The church's wonderfully luminous interior is enhanced in the **ambulatory** by the insertion of translucent alabaster and onyx in the bases of the columns.

San Quirico d'Orcia

Back on highway N°2, 15km (9 miles) east of Montalcino, this fine old town in the Orcia valley was an important stop for mediæval pilgrims heading for Rome from northern Europe, providing them with hostels and hospitals. In a later century, the Marquis de Sade complained of the accommodation, but though he did not elaborate, it may just have meant he was received with the kind of Christian virtues that did not appeal to him.

The Romanesque **Collegiate church** (just below the rank of cathedral) is a pleasing edifice with two handsomely carved **gabled portals**. In the architrave (door frame) over the 12th-century main entrance are two fighting crocodiles and, above them to the right, two sirens representing the evils and temptations present on the journey of life in general and the pilgrimage to Rome in particular. More reassuringly, supporting the portal's columns, are the lions of divine strength and justice. In the second portal (1288) on the south (right) side of the church, the two finely carved caryatids supported by lions are attributed to pupils of Giovanni Pisano. In a simple interior overpowered by an incongruous Baroque altar, seek out in the north (left) transept the **Sano di Pietro triptych** of the *Madonna and Child, Resurrection* and *Descent to Limbo*. Note, too, the admirable inlaid wooden **choir stalls** (1502) by Antonio Barili, an artist from Siena.

*T*he belfry of San Quirico d'Orcia's collegiate church acted as a beacon for pilgrims seeking refuge on their way to and from Rome. Their road was the ancient Via Cassia.

On Piazza della Libertà, opposite the Neo-Gothic church of San Francesco, are the 16th-century **Leonini Gardens**, designed in the Italian Renaissance style by Diomede Leone. Box hedges laid out in geometric patterns rise to a clump of holm oaks from which you have a good view of the Orcia valley.

Pienza

Ten kilometres (6 miles) east of San Quirico, this imposing piece of Renaissance urban planning, the first such experiment for the 'ideal city' since antiquity, is now a pleasantly tranquil Tuscan backwater. Pius II wanted to turn his modest home town of Corsignano, where he was born Enea Silvio de'Piccolomini in 1405, into a place worthy of the eminent humanist pope he had become. He called on Florentine architect Bernardo Rossellino to redesign the town with new criteria of formal harmony and classical proportions, and on principles set out by Rossellino's master, Leon Battista Alberti. It took only three years, from 1459 to 1462. Pious, perhaps, but not humble, the pope then renamed the place Pienza.

Piazza Pio II

Stroll around the middle of the square to take in Rossellino's architectural achievement. Oblique angles, a sloping pavement and subtly varying proportions in the

To keep in the good books of Pope Pius II, many of his cardinals built residences in Pienza. This is the Palazzo Ammannati, built for the Cardinal of Pavia, the pontiff's closest friend.

PIOUS PIUS

The name that Enea Silvio de'Piccolomini chose as pope represented a very deliberate change of life-style. Before he became Pius II, he had always had a weakness for the ladies. He was renowned as a humanist and court poet to the German Emperor Frederick III, but also wrote erotic verse and pornographic prose. He was a relentless libertine, with a mistress in every town he visited, leaving a dozen bastards in his wake. Rebuked by his father for a child he had had with an English lady, he wrote in reply: 'Certainly, you did not father a son of marble and iron, when you yourself were pure flesh! You know what a rooster you were, and me, I am not castrated nor numbered among the impotent.' But then he got religion, became Bishop of Trieste in 1447, then of Siena, cardinal in 1456, and pope from 1458 to 1464. He was lucky to have his nephew Francesco commission Pinturicchio to tell his life in the more decorous form of heroic frescoes in the Siena cathedral's Piccolomini Library (*see* page 235).

---

palaces have made the piazza look much larger than it is. What to some seems overcalculated is pleasing to others, who compare its overall austerity to the tangy bite of Pienza's famous *pecorino* cheese. Over to your right as you face the Duomo, the scale of the piazza is set by a delightful **Renaissance well** framed by two columns and an architrave, and emblazoned with the Piccolomini coat of arms.

Behind it, the **Palazzo Piccolomini**, with the sober elegance of its mullioned windows and simple doors, is comparable to the Rucellai Palace that Rossellino had built in Florence from an Alberti design. Its outstanding feature is on the south side where the square courtyard of Corinthian columns leads to a splendid **hanging**

garden built on three superimposed loggias. Its arrangement of evergreen hedges and trees is a consummate example of Italian Renaissance garden landscaping, linking the edifice to the countryside beyond – the Orcia valley south of Pienza.

Opposite the Duomo, the **Palazzo Comunale** honours with its tall brick tower the mediæval tradition of Tuscan civic buildings, while its lofty travertine loggia maintains the harmony of the Renaissance piazza.

Facing the Piccolomini palace, the **Palazzo Vescovile** (Bishop's Palace) was remodelled by Cardinal Roderigo Borgia (father of Cesare and Lucrezia and later Pope Alexander VI) with the family coat of arms on the corner. He walled in Gothic arches of the ground floor and added two storeys in the Renaissance style. (It is soon to be the new home of the cathedral museum.)

Duomo

In classical manner, four pilasters divide the cathedral's travertine façade into three arched bays. Pius II's garlanded coat of arms is set in the pediment above. The campanile is rather discreetly set back to the rear. The brightness bathing the spacious interior has been achieved by extending the choir out over the slope of the valley, with no painting over the high altar to obstruct the daylight through the great rear window. As compensation, in a chapel to the left of the choir, is Vecchietta's monumental *Assumption of Mary* (1461). To the right of the choir, Rossellino designed the altar for a relic of St Andrew, patron saint of Pienza. (The choir's precarious position requires extensive restoration to hold it up today).

The **Museo della Cattedrale** (cathedral museum) is at present housed opposite the

The apparent serenity of Pienza's cathedral façade conceals a considerable balancing-act for the choir at the rear, hanging out hazardously over the valley.

cathedral campanile in the former canon's residence (*Canonica*), next to its future home in the Palazzo Vescovile. Among its Sienese paintings of the 14th and 15th centuries are: Bartolo di Fredi's *Life of Jesus* in 40 episodes, and *Madonna della Misericordia* (1364); a *Madonna* triptych attributed to Sassetta; and Vecchietta's *Madonna and Child* polyptych (1463). The collection also has a polychrome terracotta tabernacle painted by Francesco di Giorgio Martini and 15th- and 16th-century Flemish tapestries.

Pieve di San Vito

A ten-minute walk west of town takes you downhill through a rustic setting of farm buildings to the little round-towered, 11th-century Romanesque parish church where Eneo Silvio de'Piccolómini was baptized in old Corsignano. Notice the floral designs and a twin-tailed siren of temptation carved on the main west entrance. Scenes from the birth of Jesus are carved over the south (right) doorway. Inside is the future pope's **baptismal font**.

Montepulciano

This attractive hill-town, 13km (8 miles) east of Pienza, is appreciated as much for its excellent local wine as for its handsome monuments. The red *Vino Nobile di Mon-* *tepulciano*, subtly smooth and earthy, is on offer in the town's numerous *cantine* (wine cellars). In a race that is more sheer grind than the dashing bravado of Siena's *Palio*, but no less fiercely contested, Montepulciano's *Bravio delle Botti* celebrates the centuries-old wine production on the last Sunday in August. The

Montepulciano's most celebrated son was the Renaissance humanist scholar, Poliziano (1454-1494). Friend and tutor to the Medici family, he saved Lorenzo the Magnificent from assassination. His poetry was illustrated by Botticelli.

town's toughs push barrels weighing 80kg (176lb), up the steep, winding main street, Via di Gracciano del Corso.

Without the formal planning of Pienza, Montepulciano's Renaissance appearance is more organically integrated into the mediæval town. It dates from the town's Florentine domination in the 15th and 16th centuries. The Medici commissioned Antonio da Sangallo the Elder to design the fortifications, most notably the massive **Porta al Prato** towering over the **Poggiofanti Gardens** at the north east end of town.

Via di Gracciano del Corso

Beyond the gate, the main street has many fine **Renaissance palazzi**. In front of the 16th-century Palazzo Avignonesi on the right (N°91), notice the Florentine **Marzocco** lion monument that in 1511 replaced the Sienese *Lupa* (She-wolf). Further along, the Palazzo Bucelli (N°73) has embedded in its façade **Etruscan urns** collected from the region by the 17th-century owner. The originally Gothic **church of Sant'Agostino** has a marble façade by Medici architect Michelozzo, making a Gothic-Renaissance transition combining classical columns with pointed-arch windows and other more Gothic sculptural ornaments over the entrance. On Piazza Michelozzo, a jolly Neapolitan *commedia dell'arte* clown tolls the hours on top of the **Torre di Pulcinella**.

Further up Via di Gracciano's steep slope, the grain merchants' 16th-century **loggia** bearing the Medici emblem leads to the **market square** on Piazza delle Erbe.

From the market, continue along Via Voltaia nel Corso past Antonio da Sangallo's fine **Palazzo Cervini** on the left (N°21, now a bank). Find some excuse like money-changing for a peep at the interior's wonderful view over the Chiana valley.

Piazza Grande

Sit for a moment on the steps of the Duomo to contemplate the nobility and warmth of the city's religious and civic centre. With its lofty crenellated tower, the formidable **Palazzo Comunale**, 14th-century but with a travertine façade remodelled, perhaps by Michelozzo, is often compared to Florence's Palazzo Vecchio. Facing the Duomo, Antonio da Sangallo's

With or without this fierce knight, Antonio da Sangallo's striking Palazzo Nobili-Tarugi stands apart from Montepulciano's more conventional Renaissance buildings.

Palazzo Nobili-Tarugi is a complex but intriguing edifice of ground-level arcading and a loggia on the upper floor. In front, on the architrave of the Renaissance **well**, the sculpted griffins of Montepulciano unite with the Marzocco lions of Florence.

Ignore the unfinished façade and ungainly campanile of the 17th-century **Duomo** and go right inside. In the **baptistery** to the north (left) of the entrance is a finely sculpted **font** (1340) by Giovanni d'Agostino and an **altar** of four saints by Andrea della Robbia with a *Madonna and Child* by a disciple of Benedetto da Maiano. In the north aisle's fourth bay is Sano di Pietro's tender *Madonna del Pilastro*. The church's main treasure, on the high altar, is the **Taddeo di Bartolo triptych** (1401), an opulent treatment of the *Assumption*.

Church of San Biagio

On the south-west corner of town at the end of an avenue of cypresses is the most beautiful of Antonio da Sangallo the Elder's Renaissance edifices for Montepulciano and for many his absolute masterpiece. It was begun in 1519 and inaugurated ten years later by the Medici pope, Clement VII. A majestic dome dominates the church's Greek-cross ground plan (four equal arms),

The woods south of Montepulciano serve only to enhance the beauty of Sangallo's great church of San Biagio. It would lose all of its theatrical impact if it had been built inside the town.

with two campaniles, one domed, the other unfinished, to the west, and a semi-circular sacristy to the east. The proportions, even in its incomplete state, and the warm tones of the stone, inside and out, are quite simply superb.

Chianciano Terme

About 7km (4 miles) south east of Montepulciano is one of Italy's major spa towns, open all year round and good for heart, liver and digestive complaints. The springs have been used since Roman times, when it was known as *Fontes Clusinae*. Even if you are not taking the waters, take a stroll in the little old village nearby, **Chianciano Vecchia.**

Sarteano

Originally an Etruscan settlement, the mediæval village 10km (6 miles) south east of Chianciano nestles up against a **Rocca** (castle) watching over it from the top of the hill. Welcoming visitors is the attractive 15th-century Renaissance-façaded **church of San Francesco**. Via Roma leads past the crumbling Palazzo Piccolomini through an archway to the **church of San Martino**. Penetrate beyond the unprepossessing neoclassical façade (1841) to a major work of Mannerist painting in the interior, **Domenico Beccafumi's** *Annunciation* (1546). At a high point in his career, the artist makes brilliant use of light and gives Mary a subtle but no less disturbing sensuality.

Chiusi

Just across the A1 *autostrada* to Rome, 12km (7 miles) east of Chianciano, this ancient town lies at the southern tip of the Valdichiana. Prospering above all else from its flourishing agriculture, it was a major member of the 12-town Etruscan Confederation. In the 5th century BC, Chiusi's King Porsenna conquered and even briefly occupied Rome. *Clevsin* in Etruscan, *Clusium* to the Romans, has preserved from that heyday ancient fortifications with fascinating underground galleries and, outside of town, an extensive necropolis of tombs with wall paintings and stone sarcophagi.

After the invasions of the Goths and Lombards, the town went into sharp decline. Like the Maremma to the west (*see* SOUTH COAST, page 267), surrounding malarial swamps ruined its agriculture until the dukes of Tuscany started land-reclamation work in the 17th century.

The **Duomo**, founded in the 6th century under the Lombards and rebuilt in the 12th, was subjected to heavy-handed restoration in 1887. The notable feature of the interior is its 18 columns of ancient Roman origin, for which restorers thought painted pastiches of ancient mosaics in nave and apse might be appropriate. The **campanile**, transformed in 1585 from a fortified tower, stands over an **Etruscan well** (*cisterna*) of the 1st century BC. To visit, apply to the Museo Archeologico (*see* below).

To the right of the church, the **Museo della Cattedrale** has an important collection of church treasures, in particular a set of 15th-century Benedictine choirbooks illustrated with miniature Sienese paintings by Francesco di Giorgio Martini and Sano di Pietro. Curiously, the museum is mainly interesting for its access, through the Episcopal Garden, to the **underground Etruscan galleries** (5th century BC). A stairway leads down to the lower levels of the imposing Etruscan fortifications, including a square bastion. It is not yet clear whether the galleries were used as water conduits or as part of the town's military defences.

The **Museo Archeologico**, Via Porsenna, has one of Tuscany's most important collections of Etruscan art. Stone sculpture of the 6th and 5th century BC includes female busts, lions, sphinxes and urns carved in bas-relief. There are also fine black Bucchero vases, painted Greek pottery, carved ivory, jewellery and household utensils. A highlight of the Roman era is the bust of Augustus.

The majority of tombs making up the **Etruscan necropolis** are located on a pretty drive 3km (2 miles) north of town, off the Via delle Tombe Etrusche. The Museo Archeologico arranges guided tours. For conservation purposes, some of the tombs may be closed, but among the most interesting and accessible are the **Tomba della Pellegrina** (3rd century BC) with urns and sarcophagi still in place, **Tomba del Leone**, recently restored, **Tomba della Scimmia** (5th century BC) with wall paintings, and **Tomba del Granduca** with eight funerary urns. East of town is the **Tomba Bonci Casuccini** (5th century BC) with its ancient doorway intact and, protected behind glass, murals of athletics and other games.

Continue north of the main Etruscan necropolis to discover a remnant of the region's distinctive marshland – now minus the deadly mosquitoes – at **Lago di Chiusi**, where rich farmland and rows of poplars surround the lake's reeds and water-lilies.

Around Monte Amiata

Ninety kilometres (56 miles) south of Siena to the west of the Via Cassia (road N°2), the extinct volcano of **Monte Amiata**, 1738m (5702ft), has left a green and fertile country, dense forests of fir, oak, chestnut and beech trees. Rich deposits of mercury have been exploited since Etruscan times. The varied countryside has made the region an increasingly active resort area both for winter and summer sports. From the peak, marked by an iron cross, there are views clear across to the islands of Elba and Corsica, north to Siena and south to lakes Bolsena and Trasimeno. That southern end of the region, approaching Umbria, has some reputed white wines.

Abbadia San Salvatore

On the eastern slope of the mountain 812m (2664ft) up along side a big chestnut forest, the town is both a modern holiday resort and a mediæval community. It takes the name of its **Benedictine abbey**, which had its heyday in the Middle Ages as a major halt on the pilgrimages from northern Europe to Rome. It was also a favourite refuge of Pope Pius II during the hot summer of 1462 which he spent supervising construction of his nearby hometown of Pienza (*see* page 247).

Two towers, the taller of them with battlements, flank the narrow façade of the 11th-century **church**, which has a triple window beneath a pointed arch. In the spacious interior, notice the fine 12th-century *Crucifixion* on the south (right) wall. Under the transept is an extensive **crypt**, one of the biggest in Tuscany. Its 32 intricately patterned columns have capitals with Lombard-Romanesque sculpture of human figures, animals and plants.

The 16th-century **cloister** houses a **museum** of ancient monastery treasures that include an 8th-century Irish reliquary and a 9th-century embroidered silk cope (ceremonial cloak) of Persian silk.

Piancastagnaio

As its name suggests, this charming little fortified village is also in chestnut forest country, just 4km (2 miles) south of Abbadia San Salvatore. To the left before entering town are a Franciscan monastery and its simple **church of San Bartolommeo**, with fragments of a 14th-century Sienese fresco depicting *the Massacre of the Innocents*. The **Rocca** is an imposing castle built by the Aldobrandeschi, local feudal lords whose origins can be traced back to Lombardy and Germany, their name being Italianized from Hildebrand.

Arcidosso

The popular winter and summer resort is 679m (2227ft) up on a ridge west of Monte Amiato. Up the hill from the modern facilities, the walled town's skyline, dominated by the fierce-looking castletower of its Aldobrandeschi **Rocca**, is little changed since it was painted in a 14th-century fresco recently uncovered in the Siena Palazzo Pubblico's Sala del Mappamondo (*see* page 230).

Santa Fiora

The most attractive views of Monte Amiato are to be had from the south slope where this beautifully kept little village is located, 7.5km (4 miles) from Arcidosso. On the main square are the resplendent Renaissance **Palazzo Sforza Cesarini**, now town hall, and the **clock-tower** remnant of an Aldobrandeschi castle.

The little Via Carolina leads to the parish church of **Santi Fiora e Lucilla** with a Romanesque rose window over its late Renaissance portal. In the otherwise simple interior, Gothic windows continue the stylistic mix, making a beguiling counterpoint to the **Andrea della Robbia's glazed terracotta** decorating the altars.

The pulpit also has bas-reliefs by della Robbia and his workshop, portraying the *Last Supper, Ascension* and *Resurrection.*

At the bottom of the hill is **La Peschiera**, an 18th-century garden where a fish pond is fed by bubbling streams from the Fiora river.

Roccalbegna

This fairytale fortress-town is in the middle of nowhere on Monte Labbro above the Albegna valley. Nevertheless, it is well worth the meandering drive 16km (10 miles) west of Santa Fiora. The **castle** of the Aldobrandeschi feudal lords is perched on *Il Sasso*, a cone-shaped rock 40m (130ft) above the rest of the village. Take the stairway to the top for the panorama. In the village, visit the **church of Santi Pietro e Paolo** for the superb **Ambrogio Lorenzetti triptych** (1340) on the high altar, a treatment of the *Madonna with St Peter and St Paul* that is at once strong and tender.

Saturnia

This elegant health resort 40km (25 miles) south of Arcidosso was originally an Etruscan settlement that the Romans colonized in the 3rd century BC. You can still see remains of the **Etruscan necropolis** and the ancient walls adjoining the **Porta Romana** (its present arch being a mediæval addition). Better than any hotel jacuzzi, located beside an old mill south of town at the *Terme di Saturnia*, is a natural **hot water-fall** – *Cascate del Gorello* – which pours over rocks whitened by the minerals gathered in natural pools.

A popular excursion 6km (3 miles) south of the *Terme* is the pretty walled village of **Montemerano** set on a hill amid groves of olive trees. In the **church of San Giorgio** are some fine 15th-century sculptures and paintings in its otherwise Baroque interior: Vecchietta's polychrome wooden bas-relief of the *Assumption* (1465) in the right aisle, his statue of *St Peter* in the left transept, and Sano di Pietro's *Madonna and Child* altarpainting in the left aisle.

Sovana

Crazy but delightful roads winding 25km (15 miles) east of Saturnia lead to this village built along a narrow ridge. In its beautiful wild setting, it consists practically of just one street running from the ruins of its 14th-century **castle** to the pretty cypress-lined piazza of the 13th-century Romanesque **Cathedral Santi Pietro e Paolo**. Much of the façade is concealed by a priests' residence, but inside are some lively if crude carvings of biblical scenes on the **column capitals**: *Abraham with Sarah and Hagar*, *Sacrifice of Isaac*, *Adam and Eve*, *Moses*, and a *Daniel* who has the lions licking his feet.

Pitigliano

The southernmost town on the itinerary, close to the Umbrian border, is a former prehistoric and Etruscan settlement today producing a much respected white wine. The terraced vineyards and wild thickets of shrubs and trees surround the town's spectacular location on a long rocky ridge, on which the outer rim of tall houses seem to form a protective wall for the centre. It was a mediæval dependency of nearby Sovana until the Aldobrandeschi lords arranged a marriage with the wealthy Orsini family in Rome and brought new money into the town. The episcopal diocese was transferred here from Sovana and Jewish merchants first arrived in the 15th century to bolster the community's prosperity.

On Piazza della Repubblica, the **Palazzo Orsini**, bearing the family coat of arms of a lion-headed bear (*orso*), is originally 14th century but was expanded by Giuliano da Sangallo's grand Renaissance design in the 16th century. In the courtyard is a hexagonal well and graceful Ionic-columned loggia. The largely 18th-century Baroque **Duomo** has a mediæval campanile. Inside, next to the sacristy, is Guidoccio Cozzarelli's *Madonna Enthroned* (1494).

Take Via Roma to explore the narrow streets of the mediæval town, notably the tiny Vicolo della Battaglia. Via Zuccarelli leads through the old quarter of the **Jewish ghetto** around the remains of a 16th-century synagogue.

Sorano

Astride its picturesque spur of volcanic tufa, 10km (6 miles) east of Pitigliano, the fortified mediæval town boasts some fine white wines. Sip a glass beneath the noble ruin of the Orsini family's 15th-century **castle** with its cylindrical tower and two inner courtyards. The monumental emblem on the main gate unites the coats of arms of the Orsini and Aldobrandeschi clans. The **Palazzo Comitale**, residence of the Orsini while they were renovating the castle, has a handsome Renaissance portal.

THE ORSINI BUNCH

For the Orsini family, Pitigliano was just a northern outpost of their Rome-based territories. They ruled by the sword, a vicious bunch of robber barons. The fact that they provided three popes did not detract from this reputation. Finally, they ran afoul of a bigger bunch of robber barons than themselves – the Borgias. They became condottiere, robber-baron consultants, so to speak.

Relax at a Resort, Explore a Nature Reserve or Share Imperial Exile on Elba

This south-west corner, ancient Etruscan gateway to the Mediterranean, is a world apart from the rest of Tuscany. The beaches and sailing harbours of the Argentario peninsula and nearby resorts have made the coast a popular weekend and summer playground for the Romans. Inland, the attraction is the natural beauty of the Maremma rather than great artistic monuments – with the brilliant exception of Massa Marittima. The island of Elba was considered remote enough to keep Napoleon out of trouble. For a while.

The prevailing landscape all along the coast and on its islands is classical Mediterranean maquis heathland (*macchia*) – splashes of pink or white myrtle blossom or purple juniper berries among the evergreen shrubs, squat holly oaks and sea pines, with the occasional porcupine, deer or wild boar scurrying away from the visitor. Migratory birds stop off at the lagoons here on the way to Africa. The fauna also include sun-worshippers congregating on sandy beaches and granite shelves of the coves and creeks at the foot of steep cliffs. Immediately behind this craggy coastline, ramblers can explore the region's natural beauty in the protected wilderness of the *Parco Naturale della Maremma*.

The region divides neatly into three separate itineraries, from south to north:

1. Around the Argentario:

*   **Orbetello**, cozy resort at centre of hilly peninsula, with fashionable sailing harbour of **Porto Ercole**, and modern resort of **Porto Santo Stefano** for embarcation to offshore islands of **Giglio** and **Giannutri**.
*   Just south of the peninsula, on the way to Lazio: **Ansedonia**, little beach-resort; **Cosa**, remains of ancient Roman seaport; and **Lake Burrano**, wildlife sanctuary.

Porto Santo Stefano is a good place to forget for a while Tuscany's cathedrals and art galleries. Just take a boat out and explore the Mediterranean, and catch a fish or two.

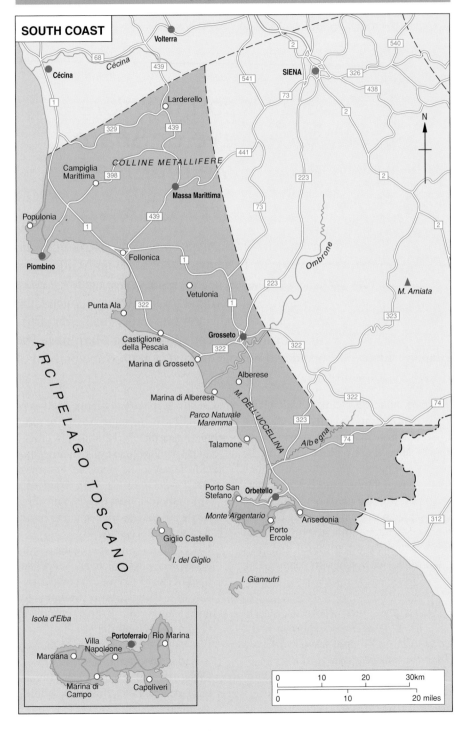

SOUTH COAST

Volterra

68 Cécina

Cécina

1

439

SIENA 326

541

438

Larderello

73

1

540

2

329

439

439

COLLINE METALLIFERE

441

223

2

Campiglia
Marittima 398

Massa Marittima

73

2

Populonia

439

223

2

1

Piombino

Follonica

1

Ombrone

Vetulonia

M. Amiata

Punta Ala 322

223

323

Castiglione
della Pescaia 322

Grosseto

322

322

Marina di Grosseto

Alberese

322

74

Marina di Alberese

M. DELL'UCCELLINA

323

Parco Naturale
Maremma

Talamone

Albegna

74

Porto San
Stefano Orbetello

Monte Argentario

Ansedonia

1 312

Porto
Ercole

Giglio Castello

ARCIPELAGO TOSCANO

I. del Giglio

I. Giannutri

Isola d'Elba

Portoferraio Rio Marina

Villa
Napoleone

Marciana

Marina di
Campo Capoliveri

0	10	20	30km
0		10	20 miles

BEATING THE BUG

The Maremma was not always a nice place to be. The broad area between the coast and Tuscany's more southerly Apennines flourished under the Etruscans and Romans thanks largely to its metal-rich hills (*Colline Metallifere*), mined principally for iron, copper and some silver. After the decline of the Roman Empire, marshes and malaria caused a centuries-long decadence (*maremma* means 'swampy coastland').

Much of the land was abandoned to mosquitoes and brigands that terrorized the few remaining inhabitants. After Siena's conquest in 1335 of Massa Marittima (*see* page 279), the new governor wrote in a report on the malaria engulfing the town that it was caused by the breath of serpents wafted in by winds from Africa. Unfortunately, he continued, there were too few human beings to emit the pure breath of good Christians powerful enough to drive out the poisonous vapours.

It was only in the 19th century that the last Dukes of Tuscany had real success in draining the marshes for agriculture and developing new industries. The deadly *Anopheles* mosquito was not eliminated here till the 1930s. The brigands have gone straight and opened up resort hotels on the coast.

2. Maremma and the Beach Resorts:
- **Talamone**, fishing village;
- southern entrance to **Maremma Nature Park** extending north to **Alberese** and its **Marina**;
- behind coast are: **Grosseto**, region's agricultural centre; **Vetulonia**, important Etruscan town; and **Massa Marittima**, architecturally beautiful.
- major beaches north of Grosseto are **Castiglione della Pescaia**, luxurious **Punta Ala** and popular **Follonica**;
- **Piombino**, industrial port important for embarcation to Elba;

- **Populonia**, excavations of ancient Etruscan iron-port.

3. Elba:
- **Portoferraio**, main port;
- **San Martino**, Napoleon's villa;
- resorts **Biodola**, **Marciana**, **Marina di Campo** and **Porto Azzurro**;
- **Capoliveri**, mining village;
- **Monte Capanne**, highest peak.

Around the Argentario

Dominating the nearby border of Tuscany with the old papal lands of Latium (*Lazio*), the fist-shaped peninsula of Monte Argentario was the main bastion of the Spanish-held *Stato dei Presidi* in the 16th and 17th centuries. Its fortresses and ramparts have left their mark on the landscape. The promontory is joined to the mainland by three narrow causeways turning west off busy highway N°1. This follows the ancient Via Aurelia that runs along the coast from Rome north to the French Riviera, putting the Argentario within easy reach for many residents of the national capital.

Orbetello

The town stands on the central causeway of the three embankments of sand and rock enclosing the salt-water **Orbetello Lagoon**. The north-westerly section of the lagoon is a nature reserve protected by the World Wildlife Fund. Birdwatchers will find there a refuge for flamingoes and spoonbills.

Since its Etruscan beginnings, the town has watched a whole stream of conquerors come and go: Romans, Byzantines, Lombards, Orsini feudal lords, Sienese, Spaniards, French and Austrians. Reconstructed after heavy bombardment in World

*T*he statue on Orbetello's cathedral façade is of Saint Biagio, a 4th-century Christian martyr. Like Francis of Assisi, he was celebrated for his gentleness with birds and animals. People suffering from throat-diseases pray to him ever since he saved a boy who swallowed a fishbone.

War II, it is now a contentedly sleepy resort with shops attracting holiday-makers from the peninsula's sailing harbours.

Its heyday as capital of the old Spanish territory becomes readily apparent as you enter through a fine 16th-century **Spanish Gate**. Other monuments of that era are the porticoed **Governor's Palace** (*Palazzo della Pretura*) on Piazza Garibaldi and, on the south-east side of town, the **Polveria**

Guzman, powder-house for the garrison's ammunition (and due to house a **museum** of Etruscan antiquities dating back to the 8th century BC and treasure from offshore shipwrecks).

Rebuilt with a 17th-century travertine façade, the **cathedral** has a carved portal from 1376 and a statue of St Biagio (St Blaise in English) up above the rose-window.

Monte Argentario

The *Strada Panoramica*, 39km (24 miles) around the promontory, takes you through the pretty *macchia* terrain of Mediterranean heathland, along sheer cliffs dotted with buff-coloured watch-towers. Steep slopes are planted with olive groves, orange and lemon trees, and vineyards producing table grapes and a modest wine. The oak and pine woods shelter peregrine falcons, nightingales and the odd wild boar. Watch out for blithe porcupines in no hurry to get out of your way on the road. Among the many fine and often secluded beaches on the far coast of the peninsula, the westernmost, **Cala Grande**, is the perfect place from which to watch the sun set – but you may not be the only one to know this. The highest point is *Il Telegrafo*, 635m (2082ft), part of a military communications post and reached by a side-road west of Orbetello, winding 13km (8 miles) uphill. At **Santa Liberata**, where the lagoon's north causeway, *Tombolo di Gianella*, meets the promontory, archaeologists have excavated remains of a Roman villa and the masonry of ancient fish-tanks.

Porto Ercole

On the south-east corner of the promontory, this charming, perennially fashionable sailing harbour has long had the favour of royalty (Queen Juliana of the Netherlands, Princess Margaret of England) and quasi-royalty (Jacqueline Kennedy, Giovanni Agnelli). Today, its 'clientèle' is a set of either casually elegant yachtsmen taking their guests on board from their Lancias, BMWs and Range Rovers or elegantly casual land-lubbers watching the action from a quayside trattoria over a plate of fine seafood. At the entrance to the town, the gateway bears a plaque commemorating the passage of a

The Marina at Porto Ercole may look crowded, but most of the boat-owners are away down in Rome. You can soon get away from the mob and find peace and quiet out in the waters around the Argentario peninsula.

genius – Caravaggio, the greatest Italian painter of his age, who died here in 1610. Get to the port early if you want to find the best bargain at the **fish market**.

The charm of the old part of town has been preserved by rebuilding the houses from their original masonry after the bombardment of World War II. Surviving Spanish fortifications include **La Rocca**, transformed from ruined castle to residential apartments overlooking the harbour, the massive **Forte Santa Barbara**, the star-shaped **Stella** and the moated **San Filippo**.

The best sandy beaches are south of town, and at isolated creeks accessible only by boat at Avolotore and Torre Ciana.

CARAVAGGIO'S END

The brilliant but violently passionate painter arrived in Porto Ercole in July, 1610, a physically broken fugitive from justice. After killing a man in a brawl four years earlier, he had fled from Rome, first to Naples, then Malta. Caravaggio's altar-painting for Malta's cathedral enabled him to join the island's Knights of St John, but when news leaked out of the killing in Rome, the knights threw him in jail. He escaped and sailed, via Sicily and Naples, to what he hoped would be the safe haven of Porto Ercole, just outside papal territory.

There, a highly placed benefactor promised him, Caravaggio could await the pope's pardon on the murder charge. However, again he was arrested, this time by the Spanish in a case of mistaken identity. He had to abandon his boat on the Porto Ercole beach. After he was released from jail a couple of days later, the boat had vanished, with all his worldly goods, including a last painting. He raged up and down the beach in the burning summer sun, contracted a fever and died 18 July, aged 39. That last painting was probably *John the Baptist*, later recovered and now hanging in Rome's Galleria Borghese.

Porto Santo Stefano

What the bigger of Argentario's two ports lacks in charm (unlike Porto Ercole, it built an entirely new town after World War II), it makes up for in the quality of its **fish market**. It is also the embarkation point for **island cruises** around Monte Argentario, the best way to take in the full beauty of the promontory.

The he local fishing industry around Argentario was hard hit by pollution, but things have greatly improved in recent years.

P orto Santo Stefano was rebuilt in modern style after being devastated by the bombardments of World War II.

Giglio and Giannutri

These most southerly islands in the Tuscan archipelago are fighting hard to preserve their wild beauty against the encroachment of modern villas. From Giglio's port, a bracing hike past vineyards and wild orange trees up to the hilltop fortress-village, **Giglio Castello**, is repaid by a magnificent view back to Argentario and the mainland. Amid the tangle of narrow streets, stairways and arches, the **parish church** has a High Renaissance statue of Christ by Giambologna. In September, a village festival recalls in wine-laden song the dreadful day when the 16th-century Turkish pirate, Barbarossa, raided Giglio and carried off most of its inhabitants as slaves. A few cruises also continue south to the tiny island of **Giannutri**, where a Roman villa has been excavated.

Ansedonia

On the mainland just south of the Orbetello lagoon, this chic little resort has grown out of the old Roman port-town of **Cosa** (founded in 273 BC). Overlooking Ansedonia, excavations have revealed the ancient hilltop walls, gates, forum and a temple. Before it silted up, the port was connected to the **Burrano lagoon**, now a marshy nature reserve just down the coast, off the Via Aurelia. Among other wildlife, it is a refuge for otter and migratory cormorants and ducks.

G̲iglio fell foul of the Turkish pirate, Barbarossa, Red Beard to us, Khayr ad-Din to the Turks. From 1533 to 1544, he was the sultan's admiral, twice defeating the great Genoese commander, Andrea Doria.

Maremma and the Beach Resorts

Along the coast north of the Argentario, when you have had your fill of beach-bumming or more hectic sporting activity in the water, visit the Maremma nature reserve (*Parco Naturale della Maremma*) for a concentrated close-up of the region's curious landscape.

Talamone

The pleasant little fishing village, 25km (15 miles) north of Orbetello, lies at the southern entrance to the Maremma park and is fast developing into a first-class resort. Looming over the port from the fortified upper village, the 15th-century greystone **Rocca** (castle) provides a great view across to the Argentario.

It houses a **Natural History Museum** (*Museo Storico Naturalistico della Maremma*) introducing visitors to the Maremma nature reserve with maps, photographs and other documentation. The museum also displays archaeological findings from the region's Roman era. They include remains of a temple commemorating the momentous battle here at Campo Reggio in 225 BC, when the Romans and Etruscans crushed Celtic invaders from the north.

In the town's **Piazza Garibaldi**, a bronze bust of the *Risorgimento* leader

After centuries of stagnating as a malarial backwater of mosquito-infested swamp, the Maremma has been almost completely drained and reclaimed as flourishing farmland. It even cultivates groves of cypresses. Welcome to Tuscany!

*C*lassical Maremma *flatlands now bloom with gorgeous carpets of sunflowers. Back in the 16th century, Duke Cosimo I de'Medici was the first Tuscan ruler to tackle seriously the problem of draining the marshes. His enlightened dream has come true.*

celebrates his stop here for arms and ammunition in 1860 on the heroic expedition of his 1000 Red Shirts, the army of national unification.

Parco Naturale della Maremma

The beautiful Maremma nature reserve runs north from Talamone to the mouth of the Ombrone river, covering a coastal strip 15km (9 miles) long and rarely more than

268

6km (4 miles) wide. The vegetation combines Mediterranean *macchia* heathland of
myrtle and juniper, marshes and forests of
pine, elms, oaks and holly oaks. Most of the
pine trees were planted in the 19th century
in the earliest period of land-reclamation.

Look out, too, for strawberry-trees with
white blossom and yellow berries turning
bright scarlet when ripe – but very acid in
taste; and midget palms along the unspoiled
beaches east of the Ombrone estuary at **Marina di Alberese**. Take a boat-cruise from
the Marina to see the cliffs formed by the
rocky slopes of the park's **Monti dell'Uccellina** (highest point 417m (1367ft).

Among the nature reserve's wildlife are
roe and fallow deer, wild boar, wild long-
horned cattle, goat, fox and wild cat. The
cattle and the region's renowned horses
are herded by the Maremma's *butteri*
cowboys, who stage an August **rodeo** at
Alberese, site of the main park-entrance.

In the middle of the park is the ruined
12th-century **monastery of San Rabano**
with a picturesque campanile. You may
also come across one of several mediæval
watch-towers. The most celebrated, at the
southern end of the park closer to Talamone, is the **Torre della Bella Marsilia**, one
remaining tower of the Sienese Marsili
family's castle destroyed in 1543 by beastly
Barbarossa. The dastardly brigand and admiral of the Turkish fleet is said to have
murdered all within the castle except the

beautiful Margherita, whom he presented to Sultan Suleiman the Magnificent. Taking the name of Khurema, she became the sultan's favourite wife, shunted aside the legitimate heir, Mustafa, and placed one of her own two sons on the throne as Selim II.

Grosseto

Emerging from the 19th- and 20th-century conquest and land-reclamation of the Maremma's malarial swamps, the provincial capital has become a major centre for agricultural production and distribution, for cattle, cereals, and fruit and vegetables. The city was rebuilt in uniformly modern style after devastating bombardment in World War II, but a compact *centro storico* has retained its 16th-century appearance inside ramparts of brick built by the Medici, the kingpin being the massive **fortress** (*Fortezza Medicea*) on the east side of the hexagon. The other bastions have been transformed into **public gardens**.

The town's most important art treasure is in the 13th-century Gothic **church of San Francesco**, off Piazza Indipendenza: **Duccio's *Crucifixion*** (1289) on the high altar, Jesus's arms outstretched beyond suffering to embrace his believers. Recent restoration has removed all the layers of

The old ramparts are the most attractive part of the otherwise strictly modern town of Grosseto. They were built as part of the Medici policy of reaching out towards the Mediterranean in the 16th century.

added paint and with it, all doubts of attribution. Notice in the church's **cloister** a monumental Renaissance well.

On Piazza Dante, the **cathedral**, with its 19th-century Neo-Gothic façade, is worth a visit for the elaborate *Madonna delle Grazie* altar in the left transept, framing Matteo di Giovanni's ornate *Assumption* (1467).

The **Museo Archeologico e d'Arte della Maremma** (archaeological and art museum), Piazza Baccarini 3, displays

Unlike the Tuscan hill-country, the flat region around Grosseto is good for bicycle-riding.

Etruscan and Roman antiquities found in the Maremma, notably a **bust of Hadrian** from Castiglione della Pescaia. The paintings include a late 13th-century *Last Judgment*, from the school of Guido da Siena, and

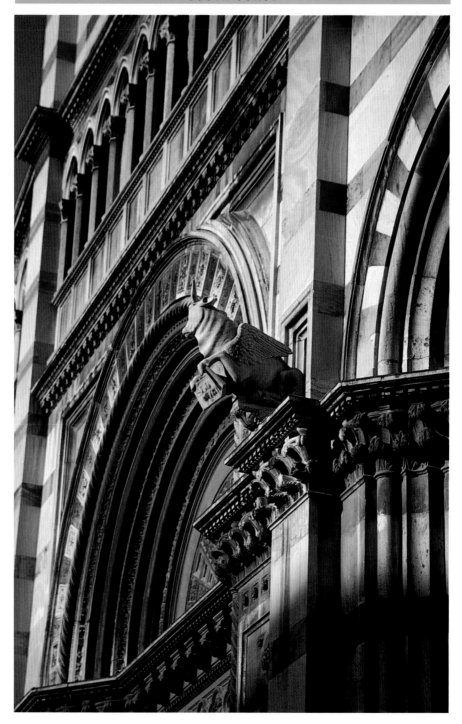

The Neo-Gothic restoration carried out on Grosseto cathedral's façade in the 19th century has tried to preserve the spirit of the ancient church. Arcades and details on the portals recall elements of the Pisan school.

Sassetta's *Madonna of the Cherries* – the 'fruit of Paradise' – from the Middle Ages.

Just 15 minutes drive west, the provincial capital's own beach, **Marina di Grosseto**, is surrounded by a pleasant grove of pines.

The Beaches

The seaside resorts of Tuscany's south coast range from the popular and often overcrowded to the secluded and simple, and the chic and downright luxurious.

Castiglione della Pescaia

This pretty resort 23km (14 miles) north west of Grosseto has a fine **sailing harbour**. It is exceedingly popular in high season, but charming in spring and autumn, particularly for the good facilities offered to fishermen, both portside and deepsea. Overlooking the harbour is the **Spanish castle** of Alfonzo of Aragon, with its Medici ramparts added in the 17th century.

The fight for a place in the sun between Brits and Germans is just not on at Castiglione della Pescaia. Don't even think of trying to reserve a beach lounger with a towel. These places cost money (following pages).

Punta Ala

Gleaming rows of immaculate white umbrellas along the equally immaculate sandy beach set the tone of this most fashionable of luxury holiday resorts. Protected from the prying eyes of intruders by thick groves of pine trees, it languishes at the southern tip of the Gulf of Follonica. Yachting, golf and polo are the preferred sports, and though sandcastles with bucket and spade are permitted, they are ruthlessly flattened by beach-sweepers at the end of each afternoon.

WHAT GOES UP

In the shade of your beach umbrella at Punta Ala, ponder the soaring rise and precipitous fall of Italo Balbo, the man who bought this beauty spot in 1929, an authentic Fascist hero. Courageous pilot in World War I, he was a leader of the March on Rome which in 1922 brought Mussolini to power. As minister of aviation, he was a dashing pioneer of long-distance flights. In 1933, he took off from an air-field at Orbetello to lead a squadron of sea-planes across the Atlantic. He landed first in New York to exhort Italian-Americans to renew pride in the old country, before flying on to Chicago for a dramatic landing at the city's centennial World Fair.

But, as we said, he was an authentic Italian Fascist hero. In his taste for the spectacular, he neglected to develop a truly viable air force for war. He was also a brute. Balbo created the Fascist militia of Black Shirts and participated enthusiastically in their vicious crushing of labour strikes. As governor general of occupied Libya, he confiscated Arab lands to be worked by peasants brought in forcibly from Italy's impoverished *Mezzogiorno*. He was killed in 1940 when his plane was shot down over Tobruk – by apparently accidental fire from Italian anti-aircraft artillery.

273

Gulf of Follonica

At the centre of the bay's broad sweep, the sandy beaches of **Follonica** itself can be recommended only to those who enjoy the jolly promiscuity of cheek-by-jowl holiday-makers hell bent on having a good time. The factory-town behind is heir to the age-old activity of foundries built by the Etruscans to work the iron ore brought in from Elba. The Medici established a monopoly here to manufacture cannon-balls.

Piombino is important principally as the port for ferries to Elba (*see* below). The harbour has been disfigured by steel-works, but if you have time to kill while waiting for your ferry, take a look at the **fortress** built by Cesare Borgia in 1501, with Medici fortifications added later by Duke Cosimo I.

A mooring at Punta Ala costs molto lire, *but the pleasures are considerable: deepsea fishing, water-skiing, but also just sitting on deck washing down your scampi with a glass of champagne.*

B efore leaving Piombino for Elba, visit the fortifications built in 1501 by Cesare Borgia. The Medici dukes of Tuscany added reinforcements over the next two centuries.

A 15km (9 mile) drive north of Piombino is the Etruscan town of **Populonia**. The **Etruscan necropolis** includes tombs from the 7th to 5th century BC. The **Museo Archeologico Gasparri**, Via di Sotto, displays a private collection of Etruscan and Greek ceramics and jewellery found in the tombs; larger objects are in the Florence museum.

Massa Marittima

A veritable architectural jewel of the Maremma, this ancient city lies 19km (12 miles) north east of Follonica. Similarly to the time of its foundation by the Etruscans, when much of the Maremma to the west was still under the sea, Massa Marittima grew very rich from the mining of copper and silver in the surrounding hills. Its elevation to the status of bishopric in the 11th century marked its rise to power and prosperity, 100 years after the town had been completely destroyed by Arab invaders. By 1225, it had become an independent republic. During its heyday, which lasted until its final conquest by Siena in 1335, it commissioned a magnificent series of art works, and also promulgated Europe's first mining code, a revolutionary document of labour protection.

The town separates into two distinct parts, the lower *Città Vecchia* (Old Town) of narrow, winding streets around the Duomo, and the *Città Nuova* (New Town) laid out up on a hill beyond the Sienese fortifications, with straight streets in a criss-crossing grid plan.

Città Vecchia

At the south-west corner of town, the irregular-shaped main town square is commonly known as Piazza del Duomo, although it is officially named Piazza Garibaldi. The great 13th-century **Duomo**,

It was from these ramparts that the soldiers of the dukes of Medici looked out for the precious cargoes of iron coming in from the island of Elba.

set theatrically on a raised stone platform of steps to counter the piazza's slope, is built in Pisan Romanesque-Gothic style. Above the blind arches of the Romanesque lower façade, a beautifully fashioned Gothic colonnade has been added, that culminates in three slender spirelets. The stone carving in the architrave over the main entrance tells the story of Massa Marittima's patron saint, St Cerbone (*see* HIDING HIS LIGHT UNDER A BUSHEL, page 280). Set back from the basilica, but in fine balance to it, is a powerful rectangular campanile. The dome over the rear was added later in the 15th century.

Inside the Duomo, the capitals on the columns have nicely carved floral and animal motifs. In a niche immediately to the left of the entrance, the 14th-century Sienese *Madonna and Child* depicts Jesus caressing his mother's chin, a mediæval symbol of their future spiritual union. It is set above a sculpted Roman sarcophagus of the 3rd century AD. Nearby, some intricately carved **bas-reliefs** from an 11th-century pulpit have been inserted into the inside west wall of the church. Over to the right of the entrance, **baptismal fonts** (1267) have been carved from one block of travertine with Girolo da Como's lovely bas-reliefs depicting the life of John the Baptist. The font's tabernacle is a 15th-century addition.

On the high altar, the ***Crucifixion*** is attributed to Giovanni Pisano; in any case it is a fine portrayal of a Jesus closed-eyed, beyond suffering. It is flanked by Vecchietta's two wooden angels as candle-bearers. Beyond the altar, the **tomb of St Cerbone** (1324) is a superb work of Gothic sculpture by Goro di Gregorio, detailing the colourful life of the 6th-century saint from suffering to glory. In the left transept, the *Madonna delle Grazie*

HIDING HIS LIGHT UNDER A BUSHEL

Strange fellow, this Cerbone. Like St Francis, he had a knack with animals, otherwise people just could not fathom him. The holy man, whose story is carved in stone in the cathedral, arrived in Tuscany from north Africa in 515. Tottila, king of the Goths, seized him and threw him to the bears. Cerbone tamed the wild beasts and was made a bishop, but soon his congregation, upset by his habit of holding mass at 2 or 3 o'clock in the morning, complained to Pope Vigilius.

Two papal legates sent to check out the story were no more willing than the good people of Massa Marittima to get up so early to take communion with Cerbone. They decided to haul him off to Rome to explain himself to the pontiff. On the way, they were stricken with a terrible thirst. 'That's what you get for not taking communion,' said Cerbone, but he took pity on them and conjured up a couple of deer to give them milk. On the outskirts of Rome, the papal legates rebuked the bishop for not having brought a gift for the pope. Not knowing such things were expected of him, he looked around and spotted a gaggle of geese, whom he asked to follow him to the Vatican.

Pope Vigilius was most happy with this gift. Cerbone, equally delighted, clapped his hands and the geese flew away. Controlling his anger, the pope asked the bishop to explain his odd timetable for celebrating mass. 'Join me at 3 o'clock tomorrow morning,' said Cerbone, 'and all will be clear.' As the two papal legates fled before he got them in on the act, too, the pope was forced to get up in the middle of the night and join Cerbone at mass. At the precise moment of the Communion, a host of angels appeared and began to sing.

'You see,' said Cerbone, 'they do this with me every time. I didn't want to frighten people by having it happen in broad daylight.'

altar-piece (1316), with scenes of the *Passion* and *Crucifixion* painted on the rear, is attributed to the school of Duccio di Buoninsegna. Further left, an early 14th-century painted wooden *Crucifixion* is perhaps by Segna di Bonaventura.

Immediately across from the cathedral, the austere travertine **Palazzo del Podestà**, which was built in 1230, houses today the **Museo Civico**. On the ground floor is a collection of Etruscan art, most notably some fine black *bucchero* vases. The collection of 14th- and 15th-century Sienese painting includes **Ambrogio Lorenzetti's** *Madonna Enthroned* (*Maestà*). In this remarkable work of supreme tenderness, notice the angels of the three virtues seated beneath the throne in order of precedence – pink-robed Charity, Hope holding a tower on her lap, and white-clad Faith carrying a Biblical painting. Another fine work on view is Sassetta's 15th-century *Archangel Gabriel* painted with a real sense of wonderment that is still more Gothic in spirit than Renaissance.

Beside the museum is the handsome little palace of the counts of Biserno, a fine Romanesque residence with two Renaissance windows incorporated into the first floor. Beyond it, on the north side of the piazza, the formidable **Palazzo Comunale**, built in the 13th century, asserts the town's civic pride at the height of its power.

Behind the Duomo, make your way down to Via Corridoni where the **Museo della Miniera** offers a fascinating undergound view of the mining activity that made the town's fortune. Guided tours are conducted through the abandoned mine, that served as an air-raid shelter in World War II, to see machines, tools and equipment, and a display of local minerals and ore from the region.

Città Nuova

From Piazza del Duomo (Garibaldi), the pretty Via Roncini climbs to the 13th-century **Torre dell'Orologio**. The truncated but still massive square clock-tower was incorporated into the Sienese fortifications (*Fortezza dei Senesi*) that divided the upper from the lower town in 1335. A huge flying arch links the tower to the gateway (*Porta alle Silici*) and **Piazza Matteotti**. Attractive old houses surround the square. The porticoed 15th-century Renaissance **Palazzetta delle Armi** provided storage for ammunition and today houses a small **museum** of Etruscan and Roman antiquities, tools, minerals and ores illustrating the local industry, along with the document of its famous mediæval mining code.

East of Piazza Matteotti, take Corso Diaz over to the **church of Sant' Agostino**. It has a Romanesque portal and an impressive 14th-century Gothic polygonal apse. Inside, in the sacristy, are 17th-century paintings by Rutilio Manetti, *Madonna* and *Visitation*, and Jacopo da Empoli, *Annunciation*.

Vetulonia

The hilltop town together with a nearby major Etruscan necropolis are located north west of Grosseto, some 30km (18 miles) via highway N°1 (Via Aurelia). Prospering from its metal mining, Vetulonia was a founding member of the Etruscan Confederation. The Etruscan and Roman town's polygonal **ramparts** are still visible, along with traces of houses, including their plumbing and sewage systems. Up the hill, apart from the town's mediæval houses and Romanesque church with handsome campanile, there is a grand view of the countryside.

To reach the **Etruscan necropolis**, take Via dei Sepolcri 3km (2 miles) north east

of town. The earliest tombs date back to the 9th century BC, but the richest finds have been made in the tombs of Vetulonia's heyday a couple of hundred years later. Their gold, silver and bronze jewellery, and terracotta are now displayed in the archaeological museums of Grosseto and Florence, but the domed tombs are still worth visiting, notably the **Tumulo della Pietrera** and **Tumulo del'Diavolino**, both 7th century BC.

Elba

Not big enough to hold Napoleon for long, the island just off the Tuscan headland of Piombino is the perfect size (27km [16 miles] long and 5km [3 miles] wide in the middle) for some lazy days on the beach, imperial grandeur be damned. The island's rugged mountains, limpid blue waters and a year-round mild, dry climate might have kept your run-of-the-mill retired emperor happy. However, the big little Corsican did not go in much for the kind of snorkelling, sailing, wind-surfing and fishing that Elba offers at Marina di Campo's resort hotels on the south coast or on the bay of Biodola on the north. Of course, a bit of surreptitious hang-gliding from Marciano might have helped him escape sooner.

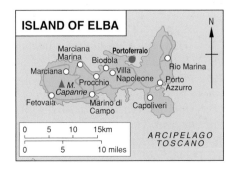

ISLAND OF ELBA

Marciana Marina, Portoferraio, Marciana, Biodola, Villa Napoleone, Rio Marina, Procchio, M. Capanne, Porto Azzurro, Fetovaia, Marino di Campo, Capoliveri

0 5 10 15km
0 5 10 miles

ARCIPELAGO TOSCANO

gate, is the older part of town around the market. An **archaeological museum** in the Fortezza della Linguella has a collection of Etruscan and Roman antiquities, and findings from offshore shipwrecks. The **Pinacoteca Foresiana**, a private collection of Tuscan paintings and prints,

For the dukes of Tuscany – and the Etruscans before them – Elba was important for its rich deposits of iron ore. It is still mined on the east side of the island at Rio Marina. The most commonly found wine of the island's vineyards is the sweet dessert *Moscato* (muscatel) or similar *Aleatico*, beautifully soporific, ideal before a siesta.

Portoferraio

To appreciate the charms of the 'Iron Port' built by Duke Cosimo I de'Medici in 1548, escape quickly from the ugly modern ferry dock. Make first for the **old port** at the head of the promontory. The harbour here is the preserve of smaller craft, motor boats and fishing vessels. Through the **Porta a Mare**, a 17th-century fortified

In the 16th century, when the Medici dukes felt less sure of their power, they needed the island of Elba's iron for their arms and ammunition factories. Portoferraio's star-shaped Forte della Stella was built to protect the shipments

is open to the public in the 16th-century Caserma de Laugier.

Above the town to the north east is the **Forte della Stella**, built by the Medici to guard the port and accessible by a flight of steps from Piazza della Repubblica (or a less steep, but longer winding road). The principal Medici fortification, watching over the open sea to the north west, is the mighty **Forte del Falcone**, worth the climb for its splendid view over the mountainous north coast of the island. The forts were built by Giovanni Battista Bellucci and Giovanni Camerini.

Napoleon's Houses

The French Emperor had two residences during his brief exile on Elba. His townhouse on the heights of Portoferraio, accessible from Piazza della Repubblica, was the **Palazzina dei Mulini**. More villa than palace, it was converted from two windmills. Napoleon's suite of rooms and the apartment of his faithful and flighty sister Pauline (*see* BROTHER AND SISTER ON ELBA, page 286) have been restored with period furniture and books from his private library at the Château of Fontainebleau. In the servants' quarters, there is a less than reverential series of caricatures, French, German and Italian.

The summer residence, **Villa San Martino**, is a 15-minute drive (or bus-ride from the ferry quay) into the hills south west of Portoferraio. Preceded by stall upon stall of Napoleonic souvenirs, the modest house stands behind the neoclassical Galleria Demidoff, built in 1851 in homage to the emperor and housing a collection of engravings. Prince Demidoff was a rich Florentine scoundrel who worshipped Napoleon. More endearing but scarcely less kitschy than the souvenirs is the decoration of Napoleon's villa – pastel-hued frescoes of his military campaign in Egypt in 1798 by court painter Vincenzo Revelli.

*After the palaces of
Fontainebleau and the Louvre, the
Palazzina dei Mulini was a bit of a
comedown for Emperor Napoleon.
Still, it was only a* pied à terre *till
he got back to Paris (left).*

*Napoleon spent little time
sleeping in this bed, though sister
Pauline brought him plenty of
ladies-in-waiting who wanted to
share it with him. His only dreams
here were of his come-back.*

BROTHER AND SISTER ON ELBA

Luckily, the emperor's beautiful sister, Pauline, was there to console him. Josephine had just died and his second wife, Marie-Louise, had gone back to her Habsburg home in Vienna.

With the English, Prussian and Russian armies at the gates of Paris in 1814, Napoleon had had no option but to abdicate and go into exile. After ruling half of Europe, he was assigned tiny Elba as his sole remaining sovereign territory, almost back where he started, within sight of Corsica. He was allowed to keep the title of emperor and was allotted an annual subsidy of 2 million francs. It served to pay 400 soldiers of his Old Guard, joined by Polish lancers and island volunteers, an army of 1600 in all.

He installed his mother Laetizia in a cottage up at Marciana, but kept Pauline with him at Portoferraio. After seeing her first husband killed by insurgents on a military expedition to Haiti, Napoleon's sister had married a Roman aristocrat and led a capricious court life as Princess Pauline Borghese. The charms of 'Paoletta,' as she was known to her numerous lovers, were famous all over Europe, enhanced by the nude sculptures of her by Antonio Canova – you can see her as *Venus* in Rome's Galleria Borghese. To Elba, she brought her carriage, trunks full of diaphanous gowns and, as a present for her brother, three ladies-in-waiting. If shy Madame Colombani resisted, Bellina and Lise le Bel happily deserted their officer-husbands to cheer up the brooding emperor. By the end of Portoferraio's Mardi Gras carnival ball, it was told, the two ladies wore only their masks to disguise their identity.

During the day, Napoleon kept himself busy riding over his pocket kingdom on horseback, sailing round the coast on his only warship, the brig *Inconstant*. He set the soldiers to build roads and modernize the town sewers and dictated regulations for agriculture and mining. But all this was make-work. Napoleon was itching. His fortune was dwindling. He feared assassination. Then news came of French dissatisfaction with the restored monarchy. On 26 February 1815, after barely nine months' exile, he sailed from Portoferraio with six small vessels, 1000 men and a few guns. Next stop: Waterloo.

And Pauline? She drowned her sorrows in Viareggio and made it the most fashionable Riviera resort of the day.

The Beaches

On the north shore west of Portoferraio, the bays of **Biodola** and **Procchio** have sandy beaches, first-rate hotels and good camping grounds. Further along the coast, in the old fishing village of **Marciano Marina**, the perfume of magnolia and oleander among the palm trees along the shore more than counters any lingering whiff of sardines on the harbour.

Elba's most popular resort, **Marina di Campo**, is on the south coast with a range of hotels and excellent water-sports facilities. For more secluded beaches, try **Fetovaia** over in the south-west corner.

On the east coast, **Porto Azzurro** nestles at the heart of a pretty bay. Its prison-like 17th-century **Spanish fortress** is indeed a prison still today. Just inland, south of the harbour, a stroll in the old mining town of **Capoliveri** offers a charming change of pace. The chief ore-port is up the coast at **Rio Marino**, with a lofty octagonal crenellated watch-tower on the harbour.

The Island Interior

From Marciana Marina, a 27km (16 mile) drive inland takes you past vineyards and up through forests of chestnut, fig and pine trees to the lovely little mediæval villages

of **Poggio** and **Marciana Alta**. In the latter, an **archaeological museum** displays prehistoric and Etruscan tools, and ceramics excavated in the area. A **cable-car** makes a spectacular trip to the bare granite summit of **Monte Capanne**, 1019m (3342ft), the highest point on the island. Hikers can follow marked trails to the top in about two hours. Birdwatchers may spot huge ravens, red-legged partridge and distinctive red-rumped swallows.

There are plenty of motor launches available for water sports at the south-coast resort of Marina di Campo. Local fishermen will take you out to the best waters for deepsea fishing. (When you come to think of it, if Napoleon had had vessels like this at his disposal, he could have made his escape from the island much sooner.)

Off the Beaten Track to the Home of Piero della Francesca and Source of the Arno

Much of eastern Tuscany, rugged and then gentle in turn, remains blessedly unspoiled. Few visitors cross the 'Berlin Wall' of the Florence to Rome autostrada to the Arno valley's Casentino forests on the Apennine slopes. Yet ancient Arezzo boasts the greatest of Piero della Francesca's masterpieces and a tournament to rival Siena's *Palio*. The upper Tiber flows unperturbed through rolling countryside that inspired the painter in his Sansepolcro home. To the south, make a loop around the Valdichiana's sunny valley to the pretty hill-town of Cortona.

Exploring eastern Tuscany can be handled without difficulty from Arezzo itself, none of the destinations being more than 50km (30 miles) from the provincial capital, and with reasonable accommodation on the way for overnight stays. We suggest four separate itineraries:

1. Arezzo – at least one day to do justice to the following:
- **San Francesco**, church: Piero della Francesca's frescoes;
- hang around **Piazza Grande**;
- visit the town's other churches, museums and historic houses;

The campanile of the parish church of Santa Maria rises above the roofs of Arezzo.

- **Passeggio del Prato, park:** leave time to relax here.

2. The Casentino – the Arno valley's forested Apennine foothills:
- begin at **Bibbiena**;
- via **Poppi** and **Pratovecchio**, porticoed towns;
- to **Romena,** with castle and Romanesque church;
- **Monte Falterona**: if you are hardy take an extra day to hike up to the source of the Arno;
- **Camaldoli**, head across to this forest and monastery;
- **La Verna**: on the way back via Bibbiena, make a side-trip to this monastery where St Francis received the stigmata;
- end at **Caprese Michelangelo**, the Renaissance giant's birthplace.

AREZZO AND EASTERN TUSCANY

Stia, Camaldoli, Eremo di Camaldoli, M. Penna, Campaldino, La Verna, Poppi, Bibbiena, Chiusi di Verna, Pieve San Stefano, M. dei Frati, Caprese Michelangelo, ALPE DI CATENAIA, Arno, M. Lori, M. Il Castello, Sansepolcro, AREZZO, Anghiari, Monterchi, Castiglion Fiorentino, Montecchio, Monte San Savino, Foiano di Chiana, Cortona, Lucignano, Farneta

258 73 bis 257 327 71 73 416 326 208 3 71 A1

N

0   10   20km
0   5   10 miles

3. Upper Tiber Valley – charmed country of Piero della Francesca on the green border with Umbria:
- **Monterchi**, on a hilltop;
- **Anghiari**, fortified;
- **Sansepolcro**, hometown of the artist with its great museum.

4. South to Cortona – a loop around the plain of the *Valdichiana* via:
- **Monte San Savino**, embellished and immortalized by its Renaissance sculptor-architect Andrea Sansovino;
- **Lucignano**, elliptical ramparts;
- **Cortona**, mediæval and Renaissance jewel: fine Etruscan museum;
- **Montecchio Vesponi**, an English mercenary's castle to visit on the way back.

*T*he statue of Petrarch, Arezzo's 14th-century poet of suffering lovers, looks across the Passeggio del Prato park at the slender steeple of the cathedral.

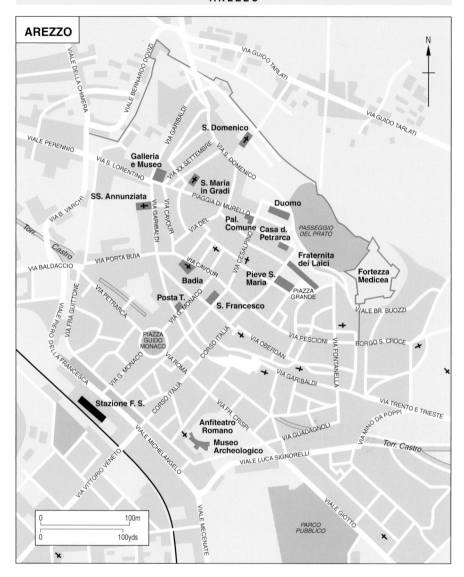

Arezzo

A settlement since the Stone Age, Arezzo, 90km (56 miles) south east of Florence, has generally plumped for the quiet life. The city was a leading member of the 12-city Etruscan Confederation created to counter the rise of Rome, but after its defeat, it became a loyal ally of the imperial capital. In the early Middle Ages, it sided with the German emperor's Ghibellines against the papal Guelphs of Florence until surrendering in 1336. Thereafter, under the Florentine umbrella, its merchants prospered and were able to build and embellish some of Tuscany's most handsome mediæval and Renaissance houses, palazzi and churches.

Arezzo was the birthplace of Petrarch, 14th-century master of the poetry of love, of Pietro Aretino, libertine humanist of the Renaissance, and of Giorgio Vasari, the Medicis' man-of-all-trades and first art historian of the Italian Renaissance.

Centro Storico

This town is a place of hidden treasures. Like many of the larger Italian cities, its characterless modern suburbs belie the real charms of its *centro storico* north of the railway station. After heavy bombardment in World War II, the restoration of Arezzo's historic monuments has benefitted from the prosperity of agricultural commerce and light industry. It is also a major focus for Italy's antique-dealers, who meet here once a month and for a big annual antiques fair in the autumn.

Church of San Francesco

The principal source of Arezzo's national and international glory – Piero della Francesca's fresco cycle of the *True Cross*, one of the artistic pinnacles of the Renaissance – is at the very heart of the old town. From the main street, Corso Italia, turn west (left as you go up hill) on Via Cavour to Piazza San Francesco. The façade of the 14th-century church has

been left unfinished in rough-hewn stone, with traces of its planned smoother granite facing only at the base.

Incrustations of the 17th and 18th centuries have been stripped away in recent years to restore a bare but bright Gothic interior. It is illuminated by the 16th-century **stained glass windows** of the Arezzo-based French artist, Guglielmo di Marcillat (Guillaume de Marseille). As a fitting prelude to the *True Cross* frescoes, the Sanctuary has a monumental painted wooden *Crucifixion* (1250), with St Francis kissing the foot of Jesus, by the anonymous Maestro di San Francesco.

Piero della Francesca's frescoes adorn the choir beyond the high altar. (He took over a commission which Bicci di Lorenzo abandoned in 1448 after executing only the

*B*ehind that plain façade of the church of San Francesco are Piero della Francesca's frescoes of The Legend of the True Cross.

*A*rezzo has cornered a privileged position in Tuscany's antique market. This shop (left) is on the Piazza Grande where an important fair is held in the autumn.

Evangelists in the choir ceiling and a *Last Judgment* on the entrance arch.) Since it was painted (1452-1459), Piero's masterpiece has suffered the assault of humidity and dirt, brutal fissures in the masonry and, not least, the distortions of clumsy restorers over the centuries, but still its magic survives and triumphs. In ten scenes, this most sophisticated of Renaissance painters illustrates key moments in the naïve popular mediæval legend of the *True Cross* with a refined intelligence and grace. He places his mathematical understanding of perspective at the service of a noble poetry infused with the most delicate and subtle colour. Notice the almost cinematographic sense with which Piero combines panoramic 'long shots' for the pageantry or battle scenes on the side walls with close-ups of more intimate moments in the vertical scenes flanking the rear window.

The episodes are presented with a certain narrative logic, but not in some simple left-to-right, top-to-bottom sequence. Ideally, to the extent that ongoing restoration allows, we suggest you look at the frescoes *twice*. First, take in the pictorial ensemble with whatever anecdotal detail catches your eye (two *Prophets*, in upper panels flanking the rear window, are also the work of Piero or a pupil). Then, if you want to understand the cycle as it relates to the actual legend, examine each panel in 'chronological' order as we present them in our account of the story (*see* LEGEND OF THE TRUE CROSS, right).

*O*n the sloping Piazza Grande, the town's rival neighbourhoods compete in an annual Giostra del Saraceno (previous pages).

LEGEND OF THE TRUE CROSS

Piero della Francesca's frescoes are an adaptation of the 13th-century *Leggenda Aurea* of the Franciscan friar Jacopo da Varagine linking the Cross back to the Creation of the world and forward to Emperor Constantine's conversion to Christianity. The story begins (*right wall, upper lunette*) with Adam on his death bed sending his son Seth to the Archangel Gabriel to get a seedling from the Tree of Knowledge in the Garden of Eden. At Adam's death, the seedling is to be planted in his mouth so that a tree can grow to provide sacred wood for the Cross. The wood is used by King Solomon for a bridge across a stream. On her visit to Israel, the Queen of Sheba has a vision of the wood's sacred destiny and kneels in adoration before meeting Solomon (*right wall, centre panel*). Solomon realizes the wood will mean the end of the kingdom of the Jews and has it buried (*right of rear window, centre panel*).

The wood is dug up and used for the Cross (not depicted). Three centuries later, an angel tells Emperor Constantine in a dream (*right of rear window, lower panel*) that he must defeat his Roman rival Maxentius in the name of the True Cross, at the battle of the Mulvian Bridge (*right wall, lower panel*).

Constantine's mother, Helena, is told by the Archangel Gabriel to seek out the True Cross in Jerusalem (classical *Annunciation* scene, *left of rear window, lower panel*). Only a Jew named Judas knows its whereabouts and he is tortured in a well to reveal his secret (*left of rear window, centre panel*). It is dug up and to prove it is the True Cross, it is used to raise a youth from the dead (*left wall, centre panel*). Subsequently stolen by Persian King Chosroes, the Cross is recaptured by Emperor Heraclius in a bloody battle ending in the execution of Chosroes (*left wall, lower panel*). Heraclius carries the Cross back to Jerusalem (*left wall, upper lunette*).

Around the Piazza Grande

The town's main square hosts a bustling antiques fair on the first Sunday of each month. On the last Sunday of August and first Sunday of September, it is also the scene of a grand pageant and tournament. Like the contest of Siena's *contrade* for the *Palio* (*see* page 225), Arezzo's historic quarters parade their gaily coloured banners and perform acrobatics before competing in the *Giostra del Saraceno* (Saracen's Joust). Horsemen in Renaissance costume ride full tilt at a pivoting statue which threatens to pivot and bash them in the back if they are not nimble enough.

Along the top of the sloping piazza, the long porticoed **Palazzo delle Logge,** with a handsome cream-and-olive façade, was built for his home town by Giorgio Vasari in 1573. At right angles to it, on the west slope, is the **Palazzo della Fraternità dei Laici** (Palace of the Lay Brotherhood) on which an airy ornate 16th-century Renaissance bell-tower crowns an elegant colonnaded loggia (1460) above the Gothic ground floor. The statues and reliefs over the entrance were sculpted by Bernardo Rossellino, who also designed the loggia. The adjacent 17th- and 18th-century **Palazzo del Tribunale** has an attractive rounded flight of steps hugging the piazza slope.

At the bottom of the slope are the remarkable semi-circular arcaded apse and campanile of the 12th-century Romanesque **Pieve** (parish church) **di Santa Maria**. Make your way round to the façade on Corso Italia. Its spectacular colonnade recalls the carved intricacies of the churches of Pisa or Lucca. A pair of binoculars will help you spot one lone human caryatid sculpted in the middle of the uppermost tier of columns. The luminous sandstone interior marks a transition to Gothic in the slightly pointed arches. Notice the imposing clustered pillars and Pisan-style capitals sculpted with rams' and lions' heads and a simple peasant figure. In the presbytery is an elaborate **Pietro Lorenzetto polyptych** (1320), recently restored, depicting the *Madonna and Child with Four Saints* beneath an *Annunciation and 12 Saints*.

Many of the mediæval houses and shops around Piazza Grande retain their old towers and wooden balconies. North of the piazza at Via dell'Orto 28, **Petrarch's house** preserves the memory of the poet with manuscripts, autographs and other mementoes. His giant **statue** (1928) stands in the nearby park, the **Passeggio del Prato**, where grassy lawns and shady pine trees offer a pleasant time-out for picnic, siesta or view of the surrounding countryside. On

---

POET OF LOVE AND PAIN

All the world's wayward lovers, that's to say, all of us, can be reassured they are not alone by one of Petrarch's celebrated lines: 'I know and love the good, yet, ah! the worst pursue.' To give the poet his full name, Francesco Petrarca (1304-74) is regarded – along with Dante and Boccaccio, his personal friend – as a founding father of Italian literature. He was born in Arezzo by political circumstance, after his lawyer father was banished from Florence, like Dante, by the fanatical Black Guelphs. When he was seven, the family followed the papal court into exile at Avignon. At 23, he fell in love with Laura, enigmatic object of his most famous poems. Probably for financial reasons, he took ecclesiastical orders, but fathered two children. Back in Italy, writing mostly in Latin, he became the first writer since antiquity to win the crown of Poet Laureate. The existential doubt that filled his work, torn between Christian constraint and humanistic freedom, made him in the eyes of many the first modern man.

the eastern edge of the park is the 16th-century **Fortezza Medicea** built by Giuliano and Andrea da Sangallo the Younger.

At the western end of the park, the elongated **Duomo**, with a façade subjected to 19th- and 20th-century restoration, is worth visiting for its Gothic interior and above all, **Piero della Francesca's** *Mary Magdalen* (1465), left of the sacristy in the north aisle. The traditionally contrite friend of Jesus is here strikingly dignified and stately. The 18th-century Capella della Madonna del Conforto in the left aisle has glazed terracotta works by Andrea della Robbia. The 16th-century **stained glass windows** are by Guglielmo di Marcillat.

From the nearby town hall (*Palazzo del Comune*), take Via Sassoverde down to the limetree-bordered piazza of the Romanesque **church of San Domenico** (1275). With its Gothic campanile, it was built by the Dominicans, as was their custom, away from the city centre as a single-naved hall for preaching. Try to ignore the stone canopy added in 1930 to the Romanesque porch with a *Madonna and Child* fresco over the door by Angelo di Lorentino. Over the high altar is a **Cimabue** *Crucifixion* (1270), one of the first known works of this precursor of the great Giotto. To the right of the altar is a fine 14th-century stone *Madonna and Child* (1339) by an unknown Sienese artist.

Continue west along Via San Domenico to **Vasari's House** at Via XX Settembre

*A*rezzo's latterday poets meet and jot down their verses on this café terrace. They continue the tradition of Petrarch and the great libertine, Pietro Aretino.

*B*eneath the cathedral's high altar is the body of the city's patron saint, Donato, who miraculously repaired a chalice broken by heathens and was martyred in 361.

PIETRO ARETINO (1492-1556)

His erotic writings proved the new Renaissance spirit of freedom and humanism could be applied to all activities of man and woman. Written in 1534 with great elegance in the then fashionable style of a Platonic dialogue, his *Ragionamenti* ('Reasonings') was a highly appreciated discourse on how to run a brothel. The scurrilous fellow is still considered too naughty to deserve a monument in his home town of Arezzo – just a Via Pietro Aretino with a car-park.

Abandoning the name of his layabout cobbler of a father, he called himself *Il Aretino* (the man of Arezzo) and went to live with his pretty bourgeois mother and her aristocratic 'protector' in Perugia. In Rome, the rich and powerful – the Chigi of Siena and Medici of Florence, including Pope Leo X – paid him to write satirical pamphlets against their enemies. However, in 1524, he ran foul of the second Medici pope, Clement VII, with his saucy sonnets on various positions in love-making to go with the engravings of Giulio Romano. He was forced to flee to Venice, more hospitable in such matters. There his satirical writing became a lucrative form of protection racket. Dubbed the 'Scourge of Princes', he was paid either by the enemies of his victims or by the potential victims themselves, hoping he would spare them. One of his most famous pay-offs was a sumptuous gold chain from French king François I.

55. The Medici court architect and painter bought the house for his Arezzo family while it was still under construction in 1540. He finished it with his own furnishing and **frescoes** in rooms devoted to Abraham, Apollo and Fame. His personal art collection here includes Andrea Sansovino's bust of Roman Emperor Galba and a Fra Bartolommeo in the family chapel.

Two Museums

The **Museo di Arte Medievale e Moderna** (Via San Lorentino 8) is housed in the handsome 15th-century Palazzo Bruni-Ciocchi. Renaissance and Mannerist art is represented by Bernardo Rossellino's terracotta *Madonna di Misericordia* and paintings by Luca Signorelli and Rosso Fiorentino. Modern works include Macchiaioli paintings by Giovanni Fattori and Telemaco Signorini. The major treasure is the exquisite **majolica collection**. This ranges from ceramics of Islamic Spain to superb creations of Faenza, Pesaro and Gubbio. A highlight is the 16th-century basin bearing the Medici coat of arms.

The **Museo Archeologico Mecenate** (Via Margaritone 10) is housed in the remodelled 14th-century monastery of San Bernardo. This follows the curve of the town's ancient **Roman amphitheatre** (visited through a separate entrance, Via Crispi 50). Starting with prehistoric exhibits, the collection highlights Arezzo's Etruscan beginnings: red-figured pottery of the 5th century BC, black Bucchero pottery, terracotta sculpture from Chiusi, a Greek wine-bowl (*krater*), Etruscan and Roman glass, and examples of the lucrative mass-produced red pottery known as Aretine ware sold throughout the Mediterranean region from the 1st century BC to the 1st century AD.

Two Renaissance Churches

Besides its predominantly Romanesque and Gothic edifices, Arezzo boasts a couple of noteworthy churches of the Renaissance era. West of the Duomo off Piaggia del Murello, **Santa Maria in Gradi** has a handsome interior designed by Bartolommeo Ammannati (1592), with an altar left of the entrance by Andrea della Robbia. Further west, on Via Garibaldi, is the early 16th-century **Santissima Annunziata**, designed by the Sangallo family while working on the town's Fortezza Medicea. In the serene grey and white interior, look in the chapel right of the high altar for Pietro da Cortona's *Madonna and St Francis*.

*T*he Palazzo del Comune is Arezzo's mediæval home of communal government from which it resisted Florentine domination until 1289.

The Casentino

Making a sharp break with the classical Tuscan landscape, the Casentino hills of the upper Arno valley are covered with dense forests of beech, fir and many other trees more common in northern than southern Europe. In place of vineyards, olive groves and rows of cypresses framing a hilltop village sleeping in the sun, you will see stark, romantic castle ruins or isolated hermitages and monasteries dramatically perched on outcroppings of rock in the woods. In these hills, the Guelphs and Ghibellines fought some of their fiercest battles.

(Starting out from Arezzo, our circuit-itinerary is little more than a day-trip. If you tackle it in reverse order from Florence, it will be slightly longer. This route follows the pretty river road along the Arno and then the Sieve.)

Bibbiena

For your first good look at the upper Arno valley, drive north of Arezzo, 33km (20 miles) along the river on road N°71, to this agricultural centre and chief town of the Casentino. As a fief of Arezzo's powerful Tarlati family, Bibbiena was a major bone of contention with Florence and was largely destroyed after the momentous battle of Campaldino in 1289 (*see* HISTORY, page 64). On Piazza Tarlati are battlemented remains of the feudal **castle**, with a grand view from the terrace over the valley and up to Monte Falterona, where the Arno has its source. Nearby is the castle's 12th-century chapel, now restored as the parish church (*Pieve*) of **Santi Ippolito e Donato**, with a *Madonna and Child* triptych by Bicci di Lorenzo and a *Crucifixion* by the school of Duccio di Buoninsegna.

Poppi

Tucked behind mediæval ramparts on a hill 5km (3 miles) north west of Bibbiena on road N°70, narrow streets of porticoed houses and a superb fortress-palace make this the most charming of the Casentino towns. At the top of its hill, the **Palazzo Pretorio** was begun in 1274 for Count Simone di Batifolle and passed into the hands of the Guidi counts, who ruled the Casentino at the end of the 13th century. With its formidable crenellated tower, the massive edifice may well have served as a first model for Florence's Palazzo Vecchio, whose architect, Arnolfo da Cambio, had worked in Poppi with his master, Lapo. The stone relief of an unhappy-looking *Marzocco* lion of Florence over the main entrance was added in 1477. Coax the guardian into letting you peep at the **inner courtyard** with its graceful balconied staircase and glazed terracotta coats of arms. In the top-floor **chapel** are frescoes (1340) by Taddeo Gaddi.

The porticoes that characterize many of the town's older streets and piazzas run the complete length of the main thoroughfare, **Via Cavour**. It leads to the 12th-century **church of San Fedele**, whose campanile is built over a tower in the town ramparts. Inside, the most noteworthy of its many paintings, otherwise mostly of the Renaissance, is a 13th-century *Madonna and Child* in the south transept.

Just north of town where the road N°70 forks west, history buffs will note the column-marker of the **Battlefield of Campaldino**, scene of a decisive victory in 1289 for the Guelphs of Florence over the Ghibellines of Arezzo. Over 20,000 infantry and cavalry fought here (including Dante), a number comparable for the age to a major battle in World War I.

Romena

Magnificently situated on the west side of the Arno valley, Romena's feudal castle and Romanesque church are reached via the town of **Pratovecchio**, 7km (4 miles) north of Poppi. Like the latter, Pratovecchio's streets are lined with attractive porticoes, notably between the pretty, tree-shaded Piazza Jacopo Landino and Piazza Paolo Uccello, named after the locally born painter. From here, the road crosses the river and forks right to **Castello di Romena**, another splendid redoubt of the Guidi counts. Built in the 11th century, three towers remain of the castle that gave refuge to the banished Dante after 1300. The castle-tour includes rooms with suits of armour, a model of the original castle and a loggia with an enchanting view of the environs.

The 12th-century **Pieva di Romena** can be reached by travelling back around the road, but the Casentino's most important Romanesque church is well worth the 15-minute walk along the more direct footpath. Built out over a slope at the rear (and above an earlier, 9th-century edifice), the chancel has two tiers of blind arcading with a couple of elongated mullioned windows in the semi-circular apse. In the interior (keys are available from house N°7 opposite the church), the columns' capitals have been sculpted with human figures, animals, plants and Christian symbols by Lombard craftsmen with a clear French influence. (Its mediæval and Renaissance paintings are undergoing restoration.)

Monte Falterona

For your pilgrimage up the mountain to the source of the Arno, start out from the pretty wool-town of **Stia**, just 3km (2 miles) north of Pratovecchio. Mountain trail maps are available from the tourist office on Piazza Tanucci. Take a look while in town at the abandoned old riverside wool factories. The bracing hike to the river's source and on to the summit – 1654m (5426ft) above sea level – takes a pleasant four hours. For the record, the Arno flows from its source for 241km (150 miles), beginning in a wide loop north of Arezzo before passing through Florence, Empoli and Pisa on its way to the Mediterranean just north of Livorno.

Forest of Camaldoli

This grandiose forest of fir and beech trees, but also birch, sycamore, oak, chestnut, poplar and alder, lies at the heart of a vast new national park. The park includes Monte Falterona to the north, and covering 11,000 hectares (27,000 acres) it stretches along the Apennine ridge to Mandrioli Pass on the border of Emilia-Romagna.

Beautiful winding roads climb through the forest east from Poppi or from Pratovecchio, each about 20km (12 miles) from the middle, where hermits and monks chose to establish two separate refuges. It was in 1012 that St Romualdo founded the order of Camaldoli, a name contracted from *campo amabile*, 'pleasant field'. At first much more austere than *amabile*, the **Camaldoli Hermitage** (*Eremo*) severed an early link with the relatively back-sliding Benedictines. Today, its dozen or so monks, though still living in hermits' cells (closed to the public), lead a more convivial life. Accordingly, their grey and white **church** has an 18th-century façade and Baroque interior of gilded stucco. About 3km (2 miles) to the south, the **Camaldoli Monastery** is a more bustling enterprise of 40 monks, some of them selling their liqueurs and herbal concoctions in the old **pharmacy**.

La Verna

Some 22km (13 miles) east of Bibbiena, this is the **monastery** where St Francis is attested to have received his stigmata in 1224. It is beautifully situated high on a rocky spur in a forest of fir trees, 1129m (3703ft) above sea level. Before beginning your visit, take in the wonderful view over the Arno valley and Casentino hills from the church terrace.

The monastery's **church** (*Chiesa Maggiore*), dating from the 14th and 15th centuries, is decorated with masterpieces of **Andrea della Robbia glazed terracotta**, notably the *Annunciation* and *Adoration of the Child Jesus* in tabernacles to the left and right of the nave. In a chapel to the left of the choir is a monumental *Ascension*.

REAL WOUNDS

In 1224, three years after his return from Palestine, Francis of Assisi retired to his La Verna mountain refuge given him earlier by a local lord. He was weary of internal dissensions in his order. At prayer one night, he had a vision of the crucifixion and his hands, feet and the side of his body were inflicted with the wounds of Jesus. Contemporary biographers stated that the stigmata bled profusely and that Francis suffered acute pain for the remaining two years of his life. His was the first and most convincingly attested case of stigmata and the only one celebrated liturgically by the Roman Catholic Church (on 17 September). Approximately 300 other cases have been attested, most of them by women, the most celebrated being St Catherine of Siena whose stigmata became visible, it was said, only after her death. The Catholic Church continues to investigate reports of stigmata, but no longer pronounces on their authenticity. Scientists suggest that the phenomenon is associated with nervous or cataleptic hysteria.

The 30 Franciscan monks hold a daily procession at 3pm from the monastery through a corridor and down a flight of steps to the **Cell of St Francis** and, just beyond, to the **Chapel of the Stigmata**. A 13th-century carved relief above the door shows the saint receiving the wounds of Jesus and an inscription in the chapel pavement marks the exact spot, protected by glass, where the apparent miracle occurred. Above the door on the inside wall is a *Madonna and Child* terracotta by Luca della Robbia, while the *Crucifixion* is by nephew Andrea.

In the valley below the monastery, **Chiusi della Verna** is a little resort providing accommodation.

Caprese Michelangelo

About 12km (7 miles) south of Chiusi della Verna, art pilgrims can visit the birthplace (in 1475) of Michelangelo. The town's **Palazzo Pretorio**, where his father, Leonardo Buonarroti, served as chief magistrate (*podestà*), houses a **museum** with photographs and plaster casts to remind you of the real thing in Florence and Rome. You are shown a room where the great baby was perhaps born. Below the castle, opposite the palazzo, is the 13th-century chapel where he was baptized.

Upper Tiber Valley

Visitors passing through London before heading for Tuscany might like to stop off in the National Gallery for a first glimpse of the country around Piero della Francesca's home in the upper Tiber valley east of Arezzo. In his *Baptism of Jesus*, you can see the little town of Anghiari (against the hill behind Jesus), the straight road that still links it to Piero's birthplace at Sansepolcro, and the sinuous Tiber river serves as a model for the Jordan in which Jesus is baptised. In the National Gallery's other masterpiece of his, the *Nativity*, the towers of Sansepolcro itself are depicted on the right, and on the left is the arid moon-like landscape north of Piero's town in the Alpe delle Luna.

To see this lovely countryside 'for real' together with the great paintings of Piero that remained in Sansepolcro and in his mother's home town of Monterchi, follow the Sansepolcro signs south east of Arezzo. The little country road winds through enchanting woods and hills of vineyards to the main eastbound road N°73.

Monterchi

At a fork on road N°73 just after the hamlet of Le Ville, 28km (17 miles) from Arezzo, take road N°221 (signposted 'Città di Castello') and the lovely little hilltop village of Monterchi will appear on the right. Orchards and vineyards nestle up against the fortifications of what was once *Mons Herculis*, much damaged by earthquakes over the centuries. The village is the revered home of a unique and sublime work of art, **Piero della Francesca's** *Madonna del Parte*, the only known depiction of the Madonna in pregnancy. It is believed by art historians to be Piero's homage to his mother, Romana di Perino, born in Monterchi. After meticulous restoration in 1993, the fresco was placed, pending final relocation, in a specially conceived room in the town's elementary school (signposted). Flanked by angels raising the flaps of her royal tent, the Madonna, in the simple majesty of her pose, is at once princess and dignified peasant. Her downward glance has communicated with countless peasant girls who traditionally come to beseech her blessing for their own pregnancy.

(From its nearby country church hit by an earthquake in 1785, the fresco was moved to a small chapel in the parish cemetery where Piero's mother is thought to be buried. The experts are seeking a more appropriately elevated location to do justice to the Madonna's downward glance.)

Anghiari

Twelve kilometres (7 miles) north of Monterchi via the Sansepolcro road, this farm town with its impressive mediæval ramparts rises above the plain where Florentine forces scored a great victory over the Milanese in 1440 (see HISTORY, page 67). Of Leonardo da Vinci's battle fresco for the Palazzo Vecchio, only preparatory sketches remain (in the royal collection at England's Windsor Castle), but Piero della Francesca may well have drawn eye-witness inspiration for his own battle-scene of *Emperor Heraclius* in the Arezzo frescoes begun a dozen years later.

On Piazza Baldaccio, in incongruous juxtaposition with the beautifully preserved old town walls, is the **Galleria Magi** steel-and-glass arcade, classical monument of the 19th-century industrial revolution. At the top of Via Trieste, the 18th-century parish church of **Santa Maria delle Grazie** has a high altar and tabernacles decorated by the workshop of Andrea della Robbia. Right of the altar is a *Madonna and Child with Saints and Angels* painted by Matteo di Giovanni, a Sansepolcro contemporary of Piero, and Tino da Camaino's polychrome wooden sculptured relief of the *Madonna and Child* (1316). Down the hill, the **Museo dell'alta Valle del Tevere** (Museum of the Upper Tiber Valley, Piazza Mameli 16) is housed in the superb Renaissance Palazzo Taglieschi. A major work in its admirable collection is the Sienese

*T*he fertile country around Monterchi was vitally important to the ancient Romans, who colonized the area. Today, Monterchi's other income is from the pilgrimage to the Madonna del Parte.

master Jacopo della Quercia's polychrome wood statue of the Madonna.

Sansepolcro

To give it its full name, *Borgo* Sansepolcro grew up around an 11th-century abbey sheltering relics from the Holy Sepulchre in Jerusalem. Today, it is a place of pilgrimage for some of the greatest creations

straight as a die, just as in Piero's *Baptism of Christ* in the London National Gallery. Just beyond the meandering Tiber, the town sits in a plain with the almost barren hills of the Alpe della Luna behind it on the horizon.

Inside the old city, laid out on an orderly rectangular plan, the pilgrimage to the *Museo Civico* (municipal museum) starts from the historic centre at **Piazza Torre di Berta**, named after an old tower destroyed in 1944. It is the scene of an annual mediæval-costumed crossbow contest, the *Palio della Balestra*, held on the second Sunday in September against the town's Umbrian rival, Gubbio. Along the broad **Via Matteotti**, notice the mediæval tower-houses, in particular the twin 12th-century towers of the Palazzo Gherardi. The **Duomo** has a fine Romanesque-Gothic interior, notable for Niccolò di Segna's *Resurrection* polyptych in the sanctuary, which Piero is said to have studied before doing his own version (in the municipal museum). Look out, too, for *Doubting Thomas* (1575) by another Sansepolcro painter, Santi di Tito (first altar in the south aisle).

Museo Civico

The municipal museum (entrance Via Aggiunti 65) is installed in the 14th-century Gothic Palazzo dei Conservatori. Its most famous work is **Piero della Francesca's Resurrection** (1463), a fresco originally painted for this palace but moved to its present room in 1480. Those who find Piero too cool and detached revise their opinion when contemplating this immensely powerful figure of Jesus rising from his tomb and ignoring the sleeping soldiers to fix with burning stare the rest of humanity. In the same room, the ***Madonna of the Misericordia* polyptych**

of the Renaissance, paintings of the town's most famous son, Piero della Francesca. Off the beaten track of the European gentry's Grand Tour – and of most tourism ever since – many of the graceful buildings of its tranquil *centro storico* remain as Piero knew them in the 15th century.

Travelling 8km (5 miles) east to Sansepolcro from Anghiari, the road still runs

Now in Lisbon's Arte Antiga museum, Piero della Francesca's St Augustine *is part of a polyptych done for Arezzo's Sant'Agostino church.*

took 15 years to complete, in 1460. The meticulous care with which the monumental work has been composed again prompts detractors to speak of mathematical calculation, but a closer look reveals intense humanity and real emotion in each of the figures. There are two other fresco fragments in this room: a pained, almost angry *St Julian*, discovered only in 1954 in the local church of Santa Chiara, and a *St Louis de Toulouse*, attributed to Piero's disciple Lorentino.

THE GREAT UNKNOWN

Piero's life is as self-effacing as his art. 12 October 1492? Of course, that was the day Christopher Columbus first set foot on American soil. But it was also the day Piero della Francesca died. Five hundred years later, while millions were commemorating the navigator's great discovery, only a few hundred devotees celebrated the anniversary of a now undisputed giant of Renaissance painting. It was only late in the 19th century that Piero began to receive anything like the recognition accorded other Renaissance masters, to the point where he is considered today as original a genius as Giotto, Masaccio or Leonardo.

He did not seek fame. After a year or so in Florence as an apprentice with Domenico Veneziano, Piero worked most of his life at home in the backwater of Sansepolcro, denying himself the spotlight of a workshop in the acknowledged art capitals of Rome, Venice or Florence itself.

Of his personal life, we know that he was born around 1420, son of a leather and wool merchant. He became a city councillor in 1442 and as a member of the militia, he patrolled the city walls at night, armed with a crossbow. The rest of his career is documented only by the dates of his paintings in and near Sansepolcro, notably Arezzo; he had rare commissions outside Tuscany to paint for the dukes of Urbino and Ferrara. One anecdote survives, but of the kind that is told of any master: his cavalry horses for the Arezzo battle frescoes were so life-like, the story goes, that when he was making a preparatory picture in a stable, one of the real horses reared up and kicked a painted rival.

Piero's death certificate records that he was buried, as he had requested in his testament, with his family *in badia*, in the abbey that is now the cathedral. Nobody today knows exactly where.

Other noteworthy works in the museum include Matteo di Giovanni's triptych for the Duomo, in which *St Peter* and *St Paul* originally flanked the central panel of Piero's *Baptism of Jesus*, now in London's National Gallery; and a *Processional Banner* (1505) by Luca Signorelli, another of Piero's pupils, with a crucifixion painted on one side and two saints on the other. There are also paintings by Pontormo, Santi di Tito and Jacopo da Empoli.

At Via Aggiunti 47, standing in front of the bell-tower of San Francesco church, is **Piero's house** (*Casa di Piero della Francesca*), which now serves as a research centre for art historians. The large palazzo may have been designed by Piero himself, borrowing architectural details in the portal, upper windows and corbels in the interior from his time spent in the great ducal palace at Urbino. In the public garden opposite is a 19th-century statue of the painter.

South to Cortona

The landscape south of Arezzo is very much a 16th- and 17th-century creation of the dukes of Tuscany where they cleared the marshy plains between the rivers Arno and Tiber. Kingpin of the irrigation is the Chiana Canal that flows into the Arno from Lake Trasimeno in Umbria. The itinerary starts with a brief incursion from Arezzo across the Florence to Rome *autostrada*.

Monte San Savino

From Arezzo, road N°73 crosses the Chiana Canal to the western edge of the valley-plain where the classical hilltop villages, olive groves and vineyards of Tuscany come back into their own. The town where sculptor-architect Andrea Sansovino was born and from where he took his name is 21km (13 miles) south west of Arezzo. It has a long tradition of ceramicists (including Andrea) and holds an annual autumn fair of its pottery and majolica.

The town's predominantly Renaissance character is affirmed as you enter through the 16th-century **Porta Fiorentina** designed by Giorgio Vasari. From here, the main street, Corso Sangallo, is lined with handsome palazzi. Andrea Sansovino's grand **Loggia dei Mercanti** (1520) is a lofty arcade on Corinthian columns. It was built for Cardinal di Monte as a pendant to his **Palazzo di Monte** across the street, now the town hall (*Palazzo Comunale*), designed five years earlier by Antonio da Sangallo the Elder. The elegant inner courtyard has two oblong wells and a hanging garden. The Corso crosses Piazza di Monte on which is Sansovino's house, marked by a plaque, and the 14th-century **church of Sant' Agostino**. Sansovino added the portal, the interior's graceful double loggia at the west end and the **cloister** next door. The artist's worn tombstone, recently discovered, is beneath the church pulpit.

Lucignano

The charming mediæval hilltop village 8km (5 miles) south of Monte San Savino is completely enclosed by elliptical ramparts. The town likes curves and the most distinctive feature of its Baroquified **Collegiata** church is the exquisite, almost circular flight of steps leading to the entrance. Beyond it in the Piazza del Tribunale, the **Museo Comunale**, housed in the town hall, includes in its collection a 13th-century Sienese *Crucifixion*, Luca Signorelli's *St Francis* and Bartoli di Fredi's *Madonna* triptych. However, its prize treasure is an unusual

14th- and 15th-century gold reliquary, the **Albero di San Francesco** (Tree of St Francis), 2.5m (over 8ft) high, decorated with carved, painted and coral miniatures.

From Lucignano, the Cortona road crosses the Valdichiana plain via the agricultural town of Foiano. Two kilometres (1 mile) beyond the Ponte di Cortona over the Chiana Canal, the Romanesque **Abbey of Farneta** has a lovely 10th-century apse of three chapels over an even more ancient crypt.

Cortona

Romantically situated on a ridge surrounded by terraces of vineyards and olive groves, this largely mediæval town of ancient Etruscan origin, 26km (16 miles) east of Lucignano, is a place to linger and dream in. On your way up the hillside, stop off to visit the 15th-century **Santa Maria delle Grazie al Calcinaio**, one of Tuscany's major Renaissance churches. A lane of cypress trees leads you to an edifice of serene simplicity, designed by Francesco di Giorgio Martini on a Latin cross ground plan beneath a handsome lofty dome. The equally simple grey-stone and whitewash interior is a marvel of clarity, illuminated by rose windows with stained glass by Guglielmo di Marcillat. The guild of leather tanners commissioned the church on what was a tannery pool (*calcinaio*), after a vision of the Madonna appeared there.

The city walls have the massive underpinning of Etruscan fortifications from the 4th century BC when Cortona was a member of the 12-city Etruscan Confederation. The town's streets are steep and narrow, but the splendid views over the Chiana valley, the Calcinaio church and down to Lake Trasimeno in Umbria make the climb

*D*isplaying an aloof charm, much of the ancient Etruscan city of Cortona is blessedly intact, particularly its mediæval centre .

well worth while. **Via Santa Margherita** offers a fine vantage point above the public gardens at the entrance to the town on its east side, especially early in the morning and again at sunset. Overlooking the gardens, the 15th-century **church of San Domenico** has a faded fresco by Fra Angelico over its portal. The 'blessed friar' lived and worked here in the early 1400s. Inside, in a chapel to the right of the high altar, is a *Madonna and Saint* (1515) by Luca Signorelli, who was born and died in Cortona (1441-1523).

Piazza della Repubblica is the historic heart of town. There, in the 13th-century Palazzo Casali, is one of Italy's most prestigious collections of antiquities, the **Museo dell'Accademia Etrusca**. Outstanding among its Etruscan bronzes, which includes figures of warriors and animals, is an elaborately carved **chandelier** (5th century BC) with 16 oil lamps surrounding the face of a gorgon. Stare at it long enough and it changes from grimace to grin and back again. There are also fine

---

DEAR JOHN

The notoriously mean citizens of Florence must have felt that this castle of Montecchio Vesponi was bonus enough for the valiant services of their English *condottiere*, Sir John Hawkwood. Having promised him an expensive marble monument after his death, they decided, once he was no longer around to object, that Paolo Uccello's fresco was all he would get.

In life, Sir John had no illusions. When two mendicant monks greeted him with the wish: 'God give you peace,' he replied: 'May God take away all the alms you've been given.' When they asked him how he could say such a thing, he replied: 'I live from war. The peace you wish me would starve me to death.'

Egyptian and Roman antiquities and some notable small paintings by Pinturicchio and Signorelli. Another Cortona-born artist, Gino Severini (1883-1966), a leader of the Futurist movement, has a special room devoted to his works.

Opposite the over-restored cathedral, the **Museo Diocesano**, occupying the former Church of Jesus (*Chiesa del Gesù*), has a remarkable collection of Tuscan artists: Pietro Lorenzetti, *Crucifixion* and *Enthroned Madonna with Angels* (1320); Sassetta, *Madonna and Child*; Fra Angelico, *Enthroned Madonna* and (in the lower church) a superb *Annunciation* (1434); and Luca Signorelli, *Deposition* and *Madonna and Child with Saints*.

For your best view of the **Etruscan Walls**, take the charming Via Dardana north of Piazza Signorelli up and then down again to the old **Porta Colonia**, where the massive stone blocks, 2400 years old, are still in place. On the northeast corner of town, at **Porta Montanina**, you can follow another stretch of Etruscan fortifications. The spectacular walk takes you this time downhill before climbing back up again, past orchards, cypress groves and the 19th-century Neo-Gothic Sanctuary of Santa Margherita, to the **Fortezza Medicea** (1556) built for Duke Cosimo I.

Montecchio Vesponi

On your way back to Arezzo, 10km (6 miles) north on road N°71, compare Cortona's Medici fortress with this 13th-century **castle** bristling with towers and battlements. It was the gift of the Florence municipality to Giovanni Acuto, better known to us as Sir John Hawkwood, the 14th-century English mercenary captain portrayed by Paolo Uccello in Florence cathedral (*see* box left).

Yes, We Can Assure You, There Is a Life after Sightseeing

It is always a relief to discover that there is more to Tuscany than its monuments. After visiting an endless stream of palazzos, museums, Etruscan ruins or Renaissance churches, beautiful as they may all be, you may be wondering what the Tuscans are doing – and feel a great urge to join them. Naturally, you may be tempted by that exquisite Italian art of *dolce far niente*, 'the sweetness of doing nothing'. However, there is plenty of shopping to do, modern sports to play and traditional festivals to enjoy, consisting of pageantry, mediæval tournaments and classical music.

Shopping

It would be nice to think that the Italians' centuries-old sense of design is now so ingrained as to be almost genetically inherited, particularly in a region so steeped in culture as Tuscany. In fact, for all the beautiful things to be found in the elegant shops of Florence, there is also a lot that is not, both in Florence itself and throughout the region. The silks, leathers and jewellery can be exquisite, the ceramics, too, though

Not all the sailboats for hire are quite as splendid as this one at Viareggio, but shop around and you'll find something to your taste.

you must distinguish between hand-crafted and mass-produced ware. But then, vulgar art for the tourist trade has reached a depth (or height, depending on your attitude) that takes it out of the realm of aesthetics into dreadful fantasy. A few years ago, one of the *Superman* films showed the horror caused in Pisa by the villain who straightened up the Leaning Tower, a disaster for the souvenir business. No joke. It nearly happened. But all is well and the magnificently awful Leaning Tower pencil-sharpeners and candlesticks are doing a roaring trade again, just like Siena's *Palio* fruit-bowls or Florence's Michelangelo *David* electric lamps and Fra Angelico *Annunciation* tea-trays.

You can, nevertheless, find truly tasteful souvenirs of your trip which you will not have to laugh off, in particular,

TUSCANY COASTAL STRIP

gourmet delicacies, not just the local produce of Tuscany, which we will deal with separately, but from all over Italy. Save such purchases for the end of your trip, to get them home as fresh as possible, but think of the cheeses, salami, Parma and San Daniele hams, home-cured *Speck* from the Tyrolean Alto Adige, Milanese sweet *panettone* brioche or Perugia's *stinchetti* almond biscuits. (All major purchases that you are not going to use during your stay, such as clothes or sports equipment, are best saved till the end, so as to avoid carrying them all over Tuscany.)

If you develop a taste for Italian coffee, why not buy a compact version of the *espresso* machine or a streamlined coffee pot that does practically the same job on the stove? Italian kitchenware is in general beautifully styled with a great sense of colour and line.

For quality goods, Italians prefer shopping in small boutiques with a long tradition, very often a family business that guarantees generations of good craftsmanship. As a result, you will not find very smart department stores, just popular, lower-price chain-stores like Upim or Rinascente. These are useful for extra T-shirts, sun-hat, suntan lotion or throw-away beach sandals.

Even when sales people do not speak English, they will bend over backwards to be helpful. If you want friendly treatment

Believe it or not, these grapes, tangerines, lemons and peaches are ceramic, but Pistoia has plenty of the real thing, too. It is, after all, in the heart of Tuscany's market-gardening region.

HOW MUCH DID YOU SAY?

Haggling is making a comeback. Uncertain economic times have persuaded shopkeepers to offer the odd *sconto* (discount), at least on larger purchases. Even in elegant jewellery stores, you may find you can round a price *down* from, say, 225,000 lire to 200,000. A good tip is to work out the price in your home currency at an advantageous rate of exchange and offer the equivalent in foreign cash – everybody these days, particularly the shopkeeper, has a pocket calculator.

in the more expensive stores, you must dress decently. Even the warmest-hearted Italian can, perhaps understandably, be snooty towards people dressed like slobs. Florentines, in particular, are notoriously intolerant of sloppiness. Credit cards work almost everywhere these days. Shops in the bigger towns are only too happy to take your foreign currency, at larcenous rates of exchange, so stock up at the bank on shopping days (*see* FACTS AND FIGURES, page 20).

Florence

If it has ceded to Milan its place as Italy's fashion capital, the old Renaissance city is still a centre of impeccable, if somewhat conservative elegance. The principal thoroughfares for the smarter **fashion** boutiques, for men and women, are Via de' Tornabuoni and Via de'Calzaiuoli.

Florentine **leather goods** remain unequalled. You can smell out Italy's, indeed Europe's, finest craftsmen at work in leather factories around San Lorenzo and Santa Croce. Watch the making of handbags, wallets, gloves, belts and desk equipment without any obligation to buy. Look out, too, for the leathercraft school tucked away behind Santa Croce's sacristy

in what were once the cells of Franciscan monks. The biggest selection and best prices are to be found in the street market by the church of San Lorenzo. There are good **cashmere sweaters** here, too.

Another good all-round market is the **Mercato Nuovo** off Via Calimala. Look for leatherware, but also souvenirs, cheaper jewellery and basketware (its original trade in the Middle Ages). If you are looking for a **flea market**, try the stalls on Piazza dei Ciompi, near Santa Croce.

Ponte Vecchio is the most picturesque place to shop for quite reasonably priced **gold**, **silver** and **jewellery**, designed with the experience of centuries of tradition and watched over by a statue of the most famous goldsmith of them all, Benvenuto Cellini.

Multicoloured glass mosaic jewellery, such as brooches, pendants, bracelets and rings, can be found all over town. Handmade in local cottage industry, they are surprisingly cheap and very attractive. **Inlaid wood** (*intarsia*) is a venerated craft here, perfected in the 16th century with the inlay of semi-precious stones and commonly seen in Renaissance church choir-stalls. Using the same techniques, **furniture** is likely to be expensive, but framed pictures of Tuscan landscapes or views of Florence are more moderately priced and, as souvenirs go, tastefully done.

Along the Arno are shops continuing the town's tradition of **bookbinding** and hand-crafted **paper stationery**. You can see the craftsmen, and buy their wares, in a workshop on the river's south bank on Via de'Bardi 17.

Antique shops are concentrated mainly along Borgo Ognissanti and Borgo San Jacopo, Via della Vigna Nuova and Via della Spada. Even if you cannot afford the mostly prohibitive prices, they are worth visiting as veritable little museums of Renaissance and

Baroque furniture and sculpture. If the original creative geniuses are long dead, master craftsmen continue the tradition of superb reproductions – prices negotiable.

Tuscany's Specialities

Local delicacies cannot always taste as good back home away from the olive groves and cypress trees, but some travel better than others. Here is a selection.

Wines

Chianti is the first but by no means only destination for your wine-buying in Tuscany. We propose two detailed itineraries in our LEISURE ROUTES AND THEMES (*see* page 103), but remind you here that **Greve**, **Radda** and **Gaiole** are major centres for Chianti Classico. Also **Siena** has excellent wine cellars covering the whole range of Tuscan wines, red and white. (**Colledi Val d'Elsa** manufactures good glassware to go with the local wines.) Beyond Chianti, **Montepulciano** and **Montalcino** are famous for their red wines, and **San Gimignano** and **Pitigliano** for their whites. **Elba** is best known for its sweet *Moscato* and *Aleatico* dessert wines. For liqueurs, try the monks' powerful tipple at **Camaldoli** in the Casentino.

Olive Oil

Nearly all the wine-towns mentioned above are very proud of their olive oil production, too, but **Lucca** would insist its oil is the finest.

Gourmet Delicacies

The great sweetmeat of **Siena** is the *panforte nero*, a dark honey-cake rich in almonds and walnuts. The best honey comes from **Montalcino** in the south and the **Garfagnana** in the north. Sharp *pecorino* cheese is a speciality of **Pienza**. For a good locally made salami, try **Montepulciano**; otherwise it is too often industrial produce from the north. Whereas **Grosseto** may justly claim a Medici origin for its *pan ducale* sweetbread, we have to take the local pastry chefs' word for it that the *torta etrusca* follows a recipe 2500 years old.

Traditional Craftwork

Siena is famous for its antique embroidery, reproductions of the grand *Palio* banners and, if you have room in your vehicle, the best billiard tables in Italy. **Sansepolcro** still makes traditional-style laceware and **Pistoia** produces fine embroidery and knitwear.

Arezzo is still turning out the much admired red Aretine pottery that made its fortune in the ancient Roman world. It also has a respected tradition in gold and silver jewellery and wood-carving. The town stages a monthly antiques market on the Piazza Grande that expands into an international fair in the autumn. **Monte San Savino** has long been a centre for ceramics – Renaissance sculptor Andrea Sansovino started his career in its workshops – and stages a major international fair in the autumn. **Chiusi** produces delightful imitations of its ancient Etruscan sculpture and ceramics, while **Cortona's** speciality is copperware, and **Montepulciano** is proud of its stone mosaics.

For chess sets, cheese boards, other ornaments and statuary, **Carrara** remains the main focus for marble products. Nearby **Pietrasanta** has particularly fine onyx, while **Volterra** and **Pisa** both produce finely carved alabaster. The

*O*n *the roads of Tuscany's hill-country, your car can always use a good extra road-horn. Somewhere, one of these crossbows may come in useful, too. All these vitally important objects are on sale in San Gimignano antique shops.*

minerals and crystals of **Elba** and **Massa Marittima** are most attractive when sold in their uncarved natural state.

Sports

Tuscans are more cool and calm about their sport than the rest of Italy, which may explain why the main professional football team, Fiorentina of Florence, does not seem to match the exploits of, say, Milan (AC and Inter), Genoa (Sampdoria),

Turin (Juventus) or more recently Parma. Typically, perhaps, Florence's most fervent match of **football** is performed in Renaissance costume as part of the *Calcio* tournament staged in June (*see* CALENDAR OF EVENTS, page 329).

More likely to stir up local enthusiasm are the **cycling races** staged throughout the year. The hilly country makes the Tour of Tuscany, usually in mid-May, one of the most gruelling races in the calendar. The two-week Tour of Italy (*Giro d'Italia*), with the race-leader wearing a pink jersey, changes its route each year but may pass through Tuscany some time from the end of May to June.

*U*n*like the Tour de France, in Italian road racing, anybody can wear a yellow shirt. For the* Giro d'Italia, *the leader's shirt is pink. Yes, that's right,* pink.

Watersports

Some of the more modern hotels are installing **swimming** pools, but the Mediterranean remains the best place in which to cool off after gruelling days among the museums and churches. The best beaches for sun-worshippers are at Viareggio and Forte dei Marmi on Tuscany's north coast, Castiglione della Pescaia and Punta Ala, to the south, and Marina di Campo, Biodola and Marciana Marina on the island of Elba. Some of these places are quite chic and charge a hefty price for beach umbrellas, mattresses and deckchairs. Pollution need not be a problem if you steer clear of industrial ports like Piombino and Livorno.

All the resorts rent equipment for **snorkelling**, **wind-surfing** and **water-skiing**, but for serious **sailing**, your best bets are further south at Porto Ercole and Porto San Stefano on the Argentario peninsula. **Scuba-diving** around the islands of Giglio, Giannutri and Elba, you may come across Etruscan or Roman antiquities: ancient anchors, wine-jars, or even sculpture. Do not even think of doing anything but reporting your find to local municipal authorities.

The vessels in which families can play around at Viareggio Harbour look very much like the lethal things provided for chase scenes in a James Bond movie.

Or do you prefer a secluded swimming pool tucked away in the middle of a pine grove on Monte Argentario peninsula (following pages)?

320

Fishing

Mediterranean offshore angling and spear-fishing are both popular, particularly around Talamone on the Maremma coast. For freshwater fishing at Lago di Chiusi or in the upper reaches of the Arno, you should get a permit from the local municipality.

Golf and Tennis

Players usually have access to local private golf courses with proof of home club membership. You will find 18-hole courses at Punta Ala and Pietrasanta on the coast, the spa resort of Montecatini Terme and Grassina in Chianti, and a couple of 9-hole courses on the island of Elba. Tennis courts are available at all the resorts, while your hotel in Florence, Siena or other major inland town can advise you about the use of municipal courts. In any case, remember to pack your own racquet or golf clubs.

Hiking and Horse-riding

There is no more inviting hiking country than the Tuscan hills, but if you find the exposed Chianti country too hot, head for the shady forests of the Casentino national park east of Florence or the Garfagnana's two nature reserves north of Lucca. In the Casentino, Poppi is the main information centre providing walking tours with trail-maps. At Castelnuovo di Garfagnana's *Comunità Montana,* you can arrange horse-riding over 350km (220 miles) of trails through the Apuan Alps to the west or the Apennines to the east.

Winter Sports

Yes, you can even try **skiing** and **skating** in Tuscany. You will find modern facilities for both south of Siena at the Monte Amiata resorts of Abbadia San Salvatore and Castel del Piano.

Entertainment

Though it lacks a major opera house or concert hall to match Milan's La Scala or Venice's Fenice, Tuscany is still an appreciable venue for classical **music** and **opera**.

Florence holds symphony concerts in the winter at its Teatro Comunale, a spring music festival, *Maggio Musicale,* 'Musical May' which may in fact go on till July, and opera in the autumn. The *Amici della Musica* (Friends of Music) organize concerts at the Teatro della Pergola in the Medici dukes' hillside villa, Poggio Imperiale, on the south bank of the Arno.

Siena's Accademia Musicale Chigiana stages open-air recitals in the courtyard of the grand Palazzo Chigi-Saraceni. You will find other summer music festivals and recitals, symphonic, chamber-music and choral, at Lucca, Massa Marittima, Arezzo and Montepulciano. Just south of Viareggio, Torre del Lago

For a peaceful change of pace, horse-riding can offer its own particular joys in the bewitching early evening light of the Lunigiana region to the north west of Carrara.

dedicates a summer opera festival to Puccini, who spent his last years there in the family villa. Look out, too, for delightful 'pocket operas' performed in other small towns like Greve in Chianti.

Open-air **jazz** and **rock concerts** are staged in public parks, particularly at the beach resorts.

Tuscany's most spectacular form of popular entertainment remains its **pageants** in mediæval and Renaissance costume. Siena's *Palio* is the most famous, but many other towns like Arezzo, Pisa, Sansepolcro and Florence stage similarly boisterous and colourful tournaments in the summer months (*see* CALENDAR OF EVENTS, page 329). These traditional festivities are above all extremely popular with the local townspeople, so that you have to contact the tourist information office in advance if you want to be sure of a good place to watch the activities.

Children

The question of 'what to do' with children in Tuscany does not have to be a constant headache. Quite apart from finding things that are specifically of interest to youngsters, the secret is to sprinkle the sightseeing with plenty of moments when visiting a monument or museum is fun in itself. Take the cathedral in Florence as an example: if they are not too small, children enjoy the adventure of climbing up to the dome. Elsewhere, the old town halls all have great towers to climb.

In any case, try to programme a few days at the beach: **Viareggio, Forte dei Marmi, Castiglione della Pescaia** or the island of **Elba**. Even if you are not staying at a resort, plan on a day-trip to the coast for a boat cruise from, say, the **Argentario** to

the islands of Giglio and Giannutri. When in doubt, *gelati* (ice cream) for everyone.

In each of the main centres, there are some sights and events that have a natural appeal to kids. Here are some suggestions: **Florence**: Boboli Gardens with its grottoes and fountains; Mercato Nuovo street-market and its bronze wild boar fountain; Ponte Vecchio's bustling jewellery market; Science History Museum with Galileo's telescopes (and his pickled finger); in the Uffizi, the Botticelli room is a great hit with little girls, the boys prefer Paolo Uccello; and the *Calcio* Renaissance football tournament.
Siena: the *Palio*, but also the great Torre del Mangia soaring above the Palazzo Pubblico; and in the cathedral, children like the action-packed frescoes of the Piccolomini Library more than you would imagine.
Pisa: the Leaning Tower is open to the

public again. Even when it's not, kids never tire of taking photos of each other leaning at the same angle. If you can combine it with a colourful regatta on the river or the Push-of-War on the Ponte di Mezzo, it's in the pocket.

Collodi: Parco di Pinnocchio theme-park.
Vinci: museum with beautiful models of Leonardo da Vinci's inventions.
Carrara: marble quarries.
Garfagnana: hiking and horse-riding in the Apuan Alps or Apennines.
Chianti: puppet theatre at Greve.
San Gimignano: the towers here are a sheer joy for kids and adults alike, the biggest, Torre Grossa in the Palazzo del Populo, being the one to climb.

There are also **castles** galore: the most spectacular: **Roccalbegna** near Monte Amiata, **Castello di Romena** in the Casentino hills and **Fosdinova** near Carrara.

*F*lorence could be a dire place for many children if it were not for the Boboli Gardens. There are plenty of opportunities for picnics and games, such as hide-and-seek around the hedges.

*I*n his home town of Vinci, the collection of the famous Leonardo's ingenious scientific inventions is one of the rare museums that both children and their parents can enjoy equally (following page).

CALENDAR OF EVENTS

Dates may vary from year to year, especially moveable religious feasts, and, apart from long-established traditions like the Siena Palio, some events announced as annual do not take place *every* year. To avoid disappointment, check with the tourist information offices both back home and locally.

1 January Castiglione di Garfagnana: mayor offers gold, incense and myrrh to church.

January Florence: concerts and opera in Teatro Comunale and Teatro della Pergola. Siena: concerts at Accademia Musicale Chigiana and Teatro dei Rinnovati.

February/March Viareggio: Mardi Gras Carnival street parade and parties, on the Thursday, Saturday and Tuesday before Lent.

19 March Siena: Feast of San Giuseppe, saint's day celebrated at church of San Giuseppe with street-fair of rice fritters and locally made toys.

2 April Lucca: costumed Liberty Festival with mass in cathedral.

Easter Florence: *Scoppio del Carro* (Explosion of the Cart), fireworks in Piazza del Duomo to celebrate Pazzi knight's return from First Crusade with Holy Sepulchre flints to light sacred fire of Easter. Prato: *Sacro Cingolo* (Mary's Waistband) ceremonially exhibited from cathedral's external Donatello pulpit.

May Massa Marittima: *Girifalco* crossbow tournament. Tour of Tuscany cycling race.

Ascension Florence: *Festa del Grillo* parade and sale of caged crickets at riverside Cascine park.

May-June *Giro d'Italia* (Tour of Italy) cycling race, usually passing through Tuscany.

May-July Florence: *Maggio Musicale* music festival.

June Florence: *Calcio* football tournament (3 days) in Renaissance costume on Piazza della Signoria after parade from Santa Maria Novella.

June-August Lucca: summer music festival.

16 June Pisa: Feast of San Ranieri, torch and candlelit parade; costumed Regatta on Arno river.

Late June Pisa: *Gioca di Ponte*, pushing heavy cart across the Arno bridge, Ponte di Mezzo.

2 July Siena: first of the summer's two *Palio* horseraces and banner-throwing pageants (*see* Siena, page 225).

July Pistoia: late-July *Giostra dell'Orso* (Joust of the Bear) mediæval costumed riders gallop full tilt at bear-emblems.

August Arezzo: *Concorso Polifonico Internazionale* music festival at Teatro Petrarca. Massa Marittima: (2nd Sunday) summer version of costumed *Girifalco* crossbow tournament. Siena: music festival at Accademia Musicale Chigiana.

16 August Siena: second version of *Palio* horse-race and banner-throwing parade.

August-September Arezzo: (last Sunday in August, 1st Sunday in September) *Giostro della Saraceno*, 14th-century costumed parade followed by joust at painted Saracen target.

September Sansepolcro: (2nd Sunday) *Balestra* crossbow tournament against traditional Umbrian rivals from Gubbio.

13-14 September Lucca: Feast of Santa Croce, candlelit procession from San Frediano to cathedral, fair on Piazza San Michele.

September-October Arezzo: Antiques Fair. Impruneta: *Festa dell'Uva* (Grape Fair). Chianti: wine-festivals at Greve, Radda, Gaiole.

October Florence to Mugello motor rally.

22 November Siena: Santa Cecilia, patron of musicians, celebrated with concerts and exhibitions.

13 December Siena: Feast of Santa Lucia, pottery fair around saint's church.

25 December Prato: Christmas Day exhibition of *Sacro Cingolo* (Mary's Waistband) from cathedral's external Donatello pulpit.

Language Guide

Staff at the major hotels and shops in the main towns and resorts usually speak some English. However, most Italians appreciate foreigners making an effort to communicate in their language, even if it is only a few words.

Just bear in mind the following tips on pronunciation:

c is pronounced like *ch* in change when it is followed by an *e* or an *i*;

ch like the *c* in 'cat';

g followed by an *e* or an *i* like the *j* in 'jet';

gh like the *g* in 'gap';

gl like *lli* in 'million';

gn like *ni* in 'onion'.

The Berlitz phrase book ITALIAN FOR TRAVELLERS covers almost all the situations you are likely to encounter in your travels in Tuscany. Also useful is the Berlitz ITALIAN–ENGLISH/ENGLISH–ITALIAN POCKET DICTIONARY.

Useful Words and Phrases

yes/no	**si/no**
please/thank you	**per favore/grazie**

*F*or a last image of Tuscany, take another look at the raw material with which so much of its genius was created: the vast expanse of the Colonnata marble quarries rising behind Carrara.

what/why/who	**che (che cosa)/ perchè**
yesterday/today/ tomorrow	**ieri/oggi/ domani**
day/week/ month/year	**giorno/settimana/ mese/anno**
(to the) right/left	**(a) destra/ (a) sinistra**
straight ahead	**sempre diritto**
near/far	**vicino/lontano**
up/down	**su/giù**
good/bad	**buono/cattivo**
big/small	**grande/piccolo**
more/less	**più/meno**
full/empty	**pieno/vuoto**
cheap/expensive	**buon mercato/caro**
hot/cold	**caldo/freddo**
open/closed	**aperto/chiuso**
free (vacant)/ occupied	**libero/ occupato**
old/new	**vecchio/nuovo**
here/there	**qui/la**
early/late	**presto/tardi**
easy/difficult	**facile/difficile**
right/wrong	**giusto/sbagliato**
Do you speak English?	**Parla Inglese?**
I don't understand.	**Non capisco.**

Excuse me	**Mi scusi**
You're welcome.	**Prego.**
How are you?	**Come sta?**
Very well, thanks.	**Molto bene, grazie.**
Goodbye.	**Arrivederci.**
Good morning.	**Buon giorno.**
Good evening.	**Buona sera.**
Good night.	**Buona notte.**
Hello/Bye.	**Ciao.**
where/when/how	**dove/quando/come**
how long/how far	**quanto tempo/ quanta dista**

Does anyone here speak English?	**C'è qualcuno qui che parla inglese?**
I don't speak (much) Italian.	**Non parla (bene) italiano.**
Could you speak more slowly?	**Può parlare più lentamente?**
Can you tell me...?	**Può dirmi...?**
Can you help me?	**Può aiutarmi?**
Where is/are...?	**Dov'è/Dove sono...?**
I'd like...	**Vorrei...**
How much does this cost?	**Quanto costa questo?**
Monday	**lunedì**
Tuesday	**martedì**
Wednesday	**mercoledì**
Thursday	**giovedì**
Friday	**venerdì**
Saturday	**sabato**
Sunday	**domenica**

In the Restaurant

What do you recommend?	**Cosa consiglia?**
Do you have a set menu?	**Avete un menù a prezzo fisso?**
I'd like a/an/some...	**Vorrei...**
beer	**una birra**
bread	**del pane**
butter	**del burro**
coffee	**un caffè**
cream	**della panna**
fish	**del pesce**
fruit	**della frutta**
ice-cream	**un gelato**
meat	**del carne**

milk	**del latte**
napkin	**un tovaglioli**
pepper	**del pepe**
potatoes	**delle patate**
salad	**dell'insalata**
salt	**del sale**
soup	**una minestra**
sugar	**dello zucchero**
tea	**un tè**
water (iced)	**dell'acqua (fredda)**
wine	**del vino**

Reading the Menu

aglio	*garlic*
agnello	*lamb*
albicocche	*apricots*
aragosta	*spiny lobster*
arancia	*orange*
bistecca	*beef steak*
braciola	*chop*
brodetto	*fish soup*
bue	*beef*
calamari	*squid*
carciofi	*artichokes*
cavolo	*cabbage*
cipolle	*onions*
coniglio	*rabbit*
costoletta	*cutlet*
cozze	*mussels*
crostacei	*shellfish*
fagioli	*beans*
fegato	*liver*
fichi	*figs*
formaggio	*cheese*
funghi	*mushrooms*

gamberi	scampi, prawns
lamponi	raspberries
manzo	beef
mela	apple
melanzana	aubergine
merluzzo	cod
ostrica	oyster
pancetta	bacon
peperoni	peppers, pimentos
pesca	peach
pesce	fish
piselli	peas
pollo	chicken
pomodoro	tomato
prosciutto	ham
rognoni	kidneys
salsa	sauce
sarde	sardines
sogliola	sole
stufato	stew
tonno	tunny (tuna)
uova	eggs
uva	grapes
vitello	veal
vongole	clams

Passaggio a livello	Level railway crossing
Pericolo	Danger
Rallentare	Slow down
Senso unico	One-way street
Senso vietato/ Vietato l'ingresso	No entry
Zona pedonale	Pedestrian zone

And Other Expressions Associated with Driving

driving licence	patente
car registration papers	libretto di circulazione
green card	carta verde
Fill the tank, please.	Per favore, faccia il pieno.
super/normal	super/normale
unleaded/ diesel	senza plombo/ gasolio
I've had a breakdown.	Ho avuto un giasto.
There's been an accident.	C'è stato un incidente.
I'd like to hire a car.	Vorrei noleggiare una macchina.
for one day/ a week	per un giorno/ una settimana

On the Road

The following are road-signs you may have to read in a hurry:

Accendere le luci	Use headlights
Deviazione	Diversion (Detour)
Divieto di sorpasso	No overtaking (passing)
Divieto di sosta	No stopping
Lavori in corso	Road works (Men working)

Accommodation

Do you have any vacancies?	Avete camere libere?
I'd like a single/ double room	Vorrei una camera singola/ doppia
with bath/shower/ private toilet.	con bagnio/doccia/ gabinetto privato

The Right Place at the Right Price

Hotels

Our Tuscany hotel listings follow the regional order of our six sightseeing chapters. Prices vary according to season, fluctuations in exchange rates and Italy's unpredictable inflation. For booking directly with hotels, we include phone and fax numbers (variably four, six, seven or eight digits), but we remind you that these are undergoing constant change with the modernization of the system. For dialling from abroad, the international area code for Italy is 39 and you should omit the 0 preceding the local area code.

At last inspection, these hotels all met international standards of cleanliness and comfort. All except some cheaper establishments have rooms with bath and most accept one or other of the major credit cards. Unless otherwise stated, they are open all year round. When checking in, be sure to ascertain that the room price quoted includes all local taxes and other charges, such as service. For our three price-range categories, we have used the following symbols (double occupancy, including service and taxes, but with meals extra):

I below 160,000 lire
II 160,000-260,000 lire
III above 260,000 lire

Florence

Albergo Mia Cara I
Via Faenza 58
50123 Florence
Tel. (055) 216 053, fax 230 2601
Clean, family-style boarding house near railway station.

Baglioni III
Piazza Unità Italian 6
50123 Florence
Tel. (055) 218 841, fax 215 695
195 rooms. Large hotel near station. Splendid view of city from roof-garden restaurant and terrace.

Bernini Palace III
Piazza San Firenze 29
50122 Florence
Tel. (055) 288 621, fax 268 272
86 rooms. Elegant and historic hotel near Palazzo Vecchio. Meeting place of Italy's first united national parliament – in the breakfast-room.

Brunelleschi III
Piazza Santa Elisabetta 3
50122 Florence
Tel. (055) 562 068, fax 219 653
94 rooms. Stylishly equipped luxury hotel near Duomo, rebuilt from 17th-century tower and mediæval church.

Croce di Malta III
Via della Scala 7
50123 Florence
Tel. (055) 282 600, fax 287 121
98 rooms. Modern luxury hotel rebuilt around old convent near Santa Maria Novella, with garden and swimming pool.

Excelsior III
Piazza Ognissanti 3
50123 Florence
Tel. (055) 264 201, fax 210 278
203 rooms. Luxury hotel in 19th-century riverside palace. Has a famous piano bar and a grand restaurant, Il Cestello. Outdoor dining on rooftop terrace in summer.

Grand Hotel III
Piazza Ognissanti 1
50123 Florence
Tel. (055) 288 781, fax 217 400
107 rooms. Riverside luxury opposite sister-hotel Excelsior, newly renovated in both modern and 1900s style.

Hermitage II
Vicolo Marzio 1
50122 Florence
Tel. (055) 287 216, fax 212 208
Tiny boarding house with riverfront terraces in a noisy neighbourhood near the Ponte Vecchio.

La Residenza II
Via Tornabuoni 8
50123 Florence
Tel. (055) 218 684, fax 284 197
Small, comfortable boarding house, handy for chic shops.

Loggiato dei Serviti II
Piazza SS Annunziata 3
50122 Florence
Tel. (055) 289 592, fax 289 595
29 rooms. Quiet hotel in beautiful Renaissance square. Bar but no restaurant.

Lungarno III
Borgo San Jacopo 14
50125 Florence
Tel. (055) 264 211, fax 268 437
*66 rooms. Fashionable modern
hotel on south bank of Arno.
Admirable modern art collection.
Bar but no restaurant.*

Morandi alla Crocetta I
Via Laura 50
50121 Florence
Tel. (055) 234 4747, fax 248 0954
*9 rooms but expanding. Renovated
old monastery near Piazza SS
Annunziata, retaining old-fashioned
charm. Bar but no restaurant.*

Pensione Beacci Tornabuoni I
Via Tornabuoni 3
50123 Firenze
Tel. (055) 212 645, fax 283 594
*30 rooms. Cozy old-fashioned
boarding house in smart shopping
district; reservation preference for
guests on half board.*

Pensione Quisisana e I
Pontevecchio
Lungarno Archibusieri 4
50122 Florence
Tel. (055) 216 692, fax 268 303
*Typical enough small Florentine
boarding house used for filming
Room with a View.*

Plaza Hotel Lucchesi III
Lungarno della Zecca Vecchia 38
50122 Florence
Tel. (055) 264 141, fax 248 0921
*97 rooms. Recently modernized
hotel, good views of city and the
Arno. Restaurant closed Sunday.*

Regency III
Piazza Massimo d'Azeglio 3
50121 Florence
Tel. (055) 245 247, fax 234 2938
*38 rooms. Elegant hotel with charm-
ing garden and renowned restaurant,
Relais le Jardin (closed Sunday).*

Sheraton Firenze III
(Off A1 Firenze Sud)
50126 Florence
Tel. (055) 64901, fax 680 747
*321 rooms. Recently opened hotel
on outskirts of Florence. Swimming
pool, tennis.*

Silla I
Via dei Renai 5
50125 Florence
Tel. (055) 234 2888, fax 234 1437
*32 rooms. Small unpretentious hotel
near the Arno. No restaurant.*

Splendor I
Via San Gallo 30
50129 Florence
Tel. (055) 483 427, fax 461 276
*Modest boarding house 10 minutes'
walk from Duomo.*

Torre di Bellosguardo III
Via Roti Michelozzi 2
50124 Florence
Tel. (055) 229 8145, fax 229 008
*13 rooms. Elegant hotel in peaceful
setting in hills above Florence,
splendid views of city and
surroundings. Beautiful garden and
swimming pool. Bar but no
restaurant.*

Villa Belvedere II
Via Benedetto Castelli 3
50124 Florence
Tel. (055) 222 501, fax 223 163
*27 rooms. Modern, quiet hotel in
lovely country just outside Florence.
Garden, swimming pool, tennis.
Open March to November.*

Villa Cora III
Viale Niccolò Machiavelli 18
50125 Florence
Tel. (055) 229 8451, fax 229 086
*48 rooms. Extravagant hillside
luxury in splendid gardens overlooking Florence, with restaurant
Machiavelli beside swimming pool.*

Villa Medici III
Via Il Prato 42
50123 Florence
Tel. (055) 238 331, fax 238 336
*103 rooms. Luxury hotel in 18th-
century villa, with completely
modernized interior. Garden,
outdoor dining and swimming pool.*

Artimino

Paggeria Medicea II
Viale Papa Giovanni XXIII 3
50040 Artimino (Florence)
Tel. (055) 871 8081, fax 871 8080
*37 rooms. Superbly restored 16th-
century residence for Medici
servants near dukes' Villa Artimino.
Tennis, swimming pool, fishing,
amid vineyards and olive groves
22km (13 miles) west of Florence.*

Fiesole

Pensione Bencistà I
Via Benedetto da Maiano 4
San Domenico, 50014 Fiesole
Tel. and fax (055) 59163
*42 rooms, Charming modest
boarding house in hillside country-*

*villa surrounded by olive trees. Half-
board obligatory, no credit cards.*

Villa Aurora III
Piazza Mino da Fiesole 39
50014 Fiesole
Tel. (055) 59100, fax 59587
*26 rooms. Centre of town, open-air
dining. Closed November to
February.*

Villa San Michele III
Via Doccia 4
50014 Fiesole
Tel. (055) 59451, fax 598 734
*28 rooms. Pleasant luxury hotel in
converted 15th-century monastery.
View of Florence and surrounding
hills. Park with heated outdoor
swimming pool. Closed December
to March.*

Poggioa a Caiano

Hermitage I
Via Ginepraia 112
50046 Poggioa Caiano-Bonistallo
Tel. (055) 877 040, fax 879 7057
*61 rooms. Convenient for visiting
Medici villas. With restaurant.*

Pisa and Northern Tuscany

Forte dei Marmi

Augustus III
Viale Morin 169
55042 Forte dei Marmi
Tel. (0584) 787 200, fax 787 102
*70 rooms. Local monument of
luxury villas in secluded park with
heated swimming pool, linked by
underpass to private beach. Closed
mid-October to April.*

Hermitage III
Via Cesare Battista 50
55042 Forte dei Marmi
Tel. (0584) 787 144, fax 787 102
*70 rooms. Modern comfort of villas
in peaceful garden setting with swimming pool. Five minutes to private
beach. Fine restaurant Il Pozzetto.
Closed October to mid-May.*

Livorno

Giardino I
Piazza Mazzini 85
57126 Livorno
Tel. and fax (0586) 806 330,
*21 rooms. Quieter hotel south of city
centre. No restaurant.*

Grand Hotel Palazzo III
Viale Italia 195
57127 Livorno
Tel. (0586) 805 371, fax 803 206
112 rooms. Big old-fashioned establishment overlooking the sea.

Gran Duca I
Piazza Micheli 18
57123 Livorno
Tel. (0586) 891 024
62 rooms. Overlooking old port. Good restaurant with terrace dining.

Rex III
Via del Litorale 34
57128 Antignano (Livorno)
Tel. (0586) 580 400, fax 509 586
62 rooms. Modern friendly seafront hotel 7km (4 miles) south of Livorno. Open-air dining.

Lucca

Albergo Diana I
Via del Molinetto 11
55100 Lucca
Tel. (0583) 490 368
Well-run boarding house near Duomo.

La Luna I
Via Fillungo-Corte Compagni 12
55100 Lucca
Tel. (0583) 493 634, fax 490 021
30 rooms. Charming hotel in old neighbourhood near Roman amphitheatre.

Pensione Cinzia I
Via della Dogana 9
55100 Lucca
Tel. (0583) 491 323
Old-fashioned little boarding house near Duomo.

Principessa Elisa IIII
Località Massa Pisana
55050 Lucca
Tel. (0583) 379 737, fax 379 019
10 rooms. Outside Lucca, handy for visiting historic villas. Elegant old-world luxury with modern comforts in 19th-century mansion, with swimming pool.

Universo I
Piazza del Giglio 1
55100 Lucca
Tel. (0583) 493 678
62 rooms. Pleasant hotel in heart of centro storico. Recently renovated. Restaurant Del Teatro (closed Thursday).

Villa la Principessa III
Via Nuova per Pisa 1616
55050 Massa Pisana (Lucca)
Tel. (0583) 370 037, fax 379 019
40 rooms. Attractive luxury in quiet 19th-century villa just outside Lucca. Outdoor swimming pool, English-style park. Restaurant closed Wednesday.

Massa-Carrara

Il Bottaccio III
Via Bottaccio
54038 Montignoso (Massa-Carrara)
Tel. (0585) 340 031, fax 340 103
Excellent restaurant also provides luxury accommodation in eight apartment suites in remodelled old mill.

Tropicana III
Viale Giuseppe Verdi 47
54039 Massa (Ronchi-Poveromo)
Tel. (0585) 309 041, fax 309 044
24 suites. At Ronchi beach resort, with heated swimming pool in garden. No restaurant. Closed November to December.

Villa Irene II
Via delle Macchie 125
54039 Massa (Ronchi-Poveromo)
Tel. (0585) 309 310, fax 308 038
38 rooms. Handsome secluded park with heated swimming pool, tennis. Restaurant for hotel-guests only. Closed November to March.

Montecatini Terme

Grand Hotel Croce di Malta III
Viale IV Novembre
51016 Montecatini Terme
Tel. (0572) 78122, fax 73352
115 rooms. More discreet of the spa's 'grand' hotels. Sauna, swimming pool in spacious park.

Grand Hotel e la Pace IIII
Via della Torretta 1
51016 Montecatini Terme
Tel. (0572) 75801, fax 78451
150 rooms. Elegant 19th-century hotel traditionally favoured by the spa resort's social élite. Park with heated outdoor swimming pool, gymnasium, tennis.

Pisa

Albergo Gronchi I
Piazza Arcivescado 1
56126 Pisa
Tel. (050) 561 823
Charming small hotel near Leaning Tower and tourist office.

Amalfitana III
Via Roma 44
56126 Pisa
Tel. (050) 29000, fax 25218
Beautifully restored 17th-century monastery with modern comforts, handy for Leaning Tower.

Ariston I
Via Maffi 42
56125 Pisa
Tel. (050) 561 834, fax 561 891
33 rooms. Modest, functional, close to Leaning Tower. No restaurant.

Arno III
Piazza della Repubblica 6
56126 Pisa
Tel. (050) 542 648, fax 543 441
Quiet, recently restored hotel near San Matteo Museum and Arno river.

Cavalieri III
Piazza Stazione 2
56125 Pisa
Tel. (050) 43290, fax 502 242
100 rooms. Comfortable modern hotel near the railway station.

Pensione Giardino I
Via Cammeo 1
56126 Pisa
Tel. (050) 562 101
Well-run boarding house near Leaning Tower with ground floor self-service restaurant.

Pensione Helvetia I
Via Don Boschi 31
56126 Pisa
Tel. (050) 553 084
Pleasant boarding house close to Leaning Tower.

Hotel Pisa II
Via Manzoni 22
56125 Pisa
Tel. (050) 44551
Impeccably clean and comfortable small hotel, 5 minutes from railway station.

Roma III
Via Bonanno Pisano 111
56126 Pisa
Tel. (050) 550 578, fax 550 164
Modern, efficient, with pleasant little garden, 6 minutes' walk from Leaning Tower.

Stefano I
Via Sant'Apollonia 35
56126 Pisa
Tel. and fax (050) 553 559
Friendly family atmosphere in quiet hotel near Leaning Tower.

Victoria ▯▯▯
Lungarno Pacinotti
56126 Pisa
Tel. (050) 502 130, fax 502 189
*Large old-fashioned hotel on Arno
river.*

Pistoia

Il Convento ▯
Via San Quirico 33
51030 Santomato (Pistoia)
Tel. (0573) 452 651, fax 453 578
*24 rooms. Converted monastery in
the hills east of town. Swimming
pool in shady garden, open-air
dining.*

Lago Verde ▯
Via Castellani 4
51030 Serravalle Pistoiese
Tel. (0573) 518 262, fax 518 227
*85 rooms. Peaceful setting in
country village west of Pistoia.
Swimming pool.*

Patria ▯
Via Crispi 8
51100 Pistoia
Tel. (0573) 25187, fax 368 168
*28 rooms. Unpretentious hotel in
heart of centro storico.*

Prato

Art Hotel Museo ▯▯
Viale della Repubblic
50047 Prato
Tel. (0574) 5787, fax 578 880
*110 rooms. Modern, efficient hotel,
tennis and sauna.*

Palace Hotel ▯▯
Via Piero della Francesca 71
50047 Prato
Tel. (0574) 592 841, fax 595 411
*85 rooms. Efficiently run hotel south
west of city centre, with swimming
pool and garden. Restaurant closed
weekends and August.*

President ▯▯
Via Simintendi 20
50047 Prato
Tel. (0574) 30251, fax 36064
*78 rooms. Functional hotel on south
edge of city centre.*

Villa Santa Cristina ▯
Via del Poggio Secco 58
50047 Prato
Tel. (0574) 595 951, fax 572 623
*23 rooms. Handsome 18th-century
villa on quiet hill overlooking town.
Swimming pool, open-air dining and
piano bar. Closed in August.*

Viareggio

Astor ▯▯▯
Viale Carducci 54
55049 Viareggio
Tel. (0548) 50301, fax 55181
*59 rooms. Classical seafront resort
hotel, near Ponente pine grove, with
swimming pool and health club.*

President ▯▯
Viale Carducci 5
55049 Viareggio
Tel. (0584) 962 712, fax 963 658
*37 rooms. Elegantly remodelled
seafront hotel. Delightful restaurant
Gaudì for open-air dining.*

Vinci

Alexandra ▯
Via dei Martiri 38
50059 Vinci
Tel. (0571) 56227, fax 56224
*26 rooms. Modest hotel handy for
visiting Leonardo da Vinci's home
and museum. Restaurant.*

Chianti and the Tuscan Hills

Castellina

Belvedere di San Leonino ▯
53011 Castellina in Chianti
Tel. (0577) 740 887, fax 740 924
*28 rooms. Amid wooded country,
vineyards and olive groves, south of
Castellina close to Siena. Swimming
pool. Restaurant closed midday.*

Salivolpi ▯
Via Fiorentina
53011 Castellina in Chianti
Tel. (0577) 740 484, fax 740 998
*19 rooms. Family-run pensione,
nicely furnished old hilltop rustic
house and modern annex, with
swimming pool. No restaurant.*

Tenuta di Ricavo ▯▯▯
53011 Castellina in Chianti
Tel. (0577) 740 221, fax 741 014
*25 rooms. A mediæval village con-
verted into luxury hotel-complex with
pool and garden north west of Castellina. Closed November to March.
Restaurant closed Wednesday.*

Villa Casalecchi ▯▯▯
53011 Castellina in Chianti
Tel. (0577) 740 240, fax 741 111
*19 rooms. Quiet location just south of
town, pool, tennis, with restaurant.
Closed November to March.*

Colle di Val d'Elsa

Arnolfo ▯
Via Campana 8
53034 Colle di Val d'Elsa
Tel. (0577) 922 020, fax 922 324
*32 rooms. 16th-century building in
historic upper town; no restaurant.
Closed mid-January to mid-
February.*

Villa Belvedere ▯▯
Località Belvedere
53034 Colle di Val d'Elsa
Tel. (0577) 920 966, fax 924 128
*15 rooms. Splendidly renovated
18th-century villa just east of town,
favourite of Habsburg archduke,
with beautiful views of Colle and
Tuscan hill country.*

Gaiole

Castello di Spaltenna ▯▯
Località Spaltenna
53013 Gaiole in Chianti
Tel. (0577) 749 483, fax 749 269
*21 rooms. Renovated mediæval
castle with reputed restaurant, pool
and handsome garden. Closed mid-
January, February.*

Park Hotel Cavarchione ▯▯
53013 Gaiole in Chianti
Tel. (0577) 749 550
*11 rooms. Pretty country setting.
Swimming pool, fine flower-garden.
Closed low-season.*

Greve

Del Chianti ▯
Piazza Matteotti 86
50022 Greve in Chianti
Tel. and fax (055) 853 763
*16 rooms. On main town square,
small garden and swimming pool.
No restaurant.*

Giovanni da Verrazzano ▯
Piazza Matteotti 28
50022 Greve in Chianti
Tel. (055) 853 189, fax 853 648
*11 rooms. Centrally located, open-
air terrace dining in summer.*

Panzano

Villa Le Barone ▯▯
Via San Leolino 19
50020 Panzano in Chianti
Tel. (055) 852 621, fax 852 277
*27 rooms. Pleasant old hillside
country villa with modern comforts.
Tennis, swimming pool in garden of
olive trees amid vineyards. Closed
November to March.*

Villa Sangiovese   II
Piazza Bucciarelli 5
50020 Panzano in Chianti
Tel. (055) 852 461, fax 852 463
*19 rooms. Country house with pool
in garden, open-air terrace dining.
Closed Christmas to February.*

Radda

Fattoria Vignale   IIII
Via Pianigiani 9
53017 Radda in Chianti
Tel. (0577) 738 300, fax 738 592
*27 rooms. Superbly furnished early
19th-century farmhouse in heart of
Chianti Classico country. Separate
restaurant and swimming pool.
Closed November to mid-March.*

La Villa Miranda   I
Strada N°429
53017 Radda in Chianti
Tel. (0577) 738 021
*40 rooms. Traditional albergo and
restaurant, with pool and tennis.*

Vescine   II
Località Vescine
53017 Radda in Chianti
Tel. (0577) 741 144, fax 740 263
*25 rooms. Handsomely restored
mediæval farm hamlet in peaceful
country setting. Pool in garden.
Closed January to February.*

San Gimignano

L'Antico Pozzo   I
Via San Matteo 87
53037 San Gimignano
Tel. (0577) 942 014, fax 942 117
*18 rooms. Nicely restored mediæval
building in which Dante is said to
have stayed. No restaurant.*

La Cisterna   II
Piazza della Cisterna 23
53037 San Gimignano
Tel. (0577) 940 328, fax 942 080
*50 rooms. Charming hotel in the
heart of town. Le Terrazze
restaurant in 15th-century décor
overlooking town and surrounding
hills. Closed November to February.
Restaurant closed Tuesday and
Wednesday lunch.*

Leon Bianco   I
Piazza della Cisterna
53037 San Gimignano
Tel. (0577) 941 294, fax 942 123
*25 rooms. Attractive, well-run hotel
in heart of centro storico. Closed
mid-January, February.*

Pescille   I
Verso Castel San Gimignano
53037 San Gimignano
Tel. and fax (0577) 940 186
*40 rooms. Handsomely
converted farmhouse looking across
to San Gimignano from the east.
Garden, swimming pool and tennis.
Outdoor dining in restaurant I
Cinque Gigli. Closed January,
February.*

Volterra

Albergo Etruria   I
Via Matteotti 32
56048 Volterra
Tel. (0588) 87377
*22 rooms. Modest, clean pensione
and one of the four lodgings in heart
of centro storico.*

San Lino   I
Via San Lino 26
56048 Volterra
Tel. and fax (0588) 85250
*44 rooms. Well-managed hotel
inside old city walls, with swimming
pool.*

Villa Nencini   I
Borgo Santo Stefano 55
56048 Volterra
Tel. (0588) 86386, fax 806 601
*14 rooms. Quiet small hotel with
pleasant garden and swimming
pool, a raity in this parched
country. No restaurant.*

Siena and Southern Tuscany

Asciano

Il Bersagliere   I
Via Roma 39
53041 Asciano
Tel. (0577) 718 629
*16 rooms. Modest hotel amid
dramatic Crete hill country,
convenient for visiting Monte
Oliveto Maggiore monastery.
Restaurant.*

Buonconvento

Roma   I
Via Soccini 14
53022 Buonconvento
Tel. (0577) 806 021
*15 rooms. Small hotel beside
ancient Roman Via Cassia.
Restaurant.*

Chianciano Terme

Michelangelo   II
Via delle Piane 146
53042 Chianciano Terme
Tel. (0578) 64004, fax 60480
*63 rooms. Classical spa hotel in
handsome park. Heated swimming
pool, tennis. Closed October to
March.*

Chiusi

La Fattoria   I
Località Paccionese
Lagio di Chiusi
Tel. (0578) 21407, fax 20644
*8 rooms. Tiny lakeside hotel with
garden and good restaurant. Closed
February.*

Montalcino

Al Brunello   I
53024 Montalcino
Tel. and fax (0577) 849 304
*18 rooms. Restaurant with
pleasant view from garden just
south of town.*

Il Giglio   I
Via S Saloni 49
53024 Montalcino
Tel. (0577) 848 167
*12 rooms. Small hotel with
restaurant. Closed January
(restaurant closed Tuesday).*

Monte Amiata

Parco Erosa   I
Via Remedi
53021 Abbadia San Salvatore
Tel. (0577) 776 326
*42 rooms. Resort hotel in garden
with mountain view, tennis. Open
for winter sports Christmas to
Easter, summer activities June to
October.*

Montepulciano

Il Riccio   I
Via Talosa 21
53045 Montepulciano
Tel. (0578) 757 713
*Pleasant little boarding-house in
old palazzo with charming terrace
at heart of centro storico.*

Il Marzocco   I
Piazza Savonarola 25
53045 Montepulciano
Tel. (0578) 757 262
*16 rooms. At north entrance to old
town. Restaurant.*

Monteriggioni

Casalta I
Località Strove
53035 Monteriggiono
Tel. (0577) 301 002
10 rooms. Quiet country hotel with restaurant just west of fortified town. Closed November to February.

Pienza

Corsignano I
Via della Madonnina 11
53026 Pienza
Tel. (0577) 748 501, fax 748 166
36 rooms. Modern comfort in friendly hotel south west of town with good restaurant. Closed 10 January to 10 March.

La Saracina III
Strada Statale 146
53026 Pienza
Tel. and fax (0578) 748 022
6 rooms. Superbly renovated 19th-century farmhouse in peaceful location 8 km (5 miles) north east of Pienza. Swimming pool and tennis. No restaurant but great American breakfast. Closed 2 January to mid-March.

San Quirico d'Orcia

Palazzuolo I
53027 San Quirico d'Orcia
Tel. and fax (0577) 897 080
45 rooms. Resort hotel with swimming pool. Outside centro storico.

Posta Marcucci II
53020 Bagno Vignoni
S of San Quirico
Tel. (0577) 887 112, fax 887 119
49 rooms. Quiet spa resort hotel with garden, heated swimming pool, tennis. Closed mid-January to mid-February.

Saturnia

Terme di Saturnia III
Via della Follonata
58050 Saturnia
Tel. (0564) 601 061, fax 601 266
92 rooms. Grand resort hotel in superb park of olive trees. Swimming pool, tennis, golf, horse-riding.

Villa Clodia I
Via Italia 43
58050 Saturnia
Tel. (0564) 601 212

10 rooms. Pleasant country villa on edge of spa resort; superb terrace view. Swimming pool, no restaurant. Closed February.

Siena

Bernini I
Via della Sapienza 15
53100 Siena
Tel. (0577) 289 047
9 rooms. Spartan but clean and friendly boarding house north west of Campo.

Cannon d'Oro I
Via Montanini 28
53100 Siena
Tel. (0577) 44321, fax 280 868
30 rooms. Excellently run pensione 10 minutes' walk north of Campo.

Certosa di Maggiano III
Via Certosa 82
53100 Siena
Tel. (0577) 288 180, fax 288 189
17 rooms. Pleasant, quiet hotel in converted 14th-century monastery just outside Siena. Heated swimming pool and tennis. Restaurant (closed Tuesday).

Duomo II
Via Stalloreggi 38
53100 Siena
Tel. (0577) 289 088, fax 43043
23 rooms. Small, centrally located, near cathedral. No restaurant.

Garden II
Via Custoza 2
53100 Siena
Tel. (0577) 47056, fax 46050
136 rooms. Just north west of town, two buildings with swimming pool and outdoor dining in garden.

Jolly Excelsior III
Piazza la Lizza 1
53100 Siena
Tel. (0577) 288 448, fax 41272
126 rooms. Modern efficient giant near sports stadium.

Palazzo Ravizza II
Pian dei Mantellini 34
53100 Siena
Tel. (0577) 280 462, fax 271 370
30 rooms. Amazingly peaceful 17th-century mansion in centro storico, yet with beautiful garden overlooking Tuscan hills. First-class family-operated boarding house.

Park Hotel Siena III
Via Marciano 18
53100 Siena
Tel. (0577) 44803, fax 49020
69 rooms. Splendid 16th-century villa designed by Renaissance master Baldassare Peruzzi, surrounded by beautiful woods just west of Siena. Swimming pool and tennis.

Santa Caterina I
Via Piccolomini 7
53100 Siena
Tel. (0577) 221 105, fax 271 087
19 rooms. Just outside Porta Romana in 18th-century villa. Summer breakfast served in large garden. No restaurant. Closed January 7 to March 7.

Villa Patrizia III
Via Fiorentina 58
53100 Siena
Tel. and fax (0577) 50431
33 rooms. Quiet location north west of town in spacious gardens with swimming pool and tennis.

Villa Scacciapensieri III
Via di Scacciapensieri 10
53100 Siena
Tel. (0577) 41422, fax 270 854
31 rooms. Comfortable converted country house just outside Siena. Summer outdoor dining in pretty garden. Park with view of city and hills. Outdoor swimming pool, tennis. Closed January to mid-March. Restaurant closed Tuesday.

South Coast

Argentario

Don Pedro I
58018 Porto Ercole
Tel. and fax (0564) 833 914
44 rooms. Comfortable hotel, outdoor dining. Closed November to March/April (open Easter).

Il Pellicano III
Località Cala dei Santi
58018 Porto Ercole
Tel. (0564) 833 801, fax 833 418
34 rooms. Luxury villa and cottages overlooking sea, amid olive trees, south west of harbour. Heated seawater swimming pool, tennis, water-skiing, horse-riding. Closed November to March/April (open for Easter).

Villa Domizia II
58010 Santa Liberata
Tel. and fax (0564) 812 735
24 rooms. Seaview hotel with beach and pleasant garden 4km (2 miles) east of Porto Santo Stefano. Closed mid-October to mid April.

Castiglione della Pescaia
L'Approdo II
Via Ponte Giorgini 29
58043 Castiglione della Pescaia
Tel. (0564) 933 466, fax 480 008
48 rooms. Well-run hotel with harbour view. Closed November and January.

Elba
Dei Coralli I
57034 Marina di Campo
Tel. (0565) 976 336, fax 977 748
62 rooms. Quiet south-coast resort hotel. Garden, swimming pool, tennis. Closed mid-October to mid-April.

Désirée III
Località Spartaia
57030 Procchio-Marciana
Tel. (0565) 907 311, fax 907 884
75 rooms. Modern resort hotel with swimming pool, tennis, private beach on north coast. Closed October to mid-April.

Hermitage III
Biodola
57037 Portoferraio (Elba)
Tel. (0565) 936 911, fax 969 984
110 rooms. Quiet north-coast resort hotel with private beach, swimming pool, garden and tennis. Restaurant. Closed October to March.

Grosseto
Bastiani II
Piarra Gioberti 64
58100 Grosseto
Tel. (0564) 20047, fax 29321
48 rooms. Efficiently run modern hotel. No restaurant.

Massa Marittima
Duca del Mare I
Piazza Dante Alighieri 1/2
58024 Massa Marittima
Tel. (0566) 902 284, fax 901 905
19 rooms. Quiet garden, outdoor dining. Restaurant closed Monday.

Punta Ala
Cala del Porto III
Via del Porto
58040 Punta Ala
Tel. (0564) 922 455, fax 920 716
41 rooms. Modern resort hotel near harbour amid shady gardens. Swimming pool, tennis, golf, water sports, private minibus to hotel beach.

Gallia Palace III
Via delle Sughere
58040 Punta Ala
Tel. (0564) 922 022, fax 920 229
100 rooms. Ultimate in resort luxury in beautiful natural setting, both beach and gardens. All water sports, tennis, golf, horse-riding.

Arezzo and Eastern Tuscany

Arezzo
Continentale I
Piazza Guido Monaco 7
52100 Arezzo
Tel. (0575) 20251, fax 350 485
74 rooms. Handy for railway station. Restaurant closed mid-July to mid-August.

Minerva I
Via Fiorentina 6
52100 Arezzo
Tel. and fax (0575) 370 390
118 rooms. Efficient comfortable hotel on Florence road west of town. Restaurant closed 1-20 August.

Cortona
San Michele I
Via Guelfa 15
52044 Cortona
Tel. (0575) 604 348, fax 630 147
32 rooms. 16th-century palazzo in very heart of centro storico. No restaurant.

Poppi
Parc Hotel I
Via Roma 214
52014 Ponte a Poppi
Tel. and fax (0575) 529 994
21 rooms. Ideal for exploring Casentino hills. Garden, swimming pool, outdoor dining. Restaurant closed Tuesday.

Sansepolcro
Fiorentino I
Via Luca Pacioli 60
52037 Sansepolcro
Tel. (0575) 740 350, fax 740 370
28 rooms. Modest hotel conveniently inside town. Restaurant.

La Balestra I
Via Montefeltro 29
52037 Sansepolcro
Tel. (0575) 735 151, fax 740 282
52 rooms. Just outside city centre, handy for exploring Piero della Francesca country. Pleasant outdoor dining. Restaurant closed Sunday night and Monday.

Restaurants

Our choice – again listed in the order of the book's six sightseeing chapters – ranges from simple trattorias to chic restaurants, and occasionally includes establishments attached to hotels. We do not list pizzerias, fast-food outlets and stand-up bars serving *tavola calda* where prices will be lower. Reservations are a good idea, if only to check on changes in closing-days – use the area code only when phoning from outside the region.

For our three price-range categories, the following symbols cover a three-course meal, 15% service, but not wine:

I below 40,000 lire
II 40,000-70,000 lire
III above 70,000 lire

Florence
Angiolino III
Via San Spirito 36
Florence
Tel. (055) 239 8976
Most charming and elegant of Arno's south-bank restaurants. First-class Tuscan cuisine. Closed Monday; and two weeks in August.

Armando di Pieralli Piero II
Borgo Ognissanti 140r
Florence
Tel. (055) 216 219

Favourite trattoria of opera singers near Excelsior hotel. Good steaks. Closed Tuesday evening, Wednesday.

Buca Mario   ‖
Piazza Ottaviani 16
Florence
Tel. (055) 214 179
Popular cellar restaurant. Closed Wednesday, Thursday lunch and during August.

Casalinga   ‖
Via dei Michelozzi 9r
Florence
Tel. (055) 218 624
Bustling new trattoria near Santo Spirito church on Arno south bank. Closed Sunday and two weeks in August.

Cavallino   ‖
Via delle Farine 6
Florence
Tel. (055) 215 818
Locally popular for summer outdoor dining, beside Palazzo Vecchio. Closed Tuesday evening, Wednesday, 3 weeks in August.

Cibreo   ‖
Via dei Macci 118
Florence
Tel. (055) 234 1100
Classic Tuscan cuisine with modern touch, elegant friendly setting in Santa Croce quarter. Closed Sunday, Monday and August.

Coco Lezzone   ‖‖
Via del Parioncino 26r
Florence
Tel. (055) 287 178
Heart of classic old neighbourhood; trattoria gone upmarket, but steaks still great. Closed Sunday and Tuesday night.

Del Carmine   ‖
Piazza del Carmine 18r
Florence
Tel. (055) 218 601
Friendly trattoria near Santa Maria del Carmine church, serving both seafood and steaks. Outdoor dining in summer. Closed Sunday and two weeks in August.

Enoteca Pinchiorri   ‖‖
Via Ghibellina 87
Florence
Tel. (055) 242 777
One of Italy's finest restaurants and wine-cellars in superb 15th-century palazzo near Michelangelo family

home. Calf's liver, lamb poems worthy of Dante. Summer dining in courtyard. Closed Sunday, Monday lunch, February, August and Christmas.

Ghibellini   ‖
Piazza San Pier Maggiore 10r
Florence
Tel. (055) 214 424
Big and noisy, popular with Florentines. Authentic bistecca alla fiorentina *and pasta in wild-boar sauce.Closed Wednesday.*

La Capannina di Sante   ‖‖
Piazza Ravenna
Florence
Tel. (055) 688 345
City's most renowned seafood restaurant. Splendid setting on banks of the Arno. Closed Sunday, Monday lunch, two weeks in August and one week at Christmas.

La Maremmana   ‖
Via dei Macci 77
Florence
Tel. (055) 241 226
Genuine old-fashioned trattoria in Santa Croce quarter, excellent fish and fixed menus. Closed Sunday.

Marione   ‖
Via della Spada 27r
Florence
Tel. (055) 214 756
Popular trattoria near Tornabuoni shops. Good pasta, fish-soup and beef dishes. Closed Sunday and mid-July to mid-August.

Nerbone   ‖
Mercato Centrale
Florence
Tel. (055) 219 949
Over a century old, robust cooking in boisterous central market. Week-day lunches only.

Pennello   ‖
Via Dante Alighieri 4r
Florence
Tel. (055) 294 848
Next door to Dante's home, local favourite for traditional cuisine, great soups, osso bucco, kidneys. Closed Sunday evening, Monday and August.

Taverna del Bronzino   ‖
Via delle Ruote 25
Florence
Tel. (055) 495 220
Neighbourhood favourite north of city centre. Closed Sunday and August.

Fiesole

Le Cave di Maiano   ‖
Via delle Cave 16
Fiesole
Tel. (055) 59133
Oasis of good cuisine among tourist-traps. Good local salami, pasta, roast chicken. Closed Thursday, and Sunday evening.

Villa San Michele   ‖‖‖
Via Doccia 4
Fiesole
Tel. (055) 59451
Elegant dining in hotel's 15th-century monastery. Summer outdoor service with superb view of Florence and hills. Great wild game in autumn. Closed mid-November to mid-March.

Pisa and Northern Tuscany

Carrara

Politeama   ‖
Via Mazzini 9
Carrara
Tel. (0585) 70861
Friendly trattoria serving excellent seafood and seasonal mushroom and truffle dishes.

Forte dei Marmi

Lo Squalo Charlie   ‖‖‖
Viale Morin 57
Forte dei Marmi
Tel. (0584) 86276
Excellent seafood restaurant, summer outdoor dining. Mid-June to mid-September, evenings only. Closed Tuesday.

Lucca

Buca di Sant'Antonio   ‖
Via della Cervia 1
Lucca
Tel. (0583) 55881
Rustic setting near Duomo. Traditional Lucca cuisine, superb pasta. Closed Sunday evening, Monday and three weeks in July.

Da Giulio in Pelleria   ‖
Via delle Conce 45
Lucca
Tel. (0583) 55948
Local peasant dishes in simple trattoria in heart of centro storico. Closed Sunday, Monday and three weeks in August.

Montecatini Terme

Enoteca da Giovanni |||
Via Garibaldi 25
Montecatini Terme
Tel. (0572) 71695
*Classical setting for refined cuisine:
seafood, pasta and lamb dishes.
Closed Monday.*

Pier Angelo ||
Viale IV Novembre 99
Montecatini Terme
Tel. (0572) 771 552
*Good seafood restaurant in heart of
town. Closed Sunday, Monday lunch
and three weeks in August.*

Pisa

Al Ristoro dei Vecchi Macelli |||
Via Volturno 49
Pisa
Tel. (050) 20424
*South of Leaning Tower towards
Arno, named after old slaughterhouse
(macelli) but serving excellent sea-
food and pasta. Closed Sunday lunch,
Wednesday and two weeks in August.*

La Mescita |
Via Cavalca 9
Pisa
Tel. (050) 544 294
*Simple country-style trattoria. Fine
pasta, seafood and grilled lamb.
Closed Saturday lunch and Sunday,
and two weeks in August.*

Lo Schiaccionoci ||
Via Amerigo Vespucci 104a
Pisa
Tel. (050) 21024
*Refined seafood in quiet, friendly
restaurant near rail station. Closed
Sunday evening, Monday and August.*

Sergio |||
Lungarno Pacinotti 1
Pisa
Tel. (050) 580 580
*Superb cuisine in elegant riverside
décor. Fine seafood, truffles in
season. Closed Sunday, and
Monday lunch, three weeks in
January, and one week in August.*

Pistoia

Leon Rosso |
Via Panciatichi 4
Pistoia
Tel. (0573) 29230
*In heart of centro storico, simple
Tuscan cuisine making robust use of
locally grown vegetables and first-
class beef.*

Prato

Il Pirańa |||
Via G Valentini 110
Prato
Tel. (0574) 25746
*Sophisticated seafood restaurant,
though no pirańa on the menu, on
southern outskirts of town. Closed
Sunday, Saturday and Monday
lunch, and August.*

Viareggio

Da Pino ||
Via Matteotti 18
Viareggio
Tel. (0584) 961 356
*Creative Sardinian seafood
cuisine in classical seafaring décor.
Closed Wednesday and Thursday
lunch, and mid-December to mid-
January.*

Montecatini ||
Viale Manin 8
Viareggio
Tel. (0584) 969 129
*Pleasant outdoor dining, seafood
but also beef and duck dishes.
Closed Monday, except mid-July to
September.*

Scintilla ||
Via Nicola Pisano 33
Viareggio
Tel. (0584) 387 096
*Good seafood trattoria south of city-
centre. Closed Sunday evening and
Monday, Christmas and ten days in
August.*

Chianti and the Tuscan Hills

Castellina

Albergaccio ||
Via Fiorentina 35
Castellina in Chianti
Tel. (0577) 741 042
*Romantic setting in renovated barn
in the middle of the wine country.
Imaginative regional cuisine.
Closed Sunday, and mid-January to
mid-February.*

Antica Trattoria in Torre |
Piazza del Comune
Castellina in Chianti
Tel. (0577) 740 236
*In centre of town, family cooking in
traditional Tuscan manner, veal a
speciality. Closed Friday and two
weeks in September.*

Certaldo

Vicario ||
Via Rivellino 3
Certaldo
Tel. (0571) 668 228
*Rustic ambience in 14th-century
house. Fine pasta, grills, bistecca
fiorentina. Closed Wednesday, and
mid-November to February.*

Colle di Val d'Elsa

Arnolfo |||
Piazza Santa Caterina 2
Colle di Val d'Elsa
Tel. (0577) 920 549
*Renowned cuisine, finest meat and
game dishes. Outdoor dining.
Closed Tuesday, mid-January to
mid-February and 10 days in
August.*

Gaiole

Castello di Spaltenna |||
Località Spaltenna (Gaiole)
Tel. (0577) 749 483
*Fine cuisine in ancient castle,
garden dining with spectacular
view. Closed Monday, and mid-
January to end February.*

Greve

Villa San Michele ||
Località Lucolena
Greve
Tel. (055) 851 034
*Hillside restaurant in forest setting
east of Greve. Outdoor dining for
traditional Tuscan and vegetarian
cuisine. Closed Monday.*

Panzano

Il Vescovino ||
Via Ciampolo da Panzano 9
Panzano in Chianti
Tel. (055) 852 464
*Creative variations on Tuscan
cuisine with finest wines. Closed
Tuesday, Wednesday lunchtime and
January, February.*

Radda

Vignale |||
Via XX Settembre 23
Radda in Chianti
Tel. (0577) 738094
*One of Chianti's finest restaurants,
superb wines and cuisine in
elegant rustic ambience. Great
soups, pigeon and rabbit. Closed
Thursday and mid-November to
February.*

Le Vigne ‖
Podere le Vigne (Radda)
Tel. (0577) 738 312
*Outdoor dining for Tuscan cuisine
amid the vineyards. Closed
Tuesday.*

San Gimignano

Bel Soggiorno ‖
Via San Giovanni 91
San Gimignano
Tel. (0577) 940 375
*Refined Tuscan cuisine in mediæval
building. Great local wines. Closed
Monday.*

Dorandò ‖‖‖
Vicolo dell'Oro 2
San Gimignano
Tel. (0577) 941 862
*Includes some ancient Etruscan
dishes on classical Tuscan menu.
Closed Monday.*

I Cinque Gigli ‖‖‖
Località Pescille
San Gimignano
Tel. (0577) 940 186
*Quiet rustic but elegant setting
with fine view of San Gimignano
towers. Excellent meat and seafood
dishes, game in season. Closed
Wednesday, and mid-January to end
February.*

La Stella ‖
Via San Matteo 75
San Gimignano
Tel. (0577) 940 444
*Traditional with fresh produce from
own farm. Closed Wednesday, and
mid-January to mid-February.*

Le Terrazze ‖‖‖
Piazza della Cisterna 23
San Gimignano
Tel. (0577) 940 328
*Romantic dining in 15th-
century décor with view over
Tuscan hills. Closed Tuesday,
Wednesday lunch, and mid-
November to mid-March.*

Volterra

Etruria ‖
Piazza dei Priori 6
Volterra
Tel. (0588) 86064
*Classical cuisine in 19th-century pal-
azzo in heart of town. Closed Thurs-
day, and November to December.*

Siena and Southern Tuscany

Asciano

La Pievina ‖
Via Lauretana 9
NW of Asciano
Tel. (0577) 718 368
*Family-run osteria reputed for
seafood and fine pasta dishes.
Closed Monday, Tuesday and
August.*

Chianciano Terme

Gallo Nero ‖
Via le Piane 54
Chianciano Terme
Tel. (0578) 63680
*Simple family-run trattoria. Closed
Thursday.*

Chiusi

La Fattoria ‖
Località Paccionese
Lagio di Chiusi
Tel. (0578) 21407
*Lakeside hotel-restaurant with
garden, first-rate traditional Tuscan
cuisine. Closed February and
Monday off-season.*

Zaira ‖
Via Arunte 12
Chiusi
Tel. (0578) 20260
*Traditional family fare. Closed two
weeks in November and Monday off-
season.*

Montalcino

Taverna dei Barbi ‖
Località Podernovi
SE of Montalcino
Tel. (0577) 849 357
*Old farmhouse, traditional cuisine.
Savoury mushroom and game
dishes. Handy for Sant'Antimo
Abbey. Closed Tuesday evening and
Wednesday.*

La Cucino di Edgardo ‖
Via Saloni 33
Montalcino
Tel. (0577) 848 232
*Creative modern Italian cuisine,
celebrated local wines. Dining in
wine-cellar. Closed Wednesday and
three weeks in January.*

Montemerano

Da Caino ‖‖‖
Via Canonica 3
Montemerano
Tel. (0564) 602 817
*Elegant setting with wine-cellar for
sophisticated cuisine. Game and
poultry specialities. Closed
Wednesday.*

Montepulciano

Sconvoltino ‖
Via dell'Opio nel Corso 30
Montepulciano
Tel. (0578) 758 229
*Pleasant little family-run restaurant
inside centro storico. Closed
Monday.*

Monteriggioni

Il Pozzo ‖
Piazza Roma 2
Monteriggioni
Tel. (0577) 304 127
*Elegant rustic décor for refined
cuisine – good pasta but also
inventive rabbit, goat, lamb dishes.
Closed Sunday evening, Monday,
three weeks in January, and 10 days
in August.*

Roccalbegna

Vecchio Castello ‖
Via della Chiesa 2
Triana, W of Roccalbegna
Tel. (0564) 989 031
*Small refined and friendly
restaurant, with old wine-cellar.
Closed Wednesday.*

Santa Fiora

Il Barilotto ‖
Via Carolina 24
Santa Fiora
Tel. (0564) 977 089
*Pleasant family-run restaurant,
traditional cuisine. Closed
Wednesday and November.*

Saturnia

I Due Cippi ‖
Piazza Vittorio Veneto 26
Saturnia
Tel. (0564) 601 074
*Summer outdoor dining in
garden. Amiable, rustic setting.
Good pasta and meat dishes. Closed
Tuesday.*

Siena

Al Marsili ‖‖
Via del Castoro 3
Siena
Tel. (0577) 47154
*Elegant dining in 15th-century
building. Closed Monday.*

Antica Trattoria Papei ‖
Piazza del Mercato 6
Siena
Tel. (0577) 280 894
*Outdoor dining in little trattoria
behind Palazzo Pubblico. Mild or
spicy cuisine, rabbit speciality.
Closed Monday.*

Cane e Gatto ‖‖
Via Pagliaresi 6
Siena
Tel. (0577) 220 751
*Creative new Italian cuisine, fine
wines. Evening service only. Closed
Thursday.*

Il Campo ‖‖‖
Piazza del Campo 50
Siena
Tel. (0577) 280 725
*Outdoor dining right on Campo.
Closed Tuesday in low season –
December to February.*

Il Giuggiolo ‖‖
Via Massetana 30
Siena
Tel. (0577) 284 295
*First-class family-run trattoria
south west of city-centre. Closed
Wednesday and August.*

La Torre ‖
Via Salicotto 7
Siena
Tel. (0577) 287 548
*Small family trattoria, traditional
cooking near Campo. Closed
Thursday.*

Medio Evo ‖‖
Via dei Rossi 40
Siena
Tel. (0577) 280 315
*Refined cuisine in mediæval
palazzo. Spicy gnocchi, grilled lamb
specialities. Closed Thursday.*

Osteria da Divo ‖
Via Franciosa
Siena
Tel. (0577) 286 054
*Rustic cuisine in mediæval setting
around ancient indoor well, near
Duomo. Closed Sunday.*

Sinalunga

Locanda dell'Amorosa ‖‖
Località Amorosa
S of Sinalunga
Tel. (0577) 280 725
*Charming restaurant in old
farmhouse. (Hotel accommodation,
10 rooms.) Closed Monday,
Tuesday lunch, and late January to
late February.*

South Coast

Castiglione della Pescaia

Corallo ‖‖
Via N. Sauro 1
Castiglione della Pescaia
Tel. (0564) 933 668
*Unusually good resort-hotel seafood
restaurant, with fresh produce from
own farm. Closed Tuesday only off-
season.*

Il Fagiano ‖‖
Piazza Garibaldi 4
Castiglione della Pescaia
Tel. (0564) 934 037
*Respectable seafood restaurant.
Closed Wednesday and February.*

Elba

Il Chiasso ‖‖
Capoliveri
Elba
Tel. (0565) 968 709
*Outdoor dining for good seafood.
Evenings only.*

L'Acqua Cheta ‖‖
Via Mellini 3
Capoliveri (Elba)
Tel. (0565) 967 071
*Stylish décor for seafood and oven-
baked meats. Off-season closed
lunchtime and Wednesday.*

Rendez-Vous da Marcello ‖‖
Piazza della Vittoria
Marciana Marina (Elba)
Tel. (0565) 99251
*Outdoor dining for good seafood
and pasta, local wines. Closed mid-
January to mid-February, Novem-
ber and Wednesday in off-season.*

Grosseto

Buca San Lorenzo ‖‖‖
Viale Manetti 1
Grosseto
Tel. (0564) 25142

*Elegant, romantic décor in Medici
ramparts of centro storico.
Imaginative country and seafood
cuisine. Closed Monday.*

Ombrone ‖‖
Viale Matteotti 71
Grosseto
Tel. (0564) 22585
*Family-run restaurant with wine-
cellar. Meat and seafood dishes.
Closed Sunday evening and
Monday.*

Porto Ercole

Il Gambero Rosso ‖‖
Lungomare Andrea Doria 60
Porto Ercole
Tel. (0564) 832 650
*Fish and seafood, outdoor dining
overlooking harbour. Closed
Wednesday and January.*

Il Gatto e la Volpe ‖‖
Via dei Canoni 3
Porto Ercole
Tel. (0564) 838 306
*Seafood restaurant, zingaresca di
pesce fish-stew speciality. Closed
November to March/April (open for
Easter).*

Il Pellicano ‖‖‖
Località Cala dei Santi
Porto Ercole
Tel. (0564) 833 801
*Spectacularly located terrace dining
overlooking sea. Closed November
to March/April (open for Easter).*

Massa Marittima

Taverna del Vecchio Borgo ‖
Via Parenti 12
Massa Marittima
Tel. (0566) 903 950
*Traditional local tavern-cooking.
Splendid soups, stuffed rabbit and
grills. Closed Sunday evening and
Monday.*

Arezzo and Eastern Tuscany

Arezzo

Buca di San Francesco ‖‖
Piazza San Francesco 1
Arezzo
Tel. (0575) 23271
*Elegant dining in cellar of 14th-
century palazzo. Closed Monday
evening, Tuesday and July.*

Le Tastevin ‖
Via de'Cenci 9
Arezzo
Tel. (0575) 28304
Refined setting (with piano bar) for traditional cuisine, good vegetable dishes. Closed Monday and August.

Casentino

Gli Accaniti ‖
Via Fiorentina 12
Pratovecchio
Tel. (0575) 583 345
Rustic but refined setting for Casentino country cooking: freshwater fish, mushroom and vegetable dishes. Closed Monday and Tuesday, two weeks in June, and two weeks in November.

La Tana degli Orsi ‖
Via Roma 1
Pratovecchio
Tel. (0575) 583 377
Attractive restaurant for good pasta and fine rabbit, pigeon, and other game dishes. Closed for lunch (except public holidays), Wednesday, two weeks June to July, and three weeks November.

Cortona

La Grotta ‖
Piazza Baldelli 3
Cortona
Tel. (0575) 604 834
Friendly restaurant for simple traditional cuisine. Closed Tuesday.

Tonino ‖
Piazza Garibaldi 1
Cortona
Tel. (0575) 630 500
Sophisticated cuisine in elegant setting. Closed Tuesday.

Sansepolcro

Da Ventura ‖
Via Aggiunti 30
Tel. (0575) 742560
Modest but good traditional Tuscan cuisine. Rooms available. Closed Saturday.

Oroscopo di Paolo e Marco ‖‖‖
Località Pieve Vecchia
NW of Sansepolcro
Tel. (0575) 734 875
In 19th-century country house, superbly presented combinations of seafood and fresh vegetables. Closed Sunday, mid-January to mid-February, and mid-June to mid-July.

Index

References to illustrations are in *italic*; those in **bold** refer to main entries; those with an asterisk refer to maps.

INDEX

INDEX

Discover the world
with **BERLITZ**®

BERLITZ DISCOVER GUIDES do more than just map out the sights – they entice you to travel with lush full-colour photography, vivid descriptions and intelligent advice on how to plan and enjoy your holiday or travel experience. Covering the world's most popular destinations, these full-colour travel guides reveal the spirit and flavour of each country or region. Use *DISCOVER* as a travel planner or as a practical reference guide. You'll find sightseeing information and suggested leisure routes, extensive full-colour maps and town plans, local hotel and restaurant listings plus special essays highlighting interesting local features. Colourful historical and cultural background is complemented by practical details such as what to visit and where to stay, where to eat and how much you should expect to pay.

No matter where you're going, make the most of your trip:

DISCOVER the world with BERLITZ.